06/14/18 Amazon $19.59 96 Sharon Williams

ISBN 978-1-331-78765-5
PIBN 10234674

1 MONTH OF
FREE
READING

at

www.ForgottenBooks.com

By purchasing this book you are eligible for one month membership to ForgottenBooks.com, giving you unlimited access to our entire collection of over 700,000 titles via our web site and mobile apps.

To claim your free month visit:

www.forgottenbooks.com/free234674

Similar Books Are Available from
www.forgottenbooks.com

———◆———

MRS. JOHN A. LOGAN.

EVERYBODY'S

GUIDE IN SOCIAL, DOMESTIC, AND BUSINESS LIFE

A TREASURY OF

USEFUL INFORMATION FOR THE MILLION.

THE CONTENTS OF ONE HUNDRED BOOKS IN A SINGLE VOLUME.

EMBRACING

ETIQUETTE, HYGIENE, HOUSEHOLD ECONOMY, BEAUTY, METHODS OF MONEY-MAKING,
CARE OF CHILDREN, NURSING OF INVALIDS, OUTDOOR SPORTS, INDOOR
GAMES, FANCY WORK, HOME DECORATION, BUSINESS, CIVIL
SERVICE, HISTORY, GEOGRAPHY, PHYSIOLOGY,
WRITING FOR THE PRESS, TEACHING,
ITALIAN ART, ETC., ETC.

PREPARED BY

Mrs. JOHN A. LOGAN,

ASSISTED BY

Prof. WILLIAM MATHEWS, CATHERINE OWEN AND WILL CARLETON.

EXPERTS IN EACH DEPARTMENT

H. J. SMITH & CO.,

CHICAGO, ILL.   PHILADELPHIA, PA.
KANSAS CITY, MO.   OAKLAND, CAL.

LIST OF SUBJECTS.

LIST OF ILLUSTRATIONS.

TABLE OF CONTENTS.

ii

HOME MANUAL.

Introduction.

THIS volume is dedicated to the millions of busy people in this
country who have no leisure to ransack libraries and peruse books,
to glean the valuable knowledge here presented in a condensed form. The
mother bending anxiously over her sick child; the sportsman who sees
his friend fall wounded by his side; the toilers in factories injured by
accident; the housekeeper to whom economy of time means additional
strength and leisure for improvement; the wife anxious to make home
beautiful for her husband ; the gay young girl who desires to know the
rules that govern the social world, the best means of enhancing her
charms, or the latest dainty device in fancy work; the woman whom
misfortune has suddenly forced into the crowded ranks of the bread-
winners; the youth who wishes to become an expert in out-door sports;
the writer uncertain how to prepare MSS; the little ones longing for
some new game—all will find the HOME MANUAL a guide, counsellor,
and friend, ever ready to aid. Who can tell from what hours of anxiety
its timely assistance may guard many a household?

Neither time nor labor has been spared in the effort to secure the latest
and best authorities in each department. With the exception of some few
pages, the text has been specially written for this volume, which is offered
to the public by its publishers with the certainty that it will receive a
cordial welcome in all American homes.

Etiquette.

TIQUETTE may be defined as a code of unwritten laws for the protection and comfort of society. Some may sneer at their value, some may possibly lay undue stress upon them; but it will invariably be found that there is a sound and sensible reason, more or less easily discoverable, underlying every rule. It is possible that a few persons may be totally indifferent to the good opinion of their fellow-mortals; but many people of refined feelings, "Nature's gentlewomen and gentlemen," have often suffered keen embarrassment and mortification, and been exposed to unkind criticism from a lack of knowledge of some little details of the customs observed among well-bred people. This department of the "Home Manual" is intended to supply, in a condensed form, ample information for the guidance of all who desire to know "just what to do" in the usual routine of business and social intercourse. The compiler has consulted the best authorities on these subjects, and is confident that no one who possesses the book will fail to find clear directions for the settlement of any doubtful points in the routine of daily life.

ETIQUETTE OF ENTERTAINMENTS.

Dinners.—A dinner party is regarded by many persons as the most formal and, at the same time, the most elegant mode of entertaining guests—it is certainly the one which most severely taxes the resources of the hostess. Any woman not positively ill-bred can fill the position of hostess at a ball; but it requires tact, readiness, and a thorough knowledge of society to make a dinner party, in the ordinary parlance, "go off well." No matter how exquisite china, glass, floral decorations, silver, and linen may be, if the hostess is a dull or awkward woman, the banquet will not be a success, for a proper selection of guests and the power of drawing them into gay and brilliant conversation is quite as needful as any of the material accessories.

2

Yet while this is the entertainment of all others most dependent upon the individuality of the host and hostess, there are certain fixed rules—as in all social matters—which must be observed, and certain suggestions may be of service.

The first point to be regarded is the choice of guests.

Invite those who will probably be agreeable to one another, and avoid including many silent or excessively loquacious persons. People who desire to monopolize conversation are as objectionable at a dinner party, as those who wrap themselves in the cloak of silence and seem utterly unconscious that anything more is expected than due attention to the dishes set before them.

If the host and hostess sit one at each end of the table, avoid having four, eight, or twelve persons, or any number which can be divided by four, because, in seating the guests, it will then be necessary to place two ladies or two gentlemen side by side, a very undesirable arrangement.

The hostess should inform each gentleman which lady he is to take in to dinner—or have cards giving this information placed on the hall-table,—and if the gentleman is not acquainted with the lady, he should request his hostess to present him.

The host should be the first to go in to dinner, his companion being either the most distinguished or the oldest lady present, the wife of the most eminent man, a stranger, or a bride.

The hostess, on the contrary, should go last; having for her companion the husband of the lady whom the host is escorting, if the dinner is given for a married couple. Otherwise her escort should be the most eminent or the oldest gentleman present, or a stranger.

The seat of honor—at the host's right hand—should be given to the lady whom he escorts to the dinner, the one on the left being assigned to the lady whose age or position entitles her to the second place.

The same rule is observed in seating gentlemen on the right and left of the hostess. A gentleman should draw out a lady's chair and assist her in moving it up to the table again, unless there is a servant to perform this duty.

In serving the dishes, the servants should begin upon the right of the master of the house, ending with the hostess, and with the guest on their mistress's right, ending with the host.

Never correct a servant in the presence of the guests; if mistakes occur, seem to be unconscious of them. Give the clearest possible instructions in advance, and unless servants are both stupid and ignorant, there will be little fear of any serious mishap. One waiter to each four persons—

if there is a butler to do the carving—is sufficient; and if really well-trained, one for every six persons will be enough. Many persons now prefer that servants should not wear gloves in waiting on the table, but use instead a napkin with one corner wrapped around the thumb, to keep his hand from touching the plates and dishes. This is a custom borrowed from our English cousins.

To insure the comfort of the guests, the following precautions should be observed. Servants should wear thin-soled shoes, the noise of their footsteps being unpleasant, and many hostesses prefer to have a dining-room carpeted, even in summer, that the sound may be still farther deadened. No clattering of plates and dishes should be allowed. Comfortable chairs should be provided, each lady being supplied with a footstool, and care should be used in keeping the room at an equal temperature, neither too cool, nor too warm. There must be ample light, but it should fall on the table from a sufficient height to prevent any glare in the eyes.

Never have the table so crowded that the waiters cannot easily attend to the needs of the guests. It is hardly necessary to say that no formal dinner should be announced by ringing a bell. A servant should enter the drawing-room and say in a low tone: "Dinner is served," or merely bow as soon as he can catch the hostess' eye.

When seated, the gloves should be removed and placed in the lap under the napkin. If the first course is raw oysters, begin to eat at once; the custom of waiting for others is out of date.

The hostess should call into requisition all her tact and knowledge of society to set her guests at ease. No accident must disturb her. If her rarest china or most precious bit of glass is broken, she must appear not to notice it. If any one has had the misfortune to arrive late, she must welcome him or her cordially, though her duties to her other guests have not permitted her to wait in the drawing-room more than the fifteen minutes permitted by etiquette to the tardy. She must think only of encouraging the timid, inducing the taciturn to talk, and enabling all to contribute their best conversational powers to the general fund of entertainment. The same rules, of course, apply to the host.

The table-cloth should be of the finest quality, ornamented with lace or embroidery, if desired; but the latest edict of fashion precludes the introduction of any colored materials that do not wash. Indeed it is well for those whose means will not permit them to follow every passing caprice of fancy to remember that fine white table linen is always suitable.

The room may be lighted with either white or colored candles or lamps. Many persons prefer to have a portion of the light fall from side brackets or sconces on the wall.

Decorations should always be arranged in such a manner that they will not interfere with the guests' view of one another. At present the preference is for low dishes of flowers of delicate perfume; all those which have a strong fragrance, such as tube-roses, etc., should be avoided, as the odor is apt to become oppressive in a warm room.

Never make an ostentatious display of plate, flowers, or ornaments of any kind; nothing is more vulgar than the appearance of a desire to impress your friends with a show of wealth.

At a large dinner, a card bearing the name of the guest should be laid beside each plate.

Each person should have a plate, two large knives, a small knife and fork for fish, three large forks, a tablespoon for soup, a small oyster-fork for raw oysters, and a goblet for water.

The knives and oyster-forks should be placed on the right, the other forks on the left of the plate, but never at the top.

Bread should be cut in thin slices, and laid on a napkin on the left of each plate. Place the glasses at the right of each plate.

Commence the dinner with raw oysters, then serve one or two soups, either a white and a clear, or a white and a brown soup; but never serve two kinds one after the other.

Follow the soup or soups with fish, serve the entrées—two may be offered at an elaborate dinner—then the roast, then the game and the salad.

Salad may be served either with the game or as a separate course. In the latter case serve cheese and bread and butter with it. The bread can be cut very thin and carefully buttered, or the butter and bread can be served separately. If preferred, the cheese can be served as a separate course.

Follow the cheese and salad with the sweet dishes and ices, then serve the fruit, and lastly the bonbons. Coffee can be served in the drawing-room, when the courses have not occupied too much time, or at the table, according to the preference of the hostess.

Black coffee, which should be made very strong and clear, must be served in very small cups, with tiny coffee-spoons.

Some vegetables, such as asparagus, sweet corn, or macaroni, can be offered by themselves; but hostesses should beware of making the meal tiresome by a needless number of courses.

It is not allowable, however, to serve more than two vegetables with one course, nor to offer anything except potatoes or potato salad with the fish.

Hot plates must be provided for hot meat courses, entrées, etc., but never for salads, cold meats, nor hot puddings, which will keep warm without help.

A fork, or knife and fork, as may be necessary, should be placed on the plate passed to each guest at each course, when the knives and forks first laid on the table have been used.

Everything except the lights and ornaments should be removed from the table before the dessert is served, the crumbs being brushed off with a crumb-scraper or a napkin, a clean one of course.

Finger bowls, set on handsome china or glass plates, with a fruit napkin or embroidered doily between, should be placed on the table for the fruit course. The dainty embroidered doilies, however, must never be used, and substantial fruit napkins should be supplied when any fruits that stain badly are served.

Where there is more than one servant, a second waiter carrying the proper vegetables should follow the first, who passes the meat or fish. The lady next the host should first be helped, and the others in turn, after which the gentlemen should be served. But when there is only one servant the guests may be helped in the order in which they sit, beginning with the lady at the host's right, then passing to the one at his left, leaving the host himself to be served last.

It should be remembered by givers of dinners that too many courses are objectionable. In the best society of our large cities fewer dishes are offered than was the case several years ago.

TEAS AND AFTERNOON RECEPTIONS.

These are among the most informal entertainments given, and the difference between a large afternoon tea and an afternoon reception is little more than the name, though the latter is perhaps a shade more formal.

The day and hour of an afternoon tea may be written on a visiting card. For an afternoon reception, an "At Home" card is used. Only simple refreshments should be served at an afternoon tea. Thin slices of bread and butter, sandwiches, fancy biscuit or cake, tea, coffee, or chocolate, ice-cream, and bouillon are offered. Punch and lemonade—but no wine of any kind—may be added if desired; and also salted almonds. cakes, candies, and other dainty trifles.

At an afternoon reception the table may be supplied with oyster-salads, pâtés, boned turkey, ice-cream, coffee, and bonbons.

Care should be taken to have the simple refreshments offered at an afternoon tea of the very best quality. English breakfast tea is now preferred, served with cream, cut white sugar, or slices of lemon for those who like tea made in the Russian style.

The hostess should shake hands with her guests and receive them cordially; any formality is out of place on an informal occasion.

If the number of guests is small, the hostess should walk about the room, talking with her visitors; if large, she should remain near the door, and have the aid of other ladies, who should entertain the guests, ask them to take refreshments, and make introductions when necessary.

At a large and elegant afternoon reception the windows may be darkened, the gas lighted, and musicians employed, if the hostess desires.

LUNCHEONS.

The hostess may make this meal as simple or as elegant as she chooses. A formal luncheon party, however, is very similar to a dinner.

If the occasion is a ceremonious one, the table is set in the same manner as for a dinner, and the dishes are handed by the servants; but the guests enter separately, instead of arm in arm.

At a large lunch-party either one long table, or several little ones may be used. If the latter method is preferred, take care that the servants have ample room to pass between them.

Each plate should have beside it two knives, two forks, one or two spoons, and a water-goblet.

The first course should consist of fruit or of raw oysters, or of bouillon or chicken consommé, served in cups, set on plates, and supplied with teaspoons.

Tea and coffee must be served at the table, but their use is optional. If the entertainment is informal, the hostess should pour them; if formal, the servant should pass them in small cups on a waiter.

If the lunch is informal, the sweets may be already on the table when the guests take their seats, if the hostess prefers; but vegetables must always be served from the side-board, and the hostess should help the chops, cold meats, etc. Many persons, however, never serve vegetables at an informal lunch, and the utmost freedom of choice in the selection of dishes is allowable. Cold meats, salads, oysters, croquettes, fish, French chops, beef-steak, and omelette are most frequently served.

When there are several courses, the plates should be changed at each course.

At formal lunches it is a pretty custom to provide a bouquet for each lady, grouping them in the center of the table to form a large central ornament, and distributing them to the guests at the close of the meal.

Many hostesses present each guest with some pretty trifle as a souvenir of the occasion, but this is not obligatory.

Guests should arrive punctually, and if the occasion is a formal one, word should be sent at once if, after accepting an invitation, any sudden occurrence prevents one from going.

Either a white or a colored table-cloth may be used, but it must be one that will wash. Both etiquette and good feeling forbid gossip or scandal at a ladies' lunch party, and nothing is more ill-bred than to afterward make ill-natured criticisms upon the hostess or the entertainment she has provided.

Cards and Calls.

IT sometimes happens that persons new to society laugh at " paste-board politeness," but a fair consideration of the convenience of cards will show that, like all the other laws of the code termed, for lack of a better word, etiquette, these little representatives of ourselves have a very sensible reason for their existence.

First, what should their style be? Plain paste-board, of good quality, engraved in fine script. Glazing, fancy designs, embossed or gilt borders or odd shapes, are considered vulgar by well-bred people.

If chance compels the use of a *written* card, let the writing be in pencil rather than in ink, thus showing that its use is a matter of accident.

The proper size for a gentleman is smaller and more oblong in shape than that chosen by ladies, and unless he has some other title, " Mr." should precede the name.

The titles properly placed on cards are those of army and navy officers, physicians, judges, and ministers of the gospel, but neither militia
nor any other complimentary titles are allowable.

Ladies now have the entire name—with the prefix of " Miss " or
" Mrs." engraved on their cards, as " Mrs. John Morris Eames," " Miss
Edith Lloyd Richardson."

Custom sanctions the engraving of the address on all visiting cards,
and some ladies add the reception day engraved in the left-hand corner.
In some cities there is one exception to this rule. A young lady, during
her first winter in society, does not use a separate visiting card, but has
her name engraved on that of her mother or chaperon.

A single gentleman, if he prefers, can have his club address engraved
on his card, instead of the number of his residence.

A widow can use on her cards either her own or her husband's name,
as choice may dictate; though she has legally no right to retain the latter,
custom sanctions it.

The oldest unmarried lady belonging to the oldest branch of a family
alone has the right to use the name prefixed by " Miss," without the
initials. For instance, in the case of an unmarried aunt and niece of the
same name, the aunt's cards should be engraved " Miss Lancaster," the
niece's " Miss Fanny Lancaster."

It is customary for a young lady to have her name placed below her
mother's or chaperon's on the same card, as

Mrs Joel Hood

Miss Hood.

A husband and wife must have separate visiting cards; the custom
of engraving the names of both on the same card is now out of date.

Black bordered cards should always be used by persons who wear
mourning.

RULES FOR LEAVING CARDS.

In making the first call of the season, a lady leaves with her own
her husband's, and those of her sons and daughters. After a dinner
party, a lady leaves her husband's cards with her own.

A married lady, when calling on another married lady, leaves two of her husband's cards with her own—one for the wife and one for the husband.

When calling at a house where there is another lady besides the hostess, the visitor should leave two cards of her own, and two bearing her husband's name.

When calling on a mother and daughters, a lady should leave two cards.

Strict etiquette directs that the caller's name should be sent up by the servant and the card left on the hall-table; but this rule is rarely observed, because few servants can repeat a name correctly.

When paying a first call to several ladies—not mother and daughters —a card should be left for each. When calling on the guest of a house, a card should be left for the hostess also, even if she is a stranger to the visitor.

When calling at a hotel, it is allowable, and even desirable, to write the name of the person for whom the visit is intended upon the card, to avoid the chance of mistakes; but this should never be done at a private residence. Cards should be left or sent on the day of a reception, if illness, a death in the family, or any other cause prevents the acceptance of the invitation.

Cards should not be turned down at the corners, nor bent over at one end—the fashion is now out of date.

In sending a first invitation to a person on whom the hostess has never called, cards should be enclosed with the invitation; but, if possible, a call should precede a first invitation.

After a proper interval of time, cards of condolence may be acknowledged (by sending mourning cards enclosed in an envelope).

In large cities, in case of a change of residence, cards are sent out bearing the new address; but this is not the custom in small places.

Persons about to quit any place, either permanently or for a long time, should leave in person or send by mail cards bearing the letters P. P. C.—"Pour prendre congé," "pays parting calls."

Invitations to an afternoon tea, reception, or wedding, if one is unable to attend, should be acknowledged by cards sent by mail, or by a messenger.

Cards may also be sent out by mail to persons living in neighboring towns, or suburbs so far away that it is difficult to pay visits in person.

When a lady has set apart a certain day during the season to receive callers, visits should be paid on that day; but when special cards have been issued for a series of reception days, it would show ignorance of etiquette, on the part of any person not invited, to call on any one on such days.

Calls should be paid within a week after the receipt of invitations to a dinner party.

Residents of large cities should call in person upon all their acquaintances at least once a year, and pay additional visits to all from whom invitations have been received.

Calls should also be made in the following cases :

When an engagement or marriage has taken place in the family of an acquaintance, or when an acquaintance has recently returned home after a long absence.

Older residents in a street or city pay the first visit to later comers, and this first visit must invariably be returned in person within a week.

If while calling a second visitor arrives, the first comer should take leave as soon as it is possible to do so without being abrupt.

Gentlemen should ask for the mistress of the house, as well as for the young ladies of the family.

Etiquette permits a gentleman—a stranger—to call upon a lady under the following circumstances : If she has invited him to do so, if he brings a letter of introduction, or if an intimate friend of the lady or of the family presents him.

A gentleman should leave his umbrella, overcoat, and overshoes in the hall; but in paying a morning call it was formerly customary—and to some extent the custom is still observed—to bring the hat and cane into the drawing-room, and either hold them or place them on the floor beside the chair; but at the present time, they are quite frequently left in the hall, and on this point the caller is free to consult his individual preference.

It is optional with the hostess whether or not to rise from her seat and cross the room to greet a visitor, or to accompany to the door a lady who is taking her departure. But in these, as in all other cases where the rules of etiquette are not imperative, it is well to remember that the course which sets the guest most at ease will always be the choice of a kindly nature.

In houses where it is the custom to have a servant open the hall-door, the hostess should ring the bell at the first signal of the visitor's departure. But where such service is desired it is better to have the servant stationed at the hall-door during calling-hours. This is especially necessary when a lady has a day set apart for receptions.

Ten or fifteen minutes is the usual length of a formal call, half an hour is the *extreme* limit.

A hostess should *never* accompany a gentleman to the door and, it is almost needless to add, that she should never pay this attention to a lady if, at the same time, other ladies are calling whom she would be obliged to leave in the drawing-room.

INVITATIONS.

Send out all invitations at the same time and in ample season; never invite any one at the last moment, except an intimate friend, who will pardon lack of ceremony. Invitations for a large reception, dinner, or luncheon should be issued one or two weeks in advance; and for a ball, in the midst of the season, two or three. But invitations to dinner and luncheon may be written, if the hostess prefers.

For any large or formal occasions, such as receptions, balls, and dinners, use plain cards, or note paper, engraved in plain script. Notes of invitation must be very carefully written on plain white paper of the best quality, but rather small size, and with due heed to the proper arrangement of words. Thus, Dr. and Mrs. A. B. Cox must be on the same line. The following may be adopted as a correct form for notes of invitations to evening parties:

Mrs. John Johns

requests the pleasure of

Mr. and Mrs. Richard Smedley's company

on Monday evening, March 6th, from nine to twelve o'clock.

A suitable form of acceptance is as follows:

Mr. and Mrs. Richard Smedley

have much pleasure in accepting

Mrs. John Johns' kind invitation

for Monday evening, March the 6th inst.

A courteous form of regret is as follows:

Mr. and Mrs. Richard Smedley
regret that a previous engagement
to drive with Mrs. Black, deprives them of the pleasure
of accepting Mrs. John Johns' kind invitation
for Monday evening, March 6th.

A prompt reply must invariably be made by all who recognize the obligations of courtesy, and it may be well to give one or two examples of an uncivil manner of replying, into which well-meaning persons sometimes fall through ignorance or carelessness

Mr. and Mrs. Claude Johnson regret that they cannot accept Mrs. Thomas White's invitation for Friday evening.

A still ruder form is: Mr. and Mrs. Claude Johnson decline Mrs. Thomas White's invitation for Friday evening.

Dinner invitations are written or engraved in the name of both husband and wife:

Mr. and Mrs. Daniel Clayton
request the pleasure of
Mr. and Mrs. Thomas White's company at dinner
February eighteenth, at seven o'clock.

An acceptance should be worded as follows:

Mr. and Mrs. Thomas White
accept, with pleasure,
Mr. and Mrs. Daniel Clayton's kind invitation to dine with them.
on Thursday, the 18th inst, at seven o'clock.

To return to regrets, the following rule is given in *London Etiquette* " All regrets from persons who are not able to accept invitations should contain a reason for regretting." This rule is as rigidly observed in the best society of America as it is in England.

Persons in mourning regret that a recent bereavement prevents them from accepting; those who are going out of town regret that intended absence prevents them from accepting. " A previous engagement" is given as an excuse when there is an engagement at home or when one has no inclination to accept ; therefore, it is always desirable for those who really regret the necessity of declining, to specify what the engagement is.

Invitations—except those to weddings and dinner parties—should be issued in the name of the hostess.

It is considered good form for a widower to send out invitations for receptions and dinners in his own name and that of his eldest daughter, if she has been several years in society, or in his own name alone. Recent custom allows hostesses to send invitations by mail, in which case two envelopes should be used.

R. S. V. P., the initials of a French phrase whose English form is " the favor of an answer is requested," may be written below an invitation on the right hand side where an answer is especially necessary. Its use, however, is becoming less and less frequent in the best circles, many well-bred persons being of the opinion that it conveys the inference that the recipient of the invitation requires a reminder of an ordinary act of courtesy. Invitations should never be addressed to Miss Jones and *escort*, or, —when sent to a gentleman and his wife or fiancée,—Mr. Smith and Lady.

Another form, though sometimes used by well-bred people, is regarded by many as objectionable, and, therefore, would better be avoided, namely, Mrs. Z. T. Lee and *family.*

Invitations to large entertainments, receptions, weddings, etc., may be sent to persons in mourning if the bereavement has not occurred within a month ; but etiquette permits them to refuse without assigning a reason, sending, however, on the day of the entertainment, black-bordered visiting cards, which announce the cause of their absence. Invitations to dinners and luncheons should never be given to persons in recent afflictions.

Always direct an answer to an invitation to the person or persons who issue it, even though they may be strangers to you. Always answer an invitation to dinner or luncheon at *once*, accepting or refusing positively. The reason is obvious, the number of seats being limited, a prompt reply gives the entertainer an opportunity to supply your place. Should illness, a death in the family, or any other reason prevent the keeping of a dinner-engagement, a letter or telegram should be immediately sent, stating the fact.

When issuing invitations to a family, direct one to the husband and wife, one to the daughters, and one to the sons. ·

Notes of invitations to a gentleman snould be addressed Mr. B. O. Hale, *never* B. O. Hale, Esq. Gentlemen must never be invited without their wives, nor ladies without their husbands, unless to entertainments given exclusively to gentlemen or to ladies.

Visiting-cards must not be used either to accept invitations or to regret the necessity of declining them.

In closing, let it be most emphatically stated that *all* invitations should be answered as promptly as possible. The French assert that it is as necessary to give an immediate answer to a note requiring a reply as it is to a verbal question.

ETIQUETTE OF MOURNING.

There is much difference of opinion in regard to the adoption of mourning dress, and excellent reasons may be advanced in support of both sides of the question.

It is expensive, dismal, injurious to the health, and depressing to the feelings at a time when the heart has most need of cheer, urge some persons, and the statements are true. Yet it is also a great protection to those who really feel that the loss they have sustained makes the fulfilment of many social duties impossible; it serves as a shield in going out on necessary errands; it checks thoughtless allusion, which might give pain, and in families which have always observed the custom, it would seem like a mark of disrespect to omit making the change of dress which habit has sanctioned.

The period of mourning, however, has been shortened of late, and the time during which it is usually worn is as follows: For a husband or wife, two years; for parent, brother or sister, one year; for a young child, six months; for an infant, three months.

For the space of a year no formal visits are paid, no gay entertainments are given in the house, nor is it considered decorous to attend the theatre or other places of public amusement while deep mourning is worn. Some persons say that a mourning veil should never be seen in a theatre, and it is certain that the sight of a person robed in deep black is extremely incongruous in any scene of gayety.

The ladies of a family, before a funeral, see no one except the most intimate friends, and if they prefer can with propriety deny themselves even to them. The gentlemen must of course see the clergyman, undertaker, and others; but no member of the family, except in a case of absolute necessity, should appear in the streets until after the funeral; there are always friends who are ready to do what is needful.

Notes of invitation are usually sent to the pall-bearers, who assemble at the house and accompany the body to the grave. It is optional with the ladies of the family whether they do or do not attend the remains to the last resting place.

After the funeral only the members of the family return to the house, and it is not expected that a widow or mother will see any one except her nearest relatives for several weeks. Whenever possible, the charge of a funeral is given to an undertaker who makes all necessary arrangements, prepares the rooms, etc. The usual custom is to dress the body in the garments worn in life; but young people are frequently laid out in white robes. Floral offerings are beautiful; but in large cities the display became so ostentatious that the request "please omit flowers" is often seen at the end of a death notice.

No invitations of any kind whatever should be left at a house of mourning until after the lapse of a month. Then cards to balls, weddings, and general entertainments may properly be sent; but when persons who have worn black are ready to resume their social life, cards should be left on all their friends and acquaintances.

Wives wear the same mourning for their husband's kindred as they would for their own, and observe the same rules.

Letters of condolence should be dispatched as promptly as possible; but, unless the writer is in mourning, black-bordered paper should not be used. It is a duty from which most persons shrink, for all who have suffered loss by death must feel how well-nigh hopeless are all attempts to console. Yet the sincere sympathy of friends can never be unwelcome to the mourner, and the message of remembrance should never be deferred.

ETIQUETTE OF LETTER WRITING.

Use thick, plain, cream-white paper, except for business letters; then ruled note paper is allowable.

Fold all letters evenly, and put the stamp in the upper right hand corner. Never use stamped or yellow envelopes, except for business correspondence. Remember to enclose a stamp when writing to a stranger concerning your own affairs.

Use sealing-wax if you understand how to make a handsome seal; but never make an impression with a thimble or similar article.

Use postal cards for ordinary business communications; never for friendly correspondence or in writing to any one who might be annoyed by having his or her occupation made public.

Take the trouble to spell correctly. Be careful to write dates, numbers and proper names plainly. Date a note, at the conclusion, on the left hand side of the page; a letter at the beginning, on the right hand.

Sign a letter with a full name, or with the last name and initials. In business correspondence sign "yours respectfully," "your obedient servant," "yours truly," or "yours sincerely." Place the name and address of your correspondent at the upper left hand corner of the page.

Let your signature suit the style of the letter—a business communication should bear a formal, a friendly note, a cordial conclusion.

Never use any title prefixed to your name. Instead, write "Please address Miss or Mrs. A. B." In directing a letter to a married woman, use her husband's full name, or last name and initials, never her own.

Never use the husband's title in directing to the wife, as Mrs. Rev. John Jones, Mrs. Gen. Paul Revere.

Always add Esq. to a gentleman's name—unless he has some other title—on all letters, *except notes of invitation.*

Never cross a letter, never put the most important part of it in a postscript, and never sign one in the first person, if the epistle has been written in the third. Never fail to answer promptly.

Always write to a hostess, after making a visit at her house, and express appreciation of her hospitality.

Never address a letter to a bishop, " Bishop of Doane ;" nor to a doctor of divinity, " Dr. Clarke ;" nor give to an Army or Navy officer a title belonging to a lower rank.

Write to a clergyman as " Rev. Jonas Sampson ;" to a doctor of divinity, " Rev. Samuel Lane, D. D. ;" to a bishop, " Right Rev. Simon Lincoln, D. D. ;" to a judge, member of Congress, mayor of a city, member of a State Legislature, etc., as " Hon. St. Clair Smith," and in the case of a member of Congress, add M. C. to the name, as " Hon. James Lamson, M. C."

Do not put " Present," " Addressed," " Kindness of Mr. Grimes," or " Favored by Mr. Jones," when a letter is to be sent by a messenger. This fashion is now nearly obsolete.

ETIQUETTE OF SPEECH.

Perhaps the two words in the English language whose use just now is most perplexing are " lady," and " gentleman," for if misapplied they become vulgarisms, and so nice is the discrimination that the employment of these terms has been pronounced the most delicate test of any person's familiarity with good society. The most simple rule that can be given, is that a man is always a man to a man, never a gentleman ; to a woman he is sometimes a man and sometimes a gentleman ; but a man would far more frequently call a woman a " woman " than he would term her " a lady." When applying an adjective, the use of the term " man," or " woman," is almost invariable, for instance : " I met an agreeable woman the other day," " He is a very clever man."

Yet a man would say, " a lady, a friend of mine," not, " a woman, a friend of mine." And he would ask : " Which of the ladies did you take in to dinner ? " by no means, " which of the women did you take in to dinner ? "

In speaking of the number of persons, one would say : " There were a great many ladies at the reception, but very few men." A lady would say : " Are there many men here who are friends of yours," not, " are there many gentleman here who are friends of yours," or, " I have invited two or three men to dinner," not, " I have invited two or three gentlemen to dinner."

" Good-morning " and " good-afternoon " are also sometimes stumbling blocks. At a morning call, the use of the words would be old-fashioned. "How do you do?" and " Good-bye," must be employed instead. But between strangers, people meeting on business affairs, or superiors and inferiors, the only proper expressions are " good-morning " and " good-afternoon."

It is hardly necessary to say that both slang and profanity should be avoided, as well as the habit of using meaningless exclamations, such as · Oh, my ! " or " goodness ! gracious ! " etc.

Pronounce distinctly—Coming, speaking, reading, writing, and similar words must not be shorn of their final consonant and converted into comin', readin', writin', etc.

Errors of pronunciation are not always committed through ignorance. Educated people frequently lapse into them from mere carelessness, and it is by no means uncommon to hear *catch* turned into *ketch*, *can* into *ken*, *fellow* into *feller*, *window* into *winder*, or *pillow* into *piller*. *Dew* and *due* become *doo*, *secretary* is often *secatary*.

Route should be pronounced as though it were written *root*, not *rout* and *tour* should be called *toor* not *tower*.

Gents for *gentlemen*, *pants* for *trousers*, *vest* for *waist-coat*, and *party* for *person* are so fully recognized as vulgarisms that perhaps a warning against them is hardly necessary.

Another frequent blunder is to use the word *sick* indiscriminately for all forms of illness. It should be applied only to nausea. Avoid what has been termed " newspaper English ;" for instance, do not say " transpire " for " happen," nor " donate " for " give," " female " for " woman " or " lady " " folks " for family."

Be careful not to drop the *h* from words in which it should be sounded, as " w'en" for " when," " w'ite " for " white," " w'ere " for " where."

Do not commit grammatical errors. One of the most common is don't for *does not*. Don't is a contraction of *do not*. Therefore the don't is not allowable. Either avoid the contraction altogether, or say doesn't.

Aint for isn't is another common blunder. Isn't is the abbreviation of *is not*. Aint, if used at all, should take the place of *am not ;* but it is always an awkward expression, and would be better omitted. A gross error, frequently committed by persons who would be expected to know bettei, are " I," or " they *done* it," for " I *did* it," " they *did* it," " I *seen* it," for " I *saw* it," and " He would have *went*," for " he would have *gone*."

An error in taste is the too frequent repetition of the word " please." Say instead, " Will you do me the favor ? " " Will you kindly," " will you oblige me," etc.; remembering that this caution is not against "please," for *occasional*, only for its *constant* use.

In conclusion avoid, as the worst possible violation of the etiquette of speech, any correction of a slip of grammar or error in pronunciation committed by another person, made in a way which could mortify or hurt the offender's feelings. If it is necessary for any reason to refer to the matter, use the utmost consideration and courtesy, choosing a time when no one else is present.

ETIQUETTE OF FAMILY LIFE.

Good manners, it has been said, are too often a cloak that is flung aside like a burden, as soon as the threshold of home is crossed. Yet, surely there is no spot on earth, where kindness and consideration for others—the foundation of etiquette—are better displayed, or more appreciated, and attention to the rules briefly given below will do much to ensure the comfort of the household.

Be as courteous in the family circle as when among strangers.

Let the house be kept in good order for daily use, not merely when guests are expected.

Have a seat at the table, a room, and a welcome for any friend who may chance to arrive.

Let the gentlemen of the family avoid smoking all over the house, or strewing cigar stumps, ashes, or burned matches on floors or tables.

Make no needless noise to disturb the rest of the household, when coming home late at night.

Do not sit between any one and the light or the fire.

Do not allow children to take possession of the most comfortable chairs or the most pleasant seats.

Do not fail to rise and offer a chair to any older person who may enter.

Never enter any one's room without knocking.

Never precede an older person in entering nor leaving a room, nor in going up-stairs.

Never fail to be as punctual as possible in attendance at the meal-hours. Never feel that sharing the expenses of the household confers a right to give needless trouble.

ETIQUETTE OF SHOPPING.

For Employees.—Never fail in courtesy to a customer; but never proffer advice to aid in making selections, unless requested to do so.

Never make any distinction between the rich and the poor.

Never forget that a customer cannot always decide what to purchase until he or she has seen the new goods, and that any one has an undoubted right to go to a store and look through the stock for a reasonable time, without buying anything.

Never talk to another employee when customers are waiting; never show temper if goods are not purchased.

Never allow any one to buy damaged goods without stating their condition.

For Customers.—Never look over goods without any intention of buying them—merely to "kill time."

Never set out on a shopping excursion without first deciding as far as possible what to buy.

Never take a costly piece of goods—nor any piece—into a better light without first asking the clerk's permission to do so.

Never let the door of a shop slam in the face of any person, nor permit a stranger to hold it open without any acknowledgment of the courtesy.

Never speak sharply nor rudely to an employee.

ETIQUETTE OF THE STREET.

Courtesy requires the return of all civil greetings—those of servants included. Only the most serious causes can justify "a cut."

In bowing, the head should be bent; a mere lowering of the eye-lids, affected by some people, is rude; but etiquette does not permit a familiar nod, except between business men, or very intimate friends. In passing and repassing on a public promenade or drive, bows are exchanged only at the first meeting. In carrying canes, umbrellas, and packages, care should be taken that they do not inconvenience others. In meeting on a street-crossing, gentlemen should make way for ladies, and younger persons for older ones.

In driving or walking, always keep to the right.

A gentleman should always offer his arm to a lady in the evening. In the day he should do so only under the following circumstances: when the pavement is slippery, when there is a crowd, or when his companion is old or needs support.

In escorting two ladies, he should offer his arm to one, and let the other walk by her side. "Sandwiches" are never desirable.

ETIQUETTE OF THE HORSE-CARS.

For Ladies.—Never accept a seat from a gentleman without acknowledging the courtesy by a bow and an *audible* expression of thanks.

Never show any sign of displeasure if, on entering a crowded car, no seat is offered.

Never—if young and strong—expect an old gentleman to resign his seat.

Never place baskets or bundles in the laps of other people.

Never hesitate, if ill or greatly fatigued, to courteously ask a gentleman if he will resign his seat, giving the reason for the request.

For Gentlemen.—Never beckon to a lady, in order to resign a seat; but rise first and offer it courteously

Never show reluctance to pass tickets or fares in cars not supplied with conductors.

Never stand on the platform of a crowded car, so that a lady will be forced to push her way off. Step down into the street if necessary.

Never take a seat while ladies are standing.

ETIQUETTE OF BUSINESS.

Never forget that time is precious to some persons, though you may be ready to waste it.

Never fail to settle all debts as promptly as possible.

Never fail to have all the details of an agreement decided so far as they can be, before the transaction is concluded.

Never forget that a contract can be broken only by the consent of all the parties concerned.

Never keep washer-women, seamstresses, nor any one dependent upon daily labor waiting for payment.

Never endorse a note, unless able and willing to pay its full amount.

Never adopt a disagreeable manner when requesting payment of a debt.

Never buy on credit, if cash can be had.

Never show false pride nor affect a manner commonly known as " being above one's business."

Never shirk labor, nor fail to devote the whole attention to the work in hand.

Never forget that a character for fair dealing is a capital that cannot be lost. Never think it unnecessary to learn the minutest details of any business, and never imagine that success in any business can be attained without a thorough training for it.

Never fail to be courteous in all business intercourse; a pleasant manner will do much to ensure success.

Never insist upon entering any business office, if told that its occupant is not at leisure.

Never address a letter to a firm in any way except Messrs. John Smith & Co., Gentlemen.

Never send a manuscript to an editor without enclosing stamps for return postage, if you desire to have it sent back if not available.

Never write business letters in a rambling nor needlessly curt style, and never place Messrs. before the signature of a firm.

Never annoy an editor by constant letters of inquiry ; remember that your manuscript is not the only one he receives, and exercise due patience.

ETIQUETTE OF TRAVELLING.

For Ladies.—Dress neatly in well made clothing of suitable material and simple style, wear as little jewelry as possible, and carry the smallest amount of baggage by hand.

Have the initials or full name on all trunks.

Never attract attention by loud talking, laughing, or constant giggling and, if under the escort of a gentleman, do not annoy him with needless requests.

Always repay a gentleman any travelling expenses, no matter how trivial.

When travelling alone, if possible, be met at the station by some friend. In arriving at a station in a large city where she is a stranger, a lady should avoid taking a hack, choose instead horse-cars, or the stages plying between stations.

Always acknowledge, by an expression of thanks, any courtesy offered, but young ladies should avoid entering into unnecessary conversation or accepting favors from men who are strangers.

Remember that in the Old World, especially on the continent of Europe, it is not the custom for ladies to walk alone in city streets.

Older ladies are privileged to offer advice or assistance, should occasion require, to young ladies travelling alone.

For Gentlemen.—It is courteous for a gentleman to offer to buy tickets, and check the baggage of a lady who is travelling under his care; but he should first take her to the ladies' waiting-room, not leave her standing on a crowded platform. He may also offer to get her refreshments, newspapers, or books, and—if the journey is a long one—invite her to walk up and down the platform at the stations. If, by any accident, the friends expected fail to meet a lady at the station, the gentleman escorting her should, if possible, go with her to her destination.

A gentleman may offer to help a lady, even if she is a stranger, whenever she seems really in need of aid. For instance, if she is laden with many parcels, or has several children with her who must be transferred from boat to car, or station to station.

Two gentlemen may talk together if agreeable to both; but it is wise to discuss only general topics.

Gentlemen may offer to open or shut a window for ladies; but should never presume upon a chance civility thus extended, by attempting to use it as a means of entering into conversation with them. While not regarded by all persons as obligatory, it is always courteous for a gentle-

man to offer his seat to a lady who is standing in any public convey-
ance.

No gentleman should smoke in cars or other places when ladies are
present, spit on the floors in cars or stations, be disobliging in a smoking-
car, by refusing to change his seat to accommodate a party who may
desire to play some game, or accept a light, or any trifling civility from
a fellow passenger, without any expression of thanks.

For Both.—Before entering boat, train, or car, give the passengers
who are in the act of leaving time to get off.

Never take a seat just vacated without waiting to see if its former
occupant intends to return.

Never grumble about the trivial discomforts that fall to every traveller's lot, nor make comparisons—unfavorable to the latter,—between one's
own home and the place where one happens to be.

Never crowd nor jostle in passing on or off cars or ferry-boats ; never
occupy more than one seat in crowded conveyances. If parcels, etc., have
been placed on an empty seat, cheerfully remove them whenever it is
needed. Never take the seat beside any person in a steam-car, without
asking if it is engaged.

Never forget that partition walls on steamers and sometimes in hotels
are very thin, and be careful to relate no family secrets for the benefit of
the person occupying the next chamber or state-room.

Never incommode fellow-travellers by opening a window which forces
them to sit in a draught—it may be an affair of life and death to delicate
persons.

ETIQUETTE OF THE TABLE.

Never lean far back in a chair nor sit on the side nor edge of it.

Never sup soup noisily, nor from the end of the spoon.

Never grasp the blade of the knife, hold it by the handle.

Never eat rapidly, and never eat with a knife.

Never cut up the food in small pieces on the plate.

Never leave a spoon in a tea-cup, pour tea into a saucer to cool, **nor**
drink from a saucer.

Never use a steel knife for fruit.

Never peel a pear or peach and then take up the juicy fruit in the fingers.

Never put food on the back of the fork.

Never tip the plate to obtain the last remnant of the soup.

Never put potato-skins, fruit parings, nor anything of the kind on the
table-cloth.

Never bite mouthfuls from bread, always break it, never cut hot bread or biscuit open.

Never hesitate to take the last piece of any dish that may be offered —to refuse would imply a doubt whether the hostess had made sufficient provision for her guests.

Never break a boiled egg into a cup nor eat it with a tea-spoon, it should always be eaten from the shell with an egg-spoon.

Never fasten a napkin at the neck, nor tuck it into a button-hole.

Never leave a napkin unfolded if the hostess folds hers.

Never leave the table until the meal is over.

Never read newspapers, books, or letters if others are at the table with you.

Never eat onions nor garlic, except when dining alone.

Never play with napkin, fork, nor any other article.

Never use a spoon to eat vegetables—a fork is the proper thing.

Never put your own knife into the butter-dish nor into any other intended for general use.

BRIEF RULES FOR THE ETIQUETTE OF THE TABLE.

In conclusion a few rules supposed to be familiar to every one, but too often ignored, may be of service. Spread the napkin over the knee, hold the fork with the handle in the hollow of the left hand ; when in the right, use it with the prongs upward, holding it between the finger and thumb.

Wipe the lips before drinking, in order not to soil the glass.

Avoid bending over the plate, drooping the head too low, thrusting the elbows out, or sitting with the back turned toward the person in the next chair.

Be careful not to take large mouthfuls nor to eat too heartily.

ETIQUETTE OF THE CLUB.

While it may be said that there are few members of clubs who do not have a sufficient knowledge of the rules of etiquette governing them, there are always some who desire information on certain points, and it is for the benefit of the latter that the following brief directions are given :

Never fail to become familiar with the regulations, and to rigidly obey them.

Never feel that you have no right to vote against the admission to a small social club of any one whose society is not agreeable to you. It would destroy the pleasure of such a club if all its members were not congenial.

Never allow personal prejudice to influence you in voting upon the admission of a new member of *a large club*.   Consider only the following points: Is the gentleman's record clear, and is he in all respects a worthy associate for gentlemen.

Never persistently propose for membership of a small club a name that has been refused.

Never be disagreeable nor disobliging to fellow-members.   A gentle· man should be as courteous in a club-house as he would be in his own.

Never talk loudly in reading-rooms or library, and never misuse books, newspapers, nor other club property.

Never seem selfish, monopolize the best arm-chair, make a practice of dining early to secure an extra share of a favorite dish, nor require special attention from waiters.

Never grow angry over political or religious discussions, and never take any property of the club away from the building.

Never mention the names of ladies in the club.

Never show curiosity about other members.

Never send an employee out of the club-house on any private errand without first requesting permission of the clerk or superintendent.

Never bring dogs or other pets to a club.

Never, while the guest of a club, take the liberty of introducing any one else; but the guest of a club is expected to avail himself of all the privileges of its members.

Wedding Invitations.

T is not the purpose of this department to go into the full descriptions of weddings and how they should be conducted, as that matter is treated in all the books of etiquette, and is also governed by the position of the parties concerned, so that every person should be governed by their position and the circumstances which surround them. The province of this department is to give the proper forms for invitations for weddings and receptions.

This is something that few books on such subjects give, and we have no doubt that our readers who are interested in such matters will appreciate.

In the first place, if possible, have your invitations engraved ; do not use a printed invitation unless you are obliged to. The difference in cost is but trifling, and the different impression in the opinion of your friends is incalculable. The invitation should be on smooth white paper, satin finished, and the size should be about 6½ x 4¼, plain script should be used in all cases. Under no circumstances allow your friends or your stationer to persuade you to use a fancy paper or type ; the envelope should match the paper exactly, and should be perfectly plain, with a long pointed flap and without gum. The outside or mailing envelope should be of good quality, and match in tint the invitation. Invitations should be mailed at least two weeks before the wedding, and it is best to give your stationer at least ten days in which to prepare them. This gives him time to do his work carefully, and also enables the invitations to get thoroughly dry, thereby preventing the blurring which will spoil the finest piece of workmanship. But in case it is not possible to give that length of time, instruct the engraver or printer to put tissue paper between each invitation and be careful to fold the tissue with each in mailing. The proper form for an invitation is :

29

Mr. & Mrs. James Brown
request your presence at the marriage
of their daughter
Fannie
TO
Mr. Henry Smith,
Thursday, March Fifth,
at four o'clock,
Christ Church, Washington, D. C.
1889.

Where a reception is given, there should be a separate card enclosed which should match the paper used in the invitation, and which should read :

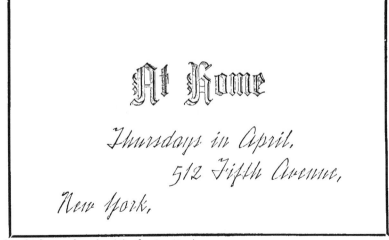

In case no reception is given, and the newly married couple wish to announce to their friends their new abode, a card reading :

should be enclosed with the invitation.

These cards are sometimes engraved at the bottom of the invitation, but it is not good form and causes inconvenience, as often many invitations are sent out to a wedding, while for many reasons only a few can be entertained at the reception. In case there is but one parent living, the invitation should read:

Mr. or Mrs. James Brown
requests, etc.,

and where the wedding is at the home of the bride, the street and number takes the place of the name of the church. It is quite the form now for weddings at the house, or when recent bereavements necessitate the wedding to be private, to ask the intimate friends by written invitations, and then send announcements to the special 400. In such cases the stationery used should be of the same quality and style as for the invitations, but should read:

Mr. & Mrs. James Brown

announce the marriage

of their daughter

Fannie

TO

Mr. Henry Smith,

Thursday, March Fifth,

Washington, D. C.

1889,

Where the parents do not make the announcement, or when the lady is an orphan, it should read:

Fannie Brown,

Henry Smith,

married

Thursday, March Fifth.

Washington. D. C.

1889.

In all cases the At Home or Reception cards are the same as with the invitation.

These forms cover nearly all cases, but if compelled to deviate from them, remember the one rule to make the invitation as concise as possible, and avoid all superfluous verbiage. Do not allow your friends to be able to make a mistake in the date or manner of their invitation.

The cost of an invitation of first-class workmanship is usually about $15.00 for the first hundred, and about $5.00 per hundred after, this in-cludes both envelopes. The printed ones cost about $5.00 for the first hundred, and about $3.00 per hundred after; the difference in the cost of the first hundred being caused by the expense of engraving the plates. The expense of the At Home and Reception cards is about $4.00 for first hundred and $1.50 per hundred after.

ETIQUETTE OF WEDDINGS.

All families do not give dinners, balls, or five o'clock teas, but nearly every house, sooner or later, throws wide its doors to wedding-guests; therefore there is no form of entertainment whose details are so generally interesting.

The styles are as varied as the circumstances of the brides, yet the simplest home wedding—to avoid criticism—demands the observance of certain rules, as well as the most gorgeous Fifth Avenue marriage. And fortunately the simplest home wedding, by the exercise of a little taste and care, may be as attractive as the stateliest ceremonial.

First, a word about the engagement. We have no formal ceremony of betrothal, such as exists among some foreign nations, but a girl's welcome by the family of her fiancé should be prompt and cordial. Any delay may cause her keen unhappiness.

It is the custom in many cities for the mother of the expectant husband to invite the fiancée and her family to a dinner as soon as possible after the engagement, and these near relatives are first informed of the probable date of the wedding-day.

In selecting the engagement ring a diamond solitaire is usually preferred, if the purse will permit; a flat gold band is the next choice.

Gifts are usually packed wherever they are bought, and are sent directly from the shop to the bride. The variety is endless, ranging from the costliest silver and jewels, clocks, lamps, fans, odd bits of furniture, camel's hair shawls, etc., down to a pretty vase, a bit of embroidery, a picture, or a piece of china painted by the hand of a friend.

No one should hesitate to send a present whose money value is small, such gifts are often the most welcome, and a present which owes its existence to the donor's own labor is regarded as especially flattering.

The display of the wedding presents is a point to be decided according to the bride's wishes. Some people think it ostentatious, others devote much time and care to their arrangement, and it is undoubtedly gratifying to many to be permitted to see them.

One rule, however, is *invariable*—the bride must acknowledge every gift by a personal note.

After the wedding invitations are issued, the bride does not usually appear in public.

The bride-groom can lavish whatever gifts he pleases on the bride, and, if a wealthy man, often presents the bridesmaids with a souvenir of the occasion, a fan, bracelet, ring, or bouquet. He buys the wedding ring and furnishes the bride's bouquet; but there his privilege or duty ends. The bride's family supply the cards, carriages, and wedding entertainment.

WEDDING IN A CITY CHURCH.

The bride at a fashionable church wedding usually wears the conventional bridal dress of some white material with train and veil. She drives to the church with her father, who gives her away; her mother and other relatives, who have arrived in advance, occupy front seats.

The bridal procession is formed by the ushers, who walk first two and two, followed by the bridesmaids, also two and two; then the child-bridesmaids, if this pretty custom is adopted, and then the bride, leaning on her father's right arm. Sometimes the children lead the others. At the altar the ushers separate, moving to the right and left, the bridesmaids do the same, thus leaving room for the bridal pair.

When the bride reaches the lowest step, the bridegroom comes forward, takes her right hand, and leads her to the altar, where both kneel.

The clergyman, who should be already in his place, motions to them to rise, and at once begins the marriage ceremony.

The newly made husband and wife pass down the aisle arm in arm, enter the carriage, and are driven home, followed by the rest of the party.

To avoid the long delay of drawing off the glove, brides now cut the finger of the one on the left hand, so that it can be slipped aside to allow the putting on of the ring; this is the routine almost invariably followed at all church weddings. The bridal procession usually enters accompanied by the music of a wedding-march, and slow music is sometimes heard while the clergyman is pronouncing the vows.

At ultra-fashionable weddings the attempt is sometimes made to follow the English fashion of a wedding-breakfast.

The etiquette of this entertainment, as yet novel on our shores, is as follows: The guests are invited a fortnight in advance, and are expected to send their replies immediately, the occasion being quite as formal as a dinner-party.

On reaching the house where the breakfast is given, the gentlemen leave their hats in the hall; but the ladies do not take off their bonnets.

INTERIOR OF CHURCH.

After speaking to the bride and groom and the host and hostess, the company chat together till breakfast is announced, when the party go to the table in the following order: First, the bride and the groom, then the bride's father escorting the groom's mother, then the groom's father with the bride's mother, then the best man with the first bridesmaid, then the rest of the bridesmaids, attended by gentlemen who have been especially invited for the purpose, and finally the remaining guests in the order directed by the bride's mother. The dishes provided are bouillon, salad, birds, oysters, ices, jellies, etc.

The health of the bride and groom is proposed by some gentleman appointed, usually the father of the groom; response is made by the father of the bride. The groom sometimes responds and proposes the health of the bridesmaids, and the best man replies. But unless all are gifted in impromptu speech-making—a rare case—the situation is apt to be awkward; and the "stand up," breakfasts are usually far pleasanter and more social. The latter plan also enables the hostess to invite more guests and the occasion is far less formal.

After remaining from one to two hours with her guests, the bride retires to change her wedding costume for her travelling dress, and is met by the groom in the hall. The father, mother, and intimate friends exchange farewell kisses with the bride, and the pair drive away amid a shower of rice and slippers.

The best man's duties are as follows: "He goes with the groom to the church and stands beside him at the altar, until the bride's arrival, then he holds the groom's hat. He attends to the payment of the clergyman's fee, follows the bridal party out of the church and, on reaching the house, aids in presenting the guests.

The bridegroom's relatives sit at the right of the altar or communion rails at the groom's left hand, and the bridemaids take their seats at the left at the bride's left hand. The bridegroom and best man take their places at the left hand of the clergyman. The groom takes the bride's right hand, and, of course, she stands at his left; her father's place is a little behind her.

At the end of the ceremony the officiating clergyman congratulates the newly married pair, the bride takes her husband's left arm and passes down the aisle with him.

Wedding-cake is no longer sent; but it is put up in boxes, neatly tied with white ribbons, and each guest, upon quitting the house, takes one, if he or she desires.

A widow must never be attended by bridesmaids, nor must she wear veil or orange blossoms; the proper dress at church is a colored silk and bonnet, and she should be accompanied by her father, brother, or some near friend.

A HOUSE-WEDDING IN THE CITY.

A fashionable wedding at home calls into requisition the services of both florist and caterer; the former to decorate the rooms, the latter to furnish the marriage feast. All sorts of floral devices are invented, from the marriage bell, monogram, and umbrella, to a bower of ferns large enough to receive the bride and bridegroom.

The part of the room to be occupied by the bridal party should be separated by a white ribbon. After the clergyman has taken his place, the bride and groom enter together, followed by the mother, father, and other friends. Hassocks should be ready for the bridal pair to kneel upon.

SIMPLE HOME-WEDDINGS.

Where money is lacking to defray the charges of florist and caterer, or in places *remote* from cities, where their assistance cannot be had, the loving hands of friends decorate the rooms with the *largesse* of foliage and blossoms nature offers, and the table may be supplied with simple dishes such as the household means can furnish. Wedding-cake, light cakes, ices, and coffee arranged on a table prettily ornamented with flowers is a sufficient entertainment at a quiet home-wedding, and let it be added, is in far better taste than a more ostentatious display which is beyond the means of the family, and leaves a burden of debt behind.

The rules for invitations, calls, etc. are the same, save of course that the wording of the invitations is varied to suit different circumstances, whether the marriage ceremony is performed at church or at home, and whether the wedding entertainment is costly or simple.

In fashionable circles after the return of the bridal party, the members of both families give a dinner in their honor, and the bridesmaids, if able to do so, give them some entertainment.

Brides sometimes announce, when sending out their wedding-cards, two or more reception days; but they do not wear their wedding-dresses, though their toilettes may be as handsome as they desire.

When invited to balls or dinners, however, the wedding-dress is perfectly appropriate for a bride to wear—of course without the wreath and veil.

Anniversary Weddings.

F late years a pleasant custom has grown up of naming the different anniversaries of the marriage-day, and celebrating them with appropriate ceremonies. The rarest of all is of course the "diamond wedding," at the close of seventy-five years of wedded life, so rare, in fact, that no description of it is necessary; next in order is the golden, the fiftieth anniversary, also very infrequent, and too often fraught with sorrowful memories of the dear ones who have passed into the shadow-land. The gifts appropriate to the occasion are, of course, gold. If any article of dress worn at the first wedding—veil, handkerchief, or fan—is still in existence, it is donned by the bride, and she carries a bouquet of white flowers.

The card of invitation is in gold letters, and a recent form runs as follows:

1839   1889

Mr. and Mrs. John Anderson

At Home,

December Fifth, 1889

Golden Wedding.

29 Madison Street

At eight o'clock.

Flowers, too, are frequently given at golden weddings—preferably yellow ones—but on a recent occasion one of the most admired floral offerings was a superb flat basket of roses, bearing in violets the dates of the marriage and its anniversary.

The silver wedding, occurring twenty-five years after the marriage-day, is apt to be a far more joyous occasion than the golden one. The bride and groom are usually still in life's prime instead of being near the end of their earthly pilgrimage; their children are in the bloom of youth, and the circle of friends is yet numerous enough to fill the places of those who have early fallen from the ranks of the battle of life. The cards are printed in silver letters, frequently in the following form:

1864.   *1889*

Mr and Mrs Cameron

Request the pleasure of your company,

On Wednesday, November the twenty=first,

At eight o'clock.

Silver Wedding.

Stuart Cameron   *Mary Brown.*

Many persons do not have their names at the end, while others order an exact copy of the marriage-notice, taken from the newspaper of the period.

Gifts of silver being inexpensive, as compared with gold, almost all who receive invitations send some present, which may be as trivial or as costly as the donor chooses. They are usually marked " Silver Wedding," or bear some appropriate motto with the initials of the couple enclosed in a true lover's knot. The variety of articles is almost endless,—silver clocks, photograph frames, belt-clasps, mirrors, brushes and combs, and other toilet articles set in solid silver, and the long array of table-ware.

The entertainment is similar to that supplied at any reception, with the addition of a large wedding-cake, containing a ring, which the bride cuts just as she did twenty-five years before.

The twentieth anniversary bears the name of the "linen wedding, but many persons consider it unlucky to celebrate it, and the Scotch have a superstition that one or the other will die within the year if any allusion to it is made. ·

The crystal wedding is celebrated on the fifteenth anniversary of the marriage. The cards of invitation are frequently crystalized, and the gifts embrace every variety of glass-ware.

"Tin weddings" are occasions of universal jollity, and much ingenuity is exercised in devising amusing gifts. One young wife received from her father-in-law a check, marked "tin," enclosed in an elaborate tin pocket-book. All the tin utensils that can be used in the kitchen and household are also lavished without stint.

Tin funnels holding bouquets of flowers and tied with ribbons are usually numerous, and the glittering metal, adorned with bows of every hue, is really very effective displayed on a table. The invitation is usually printed on a bit of tin.

The fifth anniversary is dubbed the wooden wedding, and affords an opportunity for the bestowal of beautiful gifts in wood-carving, handsome pieces of furniture and picture frames, as well as the regulation wooden rollers, chopping trays, etc., for the kitchen. Bits of birch-bark are frequently used for the invitations.

One year after the marriage is celebrated by the iron wedding, when —as its name implies—all the gifts are of this indestructible metal. This and the anniversaries previously mentioned are the ones usually celebrated; but some other dates have received the following designations:

Paper—the second anniversary.

Leather—the third.

Straw—the fourth.

Woolen—the seventh.

Pearl—the thirtieth.

Coral—the thirty-fifth.

Bronze—the forty-fifth.

Invitations to any of these occasions should be appropriate in design. For instance, the pearl wedding cards should be printed on pearl colored stationery, the coral wedding cards on pink, the bronze wedding on bronze, etc.

Society Small Talk.

WHAT TO SAY, AND WHEN TO SAY IT.

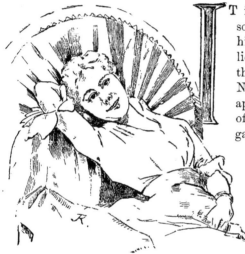

IT is true the new comer into society often discovers that his or her greatest difficulty lies in finding just the right thing to say at the right time. No one desires to sit silent and apparently stupid in the midst of a circle of people who are gaily chatting together, and, indeed, under some circumstances, the most insipid of "small talk" is far better than *no* talk at all. Fortunately it is an art which can be cultivated, and though a "brilliant conversationalist," like a genius, is born and not made, it is within the power of any one possessing average intelligence, tact, and good nature to become that welcome addition to every gathering known as "an agreeable person."

While, of course, no stereotyped phrases to suit every occasion can be given, a few suggestions may be of service to persons who desire to acquire the power of uttering graceful and pleasing things at the fitting moment, and a few general rules may aid those whose complaint is, that they "never know what to say."

There are many little topics of common interest, even among those who meet for the first time—mutual friends, similar pursuits, professions, and tastes. The art lies in their speedy discovery. In this respect, men seem to be gifted with far more readiness of perception than women.

42

The first principle of the art of making small talk is, probably, due consideration in choosing a subject which would be likely to prove agreeable to the person with whom one is to converse. The best help in ascertaining this, is to bear in mind the person's age, sex, and social position, which will almost invariably afford sufficient indications to enable one to form a tolerably accurate idea of the best subject to broach for the time.

Having secured an idea, it is better not to commence by broadly stating a fact or positively expressing an opinion, because this plan would either practically dispose of the subject, or perhaps be met with " Indeed," " Ah," or some other monosyllable, because if a different opinion was held by the person to whom the remark was made, he might not care, if a stranger, to directly contradict the view.

The object to be reached is to glide gradually into conversation, and the appearance of desiring to hear the ideas and opinions of others is far more likely to draw out their conversational powers, and afford an opportunity to display one's own, than to be curtly and egotistically explicit.

To imply by the manner an interest in the person with whom we are conversing is flattering; but to ask questions of a personal nature—evincing either idle curiosity or heedlessness—is by no means complimentary, and cannot fail to be disagreeable.

Mental exertion is as requisite to the successful mastery of the art of conversation as to the practice of any other art.

Many are prone to imagine that, without the least exertion, a sudden

torrent of brilliant ideas floods the brain of the clever talker, and envy his gifts, never dreaming that they are but the natural exercise of ordinary intelligence.

Next to the good talker ranks the good listener, who is always considered a most agreeable companion. The latter invariably appears to be deeply interested in the conversation and shows much tact in asking a question or putting in a remark just at the right time.

In conversing with new acquaintances, persons who are not reserved

MRS. GLADSTONE.

by nature often show a certain reserve manner because, having no knowledge of the tastes and ideas of the strangers, they hesitate to start any topics save the most commonplace. The power of easily making small talk dispels this reserve, and renders its fortunate possessor master or mistress of the situation.

HON. W. E. GLADSTONE.

One of the severest tests of the ability to make small talk is the morning call, because it entails fifteen minutes conversation with the person called upon, an easy matter to any one who has a ready flow of talk ; but a source of dread to those who have little idea of what ought to be said.

After the first exchange of greetings the weather usually comes to the fore ; but this topic also is speedily exhausted and one needs to introduce some subject capable of being enlarged upon. If guest or hostess has newly come to the city, either from a summer absence or a journey, the fact introduced into the talk might easily lead to a pleasant chat for the remainder of the call, the newcomer speaking of the incidents of travel or the attractions of the summer resort, the old resident, if that topic shows signs of failing, mentioning the pleasures or advantages to be obtained in the town during the winter.

If either has recently returned from a trip to Europe a wide field for talk is opened by comparing mutual experiences, or asking questions concerning the most interesting features of the principal places that have been visited.

If two or three callers are present, the hostess, even if averse to making a formal introduction, should try to render the conversation general, incidentally mentioning the names of her visitors, that each may become aware of the other's identity. When the time for leave-taking has arrived, a graceful mode of exit is to allude to any little plan that may have been formed for another meeting, as :

" Then you will let me know if I may expect you next Monday ? Good-bye."

Or, " Then I shall hope to see you at the Charity Fair on Saturday ? Good-bye." To which the hostess might reply ·

" Certainly, I will come. Good-bye "

Or, " I shall be there, if possible. Good-bye."

When there is nothing to add to the farewell, a good form is: "I think I must say good-bye," and the hostess answers:

" Good-bye, I am so glad to have seen you."

Persons who have just been introduced to each other during a call, at a tea, or on any other occasion, often have some little difficulty in starting a conversation unless aided by a suggestion from 'the person making the introduction, yet it is just at this time that pleasant, bright, " small talk " is most valuable in removing stiffness and creating a good impression.

The mention of the place from which either person comes, the fact of a recent return from a journey, or interest in any special pursuit on the part of either of the strangers by the person making the presentation is a valuable aid.

Delicate flattery, conveyed by inference, is one of the most satisfactory methods of making a good impression on a new acquaintance, reluctant as the majority of people may be to acknowledge the fact.

This, however, is not broad, blunt, insincere flattery, whose very grossness overshoots its mark ; but a pleasant, graceful manner of conveying appreciation of any special merit or talent the new acquaintance may possess. For instance: "I hope you are to sing this afternoon ; I have often heard of your lovely voice."

Or, " I am glad to meet you. Our mutual friends, the Conways, have said so many pleasant things about you."

The former remark might lead, by diverging from the owner of the " lovely voice," to a pleasant chat about music and musicians in general ; the latter would afford an opportunity for the exchange of familiar talk concerning the Conways—when they had been last met, etc.

The dinner-party is usually considered the severest test of any individual's conversational powers, and some society men—perhaps some ladies, also—make a study of collecting a store of telling little anecdotes for conversation.

Others naturally possess so ready a wit that they are always prepared to make a brilliant repartee, or an apt rejoinder. The difference is that the gay readiness of one can always keep all the guests amused, though he may have said nothing especially worth recollecting, while the witticisms of the other might be worth storing in the memory for repetition on some future occasion.

Conversation on domestic affairs and the tribulations occasioned by servants, etc., should always be avoided in general society. Few, indeed, are interested in the failures or successes of the last cook, or a minute description of infantile diseases.

A far worse error than this,—since it indicates a malicious disposition,—is ill-natured gossip concerning the affairs of others. While some thoughtless listeners may be momentarily amused, the impression left upon the mind is always unfavorable to the speaker.

Another class of remarks to be avoided is sometimes humorously mentioned as being "things one would rather not have said." Some luckless persons, either from want of tact or disregard of the feelings of others, appear to have a positive genius for the utterance of these unpleasant "home-truths," and, it is needless to say, are by no means popular in social circles.

Among such speeches may be mentioned the following: "How very badly your wife looks; she needs a warmer climate; you should send her somewhere at once; "—to a man whose narrow income renders it impossible for him to follow the advice.

Or, "What a pity your daughter's engagement is broken; Mr. Howard is such a fine fellow."

Or, "How much your little daughter looks like her Aunt Sarah, the resemblance is more striking every time I see her." "Aunt Sarah" being a notoriously plain and unattractive member of the family.

Or, again: "How very unbecoming that red bonnet is! People with auburn hair should never wear red." This to a young girl who can afford but one best bonnet a season, and who is perfectly aware that her choice has been unfortunate.

Music, the last new novel, and the last fashions in dress are frequent and usually suggestive topics to ladies, with an occasional discussion of shops and dress-makers. Young girls usually talk of their special amusements and occupations.

The small talk between persons of opposite sexes who are but slightly acquainted rarely soars above common-place topics, nor is it natural that it should do so, since its purpose is merely to pleasantly fill a few chance moments. It commonly begins with inquiries concerning absent friends —the lady, perhaps, asking if the gentleman has seen the Smiths lately. If he has, it affords him an opportunity to say where and when, mentioning any little incident connected with the meeting. If he has seen them in any city, the attractions of the place can be discussed.

A few brief imaginary conversations, illustrating the suggestions previously given, may serve to make them more clearly understood.

AT AN AFTERNOON TEA.

Strangers having been introduced, and exhausted the convenient subject of the weather, one remarks·

"What beautiful hair that little girl has."

"Yes, and the present style of wearing it is so becoming to children; it is very picturesque."

"Yes, and the Kate Greenaway costumes carry out the illusion; the little people look as if they had just stepped out of a Christmas book."

From this it would be easy to pass on to books in general, artists, or pictures, as the speakers' tastes might lead them.

AT A DINNER PARTY.

It is very desirable to fall into easy conversation immediately after any introduction; but especially so when two persons, who have previously been strangers, are sent to dinner together by the host. To maintain total silence until seated at the table will be apt to give each person the impression that his or her companion is dull and stupid.

The occasion, however, does not call for very profound remarks, almost anything will serve the purpose. For instance, the gentleman may say: "We must be careful not to step on that elaborate train," referring to the costume of a lady preceding the pair.

"Yes, indeed, that would be a mishap. But trains are graceful in spite of their inconvenience."

Her companion must answer·

"Oh! I admire them, of course. Only I have such a dread of stepping on them and bringing down the wrath of the fair wearer on my devoted head."

"Are you apt to be unlucky in that way? And do you think a woman must necessarily be enraged, if her gown is trodden upon?"

"Oh! if you want my real opinion, I should say the woman who could stand that test must be a rare exception to the generality of her sex; but here are our places. We are to sit this side, I believe."

Having seated themselves, and exchanged a few comments (of course flattering), on the table decorations, the lady, wishing to ascertain whether her companion was one of the silent diners-out, might say:

"Some people do not care to eat and talk at the same time, but prefer to let what few comments they make come in between the courses."

"A man must be a dull fellow who cannot do both, with satisfaction to his neighbor if not to himself."

"Then I may talk to you without fear of interrupting your enjoyment of your dinner? But you speak as though it were easier to please your neighbor than yourself."

"Set down that speech to my gallantry. Ladies are so good natured that they take the will for the deed, while my modesty precludes my taking credit for any efforts of mine."

"I often find that the men who are least ready to take credit are the most worthy of it; so I shall expect great things at your hands."

"I fear I have unintentionally raised your expectations, and that you will be doomed to disappointment."

"If that proves to be the case, perhaps it will be my own fault, and after all expectation is the better part of life."

"Has realization always fallen short of expectation?"

"In some degree; but I fear I am a little inclined to let my imagination soar away with me."

"Imagination is the safest companion you could have in your flight, and the one of whom you would be the least likely to grow weary."

"Do you never weary of your own thoughts—your own visions, and your own companionship?"

"Very often; but then I am more practical than poetical; you volatile feminine personages are always floating to more ethereal regions."

"I am not so foolish as to indulge in day-dreams," the lady might answer. "I think people whose lives are full of duties, have little leisure for such amusement. But to change the subject to a topic less ethereal—how delicious these Patés de Cailles are. Still, the way the poor little birds are kept alive in boxes at the markets is very cruel."

"To fatten them, I suppose. No doubt it is rather uncomfortable. You ladies are so tender-hearted. But how about the birds you wear in your hats; and the wings that deck them? Are not the gaily feathered fowl sacrificed to your vanity?"

"Perhaps so, but not tortured, etc.

MRS. GROVER CLEVELAND.

AT A MUSICALE.

Some one might remark: "That was a French song? Are you familiar with the language?"

I can read it fairly well, that is all. But my sister is an excellent French scholar. Are you not, Barbara?"

"Yes, I suppose so. But I was at school some time in Paris."

"Oh! that is such an advantage," a third speaker might remark, "I think one ought to go abroad to acquire a language."

"Do you?" a fourth might answer. "Now I think it is easiest to acquire a language in early childhood, when the mind is impressionable and the memory retentive."

A fifth might chime in: "That may be when the child has a real gift for the languages, but not otherwise."

Or, alluding to a song just finished, some one might remark: "What a fine voice Miss Seymour has! Did you ever hear her before?"

"Yes, indeed, very often. She attends a great many of these parties, I fancy. I am tolerably familiar with her list of songs, etc."

AT A RECEPTION.

"Won't you let me find you a seat somewhere? Don't you hate a crowd?" A man who was thoroughly at his ease might say to a lady to whom he had just been presented.

"Oh no, I like to see a room full of people. It looks as if they appreciated one's invitations."

"I am afraid you look at a crush from a hostess' standpoint. How you ladies always make everything a home question!"

"I'm not so sure of that. You say you hate a crowd, yet if you should come to my "at home" next

MISS AMES.

Thursday and find only a few people there, you would probably go away thinking that I must be a very unpopular woman."

"Then you want to prove that crowded rooms are the standard by which to judge of the hostess' popularity? I never regarded them from that standpoint; but you may be right. In that case I shall expect to be unable to get further than your door Thursday night."

"That is rather a far-fetched compliment. I hope you will never be kept away by a crowd when the question of seeing me is concerned; but you need have no fear this time, I have sent out very few invitations."

This is about as far as the talk could easily be carried on so slender a thread; but it could be readily turned into another direction by the question: "Is this the first entertainment of the kind you have given in your new house?"

"Why no indeed. I asked you to a party we gave three months ago, and you were out of town I believe, or something."

"Something? Why I was ill for six weeks, unable to go anywhere, and when one has been out of society for a time, it is wonderful how hard it is to fall into the routine again."

"Do you mean that people forget to send you invitations, or that you don't care to accept them?"

"A little of both, I confess that the routine of social duties is a little wearisome when one feels not quite up to the mark; there seems such a sameness and uselessness about the whole thing that one begins to wonder whether it is not a huge mistake."

"Oh, you are growing morbid. Society is well enough, so far as it goes. I would not try to set the world right, if I were you; but make the best of things as they are, that's my philosophy."

"It is an easy going view of things; but hardly the highest ground to go upon."

If the lady wished to discuss the question whether, and in what way, it is woman's mission to elevate society and remodel some of its laws, this would afford an opportunity of drawing out her companion's views and convictions; but if not, she could easily turn it into another channel, though starting with the last remark. "The highest ground? Perhaps not. But I like to be sure of my ground, and avoid dangerous subjects, opposing other people's opinions, etc. But I find one is apt to say the wrong thing."

"People who are sensitive or crotchety, are hard to get on with—one can't help rubbing them the wrong way."

'I think sensitive people, or people whose vanity and self-love are perpetually on the alert for a slight, are so much more tiresome than people with a crotchet. One can humor the crotchet aside from the individual."

"I don't know about that; I don't think you were specially inclined to humor either my crotchet or myself just now."

"Oh, that is very different. It would not be a good thing for you if I did."

"How do you know? Suppose you try it just for once, etc."

A little badinage of this sort, blended with common sense, lends, as it were, a dash of color to the conversation.

AT A BALL.

The fashion of saying, "May I have the pleasure of dancing with you?" has given place to a less formal method, and a young man now accosts a young lady with, "I hope you have kept a dance for me," "Won't you spare me a dance?" or "Shall we take a turn?" The young lady does not answer: "I shall be very happy," a reply which has disappeared with "May I have the pleasure?" but says: "I'm afraid I have none to spare except number ten, a quadrille," or "I am engaged for the next five dances; but I'll give you one, if you come for it a little later."

Another form of invitation: "Are you engaged for this dance?" Some silly girls sometimes answer by saying, "I do not think I am," while perfectly aware that they are not, and the young men are quick to see through the evasion by which the maiden seeks to conceal her lack of partners. A clever girl escapes from the dilemma by the prompt an-

swer: "I am very glad to say I am not," thus inferring that she might have been engaged, had she desired; but preferred waiting for the chance of dancing with him—a suggestion flattering to the gentleman.

Ball-room small talk is not expected to rise above the common-place. The materials supplied by the entertainment itself are very limited—the band, the flowers, the floor, the supper. Dull people usually ring the changes on these themes. For instance, "What a good band it is!" "How well the band plays!" "It's a capital band!" "What a pleasant hall-room this is!" "I think this floor is very good." "Don't you think the floor slippery, etc., etc. Such phrases, by dint of constant repetition, are apt to weary the listener, and people who can get away from them do well to branch off to vary the monotony.

In response to the query : "I suppose you are very fond of dancing?" a young lady, instead of making the usual answer: "Yes, I am, very," might say: "Yes, I am fond of it; but there are other things I like quite as much," thus giving her partner an opportunity to enquire what amusements interested her.

Simple affirmatives and negatives close the avenues of talk.

"Yes, I am," "No, I am not," "Yes, I do," "No, I do not," give little encouragement for farther efforts. If such answers are necessary, try to qualify them. Instead of a blunt "No, I am not," it would be better to say: "I do not think I am very fond of it. Do you care for it much?"

A ball-room is especially the place for airy nothings. "This is our dance, I think," a gentleman might say; "you are not afraid that I am not able to pilot you through the crowd?" If the lady answers: "No, not at all," her partner would have to seek some other opening for conversation; but were she to respond: "No, I shall believe in you till you prove my confidence misplaced," the young man could reply that "he was proud of her confidence," he "considered himself put on trial, as it were," or that she "should have no occasion to regret her trust."

If a lady wishes to compliment her partner on his waltzing, she might ask if he had spent much time in Germany. To which he would respond: "How did you guess that?" or, "No, indeed, why did you suppose so?" This would afford an opening for the reply : "Germans usually waltz so well, I thought you must have learned the art there."

Ornaments worn in a ball-room often suggest gay conversation to ready-witted people. For instance: "I envy that butterfly on your hair, close to your ear. What a chance to whisper secrets, lucky butterfly!"

The answer might be: "Oh, no, the butterfly is not so happy as you think; I shut it up in a velvet case when I go home, lest I should lose it. Now, you could not be shut up, and you wouldn't like it, if you could."

Or, the lady might reply, jestingly:

"Unlike you, my butterfly has no feeling, so it doesn't appreciate its happiness, a trait, I believe, characteristic of butterflies. You ought to know something about it."

Here the retort might follow:

"You are kind enough to anticipate my future; I haven't found my wings yet; I am still in a chrysalis state."

If the lady wanted to have the last word, she might say:

"Then you are safer to hold, if not so pretty to keep, and I think you could not do better than to remain a chrysalis for the present."

In conclusion, it may be said that in the art of small talk—as in every other art—"practice makes perfect.' No hard and fast rules to fit every occasion can be given; but persons who really desire to please, and who will take the time and trouble requisite to carry out the above suggestions, will ere long find themselves included in the class known as "people everybody is glad to meet."

CALLS.

When calling at a friend's house where there are other visitors, previously strangers to you, should you invite them to call as well as the hostess?

No. It is not necessary.

A gentleman is paying an evening call. Shortly after another visitor arrives. Should the first take leave or remain?

Take his leave by all means—not instantly, but after the interval of a few moments. Too abrupt a departure might indicate a dislike to the new-comer. But it is extremely "bad form" for one person to attempt to "sit out" another.

In going up-stairs to a parlor on the second floor, which should lead the way, the hostess or the guest?

The guest.

Two young ladies meet while paying a call at the house of a third. When one guest rises to take leave, should the other also rise and remain standing until she has taken her departure?

It would be more courteous for her to do so.

54

Is it proper for a gentleman to write to a lady with whom his acquaintance is very slight, asking permission to call at her home?

Better make the request verbally, if possible. If circumstances prevent, he may write respectfully

* *
*

A gentleman living a few miles away writes to a lady, stating that he will call on a certain evening. Should she reply?

Not unless she wishes to do so. The gentleman must take his chance of finding her at home. Yet it is perfectly proper, if she desires, to write a few lines informing him that she will be glad to receive him at the time named. If she has any engagement for the evening, a note should be sent to notify him of the fact, otherwise, the natural inference would be that she did not care to see him.

T TABLE.

How should a fork be held?

With the concave side uppermost.

* *
*

What reply should be made to the question: "Which part of the chicken do you prefer?"

"White meat," or, "Dark meat."

* *
*

At a dinner or lunch, after having been served once, would it be bad form to say: "No, thank you," in reply to the second offer of a dish?

No.

* *
*

Should one say: "No, thank you," to a servant?

Yes.

* *
*

Should the napkin be left unfolded at the end of a meal?

Yes, napkins should never be folded.

* *
*

Is it allowable for a man to eat his meals with his coat off?

Certainly not. No well-bred man would think of doing so.

Should teaspoons be placed in the holder with the bowls up or down?

It would be better to put a teaspoon on each saucer; but if a "holder" is essential, put the bowls down.

₊

In drinking tea at breakfast—from a coffee-cup—is it ever proper to leave the spoon in the cup, not in the very act of drinking, but in the intervals?

No.

₊

Is it proper to use a knife and fork in eating asparagus, or should the stalks be taken in the fingers?

Never use a knife. Many well-bred people take the stalks in the fingers. If a compromise is desired, use the fork only.

₊

Is it proper to dip a piece of bread into a coffee-cup or egg-cup to moisten it with the contents?

Not according to American ideas, but some well-bred foreigners do it.

RESS.

What costume is suitable for a gentleman to wear on board a yacht?

If on a cruise, or where the party consists exclusively of men, a blue flannel or serge suit with white waist-coat would do. If ladies are present, a black diagonal cutaway coat, white or black waist-coat, light trousers, and light derby hat.

₊

What is the proper material for a dress-suit?

Black broad-cloth or diagonal.

₊

Is it proper for young ladies to wear evening dresses while receiving calls at home in the evening?

No, a ball-dress would be an absurd costume for home wear.

₊

On what occasions is it proper for a man to wear a "tourist shirt?"

When yachting, playing ball or tennis, or in the woods.

What is the proper neck-tie to wear with a double-breasted black frock coat, at an after-noon wedding?

A silk four-in-hand.

*
* *

What kind of scarf is it proper to wear with a tweed suit?

A blue polka-dot or solid color four-in-hand.

*
* *

Is it proper to wear one, two, or three studs in a shirt front with a dress-suit?

Three studs are most generally worn, but one is perfectly allowable.

*
* *

Is it proper for a young business man to wear a high silk hat during business hours?

It is not the custom in cities. Strictly speaking, a high hat should only be worn with a frock coat or dress-suit.

*
* *

Which is the proper choice for a man calling in the evening on a lady—a black cutaway coat, waist-coat, and grey trousers, or a full-dress suit?

In winter, the dress suit. In summer, the rules of etiquette are less rigid, and there would be no objection to the former.

*
* *

Is it proper to wear a black silk hat in summer, if a man dislikes the light colored ones?

No, it is contrary to custom.

*
* *

What gloves should be chosen for street and evening wear?

For the street—the proper color is brick or tan.   For evening—
white or lavender with broad, black stitching.

⁎

Is it proper to wear a black cutaway coat at the funeral of a near
relative?

Yes.

⁎

Is it proper to wear a frock-coat at a military dinner given at
8 o'clock in the evening?

No, a dress-coat is the proper choice.

⁎

Would it be proper to attend the theatre in full dress before going
to a ball, if one occupies a box and keeps out of sight of the audience?

No, society sanctions full dress only at the opera.

⁎

Is it proper for a lady to wear diamonds when travelling?

No, nor is it good form to wear many diamonds at any time except
in full evening dress

⁎

What should a widow wear for a wedding-gown?

She may wear a bridal dress like any other bride, with the exception
of the veil and orange blossoms, but many widows prefer pearl-grey or
some other delicate shade rather than white.

NTRODUCTIONS.

Should a wife and husband be introduced as
" my wife," " my husband," or as Mr. or Mrs?

The latter, " Mrs. A., Mr. X."

⁎

If two young men meet three young ladies,
one of the young men being acquainted with
one of the young ladies, who introduces him
to her friends, should the young man present
his friend to all the young ladies, or only to
the one with whom he is acquainted?

To the one he knows.   She can then present the young man to her
friends.

Should acquaintances whom one meets hap-hazard in the street, or at a public entertainment, be introduced to one another?

No, there is no necessity for doing so.

*_**

Is it necessary to acknowledge an invitation to a church wedding?

Formerly invitations to church weddings required no answer. Of late some persons send acceptances, regrets, or failing these, their cards.

*_**

Is it allowable for a young man, on being presented to a young lady, to shake hands with her?

Not unless she first offers hers.

*_**

In introducing a lady and gentleman, whose name should be mentioned first?

The lady's.

*_**

If two ladies walking together meet a third with whom one of the two friends is unacquainted, which of the names, in making the introduction, should be mentioned first?

It makes no difference.

*_**

Should a lady be presented to a gentleman or a gentleman to a lady?

A gentleman should always be presented to a lady.

IFTS.

What is a suitable gift to send when invited to a golden wedding—if the purse will not permit the souvenir to be gold?

Flowers are always appropriate. For the occasion named, yellow ones are especially desirable.

*_**

Is it allowable for a lover to give his fiancée a bracelet instead of a ring?

Certainly, but a ring is the usual choice, because it can be constantly worn.

*_**

Is it " good form " for the bride to give the groom a present?

Yes, if she desires.

Is it proper for a gentleman to give a lady a ring to replace one she has lost?

Not unless he is engaged to her.

*
* *

What is the proper time to send a gift to a mother-in-law?

Before the wedding, at the same time the bride's is forwarded.

*
* *

In sending a birth-day card, is it proper to enclose another bearing the words "With the compliments of—"?

Yes.

*
* *

Is it allowable for a young girl to accept a gift, even the most trifling, from a young man unless a card accompanies it?

Etiquette forbids any unmarried woman to accept gifts of any value, except from men who are related to her, or from her fiancé. Flowers, fruits, or candy, however, can be received, and, if sent anonymously, the fact does not render their acceptance improper.

*
* *

What would be a suitable birth-day present for a man to send a young lady?

A bouquet of flowers or a box of nice confectionery.

Should the donors of wedding-gifts be thanked verbally or by letter?

In writing, if possible.

NGAGEMENTS.

Is it proper for a young lady who is engaged to receive evening visits regularly from former admirers?

Certainly not.

*
* *

Is it allowable for a man, who is engaged to one young lady, to take another one to the theatre, or send her flowers?

No engaged man has a right to show attention to any one except his fiancée.

*
* *

Is it necessary for a man who has been accepted by a young lady, to ask her father's consent, if he has no intention of marrying immediately?

Yes, he should ask the parents' consent at once, and frankly state his financial condition and future prospects.

Has a young lady a right to ask her lover for an engagement ring?
There could scarcely be a greater breach of etiquette.

* *
*

What is considered the most suitable engagement ring?
A diamond set in gold.

* *
*

How long is it allowable for persons to be engaged?
Until they are able to marry.

* *
*

If a man who is engaged to a lady has set no time for the wedding
can he be compelled to name a date?
No.

* *
*

Can an engaged man call on his fiancée every evening?
Certainly. He is expected to do so.

* *
*

On which finger is the engagement ring worn?
On the third finger of the left hand.

* *
*

Is it proper for an engaged couple to walk arm-in-arm in the street?
Yes, the lady is at liberty to take the arm of her fiancé, if she desires

* *
*

Is it good form for a lady to ask her fiancé to take her to drive?
It is not improper, but ladies usually wait for their lovers to take the
initiative, especially in the early days of the engagement.

* *
*

Has a man a right to break his engagement with a girl, giving her no
explanation?
Certainly not. No man, who is a gentleman, would do it.

MOURNING.

Is it improper for a man who is in mourning to wear a dress-suit to the theatre, if he
wears a black tie and studs?

By no means. A dress-suit is proper to
wear in the evening, whether the person is in
mourning or not.

* *
*

Is it improper for a person in mourning
to use mourning stationery for a business
letter?

Not improper, but unnecessary.

Is it proper for a person who is in mourning to wear colored flowers?

Hardly, but it is often done. White flowers are so easily obtained that the colored ones are not necessary.

*_**

How long should a very young widow wear a veil over her face, and, after putting the veil back, how long should it be worn?

Six months or a year over the face, and as long as she wishes afterwards, but not less than two years.

*_**

Should a man who is in mourning wear a white or a colored waist-coat?

A white waist-coat.

Are colored shirts allowable?

No.

EDDINGS.

Should the ushers at a church-wedding be invited to return after the ceremony to the house of the bride, when no reception is given and only the immediate members of the family are expected to be present?

It is not absolutely necessary, but it would be more courteous to invite them. Under the circumstance named, they would doubtless have sufficient good taste to decline.

*_**

In presenting a wedding gift, the sender being acquainted with the bridegroom, can it be addressed to the bride?

Certainly.

*_**

At a large wedding—in the country—is it allowable to use Japanese doilies instead of napkins?

Certainly not. Have a sufficient supply of napkins for the guests.

*_**

Should the bridegroom kiss the bride directly after the marriage?

Not if he desires to follow the latest rule of etiquette.

*_**

Is there any objection to invite young married men to serve in the capacity of ushers at a small home-wedding?

The sole objection is that it is not the custom. Etiquette requires that the ushers at all weddings shall be unmarried men.

**

How should cards announcing the marriage of a lady who has been divorced and taken her maiden name be worded?

In the usual way.

**

Who should invite the ushers at a wedding, the bride or the bride's parents?

Neither. It is the bridegroom's privilege to invite the ushers, but he should consult the bride's preferences.

**

What portion of the expenses of a church wedding should the bridegroom pay?

The clergyman's fee.

**

What is considered a suitable fee to give to the minister who performs the marriage ceremony?

From twenty-five to fifty dollars.

**

Is it proper to issue invitations for a wedding only two months after a death has occurred in the family?

Yes, if it is a very quiet one, limited to friends and relatives.

**

Does the best man at a church wedding precede or follow the groom?

He follows him.

**

Is it proper for an engaged man to fix the date of his marriage six or eight months ahead?

Certainly.

**

Should a bride bid her friends good-bye when departing on her wedding tour, or should she slip quietly away?

She should bid them good-bye by all means, any other course would be rude.

**

At a home-wedding is it necessary for the best man to take the maid of honor in to supper or to pay her any special attention?

**

He need not devote himself solely to her, but he should see that she is attended to.

Should the bride's mother or the groom pay for the announcement cards, if the cards bear simply the names of the bride and groom with the announcement of their marriage?

The bride's mother.

*
*

At a church-wedding, without music, is it allowable for the bride to wear a white dress and veil?

Yes, with or without music, a bride has the privilege of wearing bridal-dress.

*
*

How should a wedding invitation to a lady and her fiancé be addressed—the sender of the invitation not being acquainted with the fiancé?

Write to the lady and ask for her fiancé's address. Then send him a separate invitation.

*
*

In sending a wedding invitation to a firm, should separate invitations be addressed to the partners, including their wives, or should one be sent to the firm.

Business methods must never be introduced into social affairs. Send each member of the firm a separate invitation addressed to himself and his wife.

*
*

Is it necessary to send a wedding-present when invited only to the reception?

Not necessary, but customary.

*
*

Is it "good form," to kiss the bride at the close of the marriage ceremony?

The custom is almost obsolete.

*
*

Should wedding-cards be sent to the fiancée of the bridegroom's friend if the bridegroom is not acquainted with the lady?

Certainly.

*
*

Should a note sent to a person living in the same town be forwarded by mail or messenger or delivered in person?

Either way is perfectly proper.

*
*

In sending a present to a young lady who is to be married on the same day, should the accompanying card bear the words "with best wishes," or "with congratulations and best wishes?"

"With best wishes," congratulations should be addressed only to the groom.

*_**

Which is the proper way to address a letter, Mr. A. D. Saunders, or A. D. Saunders, Esq. ?

Until quite recently the custom has varied in this country, but the rule is now given that all letters *except notes of invitation* shall be directed to——, Esq.

*_**

When sending out announcement cards of a private wedding, is it necessary to state on what days and between what hours the bride and groom will be at home.

It is better to name certain days, but it would be perfectly proper to have the cards read : At home after June.

MISCELLANEOUS.

In entering a room at a reception or party, should the lady take the gentleman's arm ?

This was the custom some years ago; now the fashion is so decidedly obsolete that it would appear almost ridiculous.

*_**

In passing an acquaintance on the street, going in the same direction, should one turn and greet him ?

Certainly; it would be extremely rude not to do so.

*_**

Should more than one invitation be sent to a family where there are sons and daughters ?

One invitation is sufficient for each married couple in a family, and each single adult member of the family should also receive one.

*_**

On entering a public dining-room with a lady, does the gentleman precede her ?

Yes.

*_**

Is it allowable for a lady, when visiting a friend, to invite her to a matinée ?

Yes, but as a rule guests should not propose excursions, lest they should interfere with the plans of their entertainers.

*
*
*

When a lady and gentleman are travelling together, which should leave the car first?

The gentleman, to help her out.

*
*
*

Should a man offer to shake hands with a lady or leave it to her to make the offer?

As a rule a man should not offer to shake hands with a lady. In his own house, however, if he knows her well, he should welcome her with a cordial grasp of the hand.

*
*
*

On which side of a lady should a man ride?

Never on the skirt side, if possible to avoid it.

*
*
*

Is it proper for a young man well acquainted with young ladies to shake hands with them while they are standing after church waiting for their carriage, or should he merely bow and enter into conversation?

He can do either.

*
*
*

When a lady has been visiting in a friend's house, is it customary at the end of her stay to fee the servants?

Certainly. It is a matter of course.

*
*
*

If a gentleman accompanies a lady to church, is it proper for her to lead the way up the aisle and choose the seat?

Certainly.

*
*
*

If a gentleman escorts a lady to a party, is he bound to go with her to the supper-table, or is it proper for him to choose any one he desires?

He must see that the lady he accompanies is provided with supper, but he is not obliged to stay by her.

*
*
*

Should R. S. V. P. be placed on notes of invitation?

Recently it has been thought better not to do so, because the act might be interpreted as a hint that the recipient does not understand the courtesies of life. All invitations should be answered, therefore the letters R. S. V. P., which merely represent the French phrase for " please reply," are not needed.

***

Should bouillon be drunk out of the cups or sipped from a spoon?
It should be drunk out of the cups.

***

Should letters of introduction be sealed, and how should they be delivered?
They should not be sealed. If in any way connected with business, present in person; if merely social, forward by mail with the sender's card and address enclosed.

***

If a gift is presented enclosed in a box or wrapper, should it be opened in the donor's presence?
Certainly. Open the package and look at the contents in order to express the pleasure the present affords.

***

Should a lady express her thanks to a gentleman for a gift of flowers in writing or verbally?
In writing, unless she expects to see him in an hour or two.

***

What is the correct way for a gentleman to ask a lady if he can escort her home?
Say merely: "May I have the pleasure of accompanying you to your home?"

***

Which should precede in going up and down stairs, the lady or the gentleman?
The gentleman should precede the lady in going up stairs and follow her in going down.

***

Is it proper for a young man, when calling on a young lady, to present a bunch of flowers or a box of candy?
Certainly. It will be apt to make him a welcome guest.

***

Is it proper for a young man to ask a young girl at their first meeting to address him by his Christian name?
Certainly not. It would be great presumption.

Would it be proper for a lady to ask a gentleman to reimburse her for a dress he accidently soiled at a sociable, or should the gentleman offer to pay for it?

Either would be extremely improper. She should simply accept his apology courteously, and let the matter drop.

*
* *

A gentleman calling in the evening on his aunt, is presented to a young lady, who is also calling. Should he offer to escort the young lady to her home?

Certainly.

*
* *

When a lady enters a room where there are other ladies, which should speak first?

The ladies in the room.

*
* *

Is it proper for a gentleman to visit a lady more than three evenings in the week?

Certainly not, unless he is engaged to her.

*
* *

Is it good form for two young ladies to go from one city to another on the cars without an escort in the evening to meet a gentleman to attend the theatre, and then return?

By no means, unless the gentleman is a near relative, and a suitable escort is provided to meet them at the station on their return.

*
* *

On entering a theatre, concert-room, or other place of public amuse-ment, should the lady or gentleman go first?

The gentleman, unless the way is perfectly open and clear.

*
* *

Is it necessary for a lady to thank a gentleman who has escorted her home?

Certainly. Always express thanks for any courtesy.

*
* *

Is it proper for a girl of seventeen to go alone to matinées in a city?

Certainly not.

* *

Is it polite to thank a lady or gentleman for having treated one to ice-cream or soda?

Yes.

What is the proper hour in the evening for a gentleman to call on a lady?

Any time between 8 and 9:15 P. M.

***

Is it good form for a man to give a lady money to put in the contribution-box at church?

No; she is supposed to have her own funds for such purposes. If she requests a trifling loan, that alters the case.

***

If a gentleman is walking with two ladies in the evening, is it proper for him to offer his arm to one only?

Certainly; the second lady should walk by the side of her friend.

***

How should one address an unmarried lady, of whose age one is ignorant?

Dear Madam.

***

Is it allowable for a gentleman who is corresponding with a young lady to enclose postage stamps for replies?

By no means. Unless in a business correspondence, the act would be insulting.

***

Is the address " My dear friend " in a letter incorrect?

Not if it is by persons who are on terms of intimate friendship.

***

Is it rude for a man not to remove his hat when a lady enters an elevator?

If it is an office or business elevator, perhaps not. But the courtesy is always advisable; and men who desire to be ranked among gentlemen will do well to follow the rule " When in doubt, raise the hat."

***

Which arm should a gentleman offer to a lady?

Either. In the street the one which places him next to the curbstone.

***

If a man sends a lady a note by special delivery, requesting an immediate reply, is it a breach of etiquette to enclose a special delivery stamp, on the assumption that the lady would not be provided with one?

No.

***

If a man seated in a railroad car beside a lady who is a stranger to him is greeted by a male acquaintance, should he lift his hat in returning the salute (out of courtesy to her)?

It is not obligatory, but it would be courteous.

*_**

Is it bad form for a lady walking with a gentleman after dark to take his arm if he neglects to offer it?

Yes, unless he is a very intimate friend. It is of course a breach of etiquette on the gentleman's part, but she should not remind him of his error.

*_**

Is it proper for a gentleman to smoke while walking in the street with a lady?

Certainly not.

*_**

A young man in the Army, who has been intimately acquainted with a young lady, writes to her family to ask permission to correspond with her. Is it proper for her to write the first letter?

Certainly, if she desires to do so.

*_**

If a gentleman meets a lady in a large retail store and wishes to talk with her, is it allowable for him to replace his hat after removing it to bow?

Yes, for in a large store, where a number of people are passing to and fro, the same rules apply as when persons meet in the street.

*_**

A lady in calling on a friend early in the evening met the latter's brother and a stranger. On leaving the house both gentlemen went with her to the horse-cars. She bowed to the stranger and shook hands with her friend's brother. Was it a breach of etiquette not to shake hands with the stranger also?

No. A bow is sufficient for a lady to bestow on a new acquaintance.

*_**

Is it bad form to offer a gloved hand?

No.

*_**

Is it the proper thing for a gentleman to offer his arm to a lady—to whom he is neither married nor engaged—while escorting her after dark?

Certainly it is proper. Not to do so would be regarded as a lack of courtesy.

If a gentleman meets, in a restaurant, a lady with whom he is very well acquainted, is it proper for him to seat himself at the table without being invited, and if so, should he pay for her meal?

No, he should not take the seat unless invited to do so. If he *is* invited, and the lady has not already ordered her meal, he may request permission to order for both, and then pay the bill.

*
* *

Should a gentleman bow first when meeting a young lady whose acquaintance he has made at a ball?

No, it is the lady's privilege.

*
* *

After having shaken hands with a lady who is an intimate friend, should a gentleman lift his hat on taking leave of her?

Certainly.

*
* *

Is it proper for a lady to bow to a gentleman who is walking on the other side of the street, in a small town where the streets are narrow?

Perfectly proper.

*
* *

Is it allowable for a gentleman to offer his arm to a young lady on their first walk?

Yes, if the walk is taken after dark.

*
* *

Should a gentleman ask a lady to come and sit near him, or take a seat near her?

He should sit near her—it would be a gross breach of etiquette to ask her to sit near him.

*
* *

How should a gentleman ask a lady to take his arm?

He would say: " Will you take my arm?"

*
* *

Is it proper for a lady who is receiving guests at a small evening entertainment at her own house to stand in the back parlor, thus compelling the guests to pass through one room in search of her?

No, she should stand near the door where her guests enter.

*
* *

Is it necessary for a lady to invite a gentleman to call again?

Yes, if it is his first visit, otherwise not. But a lady can usually, without giving a formal invitation, find some pleasant way of expressing a desire to see a friend again.

A lady moving into a village was not called upon by a near neighbor. Later this neighbor left the place, returning some months after to visit a friend of both persons. Should the former call?

By no means. Why extend a courtesy to one who showed no desire to make the acquaintance of the new-comer?

***

Can a lady pay her own travelling expenses when escorted by a gentleman?

Certainly. She should not permit any other arrangement.

***

Is it necessary for intimate friends, at the end of an evening's or afternoon's enjoyment, to express their appreciation of it to the host or hostess?

Yes.

***

Which is the proper course—for a lady to invite a gentleman to call, or for the gentleman to ask if he may call?

It depends wholly on circumstances. The custom differs in different places.

***

What should a lady answer when a gentleman who has been presented to her says on leaving, " I've been pleased to meet you?"

A bow and a smile are a sufficient reply.

***

Is it proper for a lady to send her card to a gentleman whom she has met twice?

No. Give him a verbal invitation to call when you next meet him.

***

Should an invitation to a school concert be answered, if the recipient cannot attend and, if so, to whom should it be addressed.

Certainly, to the person who sent the invitation.

***

Is it proper for a gentleman who is accompanying a lady in a street-car to rise and give his seat to another lady?

Yes.

***

When a lady is introduced to a gentleman, should she speak, or merely bow?

Better make some pleasant remark, if she is fortunate enough to have a ready flow of small talk.

Is it " good form " for a gent. man to call on a young lady whom he has met frequently, but who has never invited him to do so?

No.

How should a letter to a young lady be addressed? With the Christian name written in full, or merely with the initials?

It is immaterial, unless the lady has unmarried sisters. In that case, if she is the oldest, omit the Christian name; if younger, it must be used.

_

In declining an invitation to an evening-party, is it necessary to put the words "with regrets" on your card?

Never use a card to decline an invitation to a party. Write a formal note in the third person.

_

A gentleman who is paying devoted attention to a young lady invites her to pay a visit at his house. Is it good form for her to go? She knows no other members of the family.

Certainly not. She must wait for a special invitation from the family.

_

If a gentleman, on meeting a lady for the first time, escorts her home, should she invite him to call?

Yes, if she has sufficient knowledge of him to be sure that he will be a desirable acquaintance. As a rule, however, invitations to call are not extended on first acquaintance.

_

When a gentleman has met a lady several times, but has received no invitation to call, is it proper for him to ask permission to do so?

Yes, if the degree of acquaintanceship warrants it, and he has no reason to suppose that the lady is reluctant to number him among her visitors.

_

In sending invitations, should the outside and inside envelopes read the same, the address only being placed on the latter?

Yes.

_

How should an envelope, containing an invitation to a brother and two sisters be addressed?

Write the brother's name on one line, and "The Misses" one line below. But it is far better to use a separate envelope for the brother.

_

Is it proper to use tooth-picks at the table?

No. Yet it is a breach of etiquette frequently committed by people otherwise well-bred.

Should a ticket given by a friend to any public affair be considered in the same light as an invitation and acknowledged by a call?

Not necessarily.

*
* *

When a gentleman escorts a lady home in the evening, should she invite him to come in?

That depends upon the hour. Not if it is later than 9.30 P. M.

*
* *

Is it proper for a lady to dance with a gentleman who has been presented to her only a few minutes before the dance begins?

Certainly.

*
* *

A society gave a reception at the house of one of its members. Several of the gentleman's friends, who were not invited to the entertainment, considering themselves slighted, cut his acquaintance. Were they right?

Certainly not, the gentleman may not have been at liberty to invite to a meeting of the society any persons who were not members. The friends showed a sad want of good sense.

*
* *

A gentleman and lady, residents of the same city, met at a summer resort. After the lady's return to town, she sent the gentleman a card. Should he consider it an invitation to call?

Yes, but it would have been better had she invited him verbally

*
* *

When giving a party to introduce a daughter into society, should all the society people of the place be invited?

No, only those on the visiting list of the lady who gives the entertainment.

*
* *

How should a man recognize his own or his friend's servants in the street?

By a nod and a pleasant word.

*
* *

Is it proper for a young man to ask a young girl whom he has invited to take a walk or a pleasure excursion to meet him at his place of business?

Certainly not. He should call at her residence.

THE PRESIDENT'S HOUSE IN 1800.

Etiquette and Entertainments in Washington.

Mrs John A Logan

N all countries the style of stationery and the form of invitations to social affairs change frequently. In our own land the size of cards of ceremony fluctuates from the very small bits of pasteboard, engraved in the finest possible script, to the large square cards of the present fashion, engraved in bold, beautiful old English or script, and often accompanied by the personal card—nearly equal in size—of the entertainers.

It must be admitted that the larger cards and text used now are more beautiful and dignified than the insignificant ones of the past. The Presidents' invitations have changed from the olden to modern times, always representing the taste of the person occupying that exalted position.

Some of our executives have paid no attention whatever to these affairs, while others have devoted much consideration to the detail and style of even these trivial matters. We have before us a number of invitations from the Executive Mansion. While all are of the larger form, the quality of paper, the style of engraving, and the taste displayed, are very different and in keeping with the progress of the last decade.

During President Grant's administration, the letter " G " was used on the stationery.

The President and Mrs. Grant,

request the pleasure of

Senator and Mrs. Logan's

company at dinner on Tuesday evening Jany 19 at

Seven o'clock

Jany 13th 1875   *An early answer is desired.*

The elegant and tasteful President Arthur used the coat-of-arms of the United States, in gold, on all invitations issued for occasions of ceremony. The stationery was of the finest quality, the tint a delicate cream color.

Official people must follow the lead of the President in matters of ceremony, and often display much taste in their elaborate menus and cards. As the current coin with which society pays its debts, these tiny pasteboards play an important part.

Thomas Jefferson was the first to issue the canons of etiquette for the society of Washington, which have, with minor changes, governed it to the present day.

All cards bear either engraved, printed, or written, the name, resi dence, and rank of the person using them, and officials add a separate card designating the office, as for instance: The Vice-President, the Chief Justice, the Secretary of State, the General of the Army, the Admiral of the Navy, etc.

At the beginning of every session of Congress all officials, or other persons holding an established social position in Washington, should pay their respects to the President and the ladies of the White House. This is done by calling and leaving a card, every one paying the first visit to the President, the Chief Justice, and the Speaker of the House of Repre- sentatives. All other officials, including the Representatives, make the first call upon the Senators. The officials of the Executive Departments, of course, call upon the President, Chief Justice, Senators, and Repre- sentatives.

These visits are always returned by the persons receiving them, the President and his family, who neither make nor return calls, being the sole exception to this rule. It is optional whether they are repeated, or the acquaintance is continued.

Persons giving entertainments should always call upon their intended guests before sending out the invitations—which should be done at least ten days prior to the occasion.

In social visiting, it is customary to turn the corners of the card to indicate the object of the call; as for instance: Turning down the upper left hand corner means a social visit; the upper right corner, a congratu- latory one; the lower left hand, a parting call; and the lower right hand corner, a call of condolence. Calls of condolence and congratulations should always be paid very promptly. Many persons are extremely care- less about making calls after accepting invitations, a negligence which is an unmistakable evidence of bad breeding. After having accepted hos- pitality from any one, politeness demands that you should speedily pay a formal visit in acknowledgment of the courtesy extended to you.

Menu cards bearing the names of the guests laid beside the plates at dinners or lunch parties, are sometimes very elaborate affairs, and afford an opportunity for the display of great taste in their selection and arrangement Some of these souvenirs are exquisite specimens of hand-painting or etching, and are really little gems in their way; the material is generally paper, but sometimes satin ribbons or choice bits of silk are used.

The President

requests the honour of the company of

Senator & Mrs. Logan

at dinner on Thursday February

14th at 7 1/2 o'clock.

To meet the Supreme Court.

In these latter days, table decorations have become marvellously beautiful; the use of flowers is so universal that the resources of the florists are often taxed to the utmost to devise acceptable novelties. In the Executive Mansion, on occasions of state dinners and ladies' luncheons given by the President and ladies of the White House, some very remarkable effects have been produced.

During President Hayes' administration, Mrs. Hayes gave an even-ing reception to the diplomatic corps, Congress, the army and navy, and other distinguished officials of Washington, which was one of the most brilliant entertainments ever witnessed in the White House. The quan-tity of flowers used in decorating the entire mansion was enormous, the corridors, East Room, Green Room, Blue Room, Red Room, state dining room, and private dining room being adorned with rare exotics. The tables in the state and private dining rooms were superbly ornamented. Every imaginable device was most exquisitely executed—floral flags, umbrellas, fountains, enormous groups of lilies-of-the-valley and violets, orchids, roses, carnations, and other fragrant flowers, made a bewilderingly beautiful scene.

Under President Arthur's administration, on various occasions, the most superb floral decorations ever beheld were displayed in the city of Washington. At one entertainment, a beautiful bridge, uniting the At-lantic and Pacific, extended almost the full length of the table; the floor was of smilax, the railings and posts of carnations, and the feathery green of the asparagus. At the end of the bridge rose a most exquisite floral column, surmounted by a beautiful gas-light, with the shade exquisitely wrought of flowers. Beneath this bridge lay a mirror, which reflected the whole structure.

Again, at a dinner party given to the Justices of the Supreme Court and Congress, the table was shaped like the letter "T," in the middle of

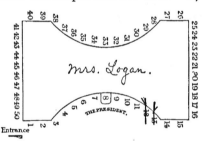

which stood the Temple of Justice, with its exquisite wreaths and festoons of rare flowers, roof of carnations, and dome of beautiful orchids, floored by a mirror with a lovely fountain in the centre. At each end were other floral designs, representing the Scales of Justice and many other appro-priate devices.

To obtain flowers enough for such elaborate decoration, the conserva-tories of Philadelphia, New York, and Boston were ransacked. We might mention, in addition, many superb entertainments that have been given by the cabinet officials, foreign ministers, and private citizens of Wash-ington, where, perhaps, more has been done in that line than in any other city in the Union.

"BENJAMIN HARRISON MCKEE.

MRS. BENJAMIN HARRISON.

THE WHITE HOUSE.

Etiquette of Washington Society.

Washington has now become the Mecca of so many Americans, who desire to pass a few weeks of the gay season in our beautiful national capital, or in the transaction of political business spend more or less time in the city, during the session of Congress, that no summary of the rules of etiquette, however brief, can be regarded as complete without mention of certain points in which its customs are peculiar to itself; because, in addition to the resident population, it contains a class of officials who are to be found nowhere else in America.

At the head of this official society stand, of course, the President of the United States and his wife, and it includes all officers elected by the people or appointed by the President in the three branches of the Government, as well as the officials appointed by the President in the various Departments, with the members of their families. This includes officers of the Army and Navy, and Marine Corps; persons holding Government offices in different States of the Union, and officers of the Diplomatic or Consular services of the United States, who may chance to be in the city.

Another class includes members of the Diplomatic and Consular Corps of foreign countries, officers of foreign governments, and officers of State or municipal governments of the United States who may be in the city.

The remaining class comprises residents from other places, visitors whose social position at home entitles them to recognition, and permanent residents—either men of wealth or those who are engaged in mercantile or professional business.

These three classes compose the complex web of what is termed Washington society, and a knowledge of its rules will tend to smooth the pathway of all who desire to enter its circle, whether for a longer or shorter period.

The order of official rank, as established by constitutional recognition, law, and usage, is as follows

82

The President.

The Vice-President, who is also the President of the Senate. If the office of Vice-President is vacant, the President of the Senate *pro tempore*.

The Chief Justice of the United States.

Senators.

The Speaker.

Representatives in Congress.

Associate Justices of the United States.

CHIEF JUSTICE MELVILLE W. FULLER.

The Members of the Cabinet, in the order of succession to the Presidency, as fixed by Act 19, 1886.

The members of the Foreign Diplomatic Corps, in the order of the presentation of their credentials to the President. Foreign members of International Commissions, and official counsel, with the Legations of their countries, take their places with the Secretary of State.

The General of the Army and the Admiral of the Navy.

The Governors of States.

The Chief Justices and Associate Justices of the Court of Claims.

Circuit and District Judges of the United States.

Chief Justices and Associates of the Territories and District of Columbia.

The Lieutenant General and Vice-Admiral.

Major-Generals, Rear Admirals, and Officers of the Staff of equal rank.

Brigadier Generals and Commodores, Chiefs of Semi-Independent Civil Bureaus, Chiefs of Departmental Bureaus in the order of their chief officers.

Colonels, Captains of the Navy, Staff officers of equal rank, the Colonel of the Marine Corps.

Consuls-General and Consuls of Foreign Governments, according to date of exequator, and the same of the United States, according to seniority of service.

Lieutenant-Colonels and Majors of the Army and Commanders and Lieutenant-Commanders of the Navy, and Staff Officers of equal rank.

The Commissioners of the District of Columbia, Governors of Territories, Lieutenants of the Army and Navy.

Captains, First and Second Lieutenants of the Army, Lieutenants, Masters, and Ensigns of the Navy, and Staff officers of equal rank.

Assistant Secretaries of Executive Departments, Secretaries of Legation, Secretaries of the Senate and House of Representatives, and Clerk of the Supreme Court.

The order of precedence in each branch of the Executive, Legislative, Judicial, Military, Naval, and Marine Services, is governed by the order of rank and regulation. The wives of persons occupying these various official positions take precedence with their husbands.

CALLS.

The President never returns calls, except those from a Sovereign, President, or ruler of an independent government, who invariably pays the first visit. The Vice-President and Senators receive first calls from the Associate Justices of the Supreme Court of the United States, the Cabinet, the Foreign Ministers, and others below them. The same rule applies to their families.

Representatives in Congress call first upon all persons in the higher grades, as also does the Speaker of the House.

The Associate Justices of the Supreme Court receive the first call from all officers except the President, Vice-President, and Senators.

The Secretary of State and other members of the Cabinet receive the

MRS. WANAMAKER.

MRS. THOMAS B. REED.

MRS. RUSK.

MRS. NOBLE.

first call from Foreign Ministers, but the families of Cabinet Ministers call first upon the families of Diplomatic Ministers.

A distinguished stranger visiting Washington pays the first call upon a resident official of equal rank.

Any newly appointed official, no matter what may be his rank, pays the first call upon those above him, and receives the first from those in lower grades.

Strangers arriving in Washington should pay the first call and leave a card, and this visit should be returned within two days. The rule applies to both social and official visits.

All these regulations in regard to calls of etiquette paid by officials apply to the ladies of their families, with the sole exception of the first call paid by the families of Cabinet Ministers upon the ladies of the Diplomatic Corps.

THE SEASON.

The *social* season begins with the receptions at the White House, and by the Cabinet Ministers on New Year's Day, and ends with the beginning of Lent.

The Congressional season commences on the first Monday in December, and ends with the session, or earlier, if it is prolonged until the summer.

RECEPTIONS.

These entertainments are usually held only during the season, and are given on fixed days by the wives of the higher officials and other ladies prominent in society. No invitations are required, and any reputable person who is suitably dressed can attend. Gentlemen may also go either with or without ladies. The host is present or absent, as inclination dictates.

The usual hours are from three to six. The reception days, allotted by the sanction of custom to the wives of the different officials, are as follows:

Mondays, the families of the Justices of the Supreme Court of the United States, and ladies living on Capitol Hill.

Tuesdays, families of the Speaker and Representatives in Congress, and of the General of the Army.

Wednesdays, families of the Cabinet Ministers.

Thursdays, families of the Vice-president and Senators of the United States.

Fridays, ladies residing in the West end, but not members of the official circle.

Saturdays, the reception of the Mistress of the White House. Ladies not in the official circle may select any one of the days mentioned, if the fact of residing in the same neighborhood with certain officials renders it more convenient for their callers. The etiquette of the reception is very simple. Hand a card to the usher, if there is one, and he will announce the visitor's name. Exchange the usual civilities, and then pass on to make way for others. If there is no one to receive the card, put it in the receiver in the hall, enter the room, and, if a stranger to the hostess, pronounce your own name clearly.

It is usual to have refreshments at these receptions, and, after exchanging a few words with the hostess, guests are expected, if they desire, to go to the dining-room and take a cup of tea, bouillon, a little salad, or an ice. But any appearance of eating a substantial lunch should be avoided.

On leaving, take leave of the host and hostess. A gentleman can hold his hat in his hand, but the overcoat should be left in the hall, and not put on till after he has paid his parting compliments to the hostess. Ladies never remove their wraps and bonnets.

The proper dress for a gentlemen is a frock coat and grey or other light trousers, tan colored gloves, and unobtrusive cravat. Ladies wear handsome street costumes.

EVENING RECEPTIONS.

The usual hours for these entertainments are from eight to twelve—often they are prolonged until still later. No one is expected to attend them except by special invitation, and the etiquette observed is the same as at a ball. Both ladies and gentlemen go in full dress—ladies wear the most elegant evening toilettes, and gentlemen the regulation evening suit —black dress coat, black trousers, white tie, pearl-colored gloves, stitched with black.

Guests on arriving are shown to dressing-rooms to remove their wraps. If there is no one to announce the names, the gentleman, if unacquainted with his host, mentions his own and then that of the lady accompanying him.

TITLES.

In addressing the President, Mr. President.

In addressing the Cabinet Ministers, Mr. Secretary, Mr. Postmaster General, etc.

Custom sanctions the use of the title Mrs. Secretary in speaking of the wives of Cabinet Ministers; but in addressing them say simply Mrs.

ORDER OF RANK OF THE CABINET MINISTERS,

As arranged by the statute fixing the order of their succession to the Presidential office in case of the death of the President, Vice-President, and President of the House of Representatives:

1. The Secretary of State.
2. The Secretary of the Treasury.
3. The Secretary of War.
4. The Attorney General.
5. The Postmaster General.
6. The Secretary of the Navy.
7. The Secretary of the Interior.

(There was no Secretary of Agriculture at the time the statute was passed.)

SATURDAY AFTERNOON RECEPTIONS.

These are held every Saturday afternoon during the season by the lady presiding over the White House, and are more especially intended for ladies, though gentlemen are not excluded. The dress is the same as for the afternoon receptions of the ladies of the Cabinet. On the way to the red parlor, leave a card in the receiver in the corridor and pass on to the blue parlor, where the receiving party will be found. The etiquette of presentation is the same as for the evening receptions given by the President.

Callers usually promenade in the East Room and visit the beautiful conservatories.

FORMS OF INVITATIONS.

Card Reception of a Cabinet Minister.

The Secretary of the Interior

and

Mrs. ----------------------------

AT HOME,

Friday evenings until March,

from nine

until twelve o'clock.

20 IOWA CIRCLE

———————

The Secretary of State

and

Mrs ----------------------------

request the pleasure of the

company of

Mr. and Mrs.----------------------------

AT DINNER,

Tuesday evening, Jan. 28th,

at eight o'clock.

10 LAFAYETTE SQUARE.

MRS. LEVI P. MORTON.

REPLY TO INVITATION OF CABINET MINISTER.

Mr. and Mrs. --------------------------------,

have the honor

to accept the invitation of

The Secretary of the Treasury

and

Mrs. --------------------------------

for Saturday evening, March 14th.

PUBLIC EVENING RECEPTIONS OF THE PRESIDENT.

The hours are from 8 to 11 P. M., and Thursday is the evening usually selected. No invitations are sent; any one suitably dressed may attend. Full evening costume is most proper; but travellers or others may wear any handsome dark dress without a bonnet.

The following routine is observed: On reaching the entrance ladies are shown to the cloak-rooms, where their wraps are left, checks being given for them. Then they join the throng, and on entering the room where the President and his wife are receiving, each person should mention his own name, and that of the lady accompanying him to the official who makes the introductions to the President. This is usually the engineer in charge of the public buildings, or the marshal of the District of Columbia.

He presents the gentleman to the President, and the former, after shaking hands, presents the lady he is escorting, and both pass on to the lady receiving, who stands at the President's right. An official stands ready to present the couple; the lady may either bow or shake hands; the gentleman should merely bow. Then pass on immediately to give place to others, leaving the reception-room without delay. Never linger for even the slightest conversation. The length of time for remaining in the White House is optional — within the hours named for the reception.

when ready to leave the house, return to the cloak-room for the wraps, and proceed to the carriage. No farewell to the President and his wife is expected. No refreshments are served.

CALLS ON THE PRESIDENT AT HIS OFFICE.

Strangers desiring to call on the President are sometimes at a loss to know what forms to observe, and a brief description may be useful.

On reaching the White House, ask for the ante-room of the Executive office, and hand a card to the official in charge, who will deliver it at the proper time. Then take a seat and wait to learn whether you can be received by the President. This may not be even on that day, if public business is urgent.

If the caller merely desires to *see* the President, he should write on his card " to pay respects." This will insure the earliest reception possible.

When shown into the Executive office mention your name and residence—if a stranger, bow, exchange a shake of the hand, and after a few words move on, making way for others. If the party includes several the first to enter should introduce the others, stating their position, if they have any local importance, and their object in coming to the Capital, but as briefly as possible.

Callers who have business must await their turn, and on entering remain standing—unless invited to sit down—and state clearly and concisely the purpose of the visit.

CALLS ON CABINET OFFICERS.

The visitor on going to the Department—which should be done between the hours of 9 and 2—proceeds to the ante-room of the Secretary's office, sends in his card, and waits for a notification that he will be received. On being shown in, observe the usual rules of a business interview, remembering that time is precious to public men.

CALLS ON SENATORS AND REPRESENTATIVES.

A visitor desiring to call on a Senator should go to the ante-room of the senate, at the east end of the senate lobby, send in his card to the official in charge, and wait a reply.

The Senators frequently desire the messenger to show the caller into the Senators' reception-room, known as the marble-room, where he joins him.

If the call is paid to a Representative, the visitor sends in his card by the door-keeper. In both cases it is well to write on the card "for Senator,"—"for Representative,"—and in the left hand "to pay respects," if the call is not on business.

If he desires to meet a Senator or Representative from another State, it would be well to send a card to one of the Members of Congress from his own State, if he knows any of them, and request an introduction either by personal presentation or by card.

MRS. JOHN TYLER.

MRS MARTHA WASHINGTON.

MRS. ABIGAIL ADAMS.

MRS. DOLLY MADISON.

MRS LOUISA CATHERINE ADAMS

MRS. MARTHA JEFFERSON.

MRS. JAMES K. POLK.

MRS. VAN BUREN.

MRS. ANDREW JACKSON.

MISS HARRIET LANE.

MRS. ABRAHAM LINCOLN.

MRS. ABIGAIL FILLMORE.

MRS. MARY A. MC ELROY.

MRS. JAMES A. GARFIELD.

MRS. ULYSSES S. GRANT.

MRS. ANDREW JOHNSON.

MISS ROSE ELIZABETH CLEVELAND.

MRS. LUCY WEBB HAYES.

MAIN ENTRANCE.

Arlington.

VISITORS to Washington rarely fail to make a pilgrimage to the national cemetery, formerly the home of General Robert E. Lee.

The main entrance is through wide gates, on either side of which stand two marble columns brought in 1873 from the portico of the building formerly occupied by the government as the war department. Three of these pillars bear the names of Scott, Lincoln, and Stanton.

There are several burial fields, but the largest one is quite near the mansion, where a level plain, many acres in extent, contains thousands of graves stretching in parallel lines almost as far as the eye can reach.

Close in the rear of the house is a huge granite tomb, near which almost every one lingers, touched by the pathos of the thought that here lie 2,111 heroes whose very names are unknown. Their bodies were gathered after the war from the road to the Rappahannock and the battle-fields of Bull Run. The entire number of the silent host interred in this " God's Acre " is 16,264.

The mansion itself was built by George Washington Parke Custis, Washington's adopted grandson, when, on attaining his majority, he came into possession of the estate. It is beautifully located on the brow of a hill on the Virginia bank of the Potomac—here a mile in width— directly opposite Washington, and its broad portico affords a superb view across the glittering "River of Swans" of the capital, dominated by the snowy marble column erected to the memory of Washington, and the majestic Capitol crowning its own hill-top two long miles away.

ARLINGTON MANSION.

The house, a two-story brick structure one hundred and forty feet long, covered with a sort of plaster stucco, painted a yellowish brown, consists of a central building with a deep, wide portico, supported by eight massive columns, and two wings. A large door opens from the portico into a wide hall running directly through to the rear and separating the rooms on the ground-floor. At the right is a large dining-room, from which open several smaller apartments, while the space on the left of the corridor is occupied by two parlors and a conservatory. The second story contains quite a number of tolerably spacious chambers, now the residence of the official who has charge of the military cemetery. The ground-floor is scantily furnished with a few chairs and desks.

Prior to Colonel Lee's departure to enter the Confederate Army, the Arlington mansion contained a very large number of Washington relics, brought by Mr. Custis—to whom they had been bequeathed by his grandmother, Lady Washington—from Mount Vernon and when in the spring of 1861 the Lee family quitted Arlington most of its treasures were left.

The United States forces soon took possession of the estate, and the government seized the relics, which may now be seen in the National Museum.

In 1869, Mrs. Lee made an attempt to regain possession of them, but Congress refused to grant her petition. Being entailed property, Arlington could not be confiscated; but as the taxes on it were not paid, it was offered for sale in January, 1864, and purchased by the government for $23,000. The National Military Cemetery was laid out in May, 1864.

Soldiers' Home.

ONE of the loveliest drives near Washington is through the grounds of the Soldiers' Home, an institution which provides a pleasant refuge for all soldiers of the regular army who have served twenty years in the ranks, or who from any cause have become permanently disabled.

The fund for the purchase was obtained by General Scott from assessments upon the large towns and cities in Mexico occupied by our troops, sales of captured government tobacco, etc., amounting in all to about $200,000, from which, after certain sums were distributed among the rank and file, and given to the wounded in hospitals, $118,000

STATUE OF GENERAL SCOTT.

SOLDIERS' HOME.

remained unused at the close of the Mexican war, and was devoted to the purchase of the farm of George W. Riggs, to which "Harewood," the property of the late W. W. Corcoran, was added.

The expenses of maintaining the place are defrayed by a tax of 12½ cents a month on the pay of every enlisted man in the army.

The grounds comprise five hundred acres of lawn and woodland, through which wind beautifully-kept roads.

The Home proper is of white marble in the form of the Roman figure I, formed of the old building known as the "Scott building" having been the first erected, and the new wing just completed called the "Anderson building." In these are barracks and the general mess-hall, which is a beautiful room; beneath it is the kitchen with its steam cooking arrangements, the billiard and card-room, carpenter and shoe shops, book-bindery,

THE PRESIDENT'S SUMMER HOME.

etc. All the work pertaining to the care of the Home and necessities of the inmates is done by the men as far as possible, thus making it self-supporting. There is also a large red brick barracks building, known as the "Sheridan building" with the library or reading hall just beyond, where well-stocked cases, tables, and easy-chairs are found. The President's cottage was the original country house of Mr. Riggs, and, on the purchase of the farm, was retained unchanged, and, owing to the necessity of the constant presence of Mr. Lincoln in Washington, was occupied by him as a summer retreat, a custom which was followed by other Presidents, Mr. Arthur being the last. Probably it may never again be used for the purpose. To keep or place it in repair, such as would be fitting our chief executive, would require an act of congress appropriating the money, as it would not be a proper expenditure of the funds raised from the tax on the soldiers, and owing to the crowded condition of the Home it will be used in the future as additional barracks, the musicians occupying it at present. When President Arthur lived there he forbade the expenditure of a dollar upon it, paying for everything from his own purse. Around the drive, to the right of the Home, are the quarters of the Governor, the Quartermaster, and the Doctor, officers in charge of the Home. The board which controls the expenditure of moneys and general management of the Home consists of the General of the Army, the Quartermaster General, the Commissary General, the Judge Advocate General, and the Governor of the Home, who is always a retired officer of the Army of the rank of Colonel.

VIEWS IN THE PARK OF SOLDIER'S HOME.

Fig. 32

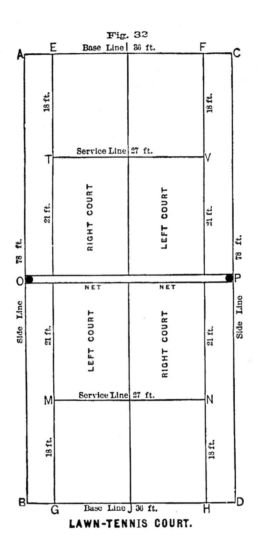

LAWN-TENNIS COURT.

Out Door Sports.

"All work and no play makes Jack a dull boy."—OLD PROVERB.

Hamlet.—" Will you play upon this pipe ?"

Guildenstern.—"I know no touch of it, my lord."—SHAKESPEARE.

The musician spends years in acquiring the skill and knowledge necessary to evoke the best music of which his chosen instrument is capable. The engineer must devote much time, thought, and energy, before he masters his profession, and can be entrusted with the sole charge of his engine. Now what musical instrument is so delicate, what mechanical device is so complicated as the human body, and yet how few children are taught the simplest rules of physical culture. The mind is trained and tasked for many hours, during many days, while the body is left to fend for itself. A slow, aimless promenade, or several hours' dance in a hot room, represent about the only exercise a girl takes after she has entered her teens; boys are better off, for most of them love the open air,

100

but how few are symmetrically developed, as they might be, did they learn to manage their bodies as the musician does his instrument and the engineer his machine.

ARCHERY.

For exercising and strengthening every muscle of the body, as well as training the eye and steadying the nerves, few, if any pastimes, excel archery. Having its origin in pre-historic times, it comes to us with an accumulation of legends, both in poetry and prose, that no other sport can boast. Italian or Spanish yew is the best material for the bow, but one of either costs $50, while a bow of lemon wood can be bought for $10. Its length should be equal to, or a little in excess of, the height of the person using it. Desirable as a good bow is, a perfect arrow is indispensable. The best target arrows have a hickory shaft, a horn nock with its notch for holding the bowstring; three peacock or goose-wing feathers or vanes set at equal distances around the shaft and just above the nock, a very hard and heavy triangular piece of wood called the *foot* at the point end of the shaft; and a steel ferrule covering the end of this foot. The English shilling is the standard of weight marked on target arrows; a fifty pound bow and a $4\frac{1}{2}$ or 5 shilling weight arrow would be suitable for the use of an athlete. To acquire the habit of drawing steadily, and always to the same distance, hold your bow in your left hand nearly vertical but a little to the right, the arrow resting upon the knuckle of your left hand, the first three fingers of your right hand closed around the string with the arrow nock between the first and the second. Extend your left arm and, with your right hand, draw string and arrow a little below the line of the chin and then loose your hold. Learn to keep the left arm perfectly steady, as the slightest movement destroys your aim. When by constant practice you have mastered these points, you are ready to learn how to shoot.

BASE BALL.

Though evolved from some of the older English games, America may justly claim base ball as her national game. Played with great celerity, the balls pitched and batted often with tremendous force, accidents unfortunately are not rare, but most of the dangers can be avoided by quickness, watchfulness, and a determination to do nothing reckless. An amateur club needs but a dozen bats and two or three balls, but the professionals add largely to this simple equipment. George E. Stackhouse, an authority on base ball, has given in print the meaning of the following:

TECHNICAL TERMS.

The game of base ball has its regular technical phraseology. An explanation of some of the terms in common use is necessary to an under- standing of the game.

Assistance on Strikes in Pitching.—The pitcher is given assistance when he strikes a batsman out. In the League the record goes into the table, but in the American Association it is credited in the summary.

Box.—The "box" is the pitcher's position, or the little square in the centre of the diamond.

Balk.—A balk entitles a base-runner to a base, and is made when the pitcher performs any of the preliminary movements in delivering the ball to the bat, but fails to throw the ball. This rule, however, is seldom if ever enforced. Nearly all the pitchers make numerous balks during a game, but the umpire seldom calls them.

Battery.—This technical term applies to the pitcher and catcher. What part of a battery a catcher is nobody has ever been able to find out.

Battery Errors.—Are the misplays of the pitcher and catcher, such as wild pitches, passed balls, called balls, and hitting the batsman.

Block.—A block ball is a ball stopped by an outsider. The ball has to be returned to the pitcher in his position before a base-runner can be put out.

Called Balls.—When a pitcher throws six balls and they are not where the batsman wants them, the batter is sent to first base on called balls.

Change of Pace.—Applies to the pitcher when he alternates in his delivery between a slow and swiftly pitched ball. Many pitchers depend largely for effectiveness upon such change of pace.

Chances.—A chance means an opportunity of a fielder to put an opponent out.

Curve.—The curve applies to the twisting or curving of the ball.

Dead Ball.—A dead ball is one that strikes the batter or his clothing or the bat, without his striking at it. It is also dead if it strikes the umpire before it reaches the catcher.

Fair Ball.—Is a ball pitched squarely over the plate at the height asked for by the batter, and whether that individual strikes at it or not it is called a strike by the umpire.

Strike.—When a batsman hits at the ball, but the bat and ball fail to collide. "Three strikes" retire a player if the catcher holds the ball.

Head Work.—The term is applied to a player who uses judgment in his work.

High Ball.—A batsman calls for a high ball when he wishes the pitcher to put the ball over the plate at a height above the waist, but below the shoulder.

Low Ball.—A fairly pitched ball which goes over the plate at a height between the player's belt and knee.

Out of Form.—Means just what one would suppose it meant. A pitcher losing his effectiveness or a batter being unable to hit the ball.

Wild Pitch.—A ball pitched out of the catcher's reach. It counts against the pitcher's record.

A. B.—In a score sheet means times at bat. Base on called balls are not counted in times at bat.

Passed Ball.—A ball fairly pitched by the pitcher, but which the catcher fumbles or allows to pass him.

R.—Stands for "runs."

1B.—In a score means "single base hits."

P. O.—In a score means "put out."

A.—Stands for assists. When a player throws a ball to a baseman who puts an opponent out, the thrower gets an assist.

T. B.—Total number of base hits.

E.—The enemy of all base ball players ; and under this head all blunders in fielding are credited.

Muffin.—Is a term applied to poor players or when a player drops or misjudges a batted or thrown ball.

Hot Balls.—The lightning like shoots thrown or hit to the infielders.

Fly Catch.—A ball caught in the air by a player.

Foul Tip.—A foul ball caught by the catcher sharp and speedy from the ball. It is a most difficult catch to make.

Napping.—When a player through carelessness or sleepy-headedness is caught off his base.

Double Play.—Two players put out on one ball, or before the ball is pitched to the bat again.

Triple Play.—The same as above, except that three players are put out instead of two.

Run Out.—When a player is caught between the bases and put out.

Wild Throw.—A ball thrown out of the reach of a player.

Running Catch.—A ball caught while running rapidly.

Dubs.—Poor players.

BOATING.

Whether the propelling power be the ancient one of oars, the more modern one of sails, or the latest invented one of steam, traversing the water has always been a favorite recreation. Though rowing was the earliest known mode of navigation, it was never accounted an amusement until the present century. Gradually the wide, heavy boats and clumsy oars, used only for transportation and commerce, have given place to the graceful canoe, light as a cockle, and the slender racing shell, long and tapering as an arrow, and almost as swift in its flight. Besides this diminution in weight two inventions have helped to add to the popularity of rowing; the first was substituting the outrigger for the oldfashioned rowlocks, the second was employing the sliding seat in place of the stationary. But rowing is an acquired art, whereas paddling comes natural; and as the racing shell is the ideal craft for the first, so the cedar canoe is the boat *par excellence* for the second, and both are preferable to yachting where exercise is the chief object; but where pleasure is the *motif* of an excursion on the water, the dancing yacht with her glistening sails, rattling cordage, luxurious seats, and breezy deck, must forever take the lead. Less romantic, but more independent than the latter, is the steam-launch with its puffing, fussy, little engine, its gay awning, and its three or four bladed screw. Like all other pleasure outfits the steam-launch will vary much in cost, from a few hundreds to many thousands of dollars. The prospective guest of a hospitable yachtsman would do well to master some of the most frequently recurring

NAUTICAL TERMS.

ABACK.—The situation when the wind blows upon the forward surface of a sail.

ABAFT or AFT.—Toward the stern.

ABOUT.—To put the vessel on the other tack.

ANCHORS.—The "bowers" are the largest anchors of a merchantman and weigh from 4,000 to 5,200 lbs; "sheet" anchors are smaller and are carried on the sides of the ship; "stream" anchors are carried inboard and vary from 300 to 1,900 lbs; "kedges" are light anchors for warping the vessel into a new position; "boat" anchors are for the ship's boats.

The anchor is "foul" when caught in the cable; "tripped" when disengaged from the ground; "apeak" when the vessel is over it and the cable perpendicular. Large vessels should ride with a length of cable out six times the depth of water. Yachts carry anchors weighing 1 to 1½ lbs. per foot of water line length.

APRON.—A timber at the back of the stem to strengthen it.

ARDENCY.—Tendency to fly up into the wind.

ATHWART.—Crosswise.

BACK STAY.—A wire or rope extending from the heads of the upper masts to the vessel's side. "*Preventer*" back stay, an extra stay while carrying heavy sail.

BALLAST.—Heavy materials placed in the hold, or built into the keel, to give the vessel stability. Iron, lead, stone, brick, gravel, and sand are used.

BANKER.—A vessel engaged in the bank fisheries.

BANDS.—Strips of canvas sewed on to prevent the sail from splitting.

BARGE.—A large and handsome rowboat, with numerous pairs of oars, for the use of flag officers and high officials. Also a large unrigged freighting vessel.

BARK.—A three-masted sailing vessel, having square sails on the fore and main masts and fore-and-aft sails on the mizzen mast.

BATEAU.—A narrow, flat-bottomed, broad skiff, sharp at both ends, with flaring sides used by lumbermen while rafting logs in the northern forests of America.

BATTEN.—A long, thin strip of wood, from one to three inches broad, used in drawing the curves while laying off the lines of a vessel.

BEAM.—Greatest width of the vessel. "*Beams*," the timbers reaching across the vessel, upon which the deck planks are nailed.

BEARDING LINE.—The inner edge of the rabbet on a vessel's stem and stern post, and the upper edge of the rabbet on the keel; it is the line where the inner surface of the planking comes in contact with those timbers.

BEATING.—Tacking to windward.

BELAY.—To fasten the end of a rope by turns around a pin or cleat.

BEND.—To make a sail fast to boom or yard, or a rope to an anchor, spar, or another rope.

BILGE.—The curvature in a ship's hull, between the side and the bottom.

BODY PLAN.—A drawing to show the vertical cross sections of a vessel.

BITTS.—Vertical posts or timbers projecting above deck.

BOATSWAIN.—A ship's officer whose duty it is to summon the crew, and see that they perform their work quickly. He is also general overseer of the rigging and canvas.

BOBSTAY.—A stay extending from the bowsprit to the cutwater.

BOLTROPE.—A superior and flexible kind of cordage for roping sails.

BOOM.—The pole which spreads the foot of a fore-and-aft sail, spinnaker, or studding sail.

BOWLINE.—A rope attached by bridles to the cringles on the windward leech of a square sail, to keep it steady, while the ship is sailing to windward.

BOWSPRIT.—The strong spar, projecting from the bow, to spread the foot of the jibs.

BOX HAULING.—Veering the ship short round on her heel, by laying the forward sails aback, and keeping the after sails full.

BRACES.—Ropes attached to the ends of the yards for hauling the yard around.

BRAILS.—Ropes to draw up the foot, leech, and other parts of fore-and-aft sails, for furling.

BRIDLES.—Short ropes attached to the bowline cringles of sails.

BRIG.—A two-masted vessel, having square sails, with the addition of a large fore-and-aft sail on the main mast.

BRIGANTINE.—A two-master, square rigged on the foremast, and sloop-rigged on the mizzen mast.

BUNT.—The middle cloths of a square sail.

BROACH TO.—To fly up into the wind.

BUNTLINES.—Ropes fastened to the foot rope or square sails and passing up over the yard, to draw up the sails with.

BURY OR HOUSING.—That part of the mast below the deck.

CANTS.—The frame timbers in bow and stern, which do not stand square to the keel.

CANVAS.—The strong flax or cotton cloth of which a sail is made; hemp canvas was used during the Civil War, but not now.

CAT-HARPINS.—The rigging close underneath the top.

CARLING.—Half-sized beams, introduced between the deck beams; and short timbers extending from one beam to another.

CAT-HEAD.—A strong short timber projecting from the side of the bow, on which the anchor is hoisted.

CAT'S-PAWS.—The spots on the surface of the water when ruffled by light puffs of wind.

CARVEL-BUILT.—When the edges of the streaks of outside planking meet each other so as to form a flush surface. " *Clinker-built* " means that the edge of one plank overlaps that of the next.

CLINKER-BUILT.—See " Carvel-BUILT."

CATAMARAN.—Two or three canoes, or canoe-like hulls, secured parallel to each other by beams and ties, which support a deck; the whole provided with a jib and fore-and-aft sail.

CHANNELS.—Short shelves of oak plank projecting from the sides of the hull to give additional spread to the shrouds.

CHOCK.—A small piece of wood fitted into or upon the top of a large timber to make good a deficiency

CROSS-JACK.—The square sail bent on to the mizzen lower yard in the merchant service ; in the navy this sail is never carried.

CUTTER.—A single-masted vessel sharp-built, with a running-in bowsprit, carrying fore-and-aft mainsail, gaff or club topsail, fore-staysail, and jib. Also, one of the medium-sized small boats of a ship, clinker built.

CLAMPS.—Heavy strakes of ceiling, covering the inside surface of the frames, underneath the beams.

COMPOSITE.—A form of vessel construction in which the frames, knees, and deck beams are of iron, and the outside planking and decking are of wood.

CAPSTAN.—A perpendicular windlass around which the cable is passed for hoisting the anchor ; it is operated by movable spokes or bars, called handspikes or capstan bars.

CEILING.—The planking on the sides and floor of the interior of the hull.

CLEATS.—Pieces of wood to which the ropes are belayed.

CLEW.—The two lower corners of square sails and fore-and-aft sails.

COMBINGS.—The raised wood work around a hatch or cockpit to prevent water washing into the hatchway.

CENTRE OF EFFORT.—That point in the sail area, where, if the whole force of the wind were concentrated, its effects would be the same as when dispersed over the whole area.

CLIPPER.—A trading vessel built for great speed, either a schooner brig, bark, or ship.

CLOSE-HAULED.—The trim of a vessel's sails when she is sailing as nearly as possible toward the quarter from which the wind blows.

CLEW-GARNETS.—Tackle attached to the clews (or lower corners) of square sails, for hauling the clews up to the yards.

COMPANION-WAY.—Ladder or steps leading to the cabin.

Courses.—The fore sail and main sail of a ship.

Chain-Plates.—The iron straps or plates on the side of a vessel, to which the shrouds and backstays are fastened.

Cringles.—Rings of ropes, formed around iron thimbles; they are fastened to the sails as a convenient means of attaching ropes.

Cross-Trees.—Bars of wood, placed athwart ships at the junction of a lower mast and topmast, to unite them and to spread the topmast stays.

Down-Helm.—To put the helm a-lee.

Davits.—Pairs of wooden or iron cranes, placed at the vessel's sides or stern for hoisting up the small boats.

Displacement.—The volume of water displaced by the immersion of a vessel's hull; the total weight of the vessel, equipment, and cargo.

Down-Haul.—A rope passing up along a stay and fastened to the upper corner of the sail, to pull it down with.

Dead-Eyes.—Wooden blocks, the lower one firmly fastened to a chain plate; the upper one to the lower end of a shroud or backstay; the two blocks are united by a small rope called the lanyard.

Draught.—The depth of water required to float a vessel.

Drag.—A vessel sails with a drag when she is deeper in the water aft, than forward.

Earings.—The upper corners of all square sails and fore-and-aft sails.

Fashion Timber.—The aftermost frame, which is secured to the ends of the transoms.

Fid.—The wooden key that holds the heel of the topmast in position.

Foot.—The lower edge of a sail.

Fore-and-Aft.—Lengthwise of the vessel.

Forecastle.—The part of a vessel before the foremast. Top gallant forecastle, the raised deck in the bow of a large vessel, built for convenience in handling the anchor and jibs.

Frigate.—A war ship with one gun deck below the main deck, and carrying from forty to fifty cannon.

Frame.—One of the ribs of the vessel, upon which the outside planking or plating, and the ceiling inside, are fastened. It is composed of "floors" which cross the keel, "futtocks" which each upward along the sides; "top-timbers," and "stanchions" which support the bulwarks.

Furling.—The operation of rolling up a sail close to the yard, stay. mast, or boom, and winding a rope or gasket around it to keep it in position.

Futtock.—See "Frame."

Gaff.—The pole to which the head of a fore-and-aft sail is bent.

GALLEY.—A war vessel propelled by oars.

GARBOARDS.—The heavy strips of outside planking next to the keel.

GASKETS.—Plaited ropes used for tying a sail to the yard when it is furled.

GOOSE-WINGS.—The clews of a square sail, which are let down (while the bunt or body remains furled), so as to show a mere scrap of sail while scudding before a storm.

GRAPNEL.—A small anchor with several claws.

GROMMETS.—Rings of rope.

GUNWALE.—The upper rail on the side of a boat or vessel.

HALLIARDS.—Ropes used for hoisting sails and yards.

HARPIN.—In shipbuilding, a temporary streak of plank nailed to the frame timbers at bow and stern to keep them in position.

HAWSE-PIPES.—The iron pipes in the bow through which the anchor cables are run out.

HOIST.—That part of a fore-and-aft sail which is extended by hoisting; a top-sail has "depth;" a course has "drops;" but "hoist" is applied to all sails by many.

HOUNDS.—The swell in the upper end of a mast, on which rests the frame of the top and the weight of the topmast and rigging.

HORSE.—A bar of iron, with a stout ring of iron on it, which spans the deck in front of the foremast or aft of the steersman, for the jib and main sheets to travel on.

JIB.—The triangular head sail, which is spread by a stay running from the head of the foremast to the end of the bowsprit. *Jib-topsail*, the headsail next forward of the jib. *Flying-jib*, the next forward of that. *Balloon-jib*, a large light headsail spread in light breezes in place of the other jibs of a yacht. *Jib-foresail*, the forestaysail of a sloop.

JIBBOOM.—A pole secured on top of the bowsprit and projecting beyond the same; used for spreading additional head sails.

JIBE.—While sailing before the wind, to bring the boom from one side over to the other.

JIGGER-MAST.—The small mast in the stern of a yawl; also, the aftermost mast in a four-masted vessel.

JIGGER-TACKLE.—A light small tackle, consisting of a double and single block for hauling up the bunt of a topsail.

JOLLY-BOAT.—One of the small boats of a large vessel; it is clinker built, and broad and bluff in form.

JURY-MAST.—A temporary mast set up in place of one that has been lost.

KEEL.—The back-bone timber of a ship, on which the whole structure is built. The stem and stern-post are virtually continuations of the keel.

KEELSON.—A heavy timber, placed upon the floor timbers over the
keel and fastened with bolts driven clean through frames and keel.

KNEE.—A natural elbow or crook of timber, used to connect the deck
beams with the side of the vessel. Hanging knees are perpendicular;
lodging knees, horizontal.

KNOT.—The nautical or geographical mile, representing one-sixtieth
part of a degree on a great circle of the earth. In order to allow for the
differences in circumference of the earth, the knot is considered by the
United States Survey as one-sixtieth of a degree on the circumference of
an exact sphere, having the same surface as the earth. The knot, or
nautical mile, is 6,080¼ feet. The land mile is 5,280 feet.

KNIGHT-HEADS.—The strong frame timbers in the bow of a vessel,
each side of the stem, rising up to the gunwale and serving to help hold
the bowsprit in position.

LACING.—The rope used to secure the heads of the sails to the yard
or gaff.

LANYARD.—The small rope rove through the holes in the dead-eyes
in setting up the shrouds of a vessel and serving to draw the shrouds taut.

LARBOARD.—The left hand side of a vessel.

LARGE.—A favoring wind when it comes upon the beam or quarter;
the vessel advances with sheets slackened or flowing and the bowlines are
not in use at all. Sailing-large is sailing with a favoring wind.

LATEEN-SAIL.—A triangular sail, hanging from a yard which is tilted
up at an angle of about 45° with the deck.

LAYING OFF, OR DOWN.—Delineation of a ship's lines to full size on a
smooth floor.

LEECH.—The sides of square sails and the after edge of a fore-and-
aft sail.

LEE HELM.—When the helm has to be kept over to the leeward side
to press the vessel's head closer into the wind.

LEEWARD.—The side away from the wind.

LININGS.—The pieces of canvas sewed on various parts of a sail to
preserve it against chafing and injury.

LOG-LINE.—The apparatus for measuring a vessel's speed.

LOG-BOOK.—The daily record of the progress of the vessel and incidents of the voyage.

LUFF.—The forward edge of a fore-and-aft sail. To luff is to steer
up into the wind.

Lug-sail.—A quadrilateral sail, spread at the top by a yard, which is hoisted to the mast by a block set on the yard about one-third of its length from the forward end.   Seen in the fishing boats of Louisiana.

Lurch.—A sudden roll of the vessel.

Marling-spike.—A round, tapering piece of wood or iron, used to separate the strands of a rope to introduce another, when splicing.

Masts.—The stout perpendicular poles which sustain the sails of a vessel.   In two-masted vessels they are called respectively the fore and main.   In three-masters they are called the fore, main, and mizzen.   A fourth mast would be called the jigger, and a fifth, the mizzen jigger.   If the height of the sails require an upper mast, the latter is called the topmast; if one above that, the topgallant mast, which is made in one spar, but is marked off into topgallant, royal, and skysail masts.

Moulding.—The width of any timber in a direction from inside the vessel outward.

Martingale or Dolphin Striker.—A short, perpendicular spar beneath the end of the bowsprit.

Metacentre.—The point where a vertical line drawn through the centre of buoyancy is met by another vertical line, drawn through the new centre of buoyancy when the vessel is inclined to one side.

Missing Stays.—Failure to go about while trying to tack.

Mizzen.—See "Mast."

Oakum.—Tarred rope picked to pieces and used for caulking seams in the planking.

Orlop Deck.—The lowest or false deck in a ship-hold; it is usually a row of beams only.   Contraction of "over-loop."

Partners.—Planks thicker than the rest of the deck to support the masts where they pierce the deck.

Peak.—The outer end of the gaff.

Points (Reef-points).—Pieces of white cordage, whose lengths are nearly double the circumference of the yard or boom, attached to the sails in rows, and used for lessening the area presented by a sail to the wind.

Pitching.—The rising and falling of a vessel, fore-and-aft, when among waves.

Port.—The larboard or left hand side of the vessel.

Plank Sheer.—The heavy plank which covers the opening between the frame timbers at the level of the deck.

Quarter.—That part of the vessel aft of the main mast.

Ribbon.—A long piece of timber four to six inches square, used to keep the frames in place while they are being planked.

Rail.—See "Gunwale."

Rake of the Masts.—The inclination backward of a mast, intended to bring the weight of the mast, sails, and rigging, and effort of the sails further aft.

Rolling.—Oscillations from side to side.

Ratlines.—Ropes fastened across the shrouds like the steps of a ladder.

Rabbet.—A groove in a piece of timber cut to receive another piece.

Reef.—A strip of the sail which is taken up and fastened to the yard or boom by the reef points in order to shorten sail. Large sails have either three or four reefs. Balance reef, the last reef.

Running Rigging.—All the running ropes and lines of a vessel attached to the sails and flags and employed in the handling of them.

Scud.—To drive before a gale.

Serving.—To wrap narrow strips of old canvas and tarred yarn around a rope to prevent it from chafing.

Schooner.—A vessel with two or more masts with fore-and-aft sails.

Sheet.—The strong rope fastened to the clew of a sail to haul and keep it in place.

Shelf.—A thick plank fastened to the inside of the frames to support the ends of the beams.

Shoulder-of-Mutton Sail.—A triangular sail, spread from the mast instead of a yard, as in the Chesapeake Bay canoes and buck-eyes.

Siding.—The width of any timber parallel to the outer surface of the vessel.

Slings.—The middle part of a yard or boom, or, more accurately, the ropes and chains fastened thereto to take its weight and promote ease of handling.

Slackness.—The tendency of the vessel's head to fall away from the wind, showing that the center of effort is too far forward of the center of lateral resistance.

Sloop.—A one-masted vessel, carrying a fore-and-aft mainsail, a gaff topsail and a large jib spread by a fixed bowsprit. In modern sloop yachts the jib is divided into a staysail, spread by a stay coming down to the knightheads, a jib and a jib topsail; and the gaff topsail is replaced by a large quadrilateral sail, with a light pole at head and foot; a spinnaker is used in light winds.

Ship.—A three-master, square-rigged on each mast.

Spanker.—The large fore-and-aft sail on the mizzen mast on large vessels. Also called Spencer and Driver.

Spinnaker.—A large triangular sail spread in light winds by sloops when sailing before the wind; it is hoisted along the mast and the foot is spread by a boom.

SPLICE.—The union of two ends of a rope by interweaving the strands.

SPRIT.—A pole for spreading a fore-and-aft sail, extending from the mast near the foot of the sail to the upper after corner of the sail.

SQUARE SAILS.—Sails spread upon yards hanging crosswise of the vessel.

STARBOARD.—The right hand side of the vessel.

STAY.—A large, strong rope extending from the head of a mast to the knightheads, or to the foot of the mast next forward of it.

STAYSAIL.—A sail spread upon a stay.

STANDING RIGGING.—The shrouds, stays, and other permanent rigging.

STEM.—The large frame timber at the extreme bow of a vessel, which is practically a continuation of the keel; the ends of the planking are secured to this timber.

STEERAGE.—That part of the space between decks, forward of the after cabin.

STERN.—The aftermost end of a vessel.

STEEVING.—The angle of elevation of the bowsprit with the level of the sea, being about 17° in large vessels.

STREAK or STRAKE.—One breadth of planking.

STABILITY.—That quality arising from the form of a vessel and the position of the weights, which, when she is inclined out of an upright position, tends to bring her back again. Stability tends to keep the vessel perpendicular to the surface of the water, whether the water is level or in the form of a wave.

STIFFNESS.—The quality which keeps a ship upright, in spite of the force of wind and waves. Too great stiffness is undesirable.

STANCHIONS.—The frame timbers which support the bulwarks.

STUDDING SAILS.—Certain sails which are set as wings to square sails, in light breezes.

STREAM ANCHOR.—See "Anchor."

SHROUDS.—The strong hemp or wire ropes, attached at the upper end to the heads of the lower masts and at the foot to the chain plates on the sides of the vessel; they secure the masts against the rolling and pitching of the vessel and the pressure of the wind upon the sails. Topmast-Shrouds—Shrouds extending from the head of the topmast to the frame of the top of the lower masts. By the aid of the ratlines tied across the shrouds, the sailors ascend from the decks to the tops and yards above.

TACK.—The lower forward corner of a fore-and-aft sail; the lower windward corner of a square sail or studding sail. The vessel is on the *starboard tack* when the wind blows against the starboard side; on the *port tack* when the wind blows on the port side.

Taut.—Stretched tight.

Taunt.—High or tall; an epithet applied to masts.

Tarpaulin.—A large piece of tarred canvas, used to protect hatchways and property from rain or spray.

Trysail.—A fore-and-aft sail, set on the fore and main lower mast of a ship. A small fore-and-aft sail for a sloop while cruising.

Treenail (pronounced trunnel).—The wooden nails, usually made of locust or white oak, used for fastening the planking and ceiling of a vessel to the frame timbers.

Tonnage.—The cubical capacity of the interior of a vessel; one ton is 100 cubic feet.

Top.—The large platform at the head´ of either the lower mast or the top mast, which affords standing room to the sailors engaged in manipulating the sails or keeping watch of the horizon for other vessels or land.

Trestle-trees.—A strong snug wooden frame placed around a mast and resting on the hounds, to secure the foot of the mast above and to take the weight of the same.

Throat.—The inner edge of the gaff against the mast.

Transom.—One of the horizontal, thwartship timbers, composing the stern frame, and fastened to the stern post on its forward side.

Topping Lift.—The strong rope brought down from a block under the top to the outer end of the boom of a fore-and-aft sail, to take the weight of the boom and lift it so that it will clear the roof of the cabins.

Vangs.—Traces used to steady the gaff extending from the gaff on each side to the bulwarks, where they are hooked and drawn tight.

Up-helm.—To put the helm to windward.

Waist.—That part of a ship between the forcastle and the quarter.

Waterway.—The large square log, laid on the ends of the beams, close against the frame timbers, and bolted to both, to give the hull rigidity.

Wear.—To come around on the other side of the wind without tacking, an operation requiring plenty of sea room. In this operation, the bow is turned away from the wind.

Wales.—The heavy outside planking above the bilge. Sometimes called the "bends."

Weather Helm.—When the vessel tends to come too close into the wind, the helm is put to windward to keep her head off.

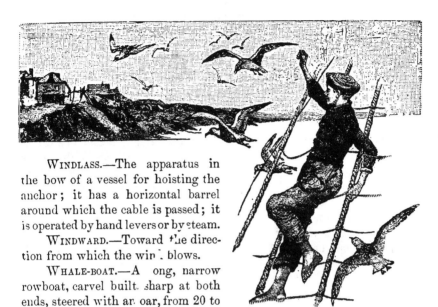

WINDLASS.—The apparatus in the bow of a vessel for hoisting the anchor; it has a horizontal barrel around which the cable is passed; it is operated by hand levers or by steam.

WINDWARD.—Toward the direction from which the wind blows.

WHALE-BOAT.—A long, narrow rowboat, carvel built, sharp at both ends, steered with an oar, from 20 to 50 feet in length and from 4 to 10 feet beam, with a small pole mast and sail, very fast and able.

YARD.—A spar suspended athwartships from a mast to spread the head of a square sail.

YAW.—To deviate from the course.

A few useful facts may be of assistance to the amateur waterman.

A suit of sails, if well taken care of, will last white and clean for three years.

Avoid stretching a new sail all it will bear at first; draw it out gradually, to prevent tearing should it be wet, while new.

The day on shipboard is divided into six periods of four hours each, and time is signalled by taps on a bell, each period ending with eight bells. The taps are as follows·

1 bell..............	12.30 o'clock.	5 bells.............	6.30 o'clock.
2 bells.............	1.00 "	6 "	7.00 "
3 "	1.30 "	"	7.30 "
4 "	2.00 "	"	8.00
5 "	2.30 "	"	8.30
6 "	3.00 "	"	9.00
7 "	3.30 "	"	9.30
8 "	4.00 "	"	10.00
1 "	4.30 "	"	10.30
2 "	5.00 "	"	11.00
3 "	5.30 "	"	11.30
4 "	6.00 "	"	12.00

CAMPING OUT.

Despite our boasted civilization and culture there is enough of the original savage in the majority of men and women to make them thoroughly enjoy a season of camping out with its hundred and one privations, its comical make-shifts, its homely occupations done in the spirit of play, but its blessed freedom from fashionable toilets, inane watering-place gossip, and ordinary, every-day, nineteenth-century routine. If one does not belong to a regular party of campers, owning an acre or so of ground with a permanent cottage erected thereon, among the mountains, on the shores of a lake, or by the restless sea, then one's camping outfit must include one or more tents according to the size of the party. A Sibley tent is conical, with an opening at the top which, affording an escape for smoke, permits of a fire being kindled, should the nights turn cold or a rainy spell set in. The ordinary A tent is less expensive and will shelter from four to six persons, but the wall-tent is best of all and will prove the most satisfactory. A buffalo robe to spread on a pile of fir, pine, or hemlock twigs, with blankets for covering, makes a bed which renders that city pest, *insomnia*, an impossibility. A coffee pot, a frying pan, and a kettle are the only cooking utensils absolutely necessary, with a portable oven, if one desires the luxury of hot bread. Besides these, the campers will need a goodly supply of servicable knives, forks, and spoons, tin cups and plates; soap, matches, candles, twine, needles and thread, a hatchet, a pair of scissors, some nails of assorted sizes, and a lantern. The kind and quantity of provisions to be transported to camp will depend upon the length of one's stay and the remoteness from civilization. Canned fruits, vegetables and soup, crackers, cheese, salt, pepper, mustard, spices, molasses, vinegar, sugar, tea, coffee, Indian meal, self-raising flour, baking soda, dried beef, rice, lemons, eggs and potatoes will none of them come amiss. In making up your party, select healthy, good tempered, congenial people, each of whom will be willing to do his or her share of the necessary work. When ready to pitch your tent choose a location having a pleasing outlook, within easy access to wood and water, and with a natural shelter, if possible, in the direction from which storms are likely to come at that season. A trench should be dug around each tent to carry off the water, should there be rain. The bill of fare will vary with the tastes of the campers and the resources of the neighborhood. An old hand at the business gives the following directions for a clam bake: "Build an oven of flat stones about three feet square. Around the edge of the oven place stones making a bin. In the oven place kindlings with larger wood placed crosswise on top. Upon this upper layer place stones about six or eight inches square. The kindlings are lighted, and when the wood has burned away, the hot stones form a bottom for the oven. Cinders should be removed with a stick or poker to prevent smoke from injuring the food. Cover the stones with fresh seaweed for a depth of two inches, and on it lay a bushel of clams which have been washed in fresh water. The fish, which are split down the back, cleaned, and seasoned with salt and pepper, are wrapped in a cloth. The onions are peeled, potatoes washed and the ends cut off. In husking the corn leave on the inner layer of the husk to keep it clean. The clams are spread so that the vegetables may be placed on them. The onions are first put on, then the potatoes, followed by the corn and the fish. A lobster is a very desirable addition. The food must be put in quickly, else the oven will cool. Cover the pile with cloth, and over all heap seaweed to confine the steam. In thirty or forty minutes remove the covering from one corner only in order to keep the bulk of the food warm. The party then help themselves. Drawn butter with pepper and salt forms a nice sauce for the clams." In making tea, allow a teaspoonful for each person, and a tablespoonful for each of coffee. Both beverages should be made with freshly boiled water, and allowed to steep ten or fifteen minutes before using.

CROQUET.

Less than fity years ago, Dr. Guyard, practicing at Pau, in the south of France, desired for his patients some out-door amusement, not too fatiguing, but with sufficient interest to keep them in the open air, and moving about for several hours at a time. Being a man of resource, he invented the game of croquet. Easily learned, requiring no violent exertion, admitting of fresh, pretty toilets and much pleasant chatting, it was a pronounced success, and its fame rapidly spread to every part of the civilized world. Played at first on any ordinary lawn, with wooden balls and long-handled mallets, science had neither part nor lot; but within the last ten years a desire for scientific playing has revolutionized the game. The grassy lawn has given place to a smooth, level, sanded court of exact dimensions, the wooden balls have been superseded by hard rubber spheres, and the long-handled mallets have been discarded in favor of short handles and long, rubber-tipped heads. The flaring arches of the old game have been replaced by narrow wickets, but little wider than the diameter of the balls. These changes render skill and fine playing possible, and have given rise to a National Association, composed at present of fifteen clubs.

CYCLING.

Beginning in Germany, with the clumsy velocipede, propelled by touching the tips of the toes to the road, human ingenuity has been at work raising the rider high above the ground, altering the location of the saddle, substituting steel wire for wooden spokes, a rubber tire for the clattering, metal-bound one, reducing the weight and increasing the speed, until to-day the ideal bicycle weighs only from 40 to 45 pounds, and causes so little fatigue that a good wheelman can travel a hundred miles a day, while a horse could carry him only about thirty or forty miles in the same time. There are three distinct styles of bicycles—a large driving wheel in front and a small trailing wheel in the rear; a small steering wheel in front, and the large driving wheel in the rear; and that having the two wheels of almost equal size. The distinguishing feature of the tricycle is that the rider sits between two wheels, of the same size; the tandem has two seats, one in front of the other; while the sociable accommodates two riders side by side. It is only necessary to add that there are now in the United States 100,000 riders of the "silent wheel," including men and women, to show how popular is this form of exercise, combined with pleasure.

FISHING.

When the disciple of Izak Walton has secured a holiday which he decides to devote to angling, his outfit, if he is not already provided, must depend upon the fishing ground selected and the variety of the finny tribe he wishes to catch. Since fly-fishing does away with angle-worms or minnows for bait, it is the favorite; and the wily fisherman will learn betimes how to make several varieties of flies that, if one kind fails to allure the prey, another may be substituted. Buy American tackle, as it is far better than the English. Though floats are cheap, a large cork will answer every purpose. Lines are of silk, linen, hemp, cotton, or silk and hair braided together. For catching such varieties as the trout, salmon, and bluefish, a reel is necessary. In selecting hooks, see that they are sharp and well barbed. Black bass bite at minnows, small frogs, crickets, etc. Large bluefish are generally trolled for; the lines are each furnished with a metal or bone squid, over which an eel skin, turned inside out, is drawn. Graylings bite at caddis worm and dark colored artificial flies. Muscalonges are trolled for with a stout linen line and a spoon hook from two and a half to three inches long. Red snappers are trolled for with a silver squid or caught with rod, strong line, and large hook, baited with porgee or mullet.

A HOME GYMNASIUM.

GYMNASTICS.

To the healthy, happy, country child spending most of the time out of doors—going for the cows, tending to the poultry, snaring rabbits, climbing trees, chopping wood, tossing hay, and a hundred similar pursuits,—gymnastic exercise is superfluous; but to the city-bred child, living perhaps in boarding-house or hotel, athletic training of some sort is a necessity. All else being equal, the stronger and healthier the body, the more vigorous the intellect. In a country where pulmonary diseases are so prevalent, and among a people so subject as the Americans to nervous complaints, whatever tends to increase the capacity of the chest will lessen the first, while such exercise as quickens the circulation and assists in renewing the tissues is the only sure cure for the second. The busiest of us may surely find an opportunity six or eight times a day to draw in a long, deep breath, retain it an instant, and then as deliberately let it escape. Raise yourself on your toes, ten, fifteen, twenty times in succession, increasing the number each day until you are able to do it a hundred times without fatigue. Acquire the habit of walking briskly and, if possible, take a run every day; but in the latter exercise, persevere in keeping the mouth shut and compelling yourself to breathe through the nose. At first you experience a feeling of suffocation and an almost irresistible desire to gasp; courage! compress your lips tightly and in a little while the disagreeable sensations pass away; you have gotten what the professionals call your second wind; your lungs fill themselves naturally and regularly, your mouth and throat remain moist instead of becoming dry and parched, as would have been the case had you yielded to the desire to pant, and you have learned the Indian's secret that enables him to run steadily for hours.

Of course, where it is practicable, systematic training under the supervision of a teacher, who will know where your weak points lie, and appoint such exercises as shall correct them, will be the best and most satisfactory. These hints are for the busy people who think they have not time for athletic training. But of whatever nature your calisthenic exercises may be, never omit the brisk rubbing down before retiring at night, it opens the pores, quickens the circulation, and removes the minute worn out particles of the scarf skin.

HORSEMANSHIP.

Horseback riding, once so universal in this country, gradually fell into disuse until the equestrian, whether man or woman, venturing to ride through the city streets to gain the shady park or quiet country roads, attracted almost as much attention as a parade or that joy of the small boy, a circus. Fortunately, however, there has been a revival of this delightful, healthgiving exercise and all who can are eagerly acquiring this most beneficial accomplishment, in choosing a horse the points of vital importance are legs, strong; hips, wide; chest, deep; back, short; with eyes and wind perfectly sound. The riding equipments demand much care in their selection; there are three kinds of bits, the snaffle, the curb, and a combination of the two. A handsome pig skin saddle is the best, as even an ordinary horse looks much better for being properly equipped. None but good riders should use a spur; for ordinary exercise a whip is all that is necessary. The proper dress for a man is a short coat and a pair of tight trousers, a high hat, jockey cap, or soft felt hat. A woman should wear a neatly fitting tailor made waist, and a skirt reaching just below the feet when in the saddle; high boots, trousers meeting the tops of these boots and a high hat. The short skirt is weighted and has two elastic straps which are adjusted after mounting, one passing over the right instep, the other under the left heel. The West Point rule for mounting, which leaves the left hand free, is the best for a man; a woman places her right hand on the pommel of the saddle, her left foot in the left hand of her assistant, her left hand on his right shoulder, and his right hand under her left armpit. Her assistant counts audibly "one, two, three," and at "three" she springs and he straightens himself thus lifting her into the saddle. Sit firmly in the saddle, expand the chest by throwing back the shoulders and keeping them equally square to the front; keep the head erect, hold the reins in the left hand and keep the arms down, the elbows just touching the sides but not pressing against them. Having mastered the art of riding, there are exciting and invigorating sports that may be indulged in; as polo, hunting buffalo, deer, wild foxes or, where none of these are practicable, a drag hunt furnishes a good excuse for a brisk ride, a good supper, and a merry time generally. In a drag hunt a bag of anise seed is dragged for several miles the day before, and left snugly hidden away.

AMATEUR PHOTOGRAPHY.

For luring the invalid into the invigorating sunshine; for developing artistic instincts, delicacy of touch, proper appreciation of the beautiful, and for the collection of pleasant souvenirs, amateur photography stands unrivalled. Though sums as large as $10,000 have been spent on this recreation, very good results have been obtained with a $10 camera; and although one may devote his life to the study and still find something to learn, the process has been so simplified that even a child can master it. A substantial and satisfactory outfit may be purchased at from $25 to $40, while the detective camera preferred by some tourists cost $50. The novice will do well to remember that the "dry plate," before being used, must never be examined by any except a red light, and the "ruby lantern" will therefore be an important item in his outfit. After a little practice, however, he will learn to adjust his plate in the holder while in absolute darkness. The plate should be touched only along the edges but must be carefully dusted before being put into the holder. Having selected his view, the operator's first care must be to adjust the legs of his tripod so that the camera is level. Next he covers his head and instrument with the "focussing cloth," uncaps the lens, and slides the movable front forward or backward until the blurred image he saw at first has grown clear and distinct; then he caps the lens, takes out the ground glass, slides in its place a plate holder; meanwhile keeping all but the front of his instrument carefully shrouded with the "focussing cloth; uncaps his lens, counts the requisite number of seconds, and replaces the cap. Cloudy days, dimly lighted rooms, and moonlight scenes require a longer exposure. As instantaneous pictures cannot be taken with a cheap lens, the device for securing such impressions is only fitted to costly cameras.

RIFLE AND SHOT-GUN.

As an amusement having a practical side, a knowledge of the use of firearms stands pre-eminent. In choosing a gun, let it be the breech-loader, selected in reference to the measurements of its prospective owner. A boy's gun may be purchased for $15, but for a man it is better policy to buy a $50 double-barreled one. Though cartridges may be bought ready-made, the thorough sportsman will delight in their manufacture. A cleaning-rod costs $1, but just as good a one can be whittled at a cost only of time and dexterity. Before experimenting with a loaded gun, practice position and aim. Having set up your target, take up your position, at say thirty yards away. Fix both eyes on the target, raise your gun, supporting the barrel with your left hand, and having the fore-finger of your right on the trigger. Notice the position when the bead on your gun is in a line with your eyes and the target. Practice this until you can take proper aim even with your eyes closed. Having learned to aim and fire, accustom yourself to treating your gun always as if it were loaded. Never draw it through a fence, from a wagon or a boat by the muzzle. Never point it at a companion, and in the field carry it over the shoulder, with barrels pointing upward, or reversed and pointing at the ground. If the weapon is a rifle, remember the increased length of range, which makes a rifle bullet dangerous a mile or two away.

Game hunted in America includes quail, snipe, grouse, woodcock, wild geese, and ducks, pigeons, plover, squirrels, raccoons, deer, elks moose, and mountain goats.

TRAPPING.

Where gunning is impracticable, trapping is often an important auxiliary for adding a dainty dish to the camper's meal or for ridding hen-house or cabbage patch of the midnight marauder. Where the trap is needed for continual use, the manufactured steel one is most satisfactory because of its greater durability, but the amateur trapper will derive much more pleasure if he makes his trap himself. For squirrels or rabbits a wooden box 24 inches long and from 8 to 10 inches wide, having the bait attached to a trigger inside, in such a manner that nibbling the bait causes the door to shut, is simple but effective. The cell trap used for muskrats, minks, and weasels has a swinging wire door hinged to the top and resting on the bottom of the trap; the door will open only inward. The hungry pest easily pushes the door open and when it falls shut he is ensnared. The professional trapper does not wash the pelt, because that rots it, nor use alum nor salt to cure it, because they would unnecessarily shrink it. If it is the skin of a deer, moose or buffalo, he dries it by stretching it on the ground, driving wooden pegs at the corners to keep it even. Pelts should always be cured in a moderately dry place, and on a flat surface.

SWIMMING.

However pleasant a pastime boating may be, it should never be indulged in until one has learned to swim. Smooth, shallow water with a shelving shore is best for the beginner. Wade out to the depth of three or four feet, wet your head, then turn your face toward the land. Return until the water is no deeper than your arm is long; support yourself by letting the tips of your fingers touch bottom, now lie down, letting the body sink below the surface, but throwing the head back so that the chin is about on a level with the surface, one arm and both legs being free practice the stroke, and occasionally raise the supporting hand, until you have gained enough confidence in the upholding power of the water to trust yourself to its buoyancy. Then wade out several feet further and attempt to swim in, putting down the supporting arm as at first, if this attempt prove a failure. Learn to swim in clothing. The ability to do so may be invaluable in an emergency; to keep the eyes open under water and, if attacked by cramp, change the manner of stroke, make several quick motions with the member affected, regardless of pain, but if the cramp continues, float back to shore, the great danger lies in becoming frightened. In learning to dive, it is well to plug the ears with oil-saturated raw cotton. Never bathe in less than two hours after a hearty meal; seldom remain in the water above 30 minutes, and always wet the head before entering the water.   Dr. Benjamin Howard, of New York, prescribes the following treatment in apparent cases of drowning

1.   Upon the nearest dry spot expose the patient to a free current of air.   Rip the clothing away from the waist and give a stinging slap upon the pit of the stomach.   If this fails to arouse the patient, proceed to force and drain away the water which has entered the chest and stomach, according to the following rule:

2.   Turn the patient upon his face, the pit of the stomach being raised upon a folded garment above the level of the mouth.   For a moment or two make steady pressure upon the back of the stomach and chest and repeat once or twice until fluid ceases to flow from the mouth.

3.   Quickly turn the patient upon his back, with the bundle of clothing beneath it, so as to raise the lower part of the breast bone higher than the rest of the body.   Kneel beside or astride of the patient, and so place your hands upon either side of the pit of the stomach and the front part of the lower ribs that the fingers fall naturally in the spaces between them and point toward the ground.   Now, grasping the waist and using your knees as a pivot, throw your whole weight forward, as if you wished to force the contents of the chest and stomach out of the mouth. Steadily increase the pressure while you count " one, two, three."   Then let go suddenly, after a final push which springs you to an erect kneeling position.   Remain erect upon your knees while you count " one, two ; " then throw your weight forward and proceed as before.   Repeat the process at first about five times a minute, increasing gradually to about fifteen times a minute, and continue it with the regularity of the natural breathing which you are trying to imitate.   If another person be present, let him with the left hand hold the tip of the tongue out of the left side of the mouth with the corner of a pocket-handkerchief, while with the right hand he grasps both wrists and pins them to the ground above the patient's head.

4.   When breathing first returns, occasionally dash a little cold water violently into the face.   As soon as breathing has been perfectly restored, strip and dry the patient rapidly and completely, and wrap him in blankets only.   Give hot brandy, a teaspoonful every five minutes, the first half hour; and a tablespoonful every fifteen minutes for an hour after that.   If the limbs are cold, apply friction.   Allow abundance of fresh air, and let the patient have perfect rest.

Practical suggestions: Avoid delay.   Promptness is of first import- ance.   A moment lost at the start may be a life lost.   Do not waste any time trying to give shelter, because shelter oftener harms than helps the patient.

Prevent crowding around the patient. However difficult it may be to enforce this rule, it must be enforced. Friends must not obstruct the circulation of air, nor engage the patient in conversation when rallying.

Take special care to avoid giving stimulants before the patient is well enough to swallow. Injudicious attempts in this direction tend to obstruct respiration and may choke the patient.

Avoid hurried and irregular motions. The excitement of the moment is always great and is likely to agitate an inexperienced man. Just as a flickering candle moved carelessly goes out, so the heart, when its beating is imperceptible, needs little cross motion or interruption to stop its action. The movements of Rule 3 should, therefore, be performed with deliberation and regularity.

Avoid an overheated room. The animal heat which is needed cannot be supplied from without; it must be generated within the system. This is best promoted by a free current of air and internal stimulants. The vital heat resulting is best retained in the patient's body by blankets alone.

Avoid giving up the patient too soon. At any time within one or two hours you may be on the very threshold of success, though no sign of it be visible. Several times success has been known to follow half an hour's apparently useless effort. Rest and careful nursing should be continued for a few days after resuscitation, because otherwise various chest troubles might ensue

LAWN TENNIS.

For more than five hundred years, some variety of tennis has been known and played. Originating in France, it was a favorite amusement in Spain and Italy before it made its way to England; yet Chaucer refers to it in 1380 as a well-established and popular game. Henry VIII and Elizabeth in England, Louis XI, Louis XII, Francis I, Charles IX, and Henry IV, of France, were all devoted to the sport of Court Tennis, from which the modern Lawn Tennis is descended. In laying out a court, let it extend from north to south with a margin of fifteen feet at the ends and ten feet at the sides. In a court of 78 feet, the base lines should be 27 feet, the service lines 21 feet from the net. Marble dust is the best material for marking. A good service is the most important feature of the game. A clever method of practice suggested by an expert is to fasten a hoop about two feet in diameter upon a three-foot stake backed by a wall. Take your station 40 feet away and practise serving through the

hoop. Unless you are left-handed, it is best to keep a little to the left of
the court. Watch your opponent's eye ; he will generally glance in the
direction he means to serve. "The proper moment to take a bounding
ball is when its upward momentum is spent, and it is about to fall."

Of all out-of-door games, lawn-tennis now ranks as prime favorite.

It is a very easy matter to learn to play ; but to fully enjoy the
exhilarating amusement, a suitable costume should be provided. The
best material for this is flannel, because it affords the most perfect protection against cold and heat. The style must be without draperies—any
catalogue of paper patterns will supply pretty designs. One of the best
is a pleated skirt, with a Jersey jacket matching it in color. Sew the
skirt on a sleeveless waist lining, which, if possible, should be of the
color of the Jersey waist. This answers several purposes, the Jersey will
fit better over it, the colored lining will prevent the white under-clothing
from showing through the meshes, as it stretches during the different
changes of position in the game, and the weight of the skirt will be
removed from the hips to the shoulders thus affording far more freedom
of movement.

The head-covering should be either a crocheted Tam O'Shanter, or a
soft cap of the dress material. The shoes, if possible, should have rubber
soles, but if these cannot be obtained, take the heels from a pair of ordinary shoes, and they will answer the purpose very tolerably.

The best ground for the court is turf, though asphalt, and earth, mixed with fine gravel, are sometimes used.

The balls must not measure less than $2\frac{15}{32}$ inches, nor more than $2\frac{1}{2}$ inches in diameter, and their weight must not be less than 1 and $\frac{15}{16}$ ounces nor more than two ounces.

The following rules have been adopted by the United States National Lawn-Tennis Association, and will enable any one who studies them to readily learn the game. It is not, however, invariably necessary to have an umpire or referee.

RULES FOR LAWN-TENNIS.

1. *The Game.*—The choice of sides, and the right to serve in the first game, shall be decided by toss; provided that, if the winner of the toss choose the right to serve, the other player shall have choice of sides, and *vice versa.* If one player choose the court, the other may elect not to serve.

2. The players shall stand on opposite sides of the net; the player who first delivers the ball shall be called the *server,* and the other the *striker-out.*

3. At the end of the first game the striker-out shall become server, and the server shall become striker-out; and so on, alternately, in all the subsequent games of the set, or series of sets.

4. The server shall serve with one foot on the base line, and with the other foot behind that line, but not necessarily upon the ground. He shall deliver the service from the right to the left courts alternately beginning from the right.

5. The ball served must drop between the service line, half-court line, and side line of the court, diagonally opposite to that from which it was served.

6. It is a fault if the server fails to strike the ball, or if the ball served drop in the net, or beyond the service line, or out of court, or in the wrong court, or if the server do not stand as directed by law 4.

7. A ball falling on a line is regarded as falling in the court bounded by that line.

8. A fault cannot be taken.

9. After a fault the server shall serve again from the same court from which he served that fault, unless it was a fault because he served from the wrong court.

10. A fault cannot be claimed after the next service is delivered.

11. The server shall not serve till the striker-out is ready. If the latter attempt to return the service, he shall be deemed ready

12. A service or fault, delivered when the striker-out is not ready, counts for nothing.

13. The service shall not be *volleyed*, i. e., taken before it has touched the ground.

14. A ball is in play on leaving the server's racket, except as provided for in law 6.

15. It is a good return, although the ball touch the net; but a service, otherwise good, which touches the net, shall count for nothing.

16. The server wins a stroke, if the striker-out volley the service, or if he fail to return the service or the ball in play; or if he return the service or the ball in play so that it drops outside of his opponent's court; or if he otherwise lose a stroke, as provided by law 18.

17. The striker-out wins a stroke, if the server serve two consecutive faults; or if he return the ball in play so that it drops outside of his opponent's court; or if he otherwise lose a stroke, as provided by law 18.

18. Either player loses a stroke, if he return the service or the ball in play so that it touches a post of the net; or if the ball touch him or anything that he wears or carries, except his racket in the act of striking; or if he touch the ball with his racket more than once; or if he touch the net or any of its supports while the ball is in play; or if he volley the ball before it has passed the net.

19. In case any player is obstiucted by any accident, the ball shall be considered *a let*.

20. On either player winning his first stroke, the score is called 15 for that player; on either player winning his second stroke, the score is called 30 for that player; on either player winning his third stroke, the score is called 40 for that player; and the fourth stroke won by either player is scored game for that player, except as below. If both players have won three strokes, the score is called *deuce ;* and the next stroke won by either player is scored *advantage* for that player. If the same player wins the next stroke, he wins the game; if he loses the next stroke, the score returns to deuce; and so on, until one player wins the two strokes immediately following the score of deuce, when game is scored for that player.

21. The player who first wins six games, wins the set; except as follows: If both players win five games, the score is called games all; and the next game won by either player is scored advantage game for

that player. If the same player wins the next game, he wins the set; if he loses the next game, the score returns to games all; and so on, until either player wins the two games immediately following the score of games all, when he wins the set. But individual clubs, at their own tournaments, may modify this rule at their discretion.

22. The players shall change sides at the end of every set; but the umpire, on appeal from either player, before the toss for choice, may direct the players to change sides at the end of every game of each set, if, in his opinion, either side has a distinct advantage, owing to the sun, wind, or any other accidental cause; but if the appeal be made after the toss for choice, the umpire can only direct the players to change sides at the end of every game of the odd or deciding set.

23. When a series of sets is played, the player who served in the last game of one set shall be striker-out in the first game of the next.

24. The referee shall call the game after an interval of five minutes between sets, if either player so order.

25. The above laws shall apply to the three-handed and four-handed games, except as below:

26. In the three-handed game, the single player shall serve in every alternate game.

27. In the four-handed game, the pair who have the right to serve in the first game shall decide which partner shall do so, and the opposing pair shall decide in like manner for second game. The partner of the player who served in the first game shall serve in the third, and the partner of the player who served in the second game shall serve in the fourth; and the same order shall be maintained in all the subsequent games of the set.

28. At the beginning of the next set, either partner of the pair which struck out in the last game of the last set may serve, and the same privilege is given to their opponents in the second game of the new set.

29. The players shall take the service alternately throughout the game; a player cannot receive a service delivered to his partner; and the order of service and striking out once established shall not be altered, nor shall the striker-out change courts to receive the service, till the end of the set.

30. It is a fault if the ball served does not drop between the service line, half-court line, and service side-line of the court, diagonally opposite to that from which it was served.

31. In matches, the decision of the umpire shall be final. Should there be two umpires, they shall divide the court between them, and the decision of each shall be final in his share of the court.

ODDS.

A *bisque* is one point which can be taken by the receiver of the odds at any time in the set except as follows:

(a) A bisque cannot be taken after a service is delivered.

(b) The server may not take a bisque after a fault, but the striker out may do so.

One or more bisques may be given to increase or diminish other odds. *Half-fifteen* is one stroke given at the beginning of the second, fourth, and every subsequent alternate game of a set.

Fifteen is one stroke given at the beginning of every game of a set.

Half-thirty is one stroke given at the beginning of the first game, two strokes given at the beginning of the second game, and so on, alternately, in all the subsequent games of the set.

Thirty is two strokes given at the beginning of every game of a set.

Half-forty is two strokes given at the beginning of the first game, three strokes given at the beginning of the second game, and so on, alternately, in all the subsequent games of the set.

Forty is three strokes given at the beginning of every game of a set.

Half-court: The players may agree into which half-court, right or left, the giver of the odds shall play, and the latter loses the stroke if the ball returned by him drop out-side any of the lines which bound that half court.

TOSS.

This pretty, new open air game, often played at lawn-parties, is very quickly learned and affords much amusement.

Provide a decorated waste-basket, two stakes, one red and one blue,— if the game is to be played by two parties,—and nine card-board circles, three blue, three white, and three red.

Set the basket on the turf and thrust the stakes into the ground directly opposite to each other and each one six feet from the basket.

The object of the players is to throw the disks into the basket. They are rated according to the color, blue counts three, white two, and red one.

When played by sides, each plays five rounds, ninety being the highest score possible for any player, but it is optional whether sides are taken or not. The account is kept by the hostess, and the player who has the highest score receives a prize.

OUT-DOOR GAMES FOR CHILDREN.

Across the ocean, in the " Vaterland," the little German children have quite a variety of games, usually played in the open air, some of which doubtless will be new to their American cousins.

CATCHING THE WEASEL.

The whole party, except one, form a circle. The one who is left out runs two or three times round the ring, and then drops a handkerchief at the feet of a playmate, who must dash swiftly forward to catch the " weasel"—namely, the one who flung down the handkerchief. While running, she sings: " Catch the weasel in the wood. Now I've lost it; now I've found it. Catch my nimble little weasel." When the game is well played, it is very lively and amusing. All the girls watch to see where the weasel drops the handkerchief, and, while running, the little weasel tries to give the pursuer as much trouble as possible by jumping to the right or left, by breaking through the ring, and leaping forward and backward. When the " weasel " is caught, the pursuer takes her place.

THE DRILL.

This is another merry little game, which makes a great deal of fun. The children stand in a row on the soft grass, with the exception o' one, who acts as captain. The game is most amusing when only two know it—the captain and the first one in the line, who is called the corporal. When all are in place, the captain stands in front and puts them through a comical drill, giving one order after another: "Cough, Laugh, Slap your cheeks, Clap your hands," etc. The whole company must obey the command at once.

After a number of orders, the captain cries: "Kneel down!" Every girl drops on her left knee, and the captain makes them all move close together, and then gives the orders: "Load! aim"—upon which every one stretches out her right arm till the command comes: "Fire!" The corporal then gives her neighbor a sudden push, and down goes the whole line on the turf.

WEAVING GARLANDS.

This graceful little game is like a dance. The girls stand in a row, with joined hands; one remains perfectly still while the others dance around until the whole line is wound into a knot, singing: "Let us lovely garlands wind." Then they dance the other way, singing: "Now the wreath we will unbind," until they form a straight line.

LITTLE WASHER-WOMEN.

This game somewhat resembles weaving garlands. The players stand opposite to one another in couples, each girl with her right hand clasping her companion's left. Then they swing their arms, slowly and gracefully, first three times toward the right and then three times toward the left, singing: "This is the way we wash the clothes, wash the clothes, wash the clothes." Then they unclasp their hands and rub them together as washer-women do in rubbing their clothes, singing: "This is the way we rub our clothes, rub our clothes."

The third movement is very pretty. The couple clasp hands just as they do at first, then raise their arms in an arch on one side and slip through so that they stand back to back, then raise their arms in the same way on the other side, and again slip through so that they stand face to face again. This must be done very quickly, thrice in succession, while the players sing: "This is the way we wring the clothes, wring the clothes, wring the clothes," and then stopping suddenly clap their hands, singing: "And hang them on the bushes." When several couples have learned the game well, it is a very pretty sight.

THE FLYING FEATHER.

In this game the little girls join hands, and dance around in a ring on the turf, trying meanwhile, by blowing a bit of down, to keep it in the air. When the players are skillful, they can often dance for fifteen minutes without letting the feather come to the earth.

BLIND MAN'S MARCH.

An open space of turf is chosen and a tree, stake, or pole selected for a goal, on which all sorts of trifles, fruit, garlands, flowers, etc., are hung as prizes. Then a circle is drawn around the goal, about six or eight feet distant. The players first dance hand in hand around the ring, then in couples around the tree, and finally form two straight lines. Lots are then drawn to decide which row shall make the blind march first, and all in that rank are blind-folded and led by the others forty or fifty paces away from the ring and formed in couples in a semi-circle. The game is prettier when a march is sung, to which the blind-folded couple keep time. Only a very few reach the goal; most go far astray. If any couples disagree about the direction to be taken, they can separate and each pursue a different path. Whoever reaches the tree, or even stands inside the circle when the game is over, receives a prize. The march is considered at an end when the singing ceases. Then all the players take off their bandages.

There is plenty of laughing, for the couples are generally standing everywhere except near the tree. The game begins again by the other side commencing the blind march.

THE BEGGAR.

A life-size pasteboard figure of a man holding a hat in his hand is needed. This hat has a hole, which serves as an opening to a calico bag. The players, standing at a certain distance, try to throw a coin or some small fruit into the beggar's hat. The one who succeeds most frequently receives some trifling prize.

THE NAUGHTY STRAW MAN.

A straw figure, completely dressed, is fastened to a tree in such a way that it hangs about a foot from the ground. He must have one arm fastened akimbo to his side, and the other hanging free. After the players have had their eyes bandaged and been furnished with a stick, the game begins. The object is to thrust the stick through the opening. Whoever succeeds in doing so can claim a prize. Of course, it often happens that the player misses, and receives a light pat for the clumsiness from the straw man's hanging arm. If any player misses the goal and passes the naughty straw man, the bandage is removed, and the player is considered out of the game.

CORONELLA.

This pretty game is played by one child, and requires an ivory or a wooden ball, fastened by a string half way down a wooden stick which ends in a point at one end and has a small leather cup at the other. The ball has a hole on the side opposite to the string, and the object is to toss it into the air as far as the string will let it go, and as it falls catch it alternately in the cup and on the point of the stick.

IN-DOOR GAMES.

THE SEERESS.

Two little girls come into the room where the others have gathered. One pretends to be a doctor, the other a somnambulist or seeress, who knows more than ordinary people. The doctor says that she can discover the deepest secrets by falling into a magnetic sleep, and then passes her hand three times over her eyes, muttering a few unintelligible words, which sound like " Hocus pocus, abracadabra," and finally ties a black handkerchief over the sleeper's eyes to keep the bright light from disturbing her.

Then the questions begin.

The doctor walks up to the nearest spectator, takes her pocket handkerchief, and then turns to the sleeper.

" Does the seeress see what I hold in my hand ? "

" A handkerchief."

" Is it white or colored ? "

" Colored."

" What is the color—black, blue, or red ? "

" Blue."

" Is it figured, plaided, or striped? "

" Plaided."

The replies usually astonish the company; but the mystery is very simple.

The doctor and seeress have agreed on certain words by which the sleeper's answers are guided. Thus *hold* is the word for handkerchief. When two things are named, as "white" or "colored," the last is always the correct one; and if three are named, the somnambulist must choose the middle one. When the game is well played, it creates a great deal of amusement.

LITTLE MARKET WOMEN.

Each player takes the character of a huckster. One sells cherries, another cakes, a third old clothes, a fourth eggs, etc.

They pace around the room, and as soon as the name of any one of them is called, she must shout her wares as loudly as possible. The buyer then enquires for the wares, and receives the answers: " I haven't it, ask somebody else." For instance: The player who begins the game calls "pears." The pear-dealer instantly screams, " Pears! Pears! Buy some fresh pears!" The first speaker then asks: " Have you apples, too? " " No," replies the pear-seller, " go to the water-carrier."

As soon as the water-carrier bears her name, she begins to shout " Water! Water! "

" Have you any raspberry vinegar? " asks the pear-seller. " No, go to the umbrella-dealer."

" Umbrellas! Umbrellas! " calls the umbrella-dealer.

" Have you sun-shades, too? " asks the water-carrier.

" No," she replies, " go to the cherry-huckster."

The cherry-huckster shouts: "Sweet cherries! Sweet cherries! Four pennies a pound."

The umbrella-dealer asks: " Have you black cherries, too? "

" No, go to the flower girl."

As soon as the flower girl hears her name, she begins to call: " Beautiful roses! Buy my roses! "

These examples will give an idea of the game which, when well played, is a very merry one. The larger the number who take part in it, the greater the fun.

Every seller who does not instantly offer her wares as soon as she hears her name must pay a forfeit, and every buyer who asks for the wrong article, for instance flowers from a fruit-dealer, must be sentenced to the same punishment.

THE COMICAL CONCERT.

This is a very lively game, and often affords much amusement, when introduced at fairs, or children's festivals.

The children stand in a circle and each one tries to imitate the music of some instrument. One pretends to play on the violin by drawing the right hand to and fro over the left arm, another raises both hands to her lips, as though blowing a horn, another drums on the table, as if it were a piano, a fourth seizes the back of the chair and touches the rounds as though it were a harp, a fifth pretends to beat a drum, a sixth to play on the guitar, a seventh to turn the handle of an organ. The greater the number of players the better. This, however, is only the beginning of the game; every musician must try to imitate the sounds of the instrument as nearly as possible. For instance:

Bum, bum, bum, for the drum,

Twang, twang, twang, for the harp,

Toot, toot, toot, for the horn, etc.

This strange mixture of sounds and gestures produces a very comical effect, when all enter into the game with spirit.

In the centre of the circle stands the "leader," whose duty it is to beat time as ridiculously as possible to make the others laugh. He or she must hold a roll of music or a baton.

In the midst of the tumult the leader must suddenly give the signal to stop, and ask:

"Why don't you play better?'

The person addressed must *instantly* give a suitable answer.

The harp-player should say:

"Because the harp-strings are too loose."

The pianist should reply:

"Because one of the piano keys won't sound."

If there is any delay in the answer, or if an unsuitable one is given, a forfeit must be paid.

THE JOURNEY TO JERUSALEM.

The players take their seats in a row, and before them stands the speaker who is to describe a journey to Jerusalem.

Each one receives a name, which must be a word that will occur frequently in the story, such as: ship, sailor, sea, island, neighborhood, nation, storm, tree, sun, air, etc. Whenever this word is uttered in the story the person who bears it must rise and turn slowly round and round, until another person's name is mentioned.

If any one whose name is called forgets to turn, she receives a blow with a handkerchief, or is obliged to pay a forfeit. Whenever the word "Jerusalem" occurs in the story, the whole group must rise and turn around.

The point is to mention all the words often enough to keep the players spinning. Of course, all sorts of adventures must be invented, the more thrilling the better. The imagination has a wide field, and if the story-teller is skillful enough to make the tale comical, the listeners may become so interested that they will forget to turn around.

How to be Beautiful.

Since no subject, it is said, interests women more than that of the best means of preserving and increasing the charms bestowed by nature, it is surely well to follow a course of treatment based upon sound hygienic rules and recommended by physicians of experience, rather than to incur the risk of injuring health and—what, alas! in the eyes of many a maiden is of far more importance—beauty, by purchasing, haphazard, any quack so-called "beautifying lotion" that may chance to be widely advertised.

The following pages have been compiled from the best authorities on a subject so important to the fair sex, if deemed trivial by the "lords of creation," and the utmost care has been used to exclude all cosmetics whose use would be injurious.

THE COMPLEXION.

Of first importance to the would-be beauty is the care of the complexion, since a sallow or muddy skin will spoil the charm of the most regular features, and to better understand the reason for the course of treatment recommended, a few words concerning the structure and functions of the skin may be valuable.

133

It consists of **two** layers, the true skin, lying underneath, and the cuticle, which covers and protects it. The true skin, besides the arteries, veins, and nerves, contains millions of little glands opening by tiny tubes upon the cuticle, through which the processes of transpiration and perspiration go on. Any check in these processes is attended with danger. Hence the injury accomplished by applying artificial varnish to the surface of the cuticle. The health and beauty of the skin depend chiefly on the freedom with which its pores can act. If they are choked by the application of foreign substances, black deposits will form, blotches will appear, nay, sometimes serious disfigurements are caused by the chemicals employed in the manufacture of certain cosmetics.

The cause of the injury to the skin occasioned by the use of "hard" water, is the presence of lime and magnesia, which, combining with the fatty acid of soap, forms a greasy substance which fills the pores of the skin, inducing them to crack and widen. Rain water is said to be the great specific for the complexion, and two of the most noted French beauties of former days are reported to have used no other cosmetic.

Besides the lotions, washes, etc., which may with benefit be used on the skin, certain general rules must be observed by those who desire to have and retain a beautiful complexion.

First, all kinds of salted and pickled food, raw or smoked meats, and rich and greasy compounds, such as pork, bologna sausage, paté de foie gras, etc., must be avoided. The more nearly the diet can be confined to milk, fruit, and farinaceous foods the better.

Over-eating is a source of much injury to the skin. Only three meals should be taken during the day, the last, three hours before retiring.

Daily exercise in the open air is essential, and thorough ventilation of the sleeping room must be secured. Shun tight lacing, and have the weight of the clothing supported by the shoulders.

These general directions may seem to some persons unnecessary, but it is of little service to apply local treatment without due observance of the laws of hygiene.

If one resides in cities, where the air is often impure, the vapor and Turkish baths, frequently taken, will be of marked benefit to the complexion. If these are not obtainable, an ordinary bath must be had every morning; but the *face* should be washed in *rain water*.

Two or three times a week the face can be washed with a lather of *absolutely pure* soap, or with a little Fuller's earth sprinkled in the hand or flesh glove. But care must be taken to wash it off thoroughly. *Never* use any of the so-called "medicated soaps," such as tar, carbolic acid, or sulphur.

An excellent cleansing lotion known as "virginal milk," to be used instead of either soap or Fuller's earth, has come down from the days of our grandmothers.

It is prepared as follows:

VIRGINAL MILK.

One quart of rose water, orange water, or elder-flower water, to which is added, drop by drop, stirring constantly, one ounce of simple tincture of benzoin. A few drops of glycerine and twelve or fifteen minims of tincture of myrrh may be added.

Care must be taken to use *simple*, not *compound* tincture of benzoin. The latter has aloes and other ingredients which would be harmful.

After washing, dry the face thoroughly with a soft towel, and then powder it; but do not use the ordinary violet or nursery powder, which is far too coarse for the purpose. Oxide of zinc is harmless, and so is magnesia, but well prepared *poudre-de-riz* "rice" powder is far better than either.

Before going to bed the face should be washed in soft water, dried, and then rubbed thoroughly from forehead to chin with cold-cream, applied with the hand, and then wiped off with a soft towel. As the cold-cream offered for sale is not always pure, it is safer to prepare it by the following directions:

            Pure white wax.........................1 ounce.
            Spermaceti ....2 ounces.
            Almond oil.............................½ pint.

Melt these ingredients slowly together, stirring constantly with a silver spoon in a glazed earthen vessel.

Then add ·   ,

            Glycerine............................ 3 ounces.
            Otto of roses........................12 drops.

Stir till nearly cold, then let the mixture settle.

This preparation should not be applied every night. The frequency of its use must depend on the condition of the skin

Steaming the skin, which may be done by the aid of a common kitchen steamer, is excellent for the preservation of the complexion, especially if the pores are choked, and the surface of the cuticle is inclined to look greasy and yellow. The effect of the steam should be aided by gentle rubbing with the hand. Five or ten minutes of this steaming and shampooing, twice or thrice a week, will do wonders in preventing premature wrinkles, and also in removing acne and "black-heads."

It is wiser to use the steam-bath at night, to avoid the danger of chill from the out-door air after the pores have been opened. Caution must of course be observed in the use of the steam. Do not let it come near enough to scald.

SEBORRHEA.

Greasiness of the Skin.—This is a very common complaint, and is caused by want of tone in the sebaceous glands, which either secrete more oily matter than can be used, giving an oily look to the skin, or if this matter is blocked in issuing, swell and show small black heads under the cuticle.

Here also local treatment will be of no avail without due observation of general hygienic rules. Saline mineral waters should be taken; fruit and salads made of dandelions and water-cresses should be eaten at breakfast; shower-baths, either lukewarm or cold, according to the season, should be used, and hot crowded rooms and rich foods scrupulously avoided. Change of climate is of the greatest value. Warm, moist climates are very injurious in these cases, while removal to high, dry, and cold regions will almost instantly benefit, and frequently cure the most obstinate diseases.

In connection with this general treatment, certain local remedies should be applied.

Stimulating and astringent washes are required. The following, to be used for bathing the face morning and evening, is excellent:

Dried rose leaves...... ....1 ounce.
White-wine vinegar........................$\frac{1}{2}$ pint.
Rose-water ....$\frac{1}{2}$ pint.

Pour the vinegar upon the rose leaves and let it stand for a week; strain and add the rose-water, throwing the leaves away. The lotion may be used either undiluted, by wetting a corner of a soft cloth with it, or a tablespoonful may be put into a cupful of rain-water.

In cases where the oiliness is excessive, apply the following, two or three times a day:

Sulphate of zinc.......... ....2 grains.
Compound tincture of lavender..............8 minims.
Water (distilled)........... ....1 ounce.

Mix the ingredients thoroughly. Sometimes the skin is so oily that it must be wiped with a soft rag dipped in benzine to cleanse it sufficiently to permit the operation of the wash.

Rubbing with flesh gloves and electric brushes, bathing with toilet vinegar, and steaming are all excellent methods of treating *seborrhea.*

The best vinegar—if obtainable—is the vinaigre-de-toilette of the Société Hygiènique. Toilet vinegars are frequently made with diluted acetic acid, into which are infused rose-leaves, lavender, verbena, or some other perfume. All toilet vinegars should be much diluted. The best time to use them is in the morning after bathing, in order to cool the skin, remove any appearance of greasiness, and give tone to the epidermis. But they must on no account be used soon after soap has been applied, because the acid of the vinegar will decompose the soap and seriously injure the skin.

Always avoid any liquid washes that contain any metallic powder in solution, or any earthy substance. Such cosmetics dry on the skin, forming a solid coating over the pores, render the complexion hard, rough, and blotched, and cause premature wrinkles and crows' feet. Speaking generally, all skin diseases should be treated by vapor baths, either once a day, or three or four times a week, as necessity may require. In addition, there must be no excess in eating or drinking ; regular hours must be kept, daily exercise must be insisted upon, good ventilation maintained, and *rain water only* used for bathing the skin.

It should also be remembered that sea-air and sea-bathing must be avoided by those who have any eruption of the skin. Persons living near the sea should move inland before essaying any form of treatment Sometimes the mere change of air will cure cutaneous diseases. In other cases, it is advisable to adopt a milk diet. If this cannot be done, all fermented drinks and butcher's meat should be given up.

ACNE.

The commonest form of eruption on the face is acne, or "black points,"—sometimes erroneously called " grubs,"—which generally appear on the nose, cheeks, and chin. The plan of squeezing out the "black points" is useless, since they are merely an oily secretion, which turns black on exposure to the air. The only mode of cure is by attention to the general hygienic rules previously given, aided by steam-baths and rubbing the affected parts with the hand while in the bath.

These baths should be taken early in the day, but never directly after breakfast or any other meal.

In addition, use the following wash, dipping a soft bit of linen into the lotion, and rubbing the pimples with it night and morning·

> Sulphur præcip.......................... ... 1 drachm.
> Spt. rectificati......·.......................... 1 ounce.

The mixture should be thoroughly shaken before using, and applied night and morning, after the face has been thoroughly washed in very hot rain-water.

Another useful lotion is made as follows:

Sulphuris præcip..	℥ ss
Etheris sulphurici......................................	℥ iv
Spiritus vini rect......................................	℥ iii–ss

It is well, also, to take an occasional dose of flowers of sulphur—two teaspoonfuls in a teacupful of warm milk about an hour before breakfast. Stir the powder until the mixture is smooth.

Or, the medicine can be taken in the form of pills—*pilula calcii sulphidi*—two or three a day.

When acne occurs in small, hard pimples, forming in groups on the forehead, chest, and back, the best remedy is to apply lotions composed of equal parts of strong spirit and water, or two parts of vinegar to one of water. Coffee, ale, beer, wines, and all rich, greasy food, pickles, and hot rolls must be avoided. The diet should consist of fresh and stewed fruit, water-cresses, lettuce, or dandelion salad, and an abundance of green vegetables and brown bread. Care must also be taken to secure thorough ventilation in the sleeping apartment.

Another less common form of acne, called *acne molluscum*, sometimes appears on the forehead and around the nose. It looks like seed-pearls sunk in the skin, and is caused by the sebaceous glands which, being unable to get rid of their contents, swell and become hard. The best remedy is to prick them with the point of a needle, press out the mass, and then bathe the empty sac with toilet vinegar, or spirit and water.

HERPES.

This is a troublesome eruption frequently seen in children and young people. Red patches appear, causing great irritation and a burning sensation. After a period varying from a few hours to one or more days, a cluster of very small blisters forms on the patch, which at last becomes a scab. Herpes usually appears at the corners of the mouth, and is then called herpes labialis.

The best remedy is a milk diet, with an occasional dose of castor oil. No local treatment is necessary.

NETTLE RASH.

This affection looks like the red marks caused by the stroke of a whip, and causes a pricking, tingling feeling, like a stinging nettle, hence its name. It is generally caused by indigestion, and some people have it after eating oat-meal or even eggs.

In its chronic form, it is almost always occasioned by some internal disease, and a physician should be consulted. If acute, use the following wash:

Carbonatis ammonia........................ ..... 1 drachm.
Plumb aeetatis................................... 2 drachms,
Aquæ rosearum................................... 8 ounces.

If the eruption is due to indigestible diet, it is well to take a dose of castor-oil, and afterward to avoid such food as shell-fish, preserved meats, salty or greasy dishes, particularly pastry. Green vegetables, salad, and ripe fruit should be freely eaten.

FLUSHING OF THE FACE.

This affection usually indicates a general disturbance of the health, and may be due to either anæmia or plethora. If the former, tonics, nourishing food, plenty of exercise, and fresh air are required. If the latter, aperient and cooling medicines, active walking, and manual labor are the best remedies. In both cases neither bandages nor laces should be allowed to impede the circulation of the blood in any part of the body, the sleeping room should be thoroughly ventilated both night and day, and a couple of ripe pears, oranges, or figs should be eaten every morning while fasting. If they cannot be had, dried figs, soaked in water over night, or stewed prunes may be substituted.

Flushing can sometimes be checked by bathing the face in very hot water, or putting the hands and feet in hot water to which a handful of mustard may be added. Extreme nervousness and hysteria cause flushing; but in this case it is only a symptom and cannot be treated except by curing the disease. Eating rapidly, reading, writing, or using the eyes and brain during or immediately after a meal frequently occasion it. No exertion should be demanded of mind or body for at least a quarter of an hour after every meal; but a nap in an arm-chair is far less beneficial than a little gentle exercise in the open air.

TAN AND FRECKLES.

These discolorations are of two kinds—summer and winter freckles. The former, due to the action of the sun's rays, soon pass away; but to aid their removal the following is an excellent lotion:

Sal-ammoniac (powdered)................. 1 drachm,
Distilled water .... 1 pint,
Eau de Cologne........................ 2 fluid drachms

Mix and apply with a rag, night and morning.

Another and more powerful wash is:

Bichloride of mercury.................. 6 grains,
Hydrochloric acid (pure) .... 1 fluid drachm,
Distilled water...... .... ¼ pint.

Mix these ingredients thoroughly, then add

Rose-water. .... } 2 fluid ounces of each.
Rectified spirit.................... }
Glycerine........................ 1 ounce.

Mix and use night and morning.

In cases where the skin is uniformly discolored and browned, the following wash will be more efficacious :

Fresh lemon juice.................... ⎫
Rose-water .... ⎬ Equal parts.
Rectified spirit................ .... ⎭

Mix thoroughly. The next day strain the clear portion through muslin, and bathe the face every night and morning with the lotion, wiping the skin afterward with a soft towel.

TO WHITEN THE SKIN.

Put one quarter of an ounce of red rose leaves into one quarter of a pint of fresh lemon juice and one quarter pint of brandy. Press, strain, and pour into bottles. It is best to decant the day after the infusion.

CHRONIC TAN AND FRECKLES.

Permanent tan and freckles are due to different causes from the sun-heat, and require different remedies. Usually there is some disorder of the liver; but there may be another disease.

If they are liver-spots the color will be yellowish-brown, the surface smooth, and the edges sharply defined. They most frequently appear on the fore-head, temples, and around the regions of the mouth. As the stains are beneath the epidermis it is difficult to remove them by external applications, yet the following lotion has often proved beneficial:

Hydragyri chlor. corrosivi .... gr. vi
Ammonii chloridi purificati................ ℥ ss
Mist. amygdalæ amar .... ℥ iv.

Mix as a lotion.

This wash should be used twice a day, and its effect aided by a "liver-pill," Podophyllum is best.

Another excellent lotion is the following:

Hydragyri chloridi corrosivi................ gr. vi
Zinci sulphatis............................ ℥ ss
Plumbi-acetatis........................... ℥ ss
Aquæ rosæ .... ℥ iv.

Mix as an ointment.

Should this wash prove irritating, use the following ointment:

Bismuthi sub-nitratis. . . . . ℥ i
Ungeneti hydrarg. ammon. . . . . ℥ i
Ungeneti aquæ rosæ ad . . . . ℥ i

ERYTHEMA.

Sometimes an eruption of small pink spots suddenly appears on the face, neck, and arms. The disorder usually lasts only a few hours, rarely longer than a day, and is often supposed to be caused by the stings of insects; but it is a mistaken idea, the trouble being due to irregularity of the bodily functions, debility, indigestion, or want of fresh air. A tonic is generally needed and quinine commonly effects a cure. The more serious cutaneous diseases, such as eczema, erysipelas, etc., need the care of a physician, therefore no form of the treatment is suggested here.

REDNESS OF THE SKIN.

Many women are much annoyed, when the season for wearing ball dresses comes around, by the red and rough appearance of their arms and necks. Powder is useless to remedy the evil, since the white coating speedily rubs off upon the broadcloth of the wearer's luckless partner. There *is* a very simple expedient, however, which only requires a little time and patience in the application. Ten minutes' friction every night with a sponge and warm water,* followed by the application of some cooling emollient, such as cold-cream, rarely fails to make the skin smooth and white, but of course some little time must be allowed for the process.

To whiten the hands, use a flesh brush and nearly *hot* water. Rub briskly, and be careful to dry thoroughly. At night apply a little almond paste, or work an almond tablet round and round as one would use soap when washing; then, after a little friction, wipe the grease lightly off, and there will be no need to sleep in gloves.

Never use scissors, except for a torn nail or some other accident, but employ instead the little pointed bone instrument which can be had at any druggist's for keeping the skin away from the nails, and cleaning the tips. For the removal of stains or trifling discolorations, rub a few drops of lemon juice on the dry hands, and work them about until nearly dry.

ON THE USE OF ROUGE.

The widest difference of opinion exists as to the desirability of using rouge, yet since there are many persons who, spite of argument, will apply it to supply their fading bloom, it is best that they should have the beautifying agent in a harmless form. And, in point of fact, there is less danger in applying many preparations of rouge than in many of the forms

* The *Crème froide aux Concombres,* sold by the Postal Toilet Co , Box 255, P. O., Washington, D. C., is the best preparation known to the writer for this purpose.

in which white face powder is offered for sale. The best rouge is manu-factured from carmine—obtained from cochineal—carthamum, and orcanet. A cheaper and inferior quality is made of red sulphur of mercury or of vermillion. The former—red sulphur of mercury—is exceedingly dan-gerous and should on no account be applied to the skin. But the use of the others cannot be said to imperil the health.

Carthamum powder is obtained from a plant known as "bastard saf-fron," and when used as rouge is usually mixed with *talc de Venise*, which is often used with benefit as a dressing for wounds, and therefore can surely be safely recommended as a cosmetic.

The best of the *liquid* rouges may be prepared as follows:

Powdered carmine.................... 1½ drachms,
Liquid ammonia..................... 5 drachms.

Put the above mixture into a bottle with a glass stopper, stand it in a cool place, and shake it well occasionally until thoroughly mixed. Then add the following, in which two drachms of essence of rose have been mixed:

Rose-water........................ 8 ounces,
Rectified spirit..................... 1½ ounces.

When completely mixed, dissolve in the liquid fine gum arabic one-half ounce, let the whole stand a few days, then bottle.

Carmine, which gives the color to the mixture, dissolves completely in liquor of ammonia, so that its purity can thus be readily ascertained. The preparation is known by the name of "Bloom of Roses."

THE FIGURE.

A perfect figure is rarer than a beautiful face, for the sin of tight lacing is sure to produce high shoulders and excessively large hips, and even the women of the present generation are slow to renounce a practice dear to their grandmothers. Corsets should support without compress-ing, and now it is fortunately an easy matter to obtain garments manu-factured to fill these requirements. Those made of canvas are best be-cause they permit the escape of perspiration.

The extremes dreaded by women who have lost the slender, yet rounded proportions of youth are obesity and leanness, and since the complaints of the victims of the former are most frequently heard, the remedies shall be first considered.

OBESITY.

Over-plumpness is frequently hereditary and often coupled with an inert and placid temperament, which renders persons indisposed to take the exercise which would tend to prevent the accumulation of fat. Peo-ple who are really determined to reduce their "too, too solid flesh," however, must resolve to do valiant battle with the demon indolence, for the first command is: Rise early in the morning.

The hours of slumber must be restricted to seven, and if the weather is pleasant, a brisk walk should be taken before breakfast; if wet, some active exercise should be had for half an hour indoors.

Breakfast should begin with ripe raw fruit. Only a small quantity of tea is allowable, without milk or cream, and as little sugar as possible. Bread, too, must be eaten very sparingly. Remember that all sugary and starchy foods are fat producing.

Substitute rusks, biscuit, or toast for ordinary bread, eat no sago tapioca, macaroni; in short, no farinaceous food of any description. Avoid sweet dishes and pastry, and never drink cocoa, beer, or wine. Use toast and water or, at dinner, half a tumbler full of lemonade. Never take more than half a tumbler full of liquid at any meal, the less liquid that can be taken the better.

Certain mineral waters are valuable, among them the Friedrichshall Bitter Water and Hunyadi Janos may be commended. Their value is doubtless due to their aperient qualities, for constipation inevitably tends to corpulence. A good remedy is a plateful of stewed prunes, or pears eaten before breakfast. Green vegetables may be included in the bill of fare; but not potatoes which, owing to their fattening power, must not be touched.

White fish, (but not salmon nor cod), raw fruit, pickles, and salad, with the herbaceous vegetables, should constitute the principal portion of food, and the salad may be dressed with vinegar and oil. If there is a necessity for more substantial food, eat from five to six ounces of cold game or poultry. But avoid pork, including ham and bacon, also white bread, especially rolls, using instead brown, and, if possible, at least a day old.

Persons in the habit of drinking wine must limit themselves to a single glass of Sherry or Bordeaux. A famous French doctor, Trousseaux, advised corpulent patients to take at each meal thirty-one grains of bicarbonate of soda.

Three meals a day must be the limit for persons who wish to rid themselves of superabundant fat, and nothing should be eaten between them. If the dinner hour is six or seven, and the hour for retiring eleven or twelve, a light supper consisting of a little toast, a tumbler of Bordeaux wine and water, is allowable.

In addition to the above regimen, Turkish baths, if obtainable, materially assist in reducing flesh. Two such baths should be taken weekly, followed by massage, and a cup of coffee as a stimulant while in the cooling-room. Meanwhile, never omit, morning and evening, to go through with a certain amount of gymnastic exercises—the best being to make the motions of briskly running without stirring from the spot. While practicing, the hands should rest on the hips, and no corsets should be worn. After leaving the bath, all the fleshy parts of the body should be rubbed, kneaded, and pounded slowly and thoroughly; but by no means with sufficient force to bruise or hurt the skin. The exercise and friction should be continued until there is a sensation of fatigue. After a time half an hour's practice will not be found too wearisome.

Before commencing this course of treatment, be weighed and test its effect by the scales every fortnight. Faithful attention to the above directions should insure a loss of from two to four pounds every three weeks. Turkish baths will greatly expedite the process. But observance of the rules is requisite; there must be no acceptance of tempting dishes, no lying in bed later than seven, and no interruption of the gymnastic exercises.

HOW TO GAIN FLESH.

Many are the methods recommended for the reduction of flesh, but it is rare to see any directions for covering bones too prominent for beauty.

The natural supposition of most persons would be that a course of treatment directly opposite to the one just recommended for obesity would secure the result desired. And in the main, this is true, yet certain explanations are required, or some very necessary details might be omitted. And here again the question of temperament must not be overlooked. A nervous, anxious person will never gain flesh like a placid, quiet one. Worry is fatal to avoirdupois. The first step toward a comfortable degree of plumpness, therefore, is to avoid fretting and irritability, and this will doubtless be more difficult for nervous persons than the hygienic rules to be observed.

The first of these is to retire early and remain in bed as late as the performance of necessary duties will permit. Before rising drink a cup of warm boiled milk or cocoa, then take a warm—not hot—bath, and dress leisurely. At breakfast drink more boiled milk, cocoa, or chocolate; but neither tea nor coffee. Eat mashed potato cooked with butter or cream or, if more palatable, sweetened wheat or oat-meal porridge. Fresh bread is better than toast, and honey and cream-cheese may be added to the bill of fare. For lunch take slightly warmed milk, mixed with an equal portion of Apollinaris or soda-water, otherwise it might be hard to digest. Eat no meat; but use instead potatoes, eggs, tapioca, sago, or custard puddings, macaroni, and salad served with plenty of oil; but neither vinegar nor pickles.

Dinner should consist of vegetable soup, fish, preferably cod, turbot, mackerel, or oysters, and puddings, sweet-meats, and fruits. Some persons who are especially desirous to gain a becoming plumpness give up flesh-meat and poultry, and adopt a diet composed solely of soup, milk, vegetables, fruits, grains, sweet-meats, fish, and eggs.

Drink nothing of an acid nature and use the sugary and oily foods as much as possible. Use very little salt; but as much mustard as may be desired. A nap either before or after dinner is beneficial. Two great aids to fattening are to eat very slowly, chewing every morsel thoroughly, and to have the meals served frequently.

Daily exercise must be regular and moderate. Horse-back riding is admirable, and singing is also extremely beneficial, because it draws an abundant supply of air into the lungs, and causes a vigorous series of contractions of the expiratory muscles, which thus renders the chest more elastic and helps to secure nutrition of the tissues.

If thinness becomes extreme, so that there is actual wasting of the flesh, and the shoulder-blades and breast-bone appear distinctly, medical aid must be obtained, for such a condition indicates actual disease.

But where there is no positive disorder, attention to the above directions will almost invariably transform an angular figure into one possessing a graceful degree of roundness.

DEVELOPMENT OF THE CHEST AND BUST.

The best local treatment is *gentle* friction—the utmost care being taken neither to chafe the skin nor to cause the slightest sensation of bruising—for five minutes, morning and evening, with a lotion compounded of equal parts of linseed oil and virginal milk. (Directions for making the latter will be found among the recipes for the improvement of the complexion.) At the same time small doses of cod-liver oil should be taken several times a day.

A valuable aid to this treatment is an hour's daily practice of scales and vocal exercises, the regular use of dumb-bells, and the performance of calisthenic exercises specially intended for the enlargement of the chest and lungs.

THE TEETH.

Any actual disease of the teeth must of course be treated by the dentist; but much may be done to delay or avert decay.

The worst foe to their preservation is excessively hot food or drinks, and strong acids are also extremely injurious. The latter, therefore,

MLLE. BERTHA SOUCARET.

should never be used as dentifrices because, though they whiten the enamel, they are sure to destroy it in time. All tooth-powders and tooth-washes should be either astringent, antiseptic, alkaline, or wholly inert. Alkalines neutralize the acidity caused by the decomposition of the food particles which accumulate around the teeth, and which, if allowed to remain, occasion the deposit of tartar, and finally the receding of the gums and the loosening and decay of the teeth.

The benefit derived from astringent and antiseptic tooth-washes and powders consists in hardening and preserving the gums, while so-called "inert" ones, such as chalk, pumice-stone, etc., have merely a medical effect. But all compositions sold as tooth-powders which contain either alum or tartaric acid should be shunned with the utmost care. A distinguished French surgeon dentist says that if one were to try to invent a preparation to destroy the teeth in the shortest possible time, nothing better could be had than a mixture of these two substances.

Very finely pulverized charcoal is one of the best tooth-powders known, because of its whitening and antiseptic properties. An excellent method of preparing charcoal tooth-powder is the following:

Areca nut charcoal........................ 5 ounces.
Cuttlefish bone............................ 2 ounces.
Raw areca nuts, pounded..... .... 1 ounce.
Pound and mix, then add two or three drops of oil of cloves or cassia.

Another excellent powder is:

Powdered bark............................ ½ ounce.
Myrrh.................................... ¼ ounce.
Camphor................................. 1 drachm.
Prepared chalk .... 1 ounce.

When the enamel on the teeth turns brown, a little lemon juice put on with a soft rag is excellent to whiten them. But it should be used very seldom, and the mouth must be thoroughly rinsed with pure soft water afterward.

Be careful always to brush the teeth before going to bed, and always pass the brush well behind the front teeth, both in the upper and the lower jaw. In the morning, after brushing, rinse the mouth with a tumblerful of water into which a few drops of tincture of myrrh has been poured.

Never permit a decayed tooth to remain in the mouth. If it cannot be filled, have it extracted; its presence is always dangerous to the sound teeth.

MOLES AND WARTS.

The former class of blemishes, satirically termed "beauty spots," are sometimes raised above the skin, sometimes on a level with it. They are sometimes merely discolorations, sometimes covered with a hairy growth. The coloring matter is deep beneath the upper skin, so that a scar remains if they are removed either by the knife or hot iron. The very best treatment for their eradication is the same as that recommended for superfluous hairs—electrolysis. The manner of operation is the same as that described for superfluous hairs, only more than one sitting is necessary, and the galvanic action should continue as long as it can be borne.

As already stated, electrolysis is the best method of removing all discolorations and excrescences on the skin, but if this treatment cannot be had, large pendent warts may be removed by winding around them a silk or silver thread and, after they shrivel and drop off, cauterizing the end with nitrate of silver. Common warts can be cured by repeatedly applying strong acetic acid, caustic potash, nitric acid, tincture of chloride of iron, or hydrochloric acid. All these remedies, however, it must be remembered, are liable to leave behind marks which may be a greater blemish than the original disfigurement. Before using them a thin layer of soft wax or spermaceti should be spread around the mole or wart to protect the skin. Children and young people of feeble constitutions often have numerous warts of all sizes on the hands and fingers. In such cases some medicine is needed in connection with the application of a paste consisting of equal parts of glacial acetic acid, precipitated sulphur, and glycerine. It should be freshly made and spread over the parts.

REMOVAL OF SUPERFLUOUS HAIR.

This blemish is frequently a source of much discomfort to brunettes, for superfluous hair not only grows much more freely on dark than on fair complexions, but is of course much more conspicuous when the hue is black.

There are two kinds, the soft, fine down called *lanugo* by some medical authorities, and the stiff, scattered hairs, resembling those in the eyebrows, which often appear on the chin and upper lip, and are specially conspicuous on moles and other local disfigurements.

Before discussing various methods of removing superfluous hair or rendering it less conspicuous, it should be said that, unless absolutely disfiguring, it is wiser not to interfere with it. Some persons are extremely sensitive to any appearance of this sort and fancy disfigurement where none exists. The slight downy line on the upper lip of a brunette frequently adds a charm by lending a piquante expression to the features. From the earliest ages various means have been employed to attain the desired object. The first, of course, were mechanical, but among the Oriental nations the secret of chemical depilatories, which will instantly and safely remove superfluous hair, has been known for centuries.

The principal mechanical method is to pluck out each individual hair with tweezers. Another way is to use a hard composition, readily softened by heat. A mass of this, in a soft condition, is pressed upon the hairs to be removed, and then allowed to cool and harden, firmly enclosing them in its substance, after which it is forcibly jerked away, bringing the hair with it. A third method is in the use of prepared pumice stone or some similar material, which rubs the hairs away piecemeal. These old plans may now be dismissed as barbarous and generally useless. By means of a properly combined chemical solvent science has rendered it possible to immediately remove all superfluous hair from the skin. But unhappily all these depilatories are not harmless, many of them containing arsenic, which should never be brought thus into contact with the skin. Persons cannot be too careful in using depilatories unless absolutely sure that they contain no harmful ingredients.

Where the growth of superfluous hair or down is not so marked as to require a depilatory, yet so noticeable as to be annoying, it may be rendered much less plainly visible by using peroxide of hydrogen, combined with an alkaline solution for toning down the color of the hair. A recipe for this bleaching process is as follows:

BLEACH FOR DOWN OR INSIGNIFICANT SUPERFLUOUS HAIR.

Equal parts of strongest solution of ammonia and absolute alcohol. This forms solution No. 1. No. 2 consists of the strongest possible solution of peroxide of hydrogen. After washing the hairs thoroughly with soap and hot water, apply No. 1 persistently for five minutes with a camel's hair brush, then, without drying, apply No. 2 with *another* brush for five minutes more.

A recipe for use as a prevention of the growth of superfluous hair where, though not yet marked, its increase is feared, is compounded as follows ·

CREAM TO BE APPLIED AFTER USING A DEPILATORY.

Oxide of zinc	80 grains.
Camphor	60 grains.
White wax	100 grains.
Sweet almond oil	2 grains.

Melt the wax and camphor in the almond oil, add the oxide of zinc and stir till cold. The hair having been removed by the non-arsenical depilatory prescribed above, a little of this cream should be thoroughly rubbed into the skin.

LOTION TO PREVENT THE APPEARANCE OF SUPERFLUOUS HAIR.

Alcohol	2 ounces.
Solution of potassium hydrate	½ ounce.
Menthol	20 grains.
Balsam of tolu	100 grains.

Rub a little, after washing at night and in the morning, well into the skin where it is feared the hair may appear.

It may be desirable to add in conclusion that attempts have recently been made to remove superfluous hair by electrolysis. But, as the electric current has to be separately applied to each individual hair, the time, labor, and expense are so great that this method will probably be used principally, if not exclusively, for the removal of the large stiff hairs which often appear on the moles and, while of very large size, are few in number

WRINKLES AND CROWS-FEET—METHODS OF TREATMENT FOR REMOVAL.

The skin of the face wrinkles exactly for the same reason and by the same mechanism that the skin of an apple shrivels. The pulp of the fruit under the skin shrinks and contracts as the juices dry up, consequently the skin, which was once tight and smooth, now being too large for the contents, shrivels and lies in folds. Similarly, when the subcutaneous fat of the cheeks and brow, which in youth is abundant, especially under the eyes and at the corners of the mouth, begins to be absorbed and to disappear, the cuticle which, so long as this fat lasted, remained smooth and even, begins to shrivel and fall into lines because it is no longer fitted to the lining which was formerly beneath it.

Crows-feet may be simply defined as the many angled wrinkles which so commonly appear beneath the eyes. Dr. Kingsford believes that, in many cases, the formation of wrinkles may be prevented, and the skin of the face kept smooth to an advanced age, by the following mechanical treatment: Having slightly oiled the fingers, the skin of the face is to be gently but firmly rubbed in a direction contrary to that the wrinkles threaten to take; that is vertically if the lines are forming horizontally, and *vice versa*. This should be done at least once daily, and the operation continued for fully five minutes at a time. The hands may be changed in case of fatigue, the fingers being twice or thrice freshly oiled, and the pressure should be even, firm, and gentle. Since this treatment was advocated, a new and valuable toilet adjunct for the treatment of crows-feet and wrinkles has been introduced in the shape of wool-fat.* This remarkable substance is the actual gloss or fatty matter of the hair and skin. Science has at last succeeded in isolating this body in a state of great purity from the fibres of the sheep's-wool! Its value consists in the fact that both the skin and the hair will greedily absorb it, whereas all ordinary oils and fats are not absorbed, bu tlie on the surface as a greasy film. It will at once be seen that this substance affords the means of restoring a full, smooth, and rounded outline of the skin by replenishing sub-cutaneous fatty tissue. This is not saying that wrinkles will now be things of the past, but by means of this wool-fat, science has afforded a wonderful aid in the prevention and removal of them. Cold cream prepared from this wool-fat and cucumber juice is very readily absorbed by the skin, and is regarded as invaluable for the removal and prevention of crows-feet and incipient wrinkles.

Another point is that those who are at all liable to wrinkles or crows-feet cannot be too careful to use soft water for washing and all toilet purposes. Hard water, that worst enemy of a good complexion, hardens and stiffens the skin by choking it with a compound of lime and soap, thus rendering it peculiarly liable to wrinkle. Full particulars of the use of water for toilet purposes will be given in another article. Free exposure to extremes of weather—heat, cold, and wind—must also be avoided.

The above remarks, however, do not apply to the few very deep and strongly marked lines visible on some faces almost from childhood. I refer to the two deep lines which sometimes exist round the mouth, or the two or three that often radiate from between the eyebrows across the forehead, or lie across the forehead horizontally. These, of course, cannot be removed or lessened by any known remedy. But when caused by any

* Lanula Cream, an excellent preparation of wool fat, can be obtained from the Postal Toilet Co., Box 255 P. O., Washington, D. C.

peculiar habit of frowning, or holding the features in any fixed position, as in reading, or looking intently at any object, or thinking profoundly, the utmost care should be taken to break the habit, to prevent the increase of these lines to a marked and disfiguring extent.

HINTS CONCERNING THE CARE OF THE HAIR.

Oils and pomades are objectionable because they soil the head, but there are lotions which contain the least possible quantity of grease and yet afford the needed nourishment. A really good quinine wash, made with bay rum and just a *suggestion* of cantharides and oil of rosemary, will not be at all greasy to use, while greatly benefiting the growth and color of the hair.

When grey hairs appear in the fringe over the brow, the choice lies between a dye and a restorer, and for this special purpose the dye has the advantage of instantly making the front hair match the back.

When the white hair is scattered over the whole head, it is almost impossible to attempt to use dye—unless a good hair-dresser is regularly employed to keep the locks the same color. This leaves one merely the choice of a restorer. Some of the latter are really only dyes under another name. If the first two or three applications color the hair, they are not restorers, and there will be great difficulty in making the back hair match the rest.

A stainless restorer, which gradually brings back the original tint, varies in effect according to the hair; but if the greyness is not caused merely by age it generally takes effect in a few weeks, and there is no unpleasant gummy feeling, and no superfluous dye to rub off upon the pillows or brushes.

When the hair is very light, and yet falls out and breaks, a quinine wash should be used nightly, as this does not darken the roots.

The fashion of wearing the hair piled on the crown of the head is injurious, but more harm is done during the night, than in the day. Instead of merely loosening it and twisting it carelessly on the top, it should be brushed downward into the natural position, the scalp sponged with bay rum or quinine, and then braided in two or three loose plaits. This insures a cool head during the night, and aids in maintaining the health of the scalp.

DYES AND RESTORERS.

When, after cases of short and severe illness or long continued ill-health, the hair falls out, as the saying goes, "by the handful," it should be cut quite short and kept clipped for at least a twelvemonth, rubbing the scalp regularly with some wash possessing tonic qualities.

Another point to be carefully noted is the manner of cutting the hair. The weakest and thinnest growth, when the hair has a marked tendency to fall out, is almost invariably along the central parting and about the crown. At these parts, therefore, the hair should be clipped more frequently than anywhere else, and the utmost care should be used to keep the hairs on the top of the head shorter, or, at any rate, as short as at the sides and back, where the growth is stronger. Unfortunately, however, the opposite course is generally pursued, the locks at the sides and back being often very closely clipped, while the hair on the crown and along the parting is left quite long.

The advantage to be derived from keeping it closely clipped is that the hair bulbs give the short hair and the new growth the nutriment that would be absorbed by the length. The air and the light, too, can penetrate to the head far more freely than when the locks are twisted up, compressed, and pinned tightly down; and friction can be much more easily applied. The value of the latter treatment, daily and regularly given, is very great, because it tends to restore vigor and tone to the hair bulbs. *Grease*, however, must never be used; it will fill the pores of the skin and injure the delicate new growth. A weak solution of the essential oils of thyme or rosemary, strong rosemary tea, or ammonia, very much diluted with water, may be rubbed in to stimulate the growth.

Many persons, when in a debilitated condition, or after fevers, are annoyed by loose " scurf " or " dandruff." An excellent preparation for its removal, and also as a cleansing wash at any time, is made as follows:

Yolk of one egg.
Rain water...................................... 1 pint.
Rosemary spirit.................. .... 1 ounce.

Beat the ingredients thoroughly together and use it warm, rubbing the lotion into the skin of the head.

The color of the hair is produced by the presence of a certain amount of some mineral ingredient in the cells. Blonde hair has magnesia; chestnut and brown hair contain a large proportion of sulphur and very little iron, while in black and dark hair iron exists in a large quantity. White and grey hair have only a very little sulphur and no iron at all. The reason that black or dark hair usually turns grey much sooner than fair hair is because the supply of iron usually fails long before the sulphur.

Acting on a theory drawn from these facts, efforts have been made to restore the color of the hair by rubbing into the roots a wash composed of sulphur or iron in a form supposed to be capable of ready absorption by the hair-bulbs. Compounds made with this object in view are termed restorers; those which color the hair itself are called dyes.

Neither iron nor sulphur can do harm applied in the above manner, but most dangerous consequences may result from the use of preparations of copper, bismuth, or lead.

As the hair almost always begins to turn grey first on the temples— some persons assert that it is because, when soap is used on the face, it comes in contact with that portion of the hair—that is the place where dye is most needed, and, alas, where any discoloration of the skin is most objectionable. The following recipe for a hair restorer or " darkener " will, therefore, be found valuable, and also has the merit of being easily prepared.

Rust of iron	1 drachm
Old ale (strong and *unsweetened*)	1 pint,
Oil of rosemary	12 drops.

Put these ingredients into a bottle, cork it very loosely, and shake it daily for ten or twelve days ; then pour off the clear part for use. Care must be taken not to let the wash come in contact with anything that rust-stain will injure.

RECIPES FOR DYEING AND CURLING THE HAIR.

Many persons, dissatisfied with the color Nature has bestowed upon their locks, resort to dyes to produce whatever hue may happen to please their fancy, and though the writer has no sympathy whatever with this course, and sincerely believes that Nature's arrangement of the coloring of hair, eyes, and complexion is rarely improved by the interference of Art, in deference to the wishes of those who desire to use such recipes the following are given:

The dyes for coloring the hair red, reddish-yellow, and auburn must be applied by an experienced hair-dresser, and as such a person can always supply the necessary preparations, it would be useless to mention them here.

If a *dark* dye is needed, the following recipe may be used ·

Green sulphate of iron	2 drachms.
Common salt	1 drachm.
Bordeaux wine	12 fluid ounces.

Let these ingredients simmer together for five minutes in a covered. *glazed* pipkin; then add :

Aleppo nut-galls (powdered)	2 drachms,

and let them simmer again, stirring occasionally. When cool, put in a table-spoonful of French brandy, cork the liquid up in a bottle, and shake well After two days, pour off the clear portion for use.

Another dye, which will color the hair light-brown, chestnut, or black, according to the degree of dilution, is made as follows:

Nitrate of silver...................... 28 grammes.
Rose-water..........................225 grammes.

Dissolve thoroughly.

To dye light-brown, dilute with twice the quantity of water; chestnut, the same quantity; for black, use undiluted. The natural color of the hair, also, has an effect upon the shade produced.

'If a very deep black is desired, use the recipe given below, but it must be made freshly just before using, or it will fail to produce the desired color:

Sulphuret of potassium...................3 drachms.
Distilled water...........................2 fluid ounces.

Moisten the hair with the mixture, let it dry, and then apply:

Nitrate of silver................... ....1½ drachms.
Distilled water.........................2 fluid ounces.
(Dissolved.)

Keep the solution of nitrate of silver in a blue bottle.

The unbound hair must be exposed to the light for a few hours before the effect will be apparent. A rag or sponge, wet with the solution of the sulphuret of potassium, slightly diluted, will remove any stains left on the skin by the dye; but, in order to avoid such stains, smear pomatum over it to avoid contact with the dye.

Before using any of the liquids named, thoroughly cleanse the hair from dust and grease, by washing it with hot water containing a pinch of soda or borax, and dry perfectly before applying the dye, which can be best put on with a soft tooth-brush. Repeat the process about once in every six weeks.

CARE OF THE EYE-LASHES.

No matter how beautiful the eye itself may be, the loss of the lashes always destroys its loveliness, and is a serious disfigurement.

One frequent cause is the formation on the lids, during sleep, of a greasy paste, which hardens, and, on being carelessly removed, pulls the lashes with it.

The remedy is to wash very delicately in the morning with cold water, and afterwards apply the following lotion, whose tonic properties are excellent. Do not let it get into the eyes:

Borax....................................4 grains.
Syrup of quinces..........................1 dr.
Distilled black-cherry water...............1 oz.

Many persons anoint the lids in the morning with a little sweet oil, before attempting to wash off the deposit.

FLUID FOR CURLING THE HAIR.

Many of the mixtures for curling the hair are injurious, but the recipe given below will be found harmless:

Dry salt of tartar (carbonate of potash).... 1 drachm.
Cochineal (powdered).................... $\frac{1}{2}$ drachm.
Liquor of ammonia....................... 1 drachm.
Essence of rose......................... 1 drachm.
Glycerine............................... $\frac{1}{4}$ ounce.
Rectified spirit........................ 1$\frac{1}{2}$ ounce.
Distilled water.........................18 ounces.

Mix the ingredients and let them stand for a week, stirring frequently, then filter. Wet the hair slightly while dressing, and as it dries the lotion will take effect.

If the hair is to be waved or curled daily, a simpler preparation is advisable.

Mix ten or twelve grains of carbonate of potash with a pint or more of warm water and soap. Pears' is excellent for the purpose. Froth the water by stirring briskly, and moisten the hair with it, dipping the brush into the mixture and damping every part. Then, before it dries, curl it on kid or wire rollers. Do this on going to bed at night, and in the morning the hair will be crisply curled. *Never* apply heated irons to the hair, they will surely injure the hair-tubes, making them wither and die.

"BABY."

How to make Children Healthy, Beautiful, and Graceful.

THE necessity of commencing physical training in the earliest childhood, in order to obtain health, grace, and beauty, was well understood by the ancient Greeks, and is now, year by year, becoming more and more recognized by the present generation.

If mothers desire handsome, well-formed, vigorous sons and daughters, they must bestow the same care and trouble on their physical as on their mental culture, never permitting the just balance between the two to be destroyed.

Beauty, strength, and health are blessings of priceless value; but the mother can do much toward securing them.

To begin with the earliest days of a child's existence, every mother, whose health will permit, should nurse her own infant. After weaning, the milk of cows, goats, or asses should, for at least a year, be the principal nourishment, with the addition of some light farinaceous food.

161

Hereditary tendencies must not be ignored; for, alas, the children must suffer for the violations of nature's laws committed by parents and grandparents.

It is also a well-known fact that a wet-nurse may transmit disease to the infant entrusted to her charge. Therefore, too much care cannot be exerted in the selection of such a person.

Having mentioned the fact that children inherit certain constitutional peculiarities from their ancestors, it is obvious that their physical training should be modified by consideration of the weaknesses and diseases of the families from which they descend.

For instance, children of families in which valvular disease of the heart is known to exist, should not be encouraged to take violent gymnastic exercise; the boys should not play base-ball, or row in University races; the girls should not play lawn-tennis.

On the other hand, children who inherit a tendency to pulmonary disease should take as much active out-door exercise as possible; nourishing food in small quantities should be frequently given, and, if circumstances will permit, they should live in a dry climate, where the soil is gravelly or sandy.

The general method to be pursued by parents who wish to train their children to be healthy men and women is as follows: First, from earliest infancy, children must have an ample supply of pure air and good food. Nurseries, if possible, should face the east, in order to have the benefit of the morning sun, and should be light, large, and thoroughly ventilated. Never let children younger than fourteen or fifteen wear stays of any kind; until then a jean waist, to support the underclothing, is all that is needed. During childhood the bones easily yield to pressure, and stricture of any kind may produce deformity; therefore, great care must be taken not to spoil or impede the development of the form by artificial bandages, either corsets, garters, waist-strings, or an excess of weight hanging from the hips. All garments made for children should hang from the shoulders. A sash tied lightly around the frock sufficiently marks the waist. Stockings should be held up by supporters. Garters impede the circulation, and thus sometimes cause varicose veins.

In variable climates, children should wear high-necked frocks and sleeves reaching at least to the elbow. Out-of-doors, stout shoes must be worn as a protection against wet, for children have an inveterate desire to wade through puddles. In-doors the feet should be as little compressed as possible, and, therefore, shoes are better than boots, unless in cases where there is any special reason for using the latter, such as cold feet, chilblains, weak ankles, etc. Under no circumstances should high-heeled or pointed boots or shoes be worn by children—all their foot-gear should be made with broad, square toes, and a simple lift at the heel, not more than a quarter, or at the most half an inch high.

During infancy, the little ones should be allowed to roll and tumble about on the floor at will. Never be anxious to make them stand; if done before the legs are strong enough to bear their weight, weak ankles, curvature of the thighs and legs, and other deformities may ensue.

Five years of age is the very earliest period at which to commence teaching them any regular gymnastic or calisthenic exercises. The object of such training is to develop muscular strength, make the limbs agile and supple, increase the capacity of the lungs, fortify the constitution, regulate the digestive functions, equalize the circulation, facilitate the development of the intellect, create and preserve beauty of figure, grace of movement, and the due proportions and roundness of the limbs.

For the above reasons both girls and boys should be trained to all kinds of physical exercises, using, of course, proper caution in regulating their training.

Swimming is one of the very best of these exercises, because it gives action to nearly every muscle of the body, requires deep and regular respiration; and, besides, healthful gymnastic movement lends a new and keen pleasure to existence. But it is an art which should be early learned and carefully taught. It is a most valuable exercise for persons of lymphatic, enfeebled, or scrofulous constitutions, and those suffering from curvature of the spine, nervous excitability, hysteria, or over-work. But it is never desirable, and sometimes dangerous, for persons who have any weakness of the lungs or heart.

Swimming should first be practiced in sea-water, because, owing to its greater density, it affords the body more support than fresh water.

The costume ought always to be made in such a way as to impede the movements of the limbs as little as possible, and a leather belt, strong enough to enable the body to be lifted by it, should occasion require, ought always to be worn.

Swimming and floating lessons should be given in nearly tepid water, and their length at first must be limited to half an hour. If headache, shivering, or coldness of the hands and feet should appear, the pupil must instantly leave the water and dress after having the body rubbed dry with warm, rough towels. Delicate girls and women who have remained a long time in the water are greatly benefited by a hot foot bath.

Gymnastic exercises are also valuable, not only for children who, living in towns, are unable to obtain much out-door exercises, but for those in the country. Mere running about over hill and dale, though beneficial in strengthening the constitution, often renders children awkward and round shouldered, unless there is a daily drill in regular, orderly movements. The body needs training as much as the mind, the eye must learn quickness, the hand steadiness, the limbs grace, the neck and head an erect carriage, the whole body ease. Out-door sports which combine physical culture with orderly motion and the discipline necessary to acquire the requisite skill are far more beneficial than the careless roaming through woods and fields which is by many considered all that is needful for their children.

Lawn tennis, now very popular, is an excellent kind of training; but, as has been said, not desirable when any weakness of the heart is known or suspected. Archery is also a most beneficial and delightful amusement. In wet or cold weather, when girls cannot enjoy out-door sports, dancing, games of battledoor or shuttlecock, graces, gymnastics, calisthenic exercises should be daily practiced. Dr. Schreber's system is excellent, and so, too, is that known as the Swedish or Ling, because they require no apparatus of any description, are easily taught, and occasion no great fatigue. Dr. Schreber's is merely a series of ryhthmic movements of the body and limbs, performed as follows:

HOME GYMNASTIC EXERCISES.

(1) Describe a circular movement with each arm twenty times in succession. Extend the arm forward, outward, and upward, thirty times in succession, drawing eight or ten deep breaths between each series.

(2) Execute a circular movement from the waist, swaying the upper part of the body slowly round—the hands meanwhile resting on the hips— thirty times.

(3) Extend the leg as nearly as possible at right angles with the body twelve times each side, taking eight or ten deep breaths between each series.

(4) Extend and bend the foot twenty times each side; perform the gesture of reaping or sawing thirty times; bend each knee rapidly twenty times; draw eight or ten deep breaths.

(5) Raise the arm swiftly and rapidly, as in the action of hurling a lance, twelve times; throw out both arms at the same time twenty or thirty times; take eight or ten deep breaths.

(6) Trot on one spot, resting the hands on the hips, and lifting the feet briskly, from one hundred to three hundred times. Draw eight or ten deep breaths.

(7) Jump with the hands on the hips, and the head and body erect fifty or a hundred times. Take eight or ten deep breaths.

These motions, whose regular execution will occupy half an hour or more, should be performed without haste, resting at intervals; if necessary, but with all the vigor, and energy that can be put into them. Each movement must be complete, thorough, and separated by a distinct pause from the preceding and following movements. The performer's strength must not be unduly taxed by the exercises; all pain and exhaustion must be avoided. Delicate girls, or those suffering from temporary or periodic indispositions, must modify or shorten the exercises. / The room where the practice takes place must be airy, cumbered with little furniture, and, if possible, uncarpeted. The dress must be light and perfectly loose, with neither tight heavy skirts, nor impeding weights, and light shoes without heels should be worn. The time for the exercises should be either before breakfast, or about an hour before the noon-day meal.

SPORTS AND OCCUPATIONS.

Another valuable means of physical training is the culture of the voice. Daily exercises in singing and reading aloud are among the very best methods of developing the lungs and chest. Where there is any tendency to consumption, catarrh, bronchitis, nothing more valuable can be recommended. At least half an hour each morning should be devoted to scales and other exercises of the voice, and an hour's reading every evening will prove of the utmost benefit. A really good reader has it in his or her power to afford as much pleasure to many persons as a fine musician, and the accomplishment is one that well repays the time necessary to acquire it.

If strong enough, the girl or boy should stand in front of a book-rest, the shoulders thrown well back, the chest forward, and the arms hanging by the side. If seated, the attitude should be comfortable and easy, with the arms resting loosely in the lap. To obtain the full advantage from the exercise, the voice must be clear and strong, and the pronunciation distinct, every syllable being plainly enunciated, the sound must not be permitted to drop toward the end of the sentence, the breath must be well sustained, and a pause of at least half a minute allowed at the end of the paragraph.

Shy, nervous children are apt to gabble, and the defect can be cured only by means of the confidence gained through constant practice.

Another desirable means of physical training is horse-back riding. It promotes muscular development and gives tone to the whole system, while

it tends to bestow confidence and grace of movement, to dispel nervousness and timidity, and to train the hand and eye. From a hygienic point
of view it is especially valuable in cases of general debility, and of any
disorder that is liable to become chronic; for instance hysteria chorea,
scrofula, hypochondria, tendency to consumption, dyspepsia, anæmia,
chlorosis and all nervous complaints.

Ten or twelve is as early as it is desirable for girls to begin to ride.
Prior to that time the bones are so soft and pliable that they are liable to
become affected by the posture in the side-saddle, and, if indulged in to
excess during early childhood, curvature of the spine or even of the
thigh-bone may be caused. When girls approach the age of fifteen care
should be taken to regulate any forms of exercise as violent as horseback
riding in accordance with possible fluctuations in their health.

After riding there is no exercise more beneficial than dancing; the
only drawbacks are the late hours, confined air, and excitement of the
ball-room. Practice in the art at home may be most earnestly recommended. If instruction in dancing is not attainable, an excellent method
of acquiring a graceful, erect carriage is to walk up and down with some
moderately large and heavy object balanced on the head.

But in the desire to give abundant physical training, do not let it
occupy an undue share of time; for it must be borne in mind that rest is
no less necessary for growing girls than exercise. Do not let children sit
on narrow benches without support; on the contrary, delicate children
will be much benefited if they can rest the spine by lying back in a convenient chair, or on a reclining board for an hour, with only a small
cushion under the head, the knees straight, and the arms either crossed
on the chest or resting by the sides. Some forms of out-door sports are
better suited for boys than for girls, and among these may be named
cricket, rowing, and cycling. In place of these, let the girls try the
exercise required by domestic work at home. No one can foresee the
vicissitudes of life, and a knowledge of the ordinary routine of the household machinery is valuable to every girl who expects in the future to
take charge of a home of her own. Yet days which might otherwise
drag wearily can be devoted to obtaining a knowledge of common daily
duties, and active girls will derive much entertainment, as well as profit,
from this important branch of a woman's education.

THE CARE OF THE COMPLEXION, TEETH, AND HAIR IN CHILDHOOD.

Very young children almost invariably possess clear, blooming complexions; but, alas! the charm often begins to fade at the age of seven,
and sometimes even earlier.

To preserve a beautiful skin, two important matters must be heeded —ventilation and the quality of the food. The first essentials for the development and preservation of beauty are pure air and sunlight. Nurseries should face the east, and be airy, spacious rooms, with high ceilings and uncurtained beds. Children ought to run about out-doors as much as possible, and be encouraged to play in the yard or garden instead of in the house.

Their fare should be of the plainest and simplest description, consisting mainly of milk and milky foods, ripe fruit, and all sorts of farinaceous dishes, such as sago, maccaroni, tapioca, rice, vermicelli, hominy, etc.; children do not need meat, seldom like it, and almost invariably prefer sweet and milky foods.

Pure water is the best drink for them; but if that cannot be had, apollinaris water may be substituted.

Coffee, tea, cocoa, and chocolate are all bad for children, making the skin thick and yellow, and often causing heartburn, indigestion, and sick-headache. Nothing is so good for children as milk and water—milk at breakfast and supper; water at the mid-day meal.

Every morning each child should have a tepid bath of rain-water, if possible. The nurse must never be allowed to wash two or more children in the same bath. The very best soap must be used, and of all kinds the best are the uncolored and unscented transparent varieties. To reap the full benefit from the bath, children must be well rubbed from head to foot with a rough Turkish towel after leaving the water. Friction is necessary in order to secure a healthy skin and good circulation.

Do not let little girls run about in the summer sun-shine with unprotected faces, or they will doubtless get freckled, and freckles are sometimes hard to remove. Large sun-bonnets or broad-brimmed hats should always be worn, and after a long walk in the summer-sun the face should be bathed with a little elder-flower water. When the children are quite young, the length and thickness of the eye lashes can be increased by carefully clipping the ends every month or six weeks. The utmost care, however, is necessary, in order to avoid harming the eye. The eye-brows may be thickened in the same way. If a child's nose has a tendency to turn up—in common speech to become a "snub"—or seems inclined to grow unduly broad at the base, it may be coaxed into better shape by careful daily pressure. In childhood the cartilage that forms the framework of the nose can easily be affected by external pressure and training.

One of the most important aids to personal beauty is a good, strong, even set of teeth. The handsomest woman's charm is spoiled as soon as she opens her mouth, if her rosy lips display bad teeth. In childhood, the enamel is extremely delicate, therefore hard brushes should never be used, and only a soft brush of badger's-hair be employed once or twice a day. Tooth-powders are quite unnecessary for children who are living on simple milk foods. A little weak myrrh and tepid water is quite sufficient to cleanse both the teeth and the gums. If the second teeth appear in an even row, they will require no attention; but if they come irregularly, they will need to be frequently pressed into position—it is better to secure the assistance of a good dentist, if possible—the first teeth, called milk-teeth, must always be removed as the second ones appear. If they are suffered to remain in the gums, they will force the second teeth from their proper places, and either make them project like tusks, or take the places of the other teeth, thus spoiling the regularity of the set, and perhaps affecting the shape of the mouth.

At the first appearance of any spot of decay, the child should be taken to the dentist to have the tooth filled.

With regard to the treatment of the hair in childhood, opinions are somewhat divided; but it would certainly seem more reasonable that the plan of keeping it short, thereby enabling the sustenance that would be distributed through the length to go to the root, is the better. Another advantage secured is the absence of the wear of curl-papers, hair-pins, etc., and the convenience of daily washing the head in warm, soft water. Neither oils nor lotions should be used on children's heads. If the hair shows a tendency to fall out, unnaturally, the use of an electric brush will be beneficial, and, with the occasional application of a quinine lotion and strict attention to general hygiene, will almost always cure the disorder.

Early hours for retiring must be rigidly enforced—an hour and a half, or two hours at the utmost, after their last meal—and they must not be allowed to rise late in the morning. Children should be up by seven, or even half past six o'clock in the summer, and by eight in winter. If they can have a little exercise out of doors before breakfast, so much the better.

CHILDISH TRICKS.

The utmost care in the observance of the directions previously given will be baffled if the tricks to which many children are addicted are not carefully watched and corrected. These, being indulged in more or less all day, or, at any rate, during the time not spent in play or study, frequently cause great disfigurement of the face, hands, or figure. Among them may be named biting the nails, sucking the thumb, rubbing the eye-brows, distorting the mouth, drawing in the lower lip, sitting with the feet turned inwards, rounding the shoulders and narrowing the chest, by sitting bent over books with the elbows thrust forward, and the chin resting on the palms. Such faults, easy to correct at first, become confirmed habits, which are extremely hard to break; and it is useless labor for the mother to try to shape by pressure the undue width of her child's nose, or to push prominent teeth into a proper position, if the child itself still more frequently thrusts its fingers into its nostrils, or by sucking the thumb thrusts the teeth forward and outward.

Older children can be reasoned with, and thus induced to correct their awkward habits; indeed, the physical education can never be thoroughly and properly carried out unless the children themselves are encouraged to aid in the work. As soon as they reach an age at which they are capable of understanding the elements of physiology and hygiene —a period that will, of course, vary with different individuals—they should receive thorough instruction in both branches. If the mother is not conversant with these sciences, she should send her children to private classes, conducted by competent teachers, who are capable of giving full explanations in clear and simple words. When this mode of education becomes more general, young girls will cease to consider unnaturally small waists desirable, high French heels ornamental to the foot, or dress-improvers a graceful addition to the human form, and there will be a corresponding decrease in the number of red noses, enlarged toe-joints, corns, and crooked spines, and in the cases of indigestion and hysteria.

Diet of Invalids.

TREATISES on the care of the sick are usually confined to the ventilation of rooms, nursing of the patient, administration of medicines, etc.; yet every physician will admit that the diet has no little share in building up a system enfeebled by disease, and as this subject has been comparatively overlooked, a few pages devoted to the explanation of the different kinds of diet and their effect upon the system may be of service to many an anxious watcher beside a sick-bed.

GENERAL DIRECTIONS.

The various foods are divided into seven classes, stimulant, laxative, astringent, tonic, emollient, analeptic, and watery. The first, the stimulant, contains foods rich in nutritive qualities, and includes all albuminous, mucilaginous, and feculent substances, whether animal or vegetable, all plants and herbs containing bitter principles; in general, all the more solid and generous foods and drinks, together with aromatic and pungent herbs, spices, and condiments.

This diet is useful where there has been loss of appetite for a long time, nervous nausea, convalescence after infectious fevers, and in cases of illness where there is prostration of the physical powers, slow circulation, faintness, and feeble digestion. But it must be carefully avoided in cases of heart disease, aneurism of the blood-vessels, liver complaint, or any tendency to apoplexy, gout, or gravel.

The tonic consists of the same foods as the first, without the herbs, spices, and condiments, and is valuable in the chronic states of exhaustion and weakness following long illnesses, which have enfeebled and shattered the system, also where the brain has been weakened by mental strain, and should be permanently used by lymphatic, scrofulous, and weak persons.

The laxative and astringent diets, of course, comprise the foods and drinks which possess these qualities, the former including fruits, stewed, baked, or raw—salads, oils, green vegetables, etc.; and is specially valuable in cases of scorbutic disease. An astringent diet is useful in chronic diarrhœa, hemorrhage, and various kinds of fluxions. A milk-diet is often employed for this purpose, with astringent herbs and grains. Rice possesses this quality and, when boiled in milk or water, will often check obstinate diarrhœa.

The emollient is known in common parlance as a "light diet," and consists mainly of vegetables, fruit, jellies, thin soups, and watery broths. It is suitable in severe illness—hemorrhage, dysentery, pleurisy, pneumonia, gastritis, typhoid fever, and during the first day or two after serious surgical operations.

The analeptic is sometimes termed a milk diet, and is one of the most useful known to the medical profession. It is extremely nutritive and emollient, and includes milk, light puddings, farinaceous soups and gruels, custards, and drinks prepared from pearl barley and other fine meals. It is used in acute stages of illness; fevers, diseases of the chest and throat, dyspepsia, cancer, kidney diseases, hysteria, rheumatism, and inflammation of the intestines.

The last, or water diet, consists of fruit and acid drinks, and includes grapes, nectarines, oranges, peaches, lemonade, and any substance combining vegetable acids with gummy or sugary qualities. This is especially useful in hot climates, and in cases of plethora, acute inflammation, repletion, brain fever, and some forms of insanity. The effect is to lower the circulation, thereby lessening any tendency to fever, and in the main to refresh, cool, and soothe an overheated or irritated system. Aneurism of the arteries and internal cancer are often greatly benefited by a fruit diet; but the effect must be carefully watched and, should exhaustion or lowering of the heart's action supervene, small quantities of albuminous or farinaceous foods must be quickly given.

In the treatment of certain violent disorders, total abstinence from food of every kind—even fruits—is necessary. For instance, apoplexy, cerebral-congestion, concussion of the brain, rupture of the blood-vessels, capital operations, and dangerous wounds of the bowels, stomach, or internal organs. Fasting is also advisable in certain stages of scarlet fever, small-pox, erysipelas, and other diseases characterized by strong febrile symptoms, that the circulatory and respiratory functions may be favorably modified, and the morbid action reduced as much as possible.

To assuage the thirst which characterizes such diseases, either demulcent or acidulated beverages should be given from time to time through the day and night.

BARLEY WATER.

The most beneficial and palatable of these drinks is made in the following way: Wash one tablespoonful of pearl barley in cold water, pour off the water, and add the barley, two or three lumps of sugar, the rind of one lemon, and the juice of half a lemon; pour over the whole a pint of boiling drinking-water, and let it stand covered on the stove or fire-place two or three hours to keep warm; then strain the mixture and let it cool.

LEMONADE.

An excellent way of preparing this refreshing drink is to cut a good sized lemon into four or five pieces, add a few lumps of loaf sugar, and pour on a pint of boiling water. Cover and let it stand until cool.

If needed at once, lemonade can be made with cold water; but the lemon juice must then be squeezed from the fruit, and the sugar melted in hot water and added to the cold water with the juice. Whether hot or cold water is used, the mixture must be strained to remove the pips and pulp of the fruit.

TOAST-WATER.

An English drink, which some invalids prefer to either of the beverages already mentioned, is made with stale bread, thoroughly browned before a clear fire. As soon as it is removed from the toasting-fork, put it into a jug, and pour over it from a pint to a quart of boiling water, according to the amount of bread. Cover and let cool.

TAMARIND WHEY.

A cooling and somewhat laxative drink is made by putting two tablespoonfuls of the fruit into a pint of milk, while it is boiling, stirring the mixture well, and then straining it. It should not be used until cool, and should always be freshly made.

ORGEAT.

This pleasant demulcent drink is made by blanching two ounces of sweet almonds and two bitter almond seeds, pounding them with sufficient orange-flower water to make a paste, and then rubbing the mixture into a quart of boiled milk and water—equal quantities of each. Strain and sweeten. This preparation is both nutritive and emollient.

RICE-WATER.

An extremely valuable drink in cases of diarrhœa, dysentery, and kindred disorders is thus prepared: Wash an ounce of Carolina rice in cold soft water, then steep for three hours in a quart of water kept simmering and slowly raised to boiling point. Strain, and cool the liquid before using.

LINSEED TEA.

A beneficial drink in acute pulmonary disorders is made as follows· Take an ounce of bruised linseed and two drachms of bruised liquorice root, put them into a jug, and pour over them one pint of boiling water. After the tea has been allowed to "draw" three or four hours, strain, sweeten to taste, and serve it hot. A little lemon peel may be added for flavoring.

Iced milk is excellent in treating diseases where nausea or diarrhœa is present, and also in diseases of the throat or stomach. As a rule ice may be freely used to relieve febrile thirst, and remove any unpleasant taste in the mouth; but in giving it to persons who are in a state of stupor or extremely weak, care must be taken that the pieces are small enough to preclude any danger of choking them. Gum-water, orange-ade, isinglass milk, or any of this class of drinks may be iced.

CORDIAL FOR EXTREME EXHAUSTION.

Where there is severe collapse or exhaustion, the following mixture will be of the utmost service. It can be quickly made, and demands no great skill in the composition. Take two ounces of first-rate cognac brandy, four ounces of cinnamon, the yolks of two fresh eggs, and half an ounce of powdered loaf sugar Beat up the eggs and sugar briskly, add the cinnamon water and brandy, stir the whole well, and administer in teaspoonful doses. In cases of great necessity the quantity of brandy may be doubled; but the patient's age, sex, constitution, and habits of life must be considered.

GENERAL RULES FOR THE FOOD OF INVALIDS.

It should always be remembered that, as a rule, nothing made for the sick-room is fit to be used a day after it has been prepared, and neither food nor drink, save in cases of absolute necessity, should be kept in the invalid's chamber, whose atmosphere and temperature are apt to hasten decomposition, especially when there is any milk in the compounds.

Another point to be borne in mind is that the food should suit the invalid's taste, be tempting in appearance, and daintily served.

Soiled or crumpled napkins should never be placed on the invalid's waiter, and the prettiest china should not be regarded as too good to hold the sufferer's food and drink.

Before serving any meal, the patient's hands and face should be washed and the mouth rinsed with water containing a few drops of tincture of myrrh.

An error frequently made in preparing dishes for the sick-room is the use of too much salt in the flavoring.

This should be very sparingly used, since it is apt to impede digestion, irritate the mucous surfaces, and cause unnatural thirst, which is especially injurious in cases of debility, tendency to fever, etc. Therefore only sufficient salt should be used to make the dishes palatable, the flavoring being given by ginger, spices, pepper, bay-leaves, parsley, mint, celery, horse-radish, and similar stimulating vegetable substances.

A distinguished English physician's study of the relative digestibility of various kinds of food led to the following conclusions, here put in the most condensed form:

Fish is the most digestible of any kind of animal food; game and poultry rank second; and then beef, mutton, pork, and veal, in the order named.

Roasting renders all meats more digestible than either boiling or frying. White fowl is more digestible than game, and fresh fish than fish salted. Milk and all milky products are more digestible than any of the articles mentioned except the fish, and boiled milk is more digestible than raw. Cream is more readily digested than butter or cheese. Eggs, when lightly cooked, are as easily digested as boiled milk. Beef tea and meat broths of all kinds are as hard to digest as pork. Feculent vegetables are as digestible as milk, eggs, and fish; bread is more difficult to digest than potatoes; starchy foods, if unmixed with grease, are very easily digested. Fresh green vegetables may be ranked in ease of digestion with poultry and, finally, the most digestible of all foods are fruits. Of all the processes of cooking for fish or flesh, boiling is best, and vegetables of every description are most digestible when steamed. A boiled potato is watery, tasteless, and lacking in nutritive qualities; a potato steamed in its skin is delicious to the taste and rich in nutrition. Asparagus, one of the best and most delicate foods for invalids, is often ruined in cooking. It should be loosely tied in a bundle and then set upright in a deep covered sauce-pan filled with just enough water to keep the stems covered; the steam is sufficient to cook the heads, and the stalks are made soft and tender by this process. Instead of the twenty minutes allotted to asparagus boiled in the usual way, this plan requires forty; but at least one-third of the stalk will be made delicious, and the heads will retain their full flavor. This mode of cooking vegetables is recommended in Sir Henry Thompson's valuable little work, "Food and Feeding," the same plan, of course, should be adopted for celery, sea-kale, vegetable marrow, cauliflower, and similar foods; but it must not be forgotten that twice as much time must be allowed as when food is cooked in the usual manner.

Lastly, it should be remembered that the peculiarities of individual cases, or the condition of the stomach, may often render it necessary to modify the above directions, for every general rule is liable to exceptions.

BROTHS.

The popular belief in the valuable nutritive qualities of beef tea is now opposed by many physicians, chemistry having proved that in the process of boiling—the usual mode of making it—the really nutritious portion—the albuminous matter—frequently escapes, and is skimmed off with the "skum" that rises to the top of the boiling mass. The chief value consists in certain stimulating and restorative qualities, which render it useful in exhausted states of the system. Many invalids, however, do not find it palatable, and a far more valuable preparation can be made from fish-stock—preferably haddock—flavored with pot herbs and other vegetables.

Fish can often be digested by persons whose stomachs will not bear the coarser kinds of animal food; and sea fish contain certain strengthening qualities of the utmost value, which can be much more easily introduced into the system in the shape of food than in that of drugs. Every one knows the value of the oil extracted from the cod's liver—which contains phosphorus, iodine, and bromine,—but it is extremely disagreeable to the taste, and often therefore fails to assimilate, so it is far preferable to obtain the same result by means of fish broth prepared in an acceptable form. To prepare such broth scientifically, with a view to obtaining the largest amount of its nutritive qualities, the fish, whilst uncooked and unboned, should be broken up in small pieces and placed in cold water. Then proceed as follows:

FISH-BROTH.

To one pound and a half of ray, skate, cod, haddock, or any other fish, put two pints of water, which should be poured over it in an earthenware jar, which must then be set in a saucepan of hot water and placed over a moderate fire to boil gently for about an hour. Meanwhile put in a stewpan with a little fresh butter, one or two small carrots and onions; cut the carrots in pieces and the onions across; cover them with slices of leeks, some sprigs of parsley, mint, thyme, marjoram, a little celery seed, a bay leaf, and a few cloves. Moisten with a little hot water, and set it to simmer over a slow fire. At the end of an hour add more hot water, and stir until the contents are well mixed and colored. Next add the fish-stock, and pass through a strainer to prevent the possibility of having any bones in the broth.

LENTIL BROTH.

A very palatable and nourishing broth can also be made without fish-stock, using instead a purée of peas or lentils. To make it, take two or three pounds of dried peas or beans, wash them, and boil them for several hours, adding water occasionally as required. Stew half a pound of rice for two hours in half a gallon of water, with a little butter, a mealy potato, a turnip, carrot, onion, head of celery, a couple of Jerusalem artichokes, and a leek or two, all cut into dice. Then add the pea broth, with a little pepper and salt, parsley, one or two bay leaves, some thyme or mint, and a few cloves. Boil, and if thickening is required, stir in a little cream just before serving.

MACARONI SOUP.

Another very nourishing and valuable soup can be made by soaking four ounces of the best macaroni in cold water for two hours, then throwing it into a pint of boiling milk and water—two parts of milk to one of water—with some salt, pepper, a tablespoonful of stale bread-crumbs, and a small onion, with a little spice. Boil all the ingredients gently together, strain through a sieve, then let the whole *simmer* and, before takiug up, add a gill of cream and a few peppercorns.

Vermicelli and sago can be used for broth in the same way.

OYSTER BROTH.

In the colder seasons of the year oyster broth is recommended as very nourishing for convalescents. Make as follows: To one pint of fish-stock add two dozen oysters, a little butter according to the taste, two ounces of flour, a little grated nutmeg, and one teaspoonful of Chili vinegar. Next add one quarter of a pint of cream or rich milk, and stir over the fire till it boils gently. Toast should be served with all these broths.

CHICKEN BROTH.

Make in the same manner as the fish broth, and serve hot with small slices of crisp, freshly made toast.

OMELETTE.

The first requisites are a china fire-proof omelette pan, with a wooden handle, and a clear, steady fire which gives out a good heat. Then break three or more fresh eggs, according to the size of the omelette—never less than three, beat the yolks and whites separately and thoroughly in a basin; have the omelette pan ready, quite hot; put in one ounce of good butter, turn in the beaten eggs, add immediately a sprinkling of fine sweet herbs chopped very small—marjorum, basil, lemon, thyme, parsley and chives—with a little pepper and salt. When the omelette has begun ᴖo settle, turn one half over on to the other with a broad silver knife, and serve at once in the omelette pan.

A richer omelette is made by adding a spoonful of cream and a little piece of butter to the eggs, and whipping the whole together before pouring .into the pan. The art of making omelettes consists in the rapidity of making, and in the quantity and quality of the heat used.

RACAHAT.

This is a delicious food for invalids, and can be obtained at most first-class pharmacists in all large cities. It is an Arabian preparation of fine lentil flour, rice, and cocoa. Directions for cooking are supplied with it, and they must be carefully followed.

OATMEAL JELLY.

Soak half a cup of oatmeal in one quart of water over night. Boil for two hours in the water in which it has been soaked. Add a quarter of a teaspoonful of salt and strain into a mould. It should be cooked in a double boiler.

CHICKEN PANADA.

Boil a young chicken half an hour. Remove the skin and, when cold, cut off the white meat and pound in a mortar to a paste, adding a little of the water in which it was boiled. Season with salt, and, if desired, a very little nutmeg. Add more of the water and boil three minutes. It should be as thick as cream.

CHICKEN JELLY.

Remove the skin from a chicken, and boil till tender. Take the meat from the bones, allowing them to remain in the water and boil longer. Chop the meat fine, season with salt, pepper, celery salt, and a very little mace or nutmeg. When the water in which the chicken boiled is reduced to a small cupful, strain and mix with the chicken. Put into a mould to harden.

BROILED SWEETBREAD.

Pour boiling water over a nice breast sweetbread, and cook five or ten minutes. Split, and wipe dry. Broil in a double broiler over a clear fire until well browned. Sprinkle with salt, and rub a little butter over it.

OYSTER TOAST.

Toast a small slice of bread and put it in a little earthen dish. Pour over it two-thirds of a cup of raw oysters, sprinkle with salt and pepper, and put a piece of butter as large as a nutmeg on the top. Set the dish in a hot oven until the oysters are cooked.

MILK JELLY.

A dainty and nourishing Italian dish is prepared as follows: Beat several eggs—from four to six—whites and yolks together, adding two dessertspoonfuls of powdered sugar or less, according to taste, then add gradually a pint of fresh milk, beating all the time. Flavor with vanilla, cinnamon, almond, or any flavoring that may be preferred. Pour into a mould and put it on the fire in a *bain marie* (often called a double boiler) till it thickens to the consistency of jelly. When cold, pour it out and serve.

ORANGE AND LEMON JELLIES.

These are pleasant to the taste, but must not be allowed to take the place of more substantial foods, as they contain little nourishment. Use isinglass, never gelatine, to stiffen them. Care should be taken, in all invalid cookery, to secure the freshest and purest ingredients. The butter, milk, and cream must have no mixture of manufactured fats, oils, or thickening material, besides being absolutely sweet and fresh to the taste and smell.

BEEF ICE.

Chop one pound of lean beef and put in a tin dish with one pint of cold water. Cover tightly, and put on the stove. Let it be fifteen minutes coming to a boil. Boil three minutes. Drain off, add salt to taste, and freeze. Patients suffering from fever can sometimes take this when they cannot relish hot beef tea.

To freeze put it into a pint pail, and set that in one a few sizes larger. Fill the space between with snow or pounded ice and fine salt. Turn the inner pail round and round a few minutes in the freezing mixture. Open it and scrape off with a silver knife the cream which has frozen to the sides of the pail. Cover again, and repeat till the mixture is sufficiently frozen. A saucer of ice cream can be frozen very quickly in this way.

HINTS AS TO THE WAY AND TIME OF GIVING FOOD TO INVALIDS.

Persons suffering from acute disorders, attended with fever, should, in the earlier and severer stages, be kept strictly on a diet of albuminous broths, and either acid or milky drinks. Any of those for whose preparation directions have been given would answer. Very little food should be eaten at a time, and there should be a pause between each spoonful. The best time to give food is in the morning, between the hours of eight and twelve o'clock, because the pulse is then more likely to be normal and the temperature lower than later in the day, so that the digestive organs are better able to assimilate nourishment.

At night nothing should be given except some light beverage, such as barley-water, lemonade, or tamarind milk, and even these should be administered with caution.

When convalescing after an acute disorder, some persons have an extraordinary appetite, and ask for solid food, which they may have liked in health; for instance—beef-steak, sausages, or even beans and bacon. Such wishes must never be indulged, for food of this sort will be almost certain to cause a relapse, which may prove dangerous. Until the health has been so far restored that the patient can take plenty of exercise in the open air, only one meal of animal food should be permitted each day, and this should not consist of anything more difficult to digest than the white meat of poultry. During the first period of convalescence, even the poultry or fish would better be omitted, and instead the patient should eat an egg lightly poached on toast, asparagus, or sea-kale, prepared by steaming in the manner previously directed and served on toast with some simple sauce, custard pudding, ground rice boiled with milk, racahat, or an omelette.

Portable Lunches.

BY CATHERINE OWEN.

WHAT to have for lunch is not a difficult question for the house-keeper, for in families of small means it usually decides itself by what is in the house; but to women breadwinners how to have some change from the fare they daily carry with them, and which, perhaps, has long since palled on their tired palates, is a very puzzling and important question.

Important because the *enjoyment* of food has more to do with health than many people think. Food that is forced on the appetite leaves the eater languid instead of invigorated. To those fortunate ones who live with their family while going out daily to store or office, it will be easy to give suggestions for appetising lunches which can be prepared by a loving mother or sister; but these very hints will seem a mockery to the woman whose only home is a boarding house, and her lunch the average cold fare to be found there; and again the lunch that costs twenty-five or thirty cents will seem equally impossible to the employee who must limit her expenditure to five or ten cents, as do the great majority of girls employed in the stores of large cities, and who, inquirers tell us, buy as David Copperfield did : " What is most filling at the price."

But, though the suggestions I shall have to make may not, certainly will not, fit all cases, I trust there may be a little help for every one—even those who cannot from circumstances change the material, may be able to change the manner of them so that they will be very different. from the accustomed fare; this may be best illustrated by taking cold meat, and bread and butter. The material may simply be a coarse lunch requiring a hearty appetite to attack it, or it may be a delicate and appetising one—this depending more often on the way it is cut and prepared, than on the quality of the bread, butter, and meat. I mean that the best quality of these will be unacceptable as a lunch, if cut in thick slices.

This brings me to the question of sandwiches, so hackneyed that it may not be thought worth attention by those seeking new ideas for lunches. But, after all, a well cut, well made sandwich is a very good thing, and will always be the main standby for packed lunches, and most women can have them, when some of the good things I shall speak of later, could only be had by women who have a home and some one to prepare their food. Although boarders may be forced to make their lunch from whatever may be given them, they can usually have the privilege of cutting it themselves; now to cut meat or bread nicely with the usual boarding-house table knife would be impossible, therefore obtain the use of the sharp carver, or else provide yourself with a sharp steel knife. Cut the bread very thin, butter it—if the butter is good and liked—liberally and evenly; do not scrape a little just over the centre; if the meat is corn-beef or ham, cut very thin slices to cover the bread and butter, season well, and lay another slice over. If the meat is cold roast beef or mutton, shave it with your sharp knife; I mean cut it so thin that it will curl as you cut it; lay several of these shavings on the bread, and, if liked, you can shave a pickle over it or sprinkle a little horseradish over; then cover with more shaved meat and another slice of bread and butter. Do not forget a proper amount of seasoning.

This is the simplest kind of sandwich within most people's power to have; the next thing is to keep them as fresh and moist as possible; for this purpose there is nothing so good as waxed paper and a tightly covered box; the waxed paper is so cheap that grocers send out butter, etc., in it, and the quality used by them, and no doubt to be obtained from them, will serve, although the pearly white paper, which comes at ten cents a quire of large sheets at the wholesale confectioners', is more dainty.

In addition to these everyday sandwiches there are others which will be an acceptable variation, some requiring a little more trouble to prepare, although others, such as those made from potted meats, are even less.

The small cans of potted ham, tongue, etc., sold at 15 cents, are very economical, as one can will make a good many sandwiches. The trouble is they are always better opened fresh or kept only a day or two, and one may get tired of them. The economical way in this, as in a good many others, lies in co-operation; let two or three who are obliged to carry their luncheon divide the trifling expense of a can of meat, and they will have at least a dozen sandwiches, costing about a cent and a half each; canned lobster, too, makes excellent sandwiches; but it requires a family at home to use up the remains in the form of devilled lobster or salad, or the same plan of co-operation. Nevertheless, where the waste of part of the can is avoided, the quantity required for half a dozen sandwiches will cost perhaps six cents.

LOBSTER SANDWICHES, NO. 1.

Take as much firm meat from a can of lobster as required, with some of the coral; the large claws are best for the purpose. Mince both meat and coral or mash them with the back of a fork, as you find best.

I am bearing in mind the possibility that I am writing for some to whom it is useless to say " pound with a potato masher," because they have only the means their lodging affords. Add butter enough to make a paste that will spread, season, and then cut neat, thin slices of stale bread, butter them, and spread one with the lobster, then, if you choose, sprinkle a little vinegar over it, or shred a small pickle very fine ; cover each sandwich with another slice of bread and butter, and then divide into convenient size. Sometimes a slice of bread cut into four fingers makes a more convenient sandwich to eat than larger ones.

LOBSTER SANDWICH, NO. 2.

Take sufficient lobster meat, chop it fine, put a rounding teaspoonful of flour and one of butter in a sauce-pan, let them melt together, stirring until they bubble. Add a gill of boiling water, stirring the while. Boil till thick and smooth, season, and then add as much of it to the lobster as will make it a rich thick hash. A few drops of vinegar may be stirred in, if liked, or lemon eaten with the sandwich. Cut two slices of stale bread not too thin, lightly toast one side of each, butter the other, then lay on the lobster mixture, place the other on top, press slightly, trim, and cut into convenient sizes.

EGG SANDWICHES.

Cut slices of bread and butter, slice hard boiled eggs, cover a slice with them, lay a few water cress tips or chopped celery over them with pepper and salt, lay another slice over and cut into shape.

Any kind of salad is a great improvement to sandwiches, but lettuce wilts before long ; if the sandwich is kept in a cool place, water cress, mustard and cress, or celery will keep quite fresh between the bread. A great improvement on any kind of meat sandwiches is to chop a little parsley and chives, or chives and water cress, or either, alone, and when quite fine mix with butter, a teaspoonful of the herb to double of butter, mix together and use this green butter for spreading the bread ; then use meat, eggs, etc., as usual.

CLAM SANDWICHES.

Chop a dozen Little Neck clams, stew them in a little water and their own liquor fifteen minutes ; the broth from this makes a strengthening drink. Strain it from the clams, pepper them slightly, stir in a piece of butter the size of a walnut, add a drop or two of Worcestershire sauce if handy, if not, vinegar ; add the yolk of an egg, stir over the fire till the egg thickens, then remove, toast slices of bread on one side, butter it, spread over it a layer of the clams, cover with another slice of bread, and cut into shape when quite cold.

OYSTER SANDWICHES.

Cut a half dozen oysters, let them plunge in their own liquor for about three minutes, pour off all but about a tablespoonful of the liquor (remembering that with a little butter and seasoning you have in it perhaps a cup of nourishing broth). Stir to the oysters a teaspoonful of butter, one of fine crumbs of cracker, pepper, and salt, and a squeeze of lemon and the yolk of an egg, or if the yolk of an egg is disliked, the white of one; stir it till thick. Let the mixture be put in a cup or bowl to cool, it may then be cut in slices and laid between bread and butter or toast.

COLD FISH SANDWICHES.

Stir in a plate the yolk of an egg, add oil gradually to it, a few drops at a time, until it thickens. When almost as thick as soft butter, season with salt, pepper, and vinegar. Stir the fish, broken small, into it, or into enough of it to make it into a mixture that will spread. Use this to cover slices of bread for sandwiches. If any of the mayonnaise is left it will keep in a cold place until the next day, when if used instead of butter to spread on bread in making sandwiches you will have a delicious change.

It will.seem almost a mockery, perhaps, to tell tired business women to do anything that will encroach on their precious time. Yet good, enjoyable food is health, and, if they are well nourished, they will be more vigorous, and perhaps feel more inclined to take a little trouble. To such as have the time I would say, then, that the most of the sandwiches for which I have given recipes can be cooked over a kerosene stove, in a tiny saucepan, over gas, or even over a spirit-lamp, by any one who knows already something of cooking. I would not recommend any one who has has never cooked to make a beginning on any make-shift contrivance,— burnt or spoiled food would probably result, because the quick heat and tin utensils used require constant attention and judgment.

Again about salad, it is difficult to procure just the little bit required for three or four sandwiches, but chives can be bought, roots and all, for a few cents a bunch in spring; so can parsley. Either flourish in a pot, and are not unsightly. Cut off the tops of the chives when you use them. Mustard and cress or pepper grass is even easier, for it only needs sprinkling thickly on wet flannel laid on a plate or tray, and kept moist by putting water under the flannel with a teaspoon. Keep it in a warm, dark spot for three days, when the seeds will have generated and will be ready to cut in a week.

I must not leave the sandwich question without mentioning two others, one a popular French lunch, and so nutritious that we hear of officers provided with a cake of chocolate, feeling independent of food supplies.

CHOCOLATE SANDWICH.

Cut thin slices of bread and butter as for other sandwiches, have a cake of sweetened chocolate in a warm spot over night, or long enough to become soft like cheese. Scrape it and spread thickly over the bread and butter, then make into sandwiches. This sandwich, when the appetite is jaded and craves variety, will be agreeable to chocolate lovers. A cake of chocolate between two crackers is another form of it.

CUCUMBER SANDWICH.

Cut cucumbers in very thin slices, dress them with oil and vinegar, mayonnaise, or whatever you prefer. Cut slices of bread, and butter, cover with two layers of the cucumber, properly seasoned, cover with another slice of bread and butter and cut into sandwiches. Eaten very cold these sandwiches are delicious in summer, either eaten alone or with a meat sandwich.

These lunches are such as could be prepared without much trouble over gas or kerosene stoves, or without heat, and suitable for those who board or lodge away from their families. Let no one for her health and youth's sake say she does not care enough about the matter to take the trouble. If her luncheon is already a satisfactory meal, which she eats with relish, she need not take the trouble to change it; but if her indifference comes from a languid appetite, that is the very reason for her to change. Unrelished food causes lack of energy.

In this article suggestions will be made, more for the friends of workers, those who like to cater tenderly for the bread-winners. I have heard such complain of the difficulty of finding variety. The English, who are famous for their love of cold dishes, have a far greater variety of such dainties than ourselves; their cold meat pies are famed the world over, and from them we may borrow a few ideas.

It is true that the unfamiliar names of some articles may not sound appetising, but let not prejudice and the fear of not liking it deprive you of a good thing.

I once spoke to a lady of that friend of the traveller in England, "Pork Pie," and the idea conjured up was so bilious that she *really* shuddered and turned pale. I am sure in her mind's eye she had a picture of a hot pie made of fat pork, perhaps salt pork at that, and reeking with grease. The fact being, however, that pork pie is far less rich than pork and beans or sausage, and is always eaten cold.

PORK PIE.

Cut one pound of fresh pork, of which one-fourth should be fat, into dice; mix with it thoroughly a teaspoonful of salt, and scant fourth of pepper. The genuine pies are made of what is called hot-paste made with milk and butter or lard made hot together, and it is only rich enough to serve as a sort of bread to eat with the meat. But as it requires experience to make it, I think any plain family paste that you are accustomed to use would be better. Line such cups as you use for popovers—about two and a half to three inches deep—with the paste a quarter of an inch thick, not less; put about one-fourth of the meat in, more if it will hold it; but while completely filling the case, do not *press* it down; shake it, then put in a little water, wet the edges, put on the cover, press the edges together so that the gravy may not boil out, brush the top with white of egg, cut a little slit in the centre, and bake in a moderate oven an hour and a quarter; when the paste begins to brown, cover the pies for the rest of the time. A pound of meat will make three to four pies, each enough for one lunch. They keep a week or more in a cold, dry place.

MELTON MOWBRAY PIES.

Prepare the pie-cases the same as for pork pies, chop half a pound of pork, the same of veal, one-fourth of the whole to be pork fat, and season with a little parsley and thyme if liked; otherwise omit; mix with a teaspoonful of salt, a quarter one of pepper, and then fill the pies with the chopped meat, which should be like sausage; pour in a tablespoonful of water, and finish the same as the pork pies. They will bake in one hour.

VEAL AND HAM PATTIES.

These are made of richer pastry—the finest puff paste or a light flaky paste. Cut the meat from the bones of a breast of veal, divide it into small pieces, let the meat and bones stew gently in a little water until the meat is nearly done, then take it up, leaving the bones to stew longer, and let it cool while you line some deep patty pans with pastry. Cut some boiled ham in dice, and to each patty put about a quarter as much ham as you have veal, mix the two meats thoroughly, use a level teaspoonful of salt, and the sixth of one of pepper for seasoning. Fill the patties with meat, piling it high in the centre. Cut the covers amply large, that they may not shrink away, wet the borders and press close together, cut a little slit in the centre with the point of a sharp knife. These will take only half an hour to cook or until the pastry is done. Having boiled the bones till the gravy is rich enough to jelly, let it cool a little, season with salt and pepper, then pour in as much as the patty will hold, through a small funnel. As the gravy will be stiff jelly when cold, there will be no trouble in packing these patties to carry.

Although the last two kinds of patties are always eaten cold by those to the manner born, they are excellent made hot, while the two next that I shall give require to be made hot; but as there are offices which have facilities for making tea or chocolate, the heating over could be easily managed in such cases.

BEEFSTEAK PATTIES.

For these use nice family paste, cut juicy round steak into half inch pieces, put the meat on to stew very gently with very little water (half a pint to a pound), pepper and salt to taste. When the meat is tender let it cool.

Line deep patty-pans or small deep dishes with pastry, fill with the meat, add a little gravy, cover the patties as usual, and then bake half an hour. When they cool pour in a little more gravy. To make them easy to pack without leaking, melt into the beef gravy just enough gelatine to make it jelly; a small teaspoonful will be enough to solidify a gill of gravy.

It must be remembered that the gravy from beefsteak or any solid beef will never form jelly. To do that requires the long boiling of bones and gristle. Shin-of-beef will make soup-stock that will form strong jelly when cold, but the finer parts of beef yield only a highly flavored broth.

Now the trouble with small pies is that they are apt to be dry, simply because no jelly is put into them, even when they ought to be eaten cold, as in the pork and veal pies, it is the savory jelly running through the meat that forms their excellence; if they lack it they are not good specimens.

SAUSAGE ROLLS.

Sausage rolls are easily made and exceedingly good and convenient.

They are properly made with puff paste, but if a plain, substantial paste is preferred, it can be substituted.

Take as many newly made pork sausages as you intend to have rolls, if sausage meat is used make into sausage form. Roll out the pastry to about the third of an inch thick, cut it in pieces *about* five inches long, (it depends on the length and thickness of the sausages) wet the edges all round, lay the sausage on one-half the paste, fold the other half over, like closing a book; then press the moistened edges of the paste together, both along the open side and the ends, so that the gravy cannot ooze out in cooking. Bake for about half an hour. These rolls, as well as all the patties, are made much more tempting in appearance by being brushed over with white of egg before they are baked, but when this is not convenient, brush them quickly with milk, taking care not to do more than moisten the surface of the paste.

It is needless to say, perhaps, that the filling for any of the patties may be varied, that any cold meat chopped and *nicely flavored*, moistened with a little soup or broth or meat gravy, make very nice patties. Canned lobster or chicken or a few oysters may be used. But of whatever they may be made, take care that the dish or patty-pan is at least two inches deep. You want plenty of meat and jelly in proportion to the crust. Many people make small pies in saucers, but though that mode may do for fruit, it is not satisfactory for meat.

LOBSTER LOAVES.

Make some rolls with a crust all round. This may not seem easy to those who have been accustomed to lay rolls close together, but by making the rolls of the finest flour and the dough stiffer than bread dough, there is no difficulty whatever. The stiff dough is allowed to rise till double its own bulk, *three times before baking*, and very well kneaded, will make much finer rolls than when made with soft dough. Break pieces the size of an egg. Take a little butter on your hands and roll them into cork shapes, rather short and thick, and also into balls, put them two inches apart on a baking sheet, let them rise to twice the size and bake in a quick oven till brown. When the loaves are cold cut off the top, scoop out part of the crumb, chop some oysters or lobster, put a dessert-spoonful of butter, in a small, thick saucepan, stir with it a teaspoonful of flour till they bubble, then add quickly three parts of a teacup of milk, stirring all the time till thick and smooth, stir in the lobster or oysters with pepper and salt. If oysters are used the liquor may be used instead of milk or half and half; cook only one minute. When cool this should form a stiff mince.

Fill the loaves, put on the slice, cut off and keep in place with a band of waxed paper, and a pin, or new carpet tack pushed into the roll through the paper.

These loaves may be filled with chicken salad, or any meat salad, with creamed fish, with any of the fillings described for patties, or with sausage, but of course everything must be cooked first.

In providing a daily lunch for anyone it must be remembered that variety is the great thing to be desired, and because the lunch eater enjoys one thing very much indeed, that is no reason for giving it two days running; if there is two days' supply let something come between. We have all heard of the husband who praised a dish of his wife's preparing, and was afraid ever to do it again, for he had it every day for a week.

Try and add some little piquant thing to the lunch basket. A few sticks of white celery rolled in a wet rag, then in a dry napkin; a few lettuce leaves in a paper candy box well sprinkled or with a wet rag laid over them keep crisp all day. A few olives or a pickle may be very refreshing. Who would ask a better lunch than cold fried oysters and a tiny gherkin? But the oysters must be very well fried, plump not hard, and crisp and brown. In making these suggestions for lunches the question of cost has not been lost sight of, and in no case should the cost be over fifteen cents, while in the majority of cases it will be much less, for instance: Four pork pies will cost 25 cents. Veal and ham perhaps 35 cents, if puff paste is used. Melton Mowbray pies 30 cents. Half a dozen oyster loaves 20 cents. In each of these cases there are three to four good lunches, such as could not be bought for three times the money.

Preservation of the Sight.

WELL-KNOWN English ophthalmic optician, in a little treatise on the subject of the treatment of the eyes, gives the following brief and simple directions, which every one would do well to follow:

1. Never look at an intensely bright light for any length of time.

2. Carefully avoid exposing the eyes to a very brilliant light after they have been in darkness, such changes being extremely injurious. In some cases blindness has resulted.

3. Persons using microscopes should incline them as much as possible in a horizontal direction. Looking down into them, when they are held upright, fills the eyes with blood by stopping the circulation in the neck.

When adjusting a very bright lamp-flame, if you wish to do it slowly, look at the flame through a slit formed by almost closing two or three fingers. This will prove a great protection to the sight.

189

HOW TO READ BY LAMP-LIGHT.

The best lamp for reading or sewing is an oil lamp moving up and down on a rod, with an opal glass shade *open underneath*, white on the inside and dark-green on the outside. The lamp should be fixed so low down on the rod that the light is reflected strongly on the object, while the flame cannot be seen by the reader. It is commonly known by the name of the German Student-lamp.

The worst possible position for either reading or writing is *facing the light*, and it will be found that while, with the back turned to the light, a person with weak eyes can read or write for two or three hours without inconvenience, half an hour in the other position will cause pain and inflammation.

The reason is perfectly simple. The light should fall on the book or the paper, while the eyes are in the shadow—the shadow of the head.

To give a practical illustration of this, let any person stand before a looking-glass and, in an otherwise dark room, hold a candle behind the head and observe in the glass the size of the black opening to the retina of the eyes. Then bring the candle round, and the contraction of the iris will at once be strikingly shown; the central black window of the eye will be reduced to half its former size. Then let the one-sided light falling from the left hand, so often recommended, be tried, and it will be found that the left iris is far less expanded than the right. That is, the eyes are forced to act irregularly, or with an unequal strain upon the exquisitely constructed system of muscular fibres constituting the sphincter pupillæ.

As the protection of the retina depends upon the ready response of these to the sight, their healthy action and preservation for old age are of the greatest importance.

In case of children there is another advantage in the back light. If the windows are fairly high, the shadow of the head falls on the book only when the pupils lean forward, and to escape it they avoid the bad habit of thus leaning and pressing the breast-bone against the edge of the desk. The *best* light of all is that which falls from above in such a manner that the eyes are protected from glare by the shadow of the forehead and eye-brows, while no shadows rest upon the books or desks. But of course this can only be obtained where there are no rooms above.

Always lean well back in reading and hold the book up. Never bend forward and face the light. Never read by fire-light, nor when lying down in bed. If, during illness, it is necessary to do so, do not hold the book up over the face; but put it on the pillow and read with the face downward, and the back turned toward the light. If the eyes are weak, never sleep in a position facing the window. Turn the side of the bed instead of its foot toward the window, and lie with your face turned away from the light.

Never read books printed in small type, if large type editions can be had, and do not read in railway trains. But those who disregard this injunction will find it much easier and less injurious if a large card or envelope is held just under each line, moving it down as each line is read.

No needle-work with dark materials should ever be done by artificial light.

When looking at pictures in a gallery, do not stand under them and raise the eyes only, stand at some distance from them and raise the whole head, or rather throw it back slightly.

GENERAL CARE OF THE EYES.

The use of tinted writing paper is very beneficial; but the colors selected should be gray, neutral, or bluish-green. Reddish-brown, pink, yellow, or strongly yellowish-green should be avoided.

Looking for any length of time through wire-gauze window-shades is injurious to the sight. The veils worn by ladies, if thick, are also harmful.

The eyes should be kept cool. It is a good plan to sluice them—keeping them closed—every morning with cold water. The constant use of this tends to strengthen and preserve the sight; but if the eyes are actually inflamed, water of the same temperature as the air in very cold weather may increase the inflammation, and tepid water will be more beneficial.

Slight inflammation in the eyes may be relieved by bathing them with cold or nearly cold tea, or a little Goulard water, to be had from any apothecary.

CARE OF INFANTS' AND CHILDREN'S EYES.

Infants should never be exposed to the full glare of the sun. Men shade their eyes with the brims of their hats, and ladies carry parasols. But infants wear nothing to protect the forehead; they are constantly to be seen in their perambulators with their faces exposed to the full glare of the sun, and I have often observed them, when left by careless nurses in this position, with their eyes closed, moving uneasily about, unable to find relief.

In schools, children usually suffer from too little light after having, while infants, been exposed to far too much of it.

By studying in school-rooms where there is a deficiency of light, children stoop over their books or take any method of bringing them nearer to their eyes to assist their imperfect vision of the letters. Thus the sight becomes strained and often seriously impaired and, if the practice is long continued, myopia or shortsightedness will result.

FATIGUE OF THE EYES.

When the eyes have been used for a long time by artificial light and become fatigued, it is useful to have at hand a wash, composed as follows :

Rose or Elder-flower water	two ounces.
Wine of Opium -	one-half drachm.
French Brandy - - - - - -	one drachm.

Mix and occasionally bathe the eyes with a fine piece of sponge, the relief will be felt at once. It will allay inflammation and preserve the sight. The eyes should be closed while being bathed, but if a small quantity of the wash gets in, it will be beneficial.

✧ HYGIENE. ✧

What to Do While Waiting for the Doctor.

EMERGENCIES.

SUFFOCATION.

UNDER this head may be enumerated all cases of loss of consciousness produced by drowning, exposure to smoke, charcoal or illuminating gas, the foul air of a sewer, old mine, or well, choking or hanging, for in every case the result is the same: air has been kept from the lungs, thus causing suffocation. The person may also have been poisoned by the nature of gas he has inhaled, but this makes no change in the treatment to be pursued.

The patient is usually wholly insensible. The breathing may be very faint or have ceased entirely, the face is often purple and swollen, and the lips livid. Yet all these signs are not always present, especially in cases where the suffocation is due to exposure of gas.

WHAT TO DO.—It is hardly necessary to say—first remove the cause of the suffocation. Take the person out of the water, cut the rope. Even if hours have passed, do not hesitate to act promptly, cases of resuscitation have occurred after the lapse of several hours, not only in apparent drowning, but when suffocation has been due to other causes.

For any case of suffocation, proceed as follows:

Dash cold water into the face, give the patient a sudden slap on the pit of the stomach, and hold ammonia under the nose. If these simple means are not sufficient to restore breathing, try artificial respiration by the following method, known as Sylvester's, and usually regarded as the most successful.

ARTIFICIAL RESPIRATION.

The chest is first made to expand, causing the air to be taken in just on the principle that a pair of bellows fills with air when opened. Then the chest is made to contract, its capacity for holding air is reduced, and the air is forced out. By causing these two movements to be performed alternately, we have first inspiration and then expiration, the two together constituting respiration or breathing Wrap the finger in one or two thicknesses of a handkerchief, and wi.pe out the mouth and back of the throat; then place the patient on his back with the shoulders resting on a roll of clothing, which should raise them sufficiently to let the head fall back and rest on the ground or floor. Then let some one seize the tongue with a dry handkerchief and draw it forward to leave the passage to the windpipe free. If there is no one to perform this office, draw the tongue well out and tie it against the lower teeth, by laying the centre of a dry strip of cloth on the tongue, crossing it under the chin, carrying the ends around the neck and tying them at the side of the throat. Or, if a rubber band is to be had, slip it over the tongue and under the chin.

Next kneel behind the unconscious person, grasp the arms just above the elbows, draw them up over his head, rather quickly, but steadily, until his hands touch the ground or floor above his head. This should be done in the time needed to count one, two. The movement expands the chest and permits the air to enter the lungs. Next lower them so that the elbows will come to the sides, and the hands cross on the pit of the stomach, and press them gently but strongly against the sides and chest. Do this in the time needed to count three, four. The movement forces the air out of the lungs. Continue these two motions—which constitute artificial respiration—very deliberately about twelve or fourteen times a minute. Do not stop until the patient breathes naturally, or until life is undoubtedly extinct.

If the patient makes an effort to breathe, even though only a gasp, wait a moment to see if he will breathe again, if not, renew the artificial respiration, but it should now be timed by his efforts to breathe. Also, when efforts at breathing commence, try putting hartshorn to the nose, dashing cold water on the patient, and slapping.

During the continuance of the movements to produce artificial respiration, the chest may be gently rubbed with warm flannel.

Artificial respiration should be kept up for an hour and a half, even if there is no sign of life, or until a physician has pronounced that life is extinct.

Failure to detect any pulse at the wrist, or to distinguish the beating of the heart by inexperienced persons, gives no certain proof of the presence of death.

As soon as natural breathing is established, the patient should be placed in a warm bed, with hot water bottles or hot bricks at each side of the body, between the thighs, under the arm-pits, at the soles of the feet and on the pit of the stomach. Use friction and warmth of all kinds till the vitality is fully restored. As soon as possible—when the patient can swallow—give warm drinks—hot tea or coffee, or whiskey and water, one teaspoonful at a time. If difficulty in breathing obstinately continues, put a large mustard plaster on the chest.

DROWNING.

When a person is taken from the water, whether really drowned or only apparently so, the face may be swollen and purple, the lips livid and the eyes bloodshot, in which case death, or unconsciousness, is probably due to suffocation by the exclusion of air from the lungs, or by drawing water into them.

In other cases the person may seem pale and flabby—then the patient has probably fainted in the water, or there has been some failure of the heart.

The treatment should be applied on the spot, unless the weather is excessively cold; when the body may be removed to any place of shelter that is near. The first thing to be done is to restore respiration, then warmth and circulation.

Send at once for a physician, blankets, dry clothing, and stimulants. Strip the patient to the waist and rub dry, letting the chest and shoulders meanwhile remain exposed to the wind. Wipe out the throat and mouth with the finger wrapped in one or two folds of a handkerchief. Then turn the body over, face downward, and resting on one arm, the abdomen being supported by a large roll of clothing or a folded blanket. Place your hands one on each side of the small of the back, and apply rather a steady pressure in order to expel any water that has been swallowed. Next turn the patient again on his back and, if breathing has not begun, try to cause it by the following simple methods. Apply smelling-salts to the nose and tickle it with a straw or feather. Dash cold water on the breast and face, or use alternately hot and cold. The sudden changes cause efforts to breathe. Give the patient a slap on the pit of the stomach with the open hand.

If natural breathing is thus restored, proceed to restore warmth and circulation by the directions given under the heading of suffocation. But they must be very quickly applied and, in case of failure, resort immediately to artificial respiration, which has been already fully described in the account of the treatment of persons who have become unconscious by suffocation.

HEAT-STROKE OR SUN-STROKE.

Long exertion in a hot, close atmosphere is even more likely to produce this condition, than direct exposure to the sun's rays. Certain symptoms precede it, which should instantly be heeded, as head-ache, a feeling of weakness at the pit of the stomach and the knees, and sometimes vomiting and dimness of vision. Sometimes loss of consciousness comes on gradually, sometimes without warning. The head, face, and body are usually burning hot, and dry. The cessation of perspiration, when one is very warm, should always be regarded as a dangerous symptom. Strip the person, wrap the body in a sheet, and keep it wet by frequent sprinkling with cold water. Continue this till consciousness returns and the body feels cool. When the above directions cannot be followed, put cloths dipped in ice-water,—or the coldest to be had,—on the head, back of the neck, and hands, loosen all tight clothing, and al ways put the sufferer in the shade and in the coolest place at hand.

BURNS.

If a person's clothing is on fire throw him or her down, wrap any woolen article such as a rug, piano cover, or coat around the body, keeping it around the throat if possible to prevent inhalation of the flames, and roll the person about till the flames are smothered, then pour on water till the last spark is out. Cut away the clothing with scissors, if any sticks to the skin make no attempt to remove it. Keep the air from burns and keep them warm. Excellent remedies are: covering with a layer of sweet oil, fresh lard, vaseline, or cold cream. Then wrap in cotton batting, flannel, or even several thicknesses of cotton cloth, if nothing else better is at hand.

BITES AND STINGS.

Dogs.—If there is the least suspicion that the dog is mad, wash the hurt with water, as hot as can be borne, and cauterize thoroughly with lunar caustic.

If on the arm or leg, tie a bandage or handkerchief around the limb, above the bite—between it and the heart—and keep it on till the doctor comes. If lunar caustic cannot be had, put common salt on the wound. If neither is at hand, bathe the injury thoroughly. Caustics should be used by the physician as soon as he arrives. Have the animal kept until the question whether it is mad is settled; but it is wise to immediately take the above precautions.

Snakes.—Instantly tie a handkerchief, bandage, or even a string very tightly a short distance above the wound. This is to delay the circulation of the poison through the system. The patient himself or some one else should immediately suck the wound, which can be done without danger, unless there is a cut or sore on the mouth or lips. Then wash the injury with warm water, apply diluted hartshorn to it, and take internally every three hours from five to fifteen drops of ammonia water—the former is a dose for a child five years old. Lunar caustic should be applied if it can be had. The poison is apt to cause sleep, so stimulants should be given —whisky is regarded as one of the best remedies for rattlesnake bites.

HEAT EXHAUSTION.

Sometimes the face, instead of being flushed, is pale, the skin is moist and even cool, the pulse quick and feeble.

Then there should be no effort to reduce heat, as in the other case; but give slight stimulants, let the patient rest in a cool, quiet room, and give the stimulants gradually. Do not use any cold applications. Put the patient in a blanket. Persons who have once been affected by heat or sun-stroke should be very careful about exposing themselves in future, as they are very liable to a second attack.

Have an extra covering within reach, in case of a sudden change of weather during the night. Never stand still out of doors after walking, especially on a street corner.

LIGHTNING STROKE.

Persons rendered unconscious by a stroke of lightning show a lessening of the strength of circulation, and a weakness of the pulse, while the breathing is slow and sighing. Give stimulants, apply heat to the body, and secure absolute rest.

FAINTING.

If in a crowded place where it is impossible to lie down, sit in a chair and drop the head between the knees as soon as the sensation of faintness comes on, and it will quickly pass off. If a person has become unconscious, fainted "dead away," place him or her flat on the floor, or on a bed or lounge, with the head lower than the body. Dash cold water into the face, apply ammonia or smelling salts to the nose, and as soon as the sufferer begins to recover, give a drink of cold water, or a little brandy.

Never let a person who has fainted remain in an erect position.

FROST BITE.

Never permit warm water, warm air, or a fire anywhere near the parts frozen until the natural temperature is nearly restored, and then the utmost care must be used to avert serious consequences. Rub the frozen part with snow—the patient being in a cold room—and apply ice-water. The circulation should be restored very slowly. When reaction comes on, warm milk containing a little stimulant of some kind should be given.

STRAINS AND DISLOCATION.

Dislocation of the Jaw.—This is by no means uncommon and may be brought on by yawning or laughing, if the accident has ever occurred to the person before.

The mouth is wide open, the chin thrown forward, the patient finds it almost impossible to speak or swallow, and an unnatural hollow may be felt behind the ear. If only one side is dislocated, the chin will be turned toward the opposite side, if *both*, the chin will be central.

Protect the thumbs with a napkin, to avoid having them cut by the teeth, and thrust them into the mouth, resting them on the upper surfaces of the back teeth of the lower jaw, then press the thumbs downward, at the same time raising the chin with the little and ring finger of both hands. If these movements are made at the same time, and with sufficient force, the jaw will slip into its place. For several following days the jaws should be kept as quiet as possible. Good soup or any other nourishing food that may be swallowed without chewing should be given. To prevent any motion of the jaw, support it by passing a cravat under it and tie the ends on the top of the head.

Dislocation of the Neck.—While this is fortunately a very rare accident, it is mentioned here because it is *absolutely necessary* to act immediately.

The cause is a heavy fall on the side of the head, which is found to be turned on one side and fixed.

Place the person on the back, then let whoever has the nerve plant one knee against each shoulder and, taking the head in a firm grasp, pull gently and, at the same time, turn it into its proper place.

Dislocation of the Shoulders.—Sometimes in these cases it is a very easy matter to replace the armbone. Lay the patient on his back and sit down by his side at the injured side, facing him. Take off the shoe from the foot nearest to the sufferer, and set the foot firmly on the arm-pit of the dislocated shoulder. Pull down the arm and, while doing, draw it over in front of his body to the other side. This process will often push the head of the bone into its place. If the elbow remains away from one side, the arm is not in place.

Dislocation of the Fingers.—The bones can usually be restored to their places by strong, steady pulling, aided by a little pressure on the parts of the bones nearest to the joint. They should be shown to a surgeon as soon as possible; but dislocations of the thumb often baffle the skill of the best medical practitioners.

SPRAINS.

Fingers and wrist.—Where the injury is inflicted on the wrist or finger, cold moist applications are usually the best. If the wrist is hurt, the hand and fore-arm must be laid on a straight splint and secured by a soft bandage, or wide strips of sticking plaster, one passing round the hand, and one or two round the arm above the wrist.

Rest of the injured part is absolutely essential; but either hot or cold applications may be used, according to the relief experienced.

Ankle.—In this case, as in all other sprains, the injury is due to the twisting or partial tearing of the ligaments about a joint; but in sprains of the ankle there is also sometimes a fracture of the ends of the bones.

If possible immerse the injured joint in water as hot as the patient can bear, keeping it at this temperature for an hour and a half by adding hot water as fast as it cools. Then put on a moderately tight bandage in such a way as to prevent any movement of the joint. Success depends on the absolute prevention of any motion.

HEMORRHAGES.

WHEN only the small blood-vessels are cut, there is merely an oozing of blood; but if a vein is opened, there is a steady flow of dark red or purple blood. If an artery is cut, the blood comes out in jets, and is bright red. This is the most serious form and requires instant care. But it often happens in a deep wound that both arteries and veins are severed, and the blood mingles, making it impossible to distinguish; therefore only those methods of stopping bleeding that will answer in all cases are given here. First, place something on the opening to stop the flow, either the fingers or thumb, or a piece of cloth folded and bound firmly on. If these methods do not succeed, the flow must be stopped by pressing the artery at some point between the heart and the wound. To do this the situation of the arteries must be learned, that persons may know where to apply the pressure. Unless the injury is in the leg or arm, the flow of blood must be checked by pressing the fingers, or a pad and bandage, directly over the bleeding point, because if the hurt is in the body the arteries conveying the blood to the wound cannot be reached.

Many a life might have been saved, had the simple means of stopping bleeding from wounds in the extremities been generally known.

In the upper arm the artery lies on the inner side of the bone, on a line with the seam of the coat, and under the biceps muscle. Press the thumb deep under the muscle toward the bone, and the bleeding will cease. In the upper part of the thigh, the artery is in front of the groin, just below the centre. By pressing firmly with both thumbs on this spot, the flow of blood from the leg will be stopped.

To stop the flow of blood to the head, press the large artery in the neck just above the collar-bone. The blood that supplies the shoulder, arm-pit, and arm flows through the artery under the collar-bone. To stop it, stand behind the injured person and press the extended fingers deep down behind the collar-bone toward the centre of the chest.

INSTANT TREATMENT OF ANY BLEEDING WOUND.

Lay the sufferer down at full length, raising the head a very little. Remove the clothing from the injury. If there is a clot of blood in the hurt, and bleeding still continues, wipe away the clot. Fold a cloth into a hard pad. If possible, bring the edges together and lay the compress over it. If this cannot be done, lay the compress on the wound and hold it until it can be fastened with a bandage. To stop a violent hemorrhage temporarily, thrust the fingers or thumb into the wound to close the openings of the vessels.

BLEEDING FROM THE LEG.

Lay the patient down, lift the foot till the limb is nearly straight. If there is a large clot of blood in the wound, wipe it out; then put on a pad and bind it firmly in place. If the flow of blood stops, do nothing till the doctor comes. If not, roll a handkerchief tightly, or get a round, flat stone, or anything else that is hard and about the size of an egg. Put it over the artery about an inch below the groin, on a line which runs from the inner crease of the groin to the inner side of the knee. Then tie another handkerchief, suspender, or strip of cloth over the pad around the thigh. Pass a stick through this, and twist till the pad is pressed deeply into the thigh, and the blood stops flowing. This is what is known in surgery as a tourniquet, and by its means any bleeding of the leg can be checked, even when a limb has been amputated.

BLEEDING FROM THE ARM.

Can be stopped in the same way. Put the tourniquet midway between the arm and the shoulder.

When there is bleeding from places where pressure cannot readily be applied, put a piece of ice on the compress, letting the cold water reach the wound. Ice helps to check bleeding, therefore use either very cold or very hot water to cleanse a bleeding wound. *Warm* water increases the flow of blood.

BRIEF RULES TO REMEMBER.

Put the injured person down at full length, raise the bleeding limb, press the wound with the fingers or a pad. If that fails, compress the main artery between the heart and the wound with the fingers or a tourniquet.

GUN-SHOT WOUNDS.

Keep cold wet cloths saturated with laudunum on the wound to prevent inflammatory swelling and, if there are symptoms of shock, give doses of whisky, wine, or brandy, and apply heat to the surface of the body. If the part is badly shattered, it is better not to apply the cloths to the wound cold. If there is much bleeding, follow directions already given

FOREIGN SUBSTANCES IN THE EYES, NOSE, EARS, STOMACH, ETC.

EYES.

EVER rub the eye. If the substance is small, the flow of tears caused by the irritation will often suffice to remove it. If not, draw down the lower lid by the fore and middle fingers, while the sufferer looks upward, and carefully examine the inner surface of the lid for the object. If not found the upper lid should be turned over, and this can be accomplished in the following way: Tell the patient to look downward, then take the centre lashes of the upper lid between the fore-finger and thumb of the left hand, drawing the lid downward and a little way from the eye-ball. Then place the smaller end of a pencil or pen-holder held in the right hand on the centre of the lid about half an inch from the margin and with a quick movement turn the lid over the point of the pencil, which should at the same moment be pressed slightly downward. Then by pressing the lid slightly backward against the eye, the whole surface is displayed. If the object is visible it can be gently wiped away with a bit of soft cloth or by a stream of soft water from a sponge. If sand or dust has got into the eye, proceed in the same way. After it has been removed, the irritation produced may make the patient imagine it is still there. Never use a poultice or thick cloth on the eyes.

Lime in the eye is a dangerous matter. Turn the lid and allow a mixture of one part vinegar to eight of warm water to run freely over the surface. Then apply a few drops of sweet or castor-oil and wash the eye thoroughly by pouring into it a stream of luke-warm water from a sponge. An oculist should be seen as soon as possible.

OBSTRUCTIONS IN THE NOSE.

Any obstruction in the nostril of a child is usually from some object thrust into it in play, such as a button, bean, pebble, or fruit-stone. To get rid of them, first try blowing the nose hard, or endeavor to produce sneezing by giving snuff or tickling the nose, or tell the child to draw in a long breath and then give him a smart slap on the back. Some one of these plans may dislodge it, if not, the sooner a physician is sent for, the better, for in some cases, for instance when peas or beans have lodged in the nose, the moisture causes them to swell and they sometimes prove very difficult to extract.

If a physician is not to be had, the attempt may be made to remove the obstruction by a bent hair-pin, a bodkin, the handle of a salt-spoon, or something of that kind. But this must be done with extreme care.

OBJECTS IN THE EAR.

The removal of objects from the ear is a far more delicate and dangerous matter than from the nose, and special instruments are usually needed. Yet, if it is impossible to obtain medical aid, something may be done. But *always* remember that the outer passage to the ear is very deep and extremely delicate. Any rough treatment may produce serious injury.

If the object is a metal or a mineral substance, syringe the ear thoroughly, the patient should meanwhile hold the head with the face bent far down, as in this position gravity lends some assistance. Very gentle efforts may be made to remove the obstruction by means of a crochet needle, a bodkin, or an ear-spoon, if the latter can be had. But always bear in mind that great harm may be done by the least harshness.

If live insects get into the ear, oil or glycerine or salt and water may be poured in. Oil, however, is pronounced by most medical authorities to be the best remedy.

STOMACH.

When coins, marbles, slate pencils, or nails are swallowed, *never* give a purgative. Give plenty of good, solid food, batter pudding, porridge, etc., so that the foreign substance will be surrounded and carried through the intestines without injuring them.

WIND-PIPE.

If any object gets lodged in the wind-pipe, a blow on the back with the palm of the hand, or a quick, strong squeeze of the chest may aid in dislodging it.

HEMORRHAGES.

The sight of blood is always alarming, and frequently so terrifies nervous people that they are unable to give the necessary help. The remedies, however, are very simple, and can be quickly and easily applied by the most inexperienced.

Nose.—Bleeding from the nose is often merely an effort of nature to get rid of an excess of blood that has accumulated in the system; but, on the other hand, it may be so great as to endanger life. If this is the case, of course medical aid should be instantly summoned; but, meantime, the

best remedy is to snuff salt and water or vinegar up the nostrils. A
strong solution of alum in warm water is also beneficial; but vinegar is
pleasanter, and will rarely fail to stop the bleeding.

Lungs.—If the hemorrhage is from the lungs, the blood is bright-red,
nearly the shade of red ink, and usually frothy. It is seldom profuse, yet,
as it is usually coughed up and received in a handkerchief, it is apt to seem
so. The stain spreading over the texture of the handkerchief makes it
difficult to estimate. The best treatment is perfect rest in bed, with the
body supported by pillows in a sitting posture, and the swallowing of
lumps of ice. If the patient is not too weak to bear it, put cold applications on the chest, and a mixture of salt and vinegar, in doses of one
teaspoonful every fifteen minutes, is often helpful.

Stomach.—When the bleeding is from the stomach, the color is usually
very dark, and it somewhat resembles coffee-grounds. If mingled with
any other contents of the stomach, its appearance may be altered. Give
ice-water or cracked ice, and teaspoonful doses of vinegar. Rest in bed is
absolutely necessary, and cold applications to the stomach may be
beneficial.

Bowels.—Give injections of ice-water, and apply ice to the abdomen.

INTERNAL HEMORRHAGES.

Where the bleeding is internal, ice-cold water should be laid on the
abdomen. The patient should be placed in bed and rest there without a
pillow, and *with the head lower than the body.*

ACCIDENTS ON RAILROADS AND IN FACTORIES.

INJURIES from machinery range from very slight and simple wounds
to the most severe ones. Many a limb or portion of a limb is cut or
torn away. Accidents of this sort very frequently occur when medical aid
cannot be obtained for some little time, and it would be desirable if some
one on every train, and in every room of a manufactory, had some idea
of the proper things to do before a doctor arrived.

Every surgeon will bear witness that the most common cause of death from severe accidents is due to the shock that follows them, and therefore directions for its treatment will be given before proceeding to an account of the means to be used for the relief of the injuries themselves.

SHOCK.

The symptoms are extreme pallor, a cold, clammy skin, very feeble pulse and breathing, pinched face, dull eyes, drooping eyelids, dilated pupils, bewilderment or dullness of the mental faculties, sometimes even stupor. A person in this condition may die very soon, and certainly will die ere long unless the vital forces can be rallied.

Prompt, energetic, and steady measures must be adopted by those who are striving to relieve them; heat must be applied at once to the *whole body*, if possible; but especially to the pit of the stomach and the region of the heart. For this purpose use a hot bath, hot fire, hot cans, hot bottles, heated blankets; in short, anything hot that can be obtained most speedily. At the same time give a teaspoonful of brandy or whisky in a tablespoonful of hot water, every ten minutes, for several hours.

This condition may be caused by fright, a blow on the pit of the stomach, sudden and severe pain, or even by drinking a great deal of ice-water. It is very common after severe gun-shot wounds.

TRIFLING INJURIES.

Under this head may be included cuts or tears.

The parts should be cleaned as gently and carefully as possible, by letting luke-warm water run freely over them. Then put any displaced skin or flesh into its proper position, and lay a clean white cloth, soaked in laudanum, or alcohol and water, on the wound. Bind on loosely with a handkerchief or anything that will serve for a bandage.

LACERATIONS OR LARGE TEARS.

First remove any dust, splinters, or fragments of clothing, then wash with lukewarm water. Nature's forceps, the thumb and finger, are in everybody's possession, and no one need be afraid to use them with proper care. A clean linen or muslin cloth or a sponge may also be used; but the utmost care must be taken to have these articles absolutely clean.

After the cleansing is completed, the injured parts must be replaced in position and retained by bandages, sticking-plaster, or the hands of some careful person. If a splint is needed, it can usually be had in a mill or on a railroad. No matter how clumsy it may be, it should be large enough to hold the injured part still and, in case of a limb, the joint above and the joint below the injury.

Sometimes these injuries occasion little pain. If, however, the suffering is severe, laudanum should be given—about thirty drops to an
adult. Cold or hot cloths—whichever afford most relief—should be applied to the wound.

CRUSHED FINGERS AND TOES.

These should be carefully washed, modeled into the proper shape,
dressed with a piece of soft white cloth soaked in hot or cold water, and
laid in a small splint.

When completely torn off, the stumps need amputation by a medical
man. While awaiting his arrival they should be cleansed, a cool, wet
dressing applied, and then left for the physician's inspection.

CRUSHED HANDS AND FEET.

Wrap them in something soft and warm, like cloth, or cotton, or
wool. Cold should never be used except when the bleeding is profuse.
Support the injured part by some kind of splint and raise it to a level
with the body. The sufferer should lie down, unless some other position
is necessary to move him, or is directed by the physician. These injuries
rarely give much pain, but are usually followed by the symptoms of
shock, for whose treatment directions have been given.

When torn or cut off by wheels, the stumps should be treated as
described, and the limb placed so that the injured part is higher than
any other.

CRUSH OF THE ARMS OR LEGS.

Treat as for the hands or feet; but the prostration is usually
greater, and the need of stimulating by warmth and heat more urgent.
Do not remove the clothing, except to cut away and replace by warm
coverings.

CRUSHES OF THE CHEST AND LOWER PARTS OF THE BODY.

These nearly always occasion death in a short time. All that can be
done is to secure rest, apply warmth and moderate stimulation. Make the
sufferer as comfortable as possible, and try to prepare him for the almost
inevitable end.

HEALTH HINTS.

Never go to bed until the feet are thoroughly dry and warm. In
passing out from any heated building into cold air, keep the mouth
tightly shut; by inhaling the air through the nose it will be warmed
before reaching the lungs, and thus prevent the sudden chills which so
often end in pneumonia or other serious diseases. Never sleep with the
head exposed to a draught from an open window.

Poisons and Antidotes.

HE remedies to be used in cases of poisoning of course vary widely; but two general directions are universally applicable—to get rid of the poison as quickly as possible, and to remember that the value of the remedy increases in the exact ratio of the promptness with which it can be obtained.

Some poisons, by irritating the lining membrane of the stomach, naturally produce vomiting, so that, by the aid of an emetic, the whole contents will be speedily ejected. Others have no tendency to cause nausea, and then the quickest methods for inducing it must be employed. Of these, the best are draughts of hot water mixed with salt or mustard, tickling the throat with a feather, thrusting the finger down it, etc.

Some poisons, however, paralyze the stomach, and the only resource is the stomach-pump. But this is sometimes difficult to obtain, and always liable to do harm if used by inexperienced hands.

VEGETABLE POISONS.

POISON OAK, IVY, AND SUMACH.

Many persons are so sensitive to the influence of these plants that, even without touching them, their mere vicinity will cause symptoms much resembling those of erysipelas.

The best remedy is said to be frequent bathing in water, as hot as can be borne. If used immediately after exposure, it will sometimes prevent the eruption. Later it relieves the itching sensation, and gradually

207

dries up the swellings.   In addition, "lead water and laudanum" is valuable as a lotion.   But persons sensitive to these poisons should be on the watch for the plants when roaming through the fields or woods.

DEADLY NIGHTSHADE.

This is found growing wild almost everywhere in the Eastern States, and cases of poisoning from eating its purplish fruit are by no means uncommon, especially among children.

Symptoms.—The enlargement of the pupil of the eye is always a prominent symptom; the limbs grow heavy and tremors run through the body.   The mucous membrane of the nose, mouth, and throat become extremely dry, and there is sometimes a singular bluish appearance of the lips.   The action of the kidneys is increased, and the drug is always to be found in the urine—indeed the chief point by which to ensure recognition of the poison is that the urine of any person suffering from the effects of belladonna (deadly nightshade) will dilate the pupil of the eye of another person or animal.

Treatment.—Give sulphate of copper or sulphate of zinc to empty the stomach, and then administer ten drops of the compound solution of iodine in a tablespoonful of water.   Opiates should be given and cold applications laid on the head.   If the strength fails, use stimulants—brandy or other alcoholic liquors.   The patient must lie down during the whole course of treatment, with the head low, so that the blood can flow toward the brain.   Hot coffee is a valuable aid, both as an antidote to the poison and on account of its stimulating properties.

STRAMONIUM, OR "JIMSON WEED."

The symptoms are the same as those produced by the poison of nightshade, and the same treatment should be pursued.

POKE BERRIES AND POKE ROOT.

This very familiar plant, though the young stalks are often used in the spring as "greens," is poisonous, and the effects doubtless would be more frequently felt if the active principle were not removed by boiling. The berries, however, are sometimes eaten by children.

Symptoms.—Excessive nausea, followed at last by vomiting, which is accompanied by great depression.   The pulse and breathing are very slow, and convulsions sometimes set in.

Treatment.—Empty the stomach at once by emetics and give liquor: fifteen drop doses of ether, or Hoffman's anodyne.   One grain dose of opium, or half a teaspoonful of laudanum, or half an ounce of paregoric may be used instead.

MONKSHOOD—WOLFSBANE.

This plant, though excessively poisonous, is cultivated in gardens for the sake of its beautiful blue flowers. When it grows wild, it has sometimes been mistaken for horse-radish, and eaten with dangerous results. It is used in medicine under the name of " aconite," and as some persons are very sensitive to its influence, cases of poisoning have occurred from taking the ordinary dose.

Symptoms.—When a fatal dose has been swallowed, the effects usually appear in from five to thirty minutes. First there is irritation and constriction of the heart, followed by tingling of the mouth, lips, and whole surface of the skin, like the pricking of chestnut-burrs, then great weakness, dimness of vision, difficult breathing, slowness of the pulse. Death is caused by the paralysis of the nerve centers.

Treatment.—Give anything containing tannin, either a solution of the tannin itself, a decoction of oak bark, or plenty of strong black tea. Administer an emetic of mustard, or sulphate of zinc, or use a stomach pump. Then milk or sweet oil should be given, and, if there is any danger of collapse, brandy, whiskey, or gin may be administered either by injection or by the mouth, and warm applications should be made to the hands, feet, spine, and stomach. It is absolutely necessary for the sufferer to lie down ; on no account must he or she rise or even sit up.

HEMLOCK OR CONIUM.

This plant, known in the most ancient times, is a native of Europe, whence it was brought to this country. It flowers in July and emits a strong mouse-like odor, long inhalation of which produces symptoms of poisoning.

Symptoms.—Weakness of the limbs, drooping of the eye-lids, drowsiness, and dizziness. The utterance is affected, and if the dose has been fatal, paralysis of the extremities follows and convulsions set in.

Treatment.—Tannin, strong tea, decoction of oak-bark, aqua ammonia, diluted with six times its bulk of water, or, if that is not at hand, a few drops of lye in plenty of water. Tickle the throat to produce vomiting, give strong coffee and compel the patient to take plenty of exercise.

DIGITALIS.

The common name is fox-glove,—the extract from the plant is known in medicine as digitalis—and it is classed among cumulative poisons, hence the danger in using it of sometimes finding it produce the effects of an over-dose.

Symptoms.—Vomiting, pain in the bowels, and purging. The grass-green color of the matter thrown off is said to be a distinctive symptom. Sometimes these symptoms immediately follow the dose, sometimes a considerable interval of time elapses. The most marked symptom is the extreme depression of the action of the heart, the pulse becomes irregular, at times almost imperceptible, the pupils are dilated, and the vision is dimmed or fails entirely. Death usually results suddenly from stoppage of the heart, caused by some trifling exertion, such as an attempt to sit up in the bed.

Treatment.—First get rid of the poison by giving emetics, warm mustard water, ipecac, etc.,—tickling the throat or using the stomach-pump; tannin or strong tea, paregoric or laudanum, wine, and large quantities of strong coffee are recommended. The patient must be kept constantly lying down, and not permitted to rise or sit up in the bed.

TOBACCO.

The first effects produced by the use of this plant have been experienced by almost every smoker.

Symptoms.—Nausea, purging, weakness, trembling, and profuse perspiration. When a fatal dose has been taken, there is also burning pain in the stomach, while the other symptoms increase. The body begins to grow cold, the trembling fits are more frequent, spasms supervene, and finally convulsions and death.

Treatment.—The first thing to be done when a large dose has been swallowed is to empty the stomach by a dose of sulphate of zinc, or any other means that may be convenient, or with a stomach-pump. Then administer tannin or strong tea—which contains it—followed by iodide of potassium in ten grain doses, or five drop doses of compound solution of iodine, well diluted with water. Brandy and ten drop doses of ammonia are beneficial in stimulating the circulation. Injections of strychnine and artificial respiration may be resorted to in extreme cases.

ARNICA.

This is a common household remedy, though of somewhat doubtful value.

Symptoms.—On first swallowing arnica there is a burning sensation in the mouth and throat, followed by greatly increased secretion of saliva. Nausea and vomiting follow, accompanied by diarrhœa, like that which attends cholera. Extreme depression of the whole system follows the first increase of respiration, circulation, and temperature, and is accompanied by violent headache, dilated pupils, and paralysis of the muscles.

STRYCHNINE—STRYCHNIA.

This poison acts upon the nervous system and throws the patient into convulsions. The time between swallowing the poison and feeling the effects varies according to the form in which it has been taken. If a solution is used, it speedily begins its deadly action on the spinal cord; if mixed with food, a longer time is necessary. If an emetic is to be of any service in cases of poisoning from strychnine, it must be administered immediately, as the convulsions prevent swallowing.

OPIUM.

This is one of the poisons most frequently taken, both from design, because it is supposed to produce an easy death, and from mistake because it is so much used as a medicine.

Symptoms.—Very soon after taking a large dose of opium the patient is overwhelmed by a stupor against which he vainly struggles and, unless some counteracting remedy is promptly given, death soon ensues.

Treatment.—There is no known antidote to opium. The first step to be taken is to administer a prompt emetic. Ten grains of sulphate of copper or a scruple of sulphate of zinc will answer, but if these cannot be had, give three tablespoonfuls of mustard in a quart of water, or the same amount of salt instead of the mustard. Keep the patient moving about, compelling exertion by every possible means, and when there is no farther hope of removing the poison, give a cathartic. If this latter attempt to clear the stomach and bowels proves thoroughly successful— otherwise it would be a fatal mistake—give some acid drink, a glass of vinegar and water or lemonade, followed by a cup of hot, strong coffee, without sugar or cream, every half hour, gradually lessening the quantity and frequency of the dose. Finally, after the effects of the drug have wholly passed away, let the patient sleep.

MORPHINE

This is the active principle of opium, of which it constitutes about ten per cent. It bears a close resemblance to quinine, which has been the cause of frequent mistakes.

Symptoms.—The same as opium, and the treatment is the same.

LAUDANUM.

This drug varies in strength from the plain tincture of opium to "black drop."

Symptoms and Treatment.—Same as for opium.

PAREGORIC.

This is camphorated tincture of opium, and is so weak that it is rarely taken in over-doses except by delicate children. Paregoric forms the basis of " soothing syrups."

Symptoms and Treatment.—Same as for opium.

MINERAL POISONS.

PHOSPHORUS.

This, one of the most fatal drugs known, is the principal ingredient in ordinary matches, and also in many of the rat and insect poisons in common use. It is slow in operation—death resulting in from two to three or four weeks after taking the poison—a fortnight being the most common period.

Symptoms.—These develop more slowly when the poison has been absorbed from matches than when it has been taken in the form of the various vermin exterminators so commonly sold. A sensation of nausea and burning, followed by vomiting, are the first symptoms. The odor of phosphorus can be frequently perceived in the matter ejected from the stomach, and it is often luminous in the dark. The stomach is painful and tender to the touch, and these sensations, with the vomiting, usually continue several days, at which time the matter thrown off contains particles not unlike coffee-grounds in appearance, constituting what is termed " black vomit." The patient may have either constipation, diarrhœa, or dysentery, and the matter cast off from the bowels may or may not be luminous in the dark. Hemorrhage from all the mucous surfaces is very common, the hands and feet become insensible, and afterwards paralyzed. Sometimes there is violent delirium, and death is usually preceded by convulsions.

Treatment.—The hope of success in saving the patient after the more serious symptoms appear is extremely slight, but if the antidotes are given early enough, the chance of prevention is very fair, especially if the poison has been taken in the solid form.

As soon as it is known that phosphorus has been swallowed, give at once in large quantities its antidote, sulphate of copper (blue vitriol), so that it may perform the double work of antidote and emetic. After the stomach has been thus thoroughly emptied, administer hydrated magnesia to cause purging, and then give small doses of the sulphate of copper. *Acid French oil of turpentine*, if obtainable, is an excellent antidote. The rectified oil, known as the spirits of turpentine, is useless. Of course, as in all cases of accident and injury, a physician should be summoned as quickly as possible.

ARSENIC.

This poison, taken in large doses, causes nausea and vomiting, which should be increased by giving ipecac, mustard and water, or salt and water.

Symptoms.—Vomiting, purging—the discharge mixed with blood—difficulty of breathing, low, feeble pulse, intense thirst, and cold extremities. If the dose is fatal, convulsions follow.

Treatment.—Large doses of chalk or magnesia, mixed with water, sugar and linseed oil, or chalk and sweet oil, should be frequently repeated for the purpose of coating the lining membrane of the stomach, and thus preventing the action of the poison. Then procure as quickly as possible, hydrated sesquioxide of iron. But, as it is absolutely necessary that this should be fresh, it is better to make it. To do this obtain from the druggist several ounces of the *Tersulphate of Iron ;* or, if that cannot be had, the *Persulphate of Iron* will answer. Put it in a glass and pour over it magnesia, soda, or ammonia. The former, as it is also an antidote, is best for the purpose. Strain the mixture through a cloth—a handkerchief will do—and give a tablespoonful or even more of the paste which will remain in the cloth. This substance is the hydrated sesquioxide of iron, and is a specific antidote to the arsenic.

If only a small dose of the poison has been swallowed, or if the treatment has been sufficiently prompt, the violent symptoms will soon pass away, after which broth or any light food may be taken. The inflammation of the stomach and bowels which will remain requires the same treatment as inflammation from any other cause; but chronic inflammation or permanent paralytic results may follow.

PARIS GREEN.

This salt of arsenic is very commonly used to destroy bugs and insects, and many cases of poisoning have resulted. The symptoms and treatment are the same as for arsenic.

Test.—A simple way of discovering whether a person has been poisoned by arsenic is to throw some of the matter ejected on a hot iron—it the fumes give out an odor resembling garlic, the presence of arsenic may be confidently believed.

COPPER.

Many cases of poisoning proceed from having eaten food cooked in copper vessels which, having been left with grease or acid standing in them, collect what is known as " verdigris," acetate of copper, or blue vitriol (sulphate of copper) a very poisonous substance which, being taken into the stomach with the food, instantly causes severe illness.

Another source of trouble arises from the practice of putting copper coins into a jar with vinegar pickles to improve their color.

Symptoms.—Severe pains in the stomach, nausea, and vomiting, the matter ejected being tinged with green or blue and tasting of copper.

Treatment.—After the stomach has been emptied by means of an emetic or stomach pump, mix the *whites* of half a dozen eggs in a quart of water and give the patient a wine-glassful every three or four minutes. When the whole has been taken, give a dose of some cathartic and apply cloths wet in hot water to allay the inflammation.

BLUE VITRIOL OR SULPHATE OF COPPER.

This is used in many disinfecting fluids, and cases of poisoning by them sometimes occur. The symptoms and treatment are the same as for copper.

MERCURY.

This is a metal very useful in medicine, yet chronic poisoning by the drug is not uncommon when given by a physician's prescription, though, occurring under his eye, it is easily checked. Ointments in which mercury forms a large ingredient, such as " blue ointment " and " red ointment " are often used without prescription, as are also the favorite cathartic medicines, blue mass and calomel. It is also used in manufactures, gilding, mirror-making, etc., and as it gives off fumes at a very low temperature, it is inhaled by persons using it and serious cases of poisoning have followed.

Symptoms.—The general symptoms are headache, loss of memory, trembling, partial loss of control over the muscles, convulsions, and finally insanity. Persons whose occupations oblige them to handle the metal should be watchful of such warnings. But before any extreme points have been reached, the symptoms of mercurial poisoning become unmistakable. The gums grow tender to the touch, the glands in the neck and throat swell, the breath is offensive, and a blue or dark slate-colored line forms between the teeth and the gums. These effects are known as salivation.

Treatment.—Where the case is chronic, stop the administration of the poison. Let the patient take nourishing food and regular exercise. A dose of from five to ten grains of iodide of potassium should be given every day.

CORROSIVE SUBLIMATE.

This mercurial salt is an intensely active poison.

Symptoms.—A feeble rapid pulse, extreme thirst, great difficulty of breathing and a bloody discharge from the stomach. It is so commonly used as a vermin and insect exterminator that accidents from its use are frequent.

Treatment.—Excite vomiting as quickly as possible by giving large draughts of warm (*not hot*) water and sugar, and by tickling the back part of the throat. Then mix the whites of a dozen eggs in a quart of water, and let the patient drink a wineglassful every two or three minutes. Fortunately white of egg is an antidote, and one which can generally be quickly and easily obtained.

RED PRECIPITATE.

Red oxide of mercury is in very common use as a poison for insects, and is sometimes swallowed by accident. The symptoms and treatment are the same as for corrosive sublimate.

LEAD.

There are many ways in which the poison may be conveyed into the system—by drinking water that has flowed through lead pipes, by eating food which has been put up in soldered jars, or, as in the case of painters, by absorbing it through the pores of the skin. When taken in the latter form, it gradually accumulates until it results in *chronic lead poisoning*, known as "lead colic" and "lead palsy."

Treatment.—First cut off the supply of poison, from whatever source it may come. Then give regularly aperient carbonated drinks, keep the bowels open by mild saline cathartics, and doses of from five to ten grains of potassium iodide, dissolved in a tablespoonful of water, administered three times each day till a cure is effected.

SUGAR OF LEAD.

Cases of poisoning by this salt, "acetate of lead," are quite frequent, as large quantities of it are contained in nearly all eye-washes and many lotions.

Symptoms.—Acute pains in the stomach and bowels, with excessive nausea and vomiting.

Treatment.—Give alum, carbonate of soda, or carbonate of potash, in warm water in large draughts to cause vomiting, which will afford relief. If these should fail, give a scruple of the sulphate of zinc (known as white vitriol), which, combining with the lead, will form a harmless salt; and destroy the activity of the poison, which may then be removed from the system by means of emetics and cathartics.

ZINC (INCLUDING CHLORIDE, ACETATE, AND SULPHATE OF ZINC).

Large doses of any of these zinc salts act as irritant and feebly caustic poisons.

Symptoms.—Burning and constriction in the throat, burning sensations in the stomach, nausea, strong metallic taste in the mouth, vomiting, profuse cold perspiration, cramps, and occasionally other nervous symptoms.

Treatment.—Like all irritant poisons, the remedies must be very promptly given. The antidotes are soap and water, baking soda in water, in the proportion of one tablespoonful to a pint, lime water, strong tea, tannin, or a decoction of oak bark, followed by mucilaginous drinks, whites of eggs, or milk to soothe the inflammation. Stimulants may be required later.

ANTIMONY—TARTAR EMETIC.

Tartar is a compound of antimony and potash, and was formerly often used in medical practice.

Symptoms.—The name of the drug being derived from its powerful emetic effects, one of the most prominent symptoms, as may be supposed, is persistent vomiting. This is followed by purging and, if violent, the discharges bear a close resemblance to the so called "rice-water" excreta of cholera. The face becomes pallid, the skin icy cold, the pulse is weak and irregular, and there is great nervous and muscular prostration. Larger doses cause still severer symptoms—intense pain at the pit of the stomach, a shrunken, anxious expression of the countenance, coldness of the breath, loss of the voice, and cramps make the case bear a close resemblance to Asiatic cholera.

Treatment.—The stomach will probably empty itself by the action of the drug, therefore no other emetic need be administered. Strong tea, decoction of tan bark, catechu, rhubarb, or best of all, tannin, should be administered at once. The application of heat to the hands, feet, spine, and pit of the stomach, and small doses of diluted brandy may also be advisable.

NITRATE OF SILVER—LUNAR CAUSTIC.

It sometimes happens that in touching ulcera in the throat with lunar caustic a piece is broken off and swallowed. In case of such an accident, instantly give the antidote, which is common table salt. Dissolve in warm water, and let the patient swallow enough to cause vomiting.

MISCELLANEOUS.

IODINE.

This is so commonly used as a medicine that accidents from it are frequent.

Symptoms.—The yellow stain of the preparation may often be seen about the lips or on the clothing. When swallowed it causes a sensation of burning in the stomach, and heat in the throat, and the pungent metallic taste is also characteristic.

Treatment.—The antidote for iodine is starch, which may be administered in the form of ordinary starch and water, flour and water, or mixed arrow-root—whichever is handiest. Vomiting should then be caused by warm water mixed with mustard, or by tickling the throat with a finger or a feather, if needful. Iodide of starch is deep blue, so the matter ejected will be of that color. Milk should be given afterward until there are no farther symptoms of inflammation.

Symptoms.—These are very marked. The face grows pale, the muscles rigid, the heart's action quick and stiff. During the paroxysms, which last some time, respiration is suspended, and the muscles are drawn into knots all over the body.

Treatment.—Remove all tight clothing from the sufferer's body, and lay him on his back in a cool, quiet place. Then fit a paper cone over his face, and in the top of it put a sponge or handkerchief saturated with chloroform, so that the air he breathes will be charged with it. Keep him under the influence until, when the chloroform is removed, the spasmodic symptoms do not return. If the dose has been large it will be several weeks before the patient can move about, and he will doubtless be obliged to take, for some time, a tonic composed of phosphates of iron, quinine, and strychnine. If chloroform cannot be had, use opium, morphine, ether, chloral, or any narcotic at hand, until the chloroform can be procured.

HYDROCYANIC ACID—PRUSSIC ACID—CYANIDE OF POTASSIUM—CYANIDE OF SILVER.

The cyanides of silver and potassium owe their poisonous qualities to prussic acid, the deadliest poison with which any human being is likely to come into contact. Few people have anything to do with the acid itself; but the cyanide of silver is largely used by photographers, and the cyanide of potassium, in spite of its deadly qualities, is sometimes applied to removing stains from linen; so poisoning by prussic acid is always a possibility. The flavor of cherry-laurel water, oil of bitter almonds, peach-kernels, etc., is caused by this poison, and their use may be dangerous—indeed, it is by no means uncommon to have children made ill by eating peach-kernels.

Symptoms.—In most cases poisoning by either the acid or its salts causes instant collapse and death, so that the only thing to be done is to decide the cause by means of the odor of bitter almonds. Small doses cause excessive weakness, nausea, and great nervous depression.

Treatment.—Ammonia, well diluted, followed by oxide of iron, should be administered immediately, and artificial respiration should be practiced, if necessary. Then give some hot stimulant, such as brandy and water. Perfect rest and quiet are needful.

CORROSIVE ACIDS—NITRIC, MURIATIC OR HYDROCHLORIC, SULPHURIC.

These acids, in the strict sense of the word, are not poisons; but in their concentrated form they destroy the tissues with which they come in contact, and are thus more fatal than many real poisons.

Symptoms.—Nitric acid stains the skin and tissues yellow; sulphuric acid turns them black. The physical sensations are intense burning pain in the mouth, throat, and stomach, accompanied by the general effects of the corrosive poisons.

Treatment.—This must be *immediate.* Give chalk and water, soap, magnesia, lime water, soda, (baking or washing) diluted lye or, if nothing else can be had, calsomine knocked from the wall and pounded up in water. These, by forming a chemical combination with the acid, neutralize its action. Then give milk, eggs, and oil, to protect the tissues. To counteract the depressing effects, give opium or morphia injections of beef-tea and brandy. Nay, it may even be necessary to inject ammonia directly into the veins, to save the patient from collapse.

CARBOLIC ACID.

This is in such general use as a disinfectant, a preventive of decomposition, and, in a weak solution, a liniment for bruises, that accidents from swallowing it are by no means infrequent.

Symptoms.—Strong carbolic acid softens the tissue of the mucous membrane till it presents a greyish-white appearance. The physical sensations are severe pain and burning in the throat and stomach, swelling of the tongue, dizziness, and finally convulsions.

Treatment.—Large quantities of olive and castor oil should be swallowed, with frequent and abundant drinks of sweet milk. If neither sweet oil nor castor oil are on hand, any other bland oil will answer the purpose till the doctor comes.

OXALIC ACID.

This preparation is familiar to housewives under the name of "salt of sorrel," "salt of lemon," and being often kept on hand for the removal of ink and other stains, is sometimes swallowed by mistake.

Symptoms.—Like other corrosive acids, oxalic acid poisoning produces burning of the throat and stomach, profuse vomiting, whose matter is sometimes mixed with blood, and extreme debility, whose effects almost amount to paralysis, while the pulse becomes so weak as to be nearly imperceptible. A strong dose will destroy life in half an hour.

Treatment.—Give lime, washing or baking soda, chalk, magnesia, or ammonia diluted with water, every three or four minutes. Magnesia is best, because it acts so quickly that no emetic is needed. Still, it is wiser, under any circumstances, to thoroughly empty the stomach by means of an emetic.

LYE—CAUSTIC SODA—CAUSTIC POTASH.

Deaths have occurred by accidental swallowing of these caustics, which act like hartshorn, only with much more quickness and severity, affecting the whole mouth, throat, and stomach. Blood appears in the discharges from the stomach and bowels, followed by cold sweat and hiccough, the immediate precursors of death.

HARTSHORN—AMMONIA—AQUA AMMONIA—SPIRITS OF AMMONIA.

This well-known fluid, if swallowed instantly, acts on the mouth, tongue, and throat, violently swelling and inflaming the mucous lining.

On reaching the stomach it quickly enters into the circulation, increasing the heart's action, and speedily causing fever.

Treatment.—When a dose of ammonia has been swallowed, follow it as soon as possible with vinegar, and then give sweet-oil, flaxseed tea, mucilage, or other familiar demulcents. A cold bath may be needed to subdue the feverish symptoms.

POISONING BY DECAYED MEAT, ETC.

Certain changes which occur in animal substances cause severe cases of poisoning. Sausages, meat-pies, fish, cheese, and various other foods have occasioned serious trouble.

Symptoms.—Nausea and headache. In fish poisoning dizziness and nettle rash usually appear. Vomiting is common, followed sometimes by collapse.

Treatment.—Emetics, alum, or mustard and water, followed by a dose of Epsom salts, followed by Vichy water, seltzer, or anything of the sort.

The Mother's Medicine Chest.

N travelling or for use at home, it is very desirable to have at hand a few remedies valuable in accidents or sudden sickness.

A small box will hold the following articles:

Absorbent cotton.

Sticking plaster—rubber plaster is best, because it requires neither heat nor moisture for its application.

Bandages of muslin or flannel.

Thread and needles.

Pins.

Vaseline.

1. Aromatic spirits of ammonia.
2. Tincture of Assafœtida.
3. Oil of cloves.
4. Hoffman's Anodyne.
5. Syrup of Ipecac.
6. Laudanum.
7. Magnesia.
8. Mustard.
9. Paregoric.
10. Spiced syrup of rhubarb.
11. Turpentine.

To these may be added, if there is room, camphor-water, essence of ginger, lime-water, and sweet spirits of nitre.

QUANTITY.

The best quantity of the eleven medicines first named would be two fluid ounces—with the exception of No. 3 (the oil of cloves) a fluid drachm of which would suffice, No. 7 (magnesia) and No. 8 (mustard) one ounce of which would be enough. See that the bottles containing the laudanum

221

and paragoric are of an entirely different shape from those which hold the
other medicines, and that they, and also the bottle containing the oil of
cloves, are marked poison. By way of still farther precaution, each one
should have tied around the neck a ribbon or string which can be felt in
the dark. See that the proper dose is marked on the label of each bottle.

DIRECTIONS FOR USE OF MEDICINES.

1. *Ammonia.*—Aromatic spirits of ammonia, not hartshorn, is extremely valuable to relieve sickness at the stomach, and even vomiting in
nervousness. Give an adult twenty-five drops, a child ten drops, in a
wine-glassful of water. This may be given every ten minutes, almost
without limit.

2. *Assafœtida.* Tincture of assafœtida is a tonic to the nerves, and
also very soothing to the bowels. Dose for an adult, one teaspoonful; for
a child, twenty drops, in a tablespoonful of water. It can often be used
as an injection, when it could not be given by the mouth. In the latter case
put for an adult a tablespoonful, and for a child, a teaspoonful in a small
tea-cupful of warm water.

3. *Cloves.* Oil of cloves is an excellent remedy to use as a local application in toothache, and also,—given in doses of three drops for an
adult, and one drop for a child—affords speedy relief for indigestion. It
may be administered rubbed into a little sugar or in a teaspoonful of
sweet oil.

Hoffmann's Anodyne is admirable in cases of hysterics, nervous fright,
or chills. The dose for an adult is one teaspoonful in a wineglassful of
water. It is a medicine rarely needed by children; but in the case of a
very nervous child, half the dose for an adult can be given.

Ipecac. Syrup of Ipecac is an emetic; but must be used in abundant quantities. The dose for an adult is a large tablespoonful, and for a
child as near a teaspoonful as possible; there should be no hesitation in
giving a sufficiently large dose. It is often of great service in cases of
poisoning, convulsions, croup, whooping-cough, and asthma.

Laudanum. Laudanum is the tincture of opium, and has all its
properties. It is one of the most valuable drugs, though a dangerous
one. But there is no fear of poisoning with any preparation of opium if
care is taken not to give more than the ordinary dose, not to give oftener
than once in half an hour, and to stop as soon as the pain lessens or there
are any symptoms of drowsiness. Occasionally small doses will cause
great alarm; but it may be considered safe to give twenty drops of
laudanum to any adult who is suffering severe pain and to repeat the

dose every half-hour till the pain is lessened or symptoms of drowsiness appear. One of the signs of the effect of opium on the system is a contraction of the pupil of the eye. On the appearance of this symptom, the use of any preparation of opium should be stopped.

One drop of laudanum given every hour will often prove successful in speedily checking diarrhœa. Yet ten or fifteen drops may be given to an adult, *after each movement*, if the smaller quantity is not sufficient.

Pure laudanum is the best possible application to cuts and bruises. A soft cloth soaked in it can be bound on, and occasionally wetted with it, without removal. It quiets pain and promotes healing. The same treatment is very soothing in faceache, toothache, and earache, even in rheumatism and neuralgia.

7. *Magnesia.* Magnesia is a remedy usually given to children for the relief of constipation. The dose is one teaspoonful, which may be administered either in water or milk. For sour stomach a pinch is sufficient.

8. *Mustard.* In using ground mustard for plasters, always mix it with an equal quantity of flour. Even then its effect is speedy, and it should be removed in a few minutes or as soon as the skin begins to redden. When it is necessary to leave a mustard plaster on for more than a few minutes, make it in the proportion of one part mustard to three or four of flour. Care should be taken to remove it as soon as the skin is red, it must not be allowed to make a blister.

As an emetic, put a teaspoonful of the ground seeds into a teacupful of lukewarm water.

9. *Puregoric.*—An opium preparation, containing, besides other ingredients, some camphor. It is the best preparation for children because the dose can be more easily measured than laudanum. An infant a few hours old can stand three drops, and in a few days, five. Any time after six months, twenty may be given. An adult can take a teaspoonful. It can be used in all cases for which laudanum is recommended.

10. *Rhubarb.*—Spiced rhubarb is an excellent laxative for the bowels. A teaspoonful is the dose for an adult or a small child. It is valuable in the early stages of diarrhœa in children, as it has a healing, soothing influence.

11. *Turpentine.*—Spirits or oil of turpentine can be used whenever mustard has been recommended for external application. Dip a soft flannel or muslin cloth in turpentine, wring out nearly dry, lay on the surface, and cover with oiled silk or a few thicknesses of dry cloth to prevent co-operation.

Red Pepper may sometimes be applied instead of mustard, though its action is more energetic. When moistened and applied to the skin, red pepper first causes a sensation of warmth and later of intense fiery burning. If left on long enough it will raise a blister, but this should be carefully avoided. Red pepper may be used in cases of colic or cholera morbus, as it quiets pain by acting as a counter irritant, and stimulates the nervous and circulatory systems. In nausea it sometimes relieves by the latter process.

LOOKING FOR PAPA.

Care and Food of Infants.

PROMINENT and very successful English physician, Dr. Chavasse, sums up the result of years of practice in the following:

FOUR RULES FOR THE TREATMENT OF INFANTS.

1. Plenty of water for the skin.
2. Plenty of milk for the stomach.
3. Plenty of fresh air for the lungs.
4. Plenty of sleep for the brain

Without an abundance of these four requisites, he says, perfect health is utterly impossible.

In reference to the first rule, he opposes the use of cold water for bathing, and denies its strengthening power, stating that it is likely to cause a chill and subsequent inflammation. Hot water he also disapproves, as having a tendency to weaken the child and make it more liable to contract diseases, and recommends as best for the purpose, tepid water used with Castile soap, which is less irritating to the skin than ordinary soaps; care being taken not to let it get into the eyes, lest it should produce inflammation, or at any rate smarting.

A sponge is better than flannel, because it enables a little stream of water to be poured over the child, thus acting like a miniature shower bath. In giving general directions for the infant's bath, he says:

"A babe ought, every morning of his life, to be thoroughly washed from head to foot; and this can only be properly done by putting him bodily either into a tub, or into a bath, or into a large nursery-basin half filled with water. The head, before placing him in the bath, should be first wetted (but not dried); then immediately put him into the water, and, with a piece of flannel well soaked, cleanse his whole body, particularly his arm-pits, between his thighs, his groins, and his hams; then take a large sponge in hand, and allow the water from it, well filled, to stream all over his body, particularly over his back and loins. Let this advice be well observed, and you will find the plan most strengthening to your child. The skin must, after every bath, be thoroughly but quickly dried with warm, dry, soft towels, first enveloping the child in one, and then gently absorbing the moisture with the towel, not roughly scrubbing and rubbing his tender skin as though a horse were being rubbed down.

"The ears must after each ablution be carefully and well dried with a soft dry napkin; inattention to this advice has sometimes caused a gathering in the ear—a painful and distressing complaint; and at othe. times it has produced deafness.

"Directly after the infant is dried, all the parts that are at all likely to be chafed ought to be well powdered. After he is well dried. and powdered, the chest, the back, the bowels, and the limbs should be gently rubbed, taking care not to expose him unnecessarily during such friction. He ought to be partially washed every evening; indeed it may be necessary to use a sponge and a little warm water frequently during the day, namely, each time after the bowels have been relieved. *Cleanliness is one of the grand incentives to health,* and therefore cannot be too strongly insisted upon. If more attention were paid to this subject, children would be more exempt from chafings, "breakings-out," and consequent suffering, than they at present are. After the second month, if the babe be delicate. the addition of two handfuls of table-salt to the water he is washed with in the morning will tend to brace and strengthen him.

"With regard to the best powder to dust an infant with, there is nothing better for general use than starch—the old-fashioned starch *made of wheaten-flour*—reduced by means of a pestle and mortar to a fine powder; or violet powder, which is nothing more than finely powdered starch scented, and which may be procured of any respectable chemist. Some mothers are in the habit of using white-lead; but as this is a poison, it ought *on no account* to be resorted to.[1]

"Remember that excoriations are generally owing to the want of water—to the want of an abundance of water. After sponging the parts where the excoriations appear with tepid *rain* water, holding him over his tub, and allowing the water from a well-filled sponge to stream over the parts, and then drying them with a soft napkin (not rubbing, but gently dabbing with the napkin), there is nothing better than dusting the parts frequently with finely powdered native carbonate of zinc. The best way of using this powder is tying up a little of it in a piece of muslin, and then gently dabbing the parts with it.

"An infant who is every morning well soused and well swilled with water, seldom suffers either from excoriations or from any other of the numerous skin diseases. Cleanliness, then, is the grand preventive of, and the best remedy for, excoriations. Naaman the Syrian was ordered 'to wash and be clean,' and he was healed, "and his flesh came again like unto the flesh of a little child, and he was clean."[2] This was, of course, a miracle; but how often does water, without any special intervention, act miraculously both in preventing and in curing skin diseases!

"An infant's clothes, napkins especially, ought never to be washed with soda; the washing of napkins with soda is apt to produce excoriations and breakings-out. 'As washer-women often deny that they use soda, it can be easily detected by simply soaking a clean napkin in fresh water and then tasting the water; if it be brackish and salt, soda has been employed.'"[3]

In regard to feeding infants, Dr. Chavasse is most positive in his opinion that nothing can be so beneficial as natural food supplied by the mother's milk. Next in order he recommends a wet nurse, then asses' milk—which, however, is difficult to obtain—and finally goat's milk. Either of the latter should be milked fresh, as wanted, and should be given by means of a feeding bottle.

If neither asses' nor goat's milk can be had, the following recipe should be given from the very commencement.

New milk, the produce of one *healthy* cow,
Warm water, of each, equal parts;
Table salt,[4] a few grains;
Lump sugar, a sufficient quantity to slightly sweeten it.

---

[1] In one case related by Koop (*Journ. de Pharm.*, xx. 603), a child was destroyed by it.
[2] 2 Kings, v. 13, 14.
[3] Communicated by Sir Charles Locock.
[4] Liebig, the great chemist, asserts that a small quantity of table salt to the food is essential to the health of children.

The milk itself ought not to be heated over the fire,[1] but should, as above directed, be warmed by the water; it must, morning and evening, be had fresh and fresh. The milk and water should be of the same temperature as the mother's milk, that is to say, at about ninety to ninety-five degrees Fahrenheit. It ought to be given by means of a feeding-bottle, and care must be taken to *scald* the bottle out twice a day, for if attention be not paid to this point the delicate stomach of an infant is soon disordered. As he grows older the milk should be gradually increased, and the water decreased, until nearly all milk be given.

"There will, in many cases, be quite sufficient nourishment in the above; I have known some robust infants brought up on it alone. But if it should not agree with the child, or if there should not be sufficient nourishment in it, then some of the following foods may be tried. The one that has been found the most generally useful is made by boiling the crumb of bread for two hours in water, taking special care it does not burn; then add a little lump sugar or brown sugar, if the bowels are constipated, to make it more palatable, add also a little new milk, the milk of one cow increasing, as the babe grows older, until it is nearly all milk, using only sufficient water to boil the bread; the milk should be poured boiling hot upon the bread.

"(2) Cut thin slices of bread into a basin, cover the bread with cold water, put it in an oven for two hours to bake; take it out, beat the bread up with a fork, sweeten slightly, and add a little milk. This is an excellent food.

"(3) If neither of the above should agree with the infant, though if properly made they almost always do—tous-les-mois—may be given. This tous-les-mois is the starch obtained from the tuberous roots of various species of canna, and is imported from the West Indies. It is very similar to arrow-root and is probably called tous-les-mois because it is good to be eaten all the year round.

"(4) Another good food is the following: Take about a pound of flour, put it into a cloth, tie it up tightly, place it in a saucepanful of water, and let it boil for four or five hours; then take it out, peel off the outer rind, and the inside will be found quite dry, which grate.

"(5) Another way of preparing an infant's food is to bake flour (biscuit-flour) in a slow oven, until it is of a light fawn color.

"(6) An excellent food for a baby is baked crumbs of bread. Crumb some bread on a plate; put it a little distance from the fire to dry, when

---

[1] It now and then happens that if the milk be not boiled, the motions of an infant are offensive; *when such is the case* let the milk be boiled, but not otherwise.

dry, rub the crumbs into a mortar, and reduce them to fine powder; pass them through a sieve, set them into a slow oven, and let them bake until a light fawn color. A small quantity, either of the boiled or of the baked flour, or of the baked crumbs of bread ought to be made into food in the same way as gruel is made, and should have a little milk added and be slightly sweetened, according to the state of the bowels—with either lump or brown sugar.

"Baked flour sometimes causes constipation. In such cases a mixture of baked flour and prepared oatmeal in the proportion of two parts of flour to one of oatmeal, will be both nourishing and regulating to the bowels. "One tablespoonful of it, mixed with a quarter of a pint of milk, or milk and water, when well boiled, flavored, and sweetened with white sugar, produces a thick, nourishing, and delicious food for infants or invalids."

"(7.) The following is also a good and nourishing food for a baby: Soak, for an hour, some *best* rice in cold water; strain, and add fresh water to the rice; then let it simmer till it will pulp through a sieve; put the pulp and the water in a saucepan, with a lump or two of sugar, and again let it simmer for a quarter of an hour; a portion of this should be mixed with one-third of fresh milk, so as to make it of the consistence of good cream.

"(8.) If a child's bowels are relaxed and weak, the milk *must* be boiled. In such conditions, the following is a good food. Into five large spoonfuls of the purest water rub smoothly one dessertspoonful of fine flour Set over the fire five spoonfuls of new milk and put two bits of sugar into it; the moment it boils, pour it into the flour and water, and stir it over a slow fire twenty minutes.

"The above recipes give a large and thoroughly tested variety of foods from which to select, as it is sometimes difficult to find one that will suit; but as soon as any one of them is found to agree, keep to it. A baby requires simplicity in food.

"Another point to be remembered is the necessity of great care and attention being observed in the preparation of any of the above articles of diet. A babe's stomach is very delicate and will revolt at ill-made, lumpy, or burnt food. Great care ought also to be observed as to the cleanliness of the cooking utensils. The above directions require the strict supervision of the mother.

"Whatever artificial food is used should be given by means of a bottle, not only because it is a more natural way of feeding a baby, as it causes him to suck as though he were drawing from the mother's breast; but the act of sucking causes the salivary glands to press out their contents, which materially aids digestion.

"The food ought to be of the consistence of good cream and should be made fresh. It ought to be given milk-warm. Attention must be paid to the cleanliness of the vessel, and care should be taken that the milk be that of *one* cow and that it be new and of good quality, otherwise it will turn acid and sour, and disorder the stomach.

"Very little sugar should be used in the food, any large quantity injures the digestion. A small pinch of table salt should be added to whatever food is used.

"Nevertheless, a child is better *without artificial food* during the first three or four months of his life, then it will be desirable to feed him twice a day, so as to gradually prepare him to be weaned, if possible, at the end of nine months. In such cases the food mentioned above will be best for him, commencing *without* the cow's milk; but gradually adding it, as less mother's milk and more artificial food is given."

Under the third rule of "plenty of fresh air for the lungs," Dr. Chavasse recommends that a child should be taken out of doors in fine summer weather a fortnight after its birth. In winter it should not go under a month and then only in the middle of the day. After two months he should breathe the open air more regularly and, after the expiration of three months, the child should be carried out *every day*, even if it is wet under foot, provided it is fine above, and the wind is neither in an easterly nor in a northeasterly direction. He must of course be well clothed; but his face should not be covered with a veil or handkerchief when he is taken out of doors. Under such circumstances it is impossible for him to receive any benefit from the invigorating effects of the fresh air.

To secure "plenty of sleep for the brain," Rule 4, Dr. Chavasse directs that the child should be in a comfortably warm, but well-ventilated room, and laid in a cradle that has no head, or on a bed whose curtains are not drawn. "He should not have a handkerchief or veil laid over his face, as either will make the air impure. If flies annoy him, put a piece of net over him, as he can readily breathe through its meshes.

"The dress, whenever a child is put down to sleep, should be loose in every part; be careful that there are no strings nor bands to cramp him

"In conclusion: If an infant from his birth be properly managed,—if he has an abundance of fresh air for his lungs,—if he has plenty of exercise for his muscles (by allowing him to kick and sprawl on the floor),— if he has a good swilling and sousing of water for his skin,—if, during the *early* months of his life, he has nothing but the mother's milk for his

stomach,—he will require very little medicine—the less the better! He
does not want his stomach to be made into a doctor's shop! The grand
thing is not to take every opportunity of administering physic, but of
using every means of withholding it! A babe who is always, without
rhyme or reason, being physicked, is sure to be puny, delicate, and un
healthy, and is ready, at any moment, to drop into an untimely grave!

Directions for the Management of the Sick-room and the Nursing of Children.

N sickness select a large and lofty room; if in the town, the back of the the house will be preferable—in order to keep the patient free from noise and bustle—as a sick-chamber cannot be kept too quiet. Be sure that there be a chimney in the room—as there ought to be in *every* room in the house—and that it be not stopped, as it will help to carry off the impure air of the apartment. Keep the chamber *well ventilated*, by, from time to time, opening the window. The air of the apartment cannot be too pure; therefore, let the evacuations from the bowels be instantly removed, either to a distant part of the house, or to an out-house, or to the cellar, as it might be necessary to keep them for the medical man's inspection.

Let there be a frequent change of linen, as in sickness it is even more necessary than in health, more especially if the complaint be fever. In an attack of fever clean sheets ought, every other day, to be put on the bed; clean body-linen every day. A frequent change of linen in sickness is most refreshing.

If the complaint be fever, a fire in the grate will not be necessary. Should it be a case either of inflammation of the lungs or of the chest, a small fire in the winter time is desirable, keeping the temperature of the room as nearly as possible at 60° Fahrenheit. Bear in mind that a large fire in a sick-room cannot be too strongly condemned; for if there be fever —and there are scarcely any complaints without—a large fire only increases it. Small fires, in cases either of inflammation of the lungs or of the chest, in the winter time, encourage ventilation of the apartment, and thus carry off impure air. If it be summer time, of course fires would be improper. A thermometer is an indispensable requisite in a sick-room.

In fever, free and thorough ventilation is of vital importance, more especially in scarlet fever; then a patient cannot have too much air; in scarlet fever, for the first few days the windows, be it winter or summer, must, to the widest extent, be opened. The fear of the patient catching cold by doing so is one of the numerous prejudices and baseless fears that haunt the nursery, and the sooner it is exploded the better it will be for human life. The valances and bed-curtains ought to be removed, and there should be as little furniture in the room as possible.

If it be a case of measles, it will be necessary to adopt a different course; then the windows ought not to be opened, but the door must from time to time be left ajar. In a case of measles, if it be winter time, a *small* fire in the room will be necessary. In inflammation of the lungs or of the chest, the windows should not be opened, but the door ought occasionally to be left unfastened, in order to change the air and to make it pure. Remember, then, that ventilation, either by open window or by open door, is most necessary in all diseases. Ventilation is one of the best friends a doctor has.

In *fever*, do not load the bed with clothes; in the summer a sheet is sufficient, in the winter a sheet and a blanket.

In *fever*, do not be afraid of allowing the patient plenty either of cold water or of cold toast and water; Nature will tell him when he has had enough. In measles, let the chill be taken off the toast and water.

In *croup*, have always ready a plentiful supply of hot water, in case a warm bath might be required.

In *child-crowing*, have always in the sick-room a supply of cold water. ready at a moment's notice to dash upon the face.

In *fever*, do not let the little patient lie on the lap; he will rest more comfortably on a horse-hair mattress in his crib or cot. If he have pain in the bowels, the lap is most agreeable to him: the warmth of the body, either of the mother or of the nurse, soothes him; besides, if he be on the lap, he can be turned on his stomach and on his bowels, which often affords him great relief and comfort. If he be much emaciated, place a pillow upon the lap when he is nursed, and let him lie upon it.

In *head affections*, darken the room with a *green* calico blind; keep the chamber more than usually quiet; let what little talking is necessary be carried on in whispers, but the less of that the better; and in *head affections*, never allow smelling salts to be applied to the nose, as they only increase the flow of blood to the head, and consequently do harm.

It is often a good sign when a child, who is seriously ill, suddenly becomes cross. It is then he begins to feel his weakness, and to give vent to his feelings. "Children are most always cross when recovering from an illness, however patient they may have been during its severest moments, and the phenomenon is not by any means confined to children."[1]

---

[1] George McDonald, M.A.

A sick child must *not* be stuffed with *much* food at a time. He will take either a tablespoonful of new milk or a tablespoonful of chicken-broth every half hour, with greater advantage than a teacupful of either the one or the other every four hours, which large quantity would very probably be rejected from his stomach, and may cause the unfortunately treated child to die of starvation!

If a sick child be peevish, attract his attention either by a toy or by an ornament; if he be cross, win him over to good humor by love, affection, and caresses, but let it be done gently and without noise. Do not let visitors see him; they will only excite, distract, and irritate him, and help to consume the oxygen of the atmosphere, and thus rob the air of its exhilarating health-giving qualities and purity; a sick-room, therefore, is not a proper place either for visitors or for gossips.

In selecting a sick-nurse, let her be gentle, patient, cheerful, quiet, and kind, but firm withal; she ought to be neither old nor young; if she be old, she is often garrulous and prejudiced, and thinks too much of her trouble; if she be young, she is frequently thoughtless and noisy; therefore choose a middle-aged woman. Do not let there be in the sick-room more than, besides the mother, one efficient nurse; a great number can be of no service—they will only be in each other's way, and will distract the patient.

Let stillness, especially if the head be the part affected, reign in a sick-room. Creaking shoes[1] and rustling silk dresses ought not to be worn in sick-chambers—they are quite out of place there. If the child be asleep, or if he be dozing, perfect stillness must be enjoined, not even a whisper should be heard.

If there be other children, let them be removed to a distant part of the house; or, if the disease be of an infectious nature, let them be sent away from home altogether.

In all illnesses—and bear in mind the following is most important advice—a child must be encouraged to try and make water, whether he ask or not, at least four times during the twenty-four hours; and at any other time, if he expresses the slightest inclination to do so. I have known a little fellow to hold his water, to his great detriment, for twelve hours, because either the mother had in her trouble forgotten to inquire, or the child himself was either too ill or too indolent to make the attempt.

See that the physician's directions are, to the very letter, carried out. Do not fancy that you know better than he does, otherwise you have no

---

[1] Nurses at these times ought to wear slippers, and not shoes.

business to employ him. Let him, then, have your implicit confidence and your exact obedience. What you may consider a trifling matter may frequently be of the utmost importance, and may sometimes decide whether the case shall end in life or death !

COMPLAINTS IN WHICH WARM BATHS ARE BENEFICIAL.

Warm Baths.—1. Convulsions: 2. Pains in the bowels, known by the child drawing up his legs, screaming violently, etc.; 3. Restlessness from teething; 4. Flatulence. The warm bath acts as a fomentation to the stomach and the bowels, and gives ease where the usual remedies do not rapidly relieve.

Precautions to be Observed in Giving Warm Baths.—Carefully ascertain, before the child be immersed in the bath, that the water be neither too hot nor too cold. Carelessness, or over anxiety to put him in the water as quickly as possible, has frequently, from his being immersed in the bath when the water was too hot, caused him great pain and suffering. From 96 to 98 degrees of Fahrenheit is the proper temperature of a warm bath. If it be necessary to add fresh warm water, let him be either removed the while, or let it not be put in when very hot; for if boiling water be added to increase the heat of the bath, it naturally ascends, and may scald him. Again, let the fresh water be put in at as great a distance from him as possible. The usual time for him to remain in a bath is a quarter of an hour or twenty minutes. Let the chest and the bowels be rubbed with the hand while he is in the bath. Let him be immersed in the bath as high up as the neck, taking care that he be the while supported under the arm-pits, and that his head be also rested. As soon as he comes out of the bath he ought to be carefully but quickly rubbed dry; and, if it be necessary to keep up the action on the skin, he should be put to bed between the blankets; or, if the desired relief has been obtained, between the sheets, which ought to have been previously warmed, where, most likely, he will fall into a sweet, refreshing sleep.

Diseases of Children.

R. CHAVASSE, while strongly opposing the doctrine of a mother *treating* serious diseases, *except in urgent cases, where no physician can be obtained, and delay may mean death,* urges the necessity of her knowing the *symptoms* of disease. He asserts that if parents were better informed on such subjects many children's lives might be saved. By her knowledge of the symptoms, "aided by having the physician's advice in time, she would nip disease in the bud, and the fight might end in favor of life, for 'sickness is a fight between life and death.'"

Sir Charles Locock, an English medical authority in the department of children's diseases, also advocates the advantage of having a mother conversant with the actual treatment of some of the more urgent infantile ailments, stating that while it is excellent advice to caution parents not to supersede the doctor, and try to manage the case themselves, much valuable and irremediable time may be lost, when *a medical man is not to be had.* "Take a case of croup," he adds, "I can speak from my own experience when I say that an emetic, *given in time,* and repeated to free vomiting, will cut short *any* case of croup. Whenever any remedy is the more valuable by its being administered *in time,* it is surely wise to give directions for its use, though in all cases a physician should be called as promptly as possible.

The *urgent* diseases which this eminent physician considers may be treated by a mother, when a doctor cannot be summoned quickly or at all, are: *Croup, child crowing, inflammation of the lungs, diphtheria, diarrhœa, dysentery* and *shivering fit.* He sums up by saying: "These directions ought to be made as complete as possible, and the objection to medical treatment being so explained as to induce mothers to try to avoid calling in a physician is not so serious as that of leaving them without any guide in those instances where every delay is dangerous, and yet where medical assistance is not to be obtained or not to be had quickly."

Full directions, as given by Drs. Chavasse and Locock for the treatment of the above named diseases, will be given in the order named, and

236

may be the means, we trust, especially in neighborhoods remote from physicians, of saving the sunshine of many a home.

CROUP.

"It is unusual for a child until he is twelve months old to have croup; but, from that time until the age of two years he is more liable to it than at any other period. The liability after two years gradually lessens, until he is ten years old, after which time it is rare.

"A child is more liable to croup in a low and damp, than in a high and dry neighborhood; indeed, in some situations, croup is almost an unknown disease; while in others it is only too well understood. Croup is more likely to prevail when the wind is either easterly or north-easterly.

"There is no disease that requires more prompt treatment than croup, and none that creeps on more insidiously. The child at first seems to be laboring under a slight cold, and is troubled with a little *dry* cough; he is hot and fretful, and *hoarse* when he cries. Hoarseness is one of the earliest symptoms of croup; and it should be borne in mind that a young child, unless he be going to have croup, is seldom hoarse; if, therefore, your child be hoarse, he should be carefully watched, in order that, as soon as the croup be detected, not a moment be lost in applying the proper remedies.

"His voice at length becomes gruff, he breathes as though it were through muslin, and the cough becomes crowing. These three symptoms prove that the disease is now fully formed. These latter symptoms sometimes come on without any previous warning, the little fellow going to bed apparently quite well, until the mother is awakened, perplexed and frightened, in the middle of the night, by finding him laboring under the characteristic cough and the other symptoms of croup. If she delay either to send for assistance, *or if proper medicines be not instantly given*, in a few hours it will probably be of no avail, and in a day or two the little sufferer will be a corpse.

"When once a child has had croup, the after attacks are generally milder. If he has once had an attack of croup, I should advise you always to have in the house medicine—a four-ounce bottle of ipecacuanha wine—to fly to at a moment's notice; but never omit, where practicable, in case of croup, whether the attack be severe or mild, to send immediately for medical aid. There is no disease in which time is more precious than in croup, and where the delay of an hour may decide either for life or for death.

"If medical aid cannot be procured, adopt the following measures. First: Look well to the goodness and purity of the medicine, for the life of the child may depend upon the medicine being genuine. This medicine is *ipecacuanha wine.*

"At the earliest dawn of the disease give a teaspoonful of ipecacuanha wine every five minutes, until free vomiting be excited. In croup, before he is safe, free vomiting must be established, and that without loss of time. If, after the expiration of an hour, the ipecacuanha wine (having given during that hour a teaspoonful of it every five minutes) is not sufficiently powerful for the purpose—although it generally is so (if the ipecacuanha wine be good)—then let the following mixture be substituted :

"Take of—Powdered Ipecacuanha, one scruple ,
            Wine of Ipecacuanha, one ounce and a half.

Make a mixture. A teaspoonful to be given every five minutes, until free vomiting be excited, first *well* shaking the bottle.

"After the vomiting, place the child for a quarter of an hour in a warm bath.[1] When out of the bath, give him small doses of ipecacuanha wine every two or three hours. The following is a palatable form for the mixture :

Take of—Wine of Ipecacuanha, three drachms ;
            Simple Syrup, three drachms ;
            Water, six drachms.

Make a mixture. A teaspoonful to be taken every two or three hours.

" But remember, the emetic which is given at *first* is *pure ipecacuanha wine, without a drop of either water or of syrup.*

" A large sponge, dipped out of very hot water, and applied to the throat, and frequently renewed, oftentimes affords great relief in croup, and ought, during the time the emetic is being administered, in all cases to be adopted.

" If it be a *severe* case of croup, and does not in the course of two hours yield to the free exhibition of the ipecacuanha emetic, apply a narrow strip of *Smith's tela vesicatoria* to the throat, prepared in the same way as for a case of inflammation of the lungs. With this only difference, let it be a narrower strip, only one-half the width there recommended, and apply it to the throat instead of to the chest. If a child has a very short, fat neck, there may not be room for the tela ; then you ought to apply it to the upper part of the chest, just under the collarbones.

---

[1] See " Warm baths,"—directions and precautions to be observed.

" Let it be understood that the tela vesicatoria is not a severe remedy ; that the tela produces very little pain—not nearly so much as the application of leeches; although, in its action, it is much more beneficial, and is not nearly so weakening to the system.

Keep the child from all stimulants; let him live on a low diet, such as milk and water, toast and water, arrow-root, etc. ; and let the room be, if practicable, at a temperate heat—60 degrees Fahrenheit, and be well ventilated.

" Thus it is evident that the *treatment* of croup is very simple, and the plan might be carried out by an intelligent mother. Nevertheless, it is a duty, at the very *onset* of the disease, to obtain a physician, if possible.

" Another point to be emphasized is that, if the child is to be saved, the *Ipecacuanha Wine must be genuine and good.* This can only be assured by having the medicine from a thoroughly reliable druggist. Again, if a child has ever had croup, *always* keep in the house a four-ounce bottle of ipecacuanha wine, which may be resorted to at a moment's notice, in case there is the slightest return of the disease.

" Unfortunately, ipecacuanha wine is not a medicine that keeps well ; therefore a fresh bottle ought to be obtained every three or four months, either from a physician or a druggist. As long as the wine remains *clear* it is good ; but as soon as it becomes *turbid* it is bad, and ought to be replaced by a fresh supply.

" *What not to do.*—Do not give emetic tartar ; do not apply leeches ; do not keep the room very warm ; do not give stimulants ; do not omit to have always in the house a four-ounce bottle or three or four one-ounce bottles of ipecacuanha wine."

CHILD-CROWING OR SPURIOUS CROUP.

" This is a disease sometimes mistaken for *genuine croup.* But it is of more frequent occurrence than the latter, and requires a different plan of treatment. The ailment very rarely occurs except during teething, and is *most dangerous.* But if a child who is subject to it can escape suffocation until he has cut the whole of his first set of teeth—twenty—he is then as a rule safe.

" Child-crowing comes on in paroxysms. The breathing in the intervals is quite natural—indeed, the child seems perfectly well. Thus the dangerous nature of the disease is overlooked till an unusually severe paroxysm recurs, and the little patient dies of suffocation.

" The symptoms in a paroxysm of child-crowing are as follows: The child suddenly loses and fights for his breath, and in doing so makes a noise very much like that of crowing; hence the name child-crowing. The face during the paroxysm becomes bluish or livid. In a favorable case, after either a few seconds, or even, in some instances, a minute, and a frightful struggle to breathe, he regains his strength, and is, until another paroxysm occurs, perfectly well. In an unfavorable case, the upper part (chink) of the windpipe remains for a minute or two closed, and the child, not being able to breathe, drops a corpse in his nurse's arms. Many children, who are said to have died of fits, have really died of child-crowing.

"The description has been intentionally made full, because many lives might be saved if a mother knew the nature of the complaint, and the *great need during the paroxysms of prompt and proper measures.* Too often, before a physician has had time to arrive, the child has breathed his last, the mother being perfectly ignorant of the necessary treatment."

"Hence, it is vitally important to give clear information in a work of this kind.

Treatment of Child-Crowing.—"The first thing, of course, to be done is to send immediately for a medical man. Have a plentiful supply of cold and of hot water always at hand, ready at a moment's notice for use. The instant the paroxysm is upon the child, plentifully and perseveringly dash cold water upon his head and face. Put his feet and legs in hot salt, mustard, and water; and, if necessary, place him up to his neck in a hot bath, still dashing water upon his face and head. If he does not come round, sharply smack his back and buttocks.

" As soon as a physician arrives, he will lose no time in thoroughly lancing the gums and in applying other appropriate remedies.

" Great care and attention ought, during the intervals, to be paid to the diet. If the child is breathing a smoky, close atmosphere, he should be immediately removed to a pure one. In this disease, indeed, there is no remedy equal to a change of air—to a dry, bracing neighborhood. Change of air, even if it be winter, either to the coast or to a healthy farm-house, is the best remedy. Where, in a case of this kind, it is not practicable to send a child from home, then let him be sent out of doors the greater part of the day; let him, in point of fact, almost live in the open air. I am quite sure, from an extensive experience, that in this disease, fresh air, and plenty of it, is the best and principal remedy."

INFLAMMATION OF THE LUNGS.

" If the child has had a shivering fit, if his skin be very hot and very dry; if his lips be parched; if there be great thirst; if his cheeks be flushed; if he be dull and heavy, wishing to be quiet in his crib or cot; if his appetite be diminished; if his tongue be furred; if his mouth be burning hot and dry; if his urine be scanty and high-colored, staining the napkin or the linen; if his breathing be short, panting, hurried, and oppressed; if there be a hard, dry cough, and if his skin be burning hot, then there is no doubt that inflammation of the lungs has taken place.

"No time should be lost in sending for medical aid; indeed, the hot, dry mouth and skin, and short, hurried breathing, would be sufficient cause for your procuring immediate assistance. If inflammation of the lungs were properly treated at the onset, a child would scarcely ever be lost by that disease.

'*Treatment of Inflammation of the Lungs.*—Keep the child to one room, to his bed-room, and to his bed. Let the chamber be properly ventilated. If the weather be cool, let a small fire be in the grate; otherwise, he is better without a fire. Let him live on a low diet, such as weak black tea, milk and water, and toast and water, thin oatmeal gruel, arrow-root, and such simple beverages, and give him the following mixture: "

> Take of—Wine of Ipecacuanha, three drachms;
> Simple Syrup, three drachms;
> Water, six drachms:

Make a mixture. A teaspoonful of the mixture is to be taken every four hours.

"Be careful that you go to a respectable chemist, in order *that the quality of the ipecacuanha wine may be good, as the child's life may depend upon it.*

"If the medicine produces sickness, so much the better; continue it regularly until the short, oppressed, and hurried breathing has subsided, and has become natural.

"If the attack be very severe, in addition to the above medicine, at once apply a blister, not the common blister, but *Smith's tela vesicatoria* —a quarter of a sheet, which ought to be fastened on to a piece of sticking-plaster, taking care to apply the tela vesicatoria (which is on paper) to the warmed plaster, so as to securely fasten the tela vesicatoria on the sticking-plaster. The plaster should be rather larger than the blister, so as to leave a margin. Any respectable chemist will understand the above directions, and will prepare the tela ready for use. If the child be a year old, the blister ought to be kept on for three hours, and then a piece of thin, dry, soft linen rag should be applied for another three hours. At the end of which time—six hours—there will be a beautiful blister, which must then, with a pair of scissors, be cut, to let out the water; and then the blister is to be dressed, night and morning, with simple cerate on lint.

"If the little patient be more than a year, say two years old, let the tela remain on for five hours, and the dry linen rag for five hours longer, before the blister, as above recommended, be cut and dressed.

"If in a day or two the inflammation still continues violent, let another tela vesicatoria be applied, not over the old blister, but let a narrow strip of it, on sticking-plaster, be applied on each side of the old blister, and managed in the same manner as before directed."

"It would be difficult to speak too highly of Smith's tela vesicatoria. It has saved the lives of scores of children, and is very far superior to the old-fashioned blistering plaster. If the above rules are observed, it seldom fails to rise; it gives much less pain than the common blister, and when the effect desired has been produced, it readily heals, which cannot be said of the common fly-blister, more especially with children.

"The sheet anchors then, in cases of the inflammation of the lungs of children, are ipecacuanha wine and Smith's tela vesicatoria. But, as has already been stated, the *utmost care* must be observed in having the ipecacuanha wine genuine and good. This can only be done by getting the medicine from a thoroughly reliable chemist.

"Ipecacuanha wine, when genuine and good, is, in many children's diseases, one of the most valuable of medicines.

What must not be done.—"Do not, on any account," Dr. Chavasse urges, apply leeches. They draw out the life of the child, but not the disease, avoid—let this be carefully heeded—giving emetic tartar. It is one of the most lowering and death-dealing medicines that can be given to either an infant or a child. Whoever tries a dose will never be inclined to poison a baby with such a preparation. Many years ago, I myself gave it in inflammation of the lungs and lost many children. Since leaving it off, the recoveries of patients by the ipecacuanha treatment, combined with the external application of Smith's tela vesicatoria, have been in many cases marvelous.

"Avoid broths and wine, and all stimulants. Do not put the child into a warm bath, it only oppresses the already oppressed breathing. Moreover, after he is out of the bath, it causes a larger quantity of blood to rush to the head and back to the lungs and to the bronchial tubes, and thus feeds the inflammation. Do not, by a large fire, keep the temperature of the room high. A small fire, in the winter time, encourages ventilation, and in such a case does good. When the little patient is on the mother's or on the nurse's lap, do not burden him with a heavy blanket or with a thick shawl. Either a child's thin blanket, or a thin woolen shawl, in addition to his usual night-gown, is all the clothing necessary."

DIPHTHERIA.

" This dreaded disease, which by many is supposed to be of modern origin, was known in very ancient times. Homer, and Hippocrates, the father of physic, have both described it. Diphtheria first appeared in England in the beginning of the year 1857, since which time it has never left its shores.

" The symptoms are as follows: The little patient, before the disease really shows itself, feels poorly, and is " out of sorts." A shivering fit, though not severe, may generally be noticed. There is heaviness and slight head ache, principally over the eyes. Sometimes, but not always, there is a mild attack of delirium at night. The next day he complains of slight difficulty of swallowing. If old enough, he will complain of constriction about the swallow. On examining the throat, the tonsils will be found to be swollen and redder—more darkly red than usual. Slight specks will be noticed on the tonsils. In a day or two an exudation will cover them, the back of the swallow, the palate, the tongue, and sometimes the inside of the cheeks and the nostrils. This exudation of lymph gradually increases until it becomes a regular membrane. which puts on the appearance of leather; hence its name diphtheria. This membrane peels off in pieces; and if the child be old and strong enough he will sometimes spit it up in quantities, the membrane again and again rapidly forming as before. The discharges from the throat are occasionally, but not always offensive. There is danger of croup from the extension of the membrane into the windpipe. The glands about the neck and under the jaw are generally much swollen; the skin is rather cold and clammy; the urine is scanty and usually pale; the bowels at first are frequently relaxed. This diarrhœa may or may not cease as the disease advances.

" The child is now in a perilous condition, and it becomes a battle between his constitution and the disease. If, unfortunately, as is too often the case—diphtheria being more likely to attack the weakly—the child be very delicate, there is but slight hope of recovery. The danger of the disease is not always to be measured by the state of the throat. Sometimes, when the patient appears to be getting well, a sudden change for the worse rapidly carries him off. Hence the importance of great caution, in such cases, in giving an opinion as to ultimate recovery.

" Enough has been said to show the terrible nature of the disease, and the duty of summoning (at the earliest possible moment) an experienced physician.

" There is no doubt of the contagious character of the sickness. Therefore, when practicable, the rest of the children ought instantly to be removed from the room to a distance. I say children, for it is emphatically a disease of childhood. When adults have it, it is the exception, and not the rule.

"*Treatment to Pursue.*—Examine well into the ventilation, for as diphtheria is frequently caused by deficient ventilation, the best remedy is thorough ventilation. Look well both to the drains and to the privies, and see that the drains from the water-closets and from the privies do not in any way contaminate the pump-water. If the drains be defective or the privies be full, the disease in your child will be generated, fed, and fostered. Not only so, but the disease will spread in your family and all around you.

" Keep the child to his bed-room and to his bed. For the first two or three days, while the fever runs high, put him on a low diet, such as milk, tea, arrow-root, etc.

" Apply to his throat every four hours a warm barm and oatmeal poultice. If he be old enough to have the knowledge to use a gargle, the following will be found serviceable: "

> Take of—Powdered alum, one drachm;
> Simple syrup, one ounce;
> Water, seven ounces:

To make a gargle.

" The best medicine for the first few days of the attack is one of the following mixtures: "

> Take of—Chlorate of potash, two drachms;
> Boiling water, seven ounces and a half;
> Syrup of red poppy, half an ounce:

To make a mixture. A tablespoonful to be taken every four hours.

Or,

> Take of—Diluted sulphuric acid, one drachm;
> Simple syrup, one ounce and a half;
> Infusion of roses,[1] four ounces and a half;

To make a mixture. A tablespoonful to be given every four hours.

---

[1] Let the infusion of roses be made merely with the rose leaves and boiling water.

As soon as the skin has lost its preternatural heat, beef tea and chicken broth ought to be given. Or, if great prostration should supervene, in addition to the beef tea, port wine, a tablespoonful every four hours, should be administered. If the child be cold, and there be great sinking of the vital powers, brandy and water should be substituted for the port wine. Remember, in *ordinary* cases, port wine and brandy are not necessary, *but in cases of extreme exhaustion* they are most valuable.

As soon as the great heat of the skin has abated and the debility has set in, one of the following mixtures will be found useful:

> Take of—Wine of iron, one ounce and a half;
> Simple syrup, one ounce;
> Water, three ounces and a half·

To make a mixture. A tablespoonful to be taken every four hours.

Or,

> Take of—Muriated tincture of iron, half a drachm;
> Simple syrup, one ounce;
> Water, three ounces:

To make a mixture. A tablespoonful to be taken three times a day.

"If the disease should travel downward, it will cause all the symp toms of croup, then it must be treated as croup; with this only difference, that a blister (*tela vesicatoria*) must *not* be applied, or the blistered surface may be attacked by the membrane of diphtheria, which may either cause death or hasten that catastrophe. In every other respect treat the case as croup, by giving an emetic, a teaspoonful of ipecacuanha wine every five minutes, until free vomiting be excited, and then administer smaller doses of ipecacuanha wine every two or three hours, as I recommended for the treatment of croup.

" *What not to do.*—Do not, on any account, apply either leeches or a blister. If the latter be applied, it is almost sure to be covered with the membrane of diphtheria, similar to that inside of the mouth and of the throat, which would be a serious complication. Do not give either calomel or emetic tartar. Do not depress the system by aperients, for diphtheria is an awfully depressing complaint of itself; the patient, in point of fact, is laboring under the depressing effects of poison, for the blood has been poisoned either by the drinking water being contaminated by fecal matter from a privy or from a water-closet; by some horrid drain; by proximity to a pig-sty; by an overflowing privy, especially if vegetable matter be rotting at the same time in it; by bad ventilation, or by contagion. Diphtheria may generally be traced either to the one or

to the other of the above causes; therefore let me urgently entreat you
to look well into all these matters, and thus to stay the pestilence.   Dip-
theria might long remain in a neighborhood, if active measures be not
used to exterminate it.

    " The causes are: Bad and imperfect drainage; want of ventilation;
overflowing privies, low neighborhoods in the vicinity of rivers; stagnant
waters; indeed, everything that vitiates the air, and thus depresses the
system, more especially if the weather be close and muggy; poor and
improper food; and last, though not least, contagion. . Bear in mind, too,
that a delicate child is much more predisposed to the disease than a
strong one.

DIARRHŒA.

    If at first there are abundant and loose discharges, rest and a milk
diet will frequently effect a cure. If the discharges are small, give
tincture of rhubarb or castor oil. The patient should be kept quiet and
if possible on his back. If after the medicine has operated, the disease
continues, give chalk mixture and tincture of kino, in the proportion of
three-fourths chalk mixture to one-fourth tincture of kino, and if there
is much pain, add a few drops of paregoric to each teaspoonful. Dose
of the mixture for a child three years old, one teaspoonful every three
hours. The medicine should be well shaken before using. A little
Jamaica ginger and the essence of peppermint may be given in water.
A mixture used by Dr. Francis Minot, of Boston, has been very successful in the early stages of this disease and, if a physician's aid cannot be
obtained, should be given.

> Tincture of Rhubarb............................1 ounce.
> Sulphate of Magnesia...........................1 ounce.
> Syrup of Ginger................................½ ounce.
> Cinnamon Water.................... ....1½ ounces.

    Mix thoroughly. DOSE—One teaspoonful in water every three hours for
a child of three or four years.

    As soon as possible consult a physician, and try to ascertain the causes.
The most common ones are bad drainage, bad air in the sleeping-room, hot
weather, exposure to cold, raw winds or to dampness, especially toward
dusk and in early autumn. Improper food, too, is frequently at fault, such
as unripe fruit, cake, or other indigestible things. If the child has a wet-
nurse, a change may be required. A cure is often very rapidly effected
by removing the little invalid to the country. For infants using the
bottle, Mellin's Food is best.

DYSENTERY.

This painful disorder is often caused by a neglected diarrhœa. It is more dangerous than the latter because its character is inflammatory, and as it often attacks a delicate child, it requires skillful treatment; hence great care and experience are needed by those who have charge of the patient.

Symptoms.—"The child has probably had an attack of diarrhœa—or bowel complaint as it is often called—for several days, having had a dozen or two of motions, many of them slimy and frothy like "frog-spawn," during the twenty-four hours. Suddenly the character of the motion changes—from being principally stool it becomes almost entirely blood and mucus; he is dreadfully griped, which causes him to strain violently every time he has a motion—screaming and twisting about, evidently in the greatest pain, drawing his legs up to his belly, and writhing in agony. Sickness and vomiting are always present, helping to rob him of his remaining strength. His face is the picture of distress. If he has been a plump, healthy little fellow, you will see his face in a few days become old-looking, care worn, haggard, and pinched. Day and night the enemy tracks him (unless proper remedies be administered); no sleep, or, if he sleep, he is every few minutes roused. It is heart-rending to have to attend a bad case of dysentery in a child—the writhing, the screaming, the frequent vomiting, the pitiful look, the rapid wasting and exhaustion, make it more distressing to witness than almost any other disease a doctor attends; but if no physician can be had, pursue the following directions.

"*What to do.*—If the child be at the breast, keep him to it, and let him have nothing else, for dysentery is frequently caused by improper. feeding. If your milk be not good, or if it be scanty, *instantly* procure a healthy wet-nurse. *Lose not a moment;* for in dysentery moments are precious. But, suppose that you have no milk, and that no wet-nurse can be procured: what then? Feed him entirely on cow's milk—the milk of *one* healthy cow; let the milk be unboiled, and be fresh from the cow. Give it in small quantities at a time, and frequently, so that it may be retained on the stomach. If a tablespoonful of the milk make him sick, give him a dessertspoonful; if a dessertspoonful cause sickness, let him only have a teaspoonful at a time, and let it be repeated every quarter of an hour. But remember, in such a case the breast milk—the breast milk alone—is incomparably superior to any other milk or to any other food whatever.

"If he be a year old and weaned, then feed him, as above recom mended, on the cow's milk. If there be extreme exhaustion and debility, let fifteen drops of brandy be added to each tablespoonful of new milk, and let it be given every half hour.

"Now with regard to medicine. I approach this part of the treatment with some degree of reluctance—for dysentery is a case requiring opium, and opium I never like a mother of her own accord to administer. But suppose a medical man cannot be procured in time, the mother must then prescribe or the child will die! *What then is to be done?* Sir Charles Locock considers 'that in severe dysentery, especially where there is sickness, there is no remedy equal to pure calomel, in a full dose, without opium.'" Therefore, at the very *onset* of the disease, let from three to five grains (according to the age of the patient) of calomel, mixed with an equal quantity of powdered white sugar, be put dry on the tongue. In three hours after let the following mixture be administered:

> Take of—Compound Ipecacuanha Powder, five grains;
> Ipecacuanha Wine, half a drachm ·
> Simple Syrup, three drachms;
> Cinnamon Water, nine drachms:

To make a mixture.[1] A teaspoonful to be given every three or four hours, first *well* shaking the bottle.

Supposing he cannot retain the mixture—the stomach rejecting it as soon as swallowed—what then? Give the opium, mixed with small doses of mercury with chalk and sugar, in the form of powder. and put one of the powders *dry* on the tongue every three hours:

> Take of—Powdered Opium, half a grain;
> Mercury with Chalk, nine grains;
> Sugar of Milk, twenty-four grains:

Mix well in a mortar, and divide into twelve powders.

Now, suppose the dysentery has for several days persisted, and that during that time, nothing but mucus and blood—that no real stool—has come from the bowels, then a combination of castor oil and opium[2] ought, instead of the medicine recommended above, to be given.

---

[1] Let this mixture, or any other medicine that may be prescribed, be always made by a respectable druggist.

[2] The late Dr. Baly of England, who had made dysentery his particular study, considered the combination of opium and castor oil very valuable in dysentery.

Take of—Mixture of Acacia, three drachms;
Simple Syrup, three drachms;
Tincture of Opium, ten drops (*not* minims);
Castor Oil, two drachms;
Cinnamon Water, four drachms:

Make a mixture. A teaspoonful to be taken every four hours, first *well* shaking the bottle.

A warm bath, at the commencement of the disease, is very efficacious; but it must be given at the *commencement*. If he has had dysentery for a day or two, he will be too weak to have a warm bath; then, instead of the bath, try the following: Wrap him in a blanket which has been previously wrung out of hot water, over which envelop him in a *dry* blanket. Keep him in this hot, damp blanket for half an hour; then take him out, put on his night-gown and place him in bed, which has been, if it be winter time, previously warmed. The above " blanket treatment " will frequently give great relief, and will sometimes cause him to fall into a sweet sleep. A flannel bag filled with hot powdered table salt, made hot in the oven, applied to the bowels, will afford much comfort.

What not to do.—Do not give aperients, unless it be, as before advised, the castor oil guarded with the opium; do not stuff him with artificial food; do not fail to send for a judicious and an experienced medical man; for, remember, it requires a skillful doctor to treat a case of dysentery, more especially in a child.

SHIVERING FIT.

This is something demanding *immediate* attention, as nearly all *serious* illnesses commence with it. Severe colds influenza, inflammation of different organs, scarlet fever, measles, small-pox, etc. Therefore send for a doctor *instantly* if one can be had, a few hours of judicious treatment, at the commencement of an illness, are frequently of more avail than days and weeks after the disease has gained a firm footing.

Treatment to pursue.—*Instantly* have the bed warmed and put the child to bed. Apply either a hot bottle or a hot brick, wrapped in flannel, to the soles of his feet. Put an extra blanket on his bed, and give him a cup of hot tea.

As soon as the shivering fit is over, and he has become hot, gradually lessen the *extra* quantity of clothes on his bed, and take away the hot bottle or the hot brick from his feet.

What not to do.—Do not give either brandy or wine, as inflammation of some organ might be about taking place. Do not administer opening medicine, as there might be some "breaking out" coming out on the skin, and an aperient might check it.

While it may be said that all diseases are *urgent,* in the sense that, in all cases, the more promptly proper remedies can be used the more rapid will be the recovery; those above mentioned require especially speedy action. There are, however, several other so-called "childish diseases," a knowledge of whose symptoms and treatment may be of infinite value to mothers, though the advice cannot be too often and too emphatically reiterated, that a physician should *always* be secured as soon as possible.

Among this latter class of ailments, the most dreaded are scarlet fever and scarlatina, which are, in fact, one and the same disease, scarlatina being the Latin name of scarlet fever and used commonly to designate a mild form.

CHILDISH DISEASES.

MEASLES.

"Measles commences with symptoms of a common cold; the patient is at first chilly, then hot and feverish; he has a running at the nose, sneezing, watering and redness of the eyes, headache, drowsiness, a hoarse and peculiar ringing cough, which nurses call 'measle-cough,' and difficulty of breathing. These symptoms usually last three days before the eruption appears; on the fourth it (the eruption) generally makes its appearance, and continues for four days and then disappears, lasting altogether, from the commencement of the symptoms of cold to the decline of the eruption, seven days. It is important to bear in mind that the eruption consists of *crescent-shaped—half-moon shaped—patches;* that they usually appear first about the face and the neck, in which places they are the best marked; then on the body and on the arms; and, lastly, on the legs, and that they are slightly raised above the surface of the skin. The face is swollen, more especially the eyelids, which are sometimes for a few days closed.

"Well, then, remember, *the running at the nose, the sneezing, the peculiar hoarse cough, and the half-moon shaped patches* are the leading features of the disease, and point out for a certainty that it is measles.

"The principal danger in measles is the affection of the chest. The mucous lining membrane of the bronchial tubes is always more or less inflamed and the lungs themselves are sometimes affected. The only way to 'throw out the eruption,' as it is called, is to keep the body comfortably warm, and to give the beverages ordered by the physician with the chill off.

"*Treatment to pursue.*—The child ought to be confined both to his room and to his bed, the room being kept comfortably warm; therefore, if it be winter time, there should be a small fire in the grate; in the summer time, a fire would be improper. The child must not be exposed to draughts; notwithstanding, from time to time, the door ought to be left a little ajar, in order to change the air of the apartment; for proper ventilation, let the disease be what it may, is absolutely necessary.

"Let the child, for the first few days, be kept on a low diet, such as milk and water, arrow-root, bread and butter, etc.

"If the attack be mild, that is to say, if the breathing be not much affected (for in measles it always is more or less affected), and if there be not much wheezing, the acidulated infusion of roses' mixture[1] will be all that is necessary.

"But suppose that the breathing is short, and that there is a great wheezing, then, instead of giving him the mixture just advised, give him a teaspoonful of a mixture composed of ipecacuanha wine, syrup, and water,[2] every four hours. And if, on the following day, the breathing and the wheezing be not relieved, in addition to the ipecacuanha mixture, apply a tela vesicatoria, as advised under the head of inflammation of the lungs.

"When the child is convalescing, batter puddings, rice, and sago puddings, in addition to the milk, bread and butter, etc., should be given; and, a few days later, chicken, mutton-chops, etc.

The child ought not, even in a mild case of measles, and in favorable weather, to be allowed to leave the house under a fortnight, or it might bring on an attack of bronchitis.

---

[1] Prescription given in directions for treatment of diphtheria, page 235.

[2] Prescription given in directions for treatment of inflammation of the lungs, page 232.

" *What not to do.*—Do not give either 'surfeit water' or wine. Do not apply leeches to the chest. Do not expose the child to the cold air. Do not keep the bed-room very hot, but comfortably warm. Do not let the child leave the house, even under favorable circumstances, under a fortnight. Do not, while the eruption is out, give aperients. Do not, ' to ease the cough,' administer either emetic tartar, or paregoric—the former drug is awfully depressing; the latter will stop the cough, and will thus prevent the expulsion of the phlegm."

SCARLET FEVER.

Symptoms.—The patient is generally chilly, languid, drowsy, feverish and poorly for two days before the eruption appears. At the end of the second day, the characteristic bright scarlet fever efflorescence, somewhat similar to the color of a boiled lobster, usually first shows itself. The scarlet appearance is not confined to the skin; but the tongue, the throat, and the whites of the eyes put on the same appearance; with this only difference, that on the tongue and on the throat the scarlet is much darker; and, as Dr. Elliotson accurately describes it,—" the tongue looks as if it had been slightly sprinkled with Cayenne pepper." The eruption usually declines on the fifth, and is generally indistinct on the sixth day; on the seventh it has completely faded away. There is usually, after the first few days, great itching on the surface of the body. The skin, at the end of the week, begins to peel and to dust off, making it look as though meal had been sprinkled upon it.

The question: what is the difference between scarlatina and scarlet fever? is often asked. They are, in fact, one and the same disease, scarlatina being the Latin for scarlet fever. But in a popular sense, when the disease is mild, it is usually called scarlatina. The latter term does not sound so formidable to the ears of patients or of parents.

There are three forms of scarlet fever,—the one where the throat is little, if at all affected, and this is a mild form of the disease; the second, which is generally, especially at night, attended with delirium, where the throat is much affected, being often greatly inflamed and ulcerated; and the third (which is, except in certain unhealthy districts, comparatively rare, and which is very dangerous), the malignant form.

"Aperient medicines," says Dr. Chavasse, from whose valuable work this description of scarlet fever and its treatment—in which he has been marvellously successful—is taken, " should never be given. They are in my opinion highly improper and dangerous, both before and during the period of eruption. It is my firm conviction that the administration of opening medicine, at such times, is one of the principal causes of scarlet fever being so frequently fatal. This, is, of course, more applicable to the poor, and to those who are unable to procure a skilful medical man.

"The principal dangers in scarlet fever are: The affection of the throat, the administration of the opening medicine during the first ten days, and a peculiar disease of the kidneys ending in anasarca (dropsy), on which account, the physician ought, when practicable, to be sent for at the onset, that no time may be lost in applying proper remedies."

HOW TO DISTINGUISH BETWEEN SCARLET FEVER AND MEASLES.

It is of the utmost importance to distinguish between the above men-tioned diseases, the treatment required being radically different. In measles the patient ought to be kept *moderately* warm, and the drinks should be given with the chill off; while in scarlet fever the patient ought to be kept cool—indeed for the first few days, *cold ;* and the drinks, such as spring water, toast water, etc., should be administered quite cold.

The following are the points to be noted: Measles commences with symptoms of a common cold; scarlet fever does not. Measles has a peculiar *hoarse* cough ; scarlet fever has not. The eruption of measles is in patches of a half-moon shape, and is slightly raised above the skin ; the eruption of scarlet fever is *not* raised above the skin at all, and is one continued mass. The color of the eruption is much more vivid in scarlet fever than in measles. The chest is the part principally affected in measles, and the throat in scarlet fever.

"There is an excellent method of determining, for a certainty, whether the eruption be that of scarlatina or otherwise. I myself, have, in several instances, ascertained the truth of it: 'For several years M. Bouchut has remarked in the eruption of scarlatina a curious phenomenon, which serves to distinguish this eruption from that of measles, erythema, erysipelas, etc., a phenomenon essentially vital, and which is connected with the excessive contractability of the capillaries. The phenomenon in question is a *white line*, which can be produced at pleasure by drawing the back of the nail along the skin where the eruption is situated. On drawing the nail, or the extremity of a hard body (such as a pen-holder), along the eruption, the skin is observed to grow pale, and to present a white trace, which remains for one or two minutes, or longer, and then disappears. In this way the diagnosis of the disease may be very dis-tinctly written on the skin; the word "Scarlatina" disappears as the eruption regains its uniform tint.'"

"If," says Dr. Chavasse, "the following rules are carried out, and my directions .obeyed to the letter, I can promise that *if the scarlet fever be neither malignant, nor complicated with diphtheria,* the plan I am about to advise will, with God's blessing, usually be successful."

"Send the child to bed, throw open the windows, be it winter or summer, and have a thorough ventilation; for the bed-room must be kept cool, I may say cold. Do not be afraid of fresh air, for the first few days, it is essential to recovery. *Fresh air, and plenty of it, in scarlet fever, is the best doctor a child can have,* let these words be written legibly on your mind.

"Now for the throat—The best *external* application is a barm and oatmeal poultice. How ought it to be made, and how applied? Put half a teacupful of barm into a saucepan, put it on the fire to boil; as soon as it boils take it off the fire, and stir oatmeal into it, until it is of the consistence of a nice soft poultice; then place it on a rag, and apply it to the throat; carefully fasten it on with a bandage, two or three turns of the bandage going round the throat, and two or three over the crown of the head, so as nicely to apply the poultice where it is wanted—that is to say, to cover the tonsils. Tack the bandage: do not pin it. Let the poultice be changed three times a day. The best medicine is the acidulated infusion of roses, sweetened with syrup.[1] It is grateful and refreshing, it is pleasant to take, it abates fever and thirst, it cleans the throat and tongue of mucus, and is peculiarly efficacious in scarlet fever; as soon as the fever is abated it gives an appetite. My belief is that the sulphuric acid in the mixture is a specific in scarlet fever, as much as quinine is in ague, and sulphur in itch. I have reason to say so, for, in numerous cases, I have seen its immense value.

"Now, with regard to food—if the child be at the breast, keep him entirely to it. If he be weaned and under two years old, give him milk and water, and cold water to drink. If he be older, give him toast and water, and plain water from the pump, as much as he chooses; let it be quite cold—the colder the better. Weak black tea, or thin gruel, may be given, but not caring, unless he be an infant at the breast, if he take nothing but *cold* water. If the child be two years old and upwards, roasted apples with sugar, and grapes will be very refreshing, and will tend to cleanse both the mouth and throat. Avoid broths and stimulants of every kind.

"When the appetite returns, you may consider the patient to be safe. The diet ought now to be gradually improved. Bread and butter, milk

---

[1] For the prescription of the acidulated infusion of roses with syrup, see page 235.

and water, and arrow-root made with equal parts of new milk and water, should for the first two or three days be given. Then a light batter or rice pudding may be added, and in a few days afterward, either a little chicken or a mutton-chop.

"The essential remedies, then, in scarlet fever, are, for the first few days—(1) plenty of fresh air and ventilation, (2) plenty of cold water to drink, (3) barm poultices to the throat, and (4) the acidulated infusion of roses' mixture as a medicine.

"Now, then, comes very important advice. After the first few days, probably five or six, sometimes as early as the fourth day, *watch carefully and warily, and note the time, the skin will suddenly become cool*, the child will say that he feels chilly; then is the time you must now change your tactics—*instantly close the windows, and put extra clothing*, a blanket or two, on his bed. A flannel night-gown should, until the dead skin has peeled off, be now worn next to the skin, when the flannel night-gown should be discontinued. The patient ought ever after to wear, in the day-time, a flannel waistcoat. His drinks must now be given with the chill off; he ought to have a cup of warm tea, and gradually his diet should, as I have previously recommended, be improved.

"There is one important caution I wish to impress upon you,—*do not give opening medicine during the time the eruption is out*. In all probability the bowels will be opened: if so, all well and good; but do not, on any account, for the first ten days, use artificial means to open them. It is my firm conviction that the administration of purgatives in scarlet fever is a fruitful source of dropsy, of disease, and death. When we take into consideration the sympathy there is between the skin and the mucous membrane, I think that we should pause before giving irritating medicines, such as purgatives. The irritation of aperients on the mucous membrane may cause the poison of the skin disease (for scarlet fever is a blood poison) to be driven internally to the kidneys, to the throat, to the pericardium (bag of the heart), or to the brain. You may say, 'Do you not purge, if the bowels be not open for a week?' I say emphatically, 'No!'

"I consider my great success in the treatment of scarlet fever to be partly owing to my avoidance of aperients during the first ten days of the child's illness.

"If the bowels, after the ten days, are not properly opened, a dose or two of the following mixture should be given:

> Take of—Simple syrup, three drachms;
> Essence of senna, nine drachms.

To make a mixture. Two teaspoonfuls to be given early in the morning occasionally, and to be repeated in four hours, if the first dose should not operate.

"Let us now sum up the plan I adopt:

"1. Thorough ventilation, a cool room, and scant clothes on the bed for the first five or six days.

"2. A change for temperature of the skin to be carefully regarded. As soon as the skin is cool, closing the windows, and putting additional clothing on the bed.

"3. The acidulated infusion of roses' syrup is the medicine for scarlet fever.

"4. Purgatives to be religiously avoided for the first ten days at least, and even afterward, unless there be absolute necessity.

"5. Leeches, blisters, emetics, cold and tepid spongings, and painting the tonsils with caustic, inadmissible in scarlet fever.

"A strict antiphlogistic (low) diet for the first few days, during which time cold water to be given *ad libitum.*

"The patient not to leave the house in the summer under the month; in the winter, under six weeks.

"*What not to do.*—Do not, then, apply either leeches or blisters to the throat; do not paint the tonsils with caustic; do not give aperients; do not, for the first few days of the illness, be afraid of cold air to the skin, and of cold water as a beverage; do not, emphatically let me say, do not let the child leave the house for at least a month from the commencement of the illness.

"My firm conviction is, that purgatives, emetics, and blisters, by depressing the patient, sometimes causes ordinary scarlet fever to degenerate into malignant scarlet fever.

"He must not be allowed to go out for at least a month from the commencement of the attack, in the summer, and six weeks in the winter; and not even then without the express permission of a physician. It might be said that this is an unreasonable recommendation, but when it is considered that the whole of the skin generally desquamates, or peels off, and consequently leaves the surface of the body exposed to cold, which cold flies to the kidneys, producing a peculiar and serious disease in them, ending in dropsy, this warning will not be deemed unreasonable.

"Scarlet fever dropsy, which is really a formidable disease, generally arises from the carelessness, the ignorance, and the thoughtlessness of parents in allowing a child to leave the house before the new skin is properly formed and hardened. Prevention is always better than cure.

" During the last seventeen years I have never had dropsy scarlet fever, and I attribute it entirely to the plan of treatment recommended, and in not allowing my patients to leave the house under the month,—until, in fact the skin that has peeled off has been renewed.

" Thus far with the regard to the danger to the child himself. Now, if you please, let me show you the risk of contagion that you inflict upon families, in allowing your child to mix with others before a month at least has elapsed. Bear in mind, a case is quite as contagious, if not more so, while the skin is peeling off, as it was before. Thus, in ten days or a fortnight, there is as much risk of contagion as at the beginning of the disease, and when the fever is at its height. At the conclusion of the month, the old skin has generally all peeled off, and the new skin has taken its place; consequently there will then be less fear of contagion to others. But the contagion of scarlet fever is so subtle and so uncertain in its duration, that it is impossible to fix the exact time when it ceases.

" Let me most earnestly implore you to ponder well on the above important facts. If these remarks should be the means of saving only one child from death or from broken health, my labor will not have been in vain."

MODE OF PURIFYING A HOUSE FROM THE CONTAGION OF SCARLET FEVER.

Let every room be lime-washed and then white-washed; if the contagion has been virulent, let every bed-room be freshly papered (the walls having been previously stripped of the old paper and then lime-washed); let the bed, the bolsters, the pillows, and the mattresses be cleansed and purified; let the blankets and coverlids be thoroughly washed, and then let them be exposed to the open air—if taken into a field, so much the better; let the rooms be well scoured; let the windows, top and bottom, be thrown wide open; let the drains be carefully examined; let the pump water be scrutinized to see that it be not contaminated by fecal matter, either from the water-closet or from the privy; let privies be emptied of their contents—remember this is most important advice—then put into the empty places lime and powdered charcoal, for it is a well-ascertained fact that it is frequently impossible to rid a house of the infection of scarlet fever without adopting such a course.

Let the children who have not had, or who do not appear to be sickening from scarlet fever, be sent away from home—if to a farm-house so much the better. Indeed, leave no stone unturned, no means untried, to exterminate the disease from the house and from the neighborhood.

WHOOPING COUGH.

"This disease is not inflammatory, but purely spasmodic. It is, however, usually accompanied with more or less bronchitis—inflammation of the mucous membrane of the bronchial tubes—for which reason it is necessary *in all cases* to consult a physician, that he may watch the progress of the disease and nip inflammation in the bud.

Whooping-cough is emphatically a disease of the young; it is rare for adults to have it; if they do, they usually suffer more severely than children. A child seldom has it but once in life. It is highly contagious, and therefore frequently runs through a whole family of children, giving much annoyance, anxiety, and trouble to the mother and the nurses; hence whooping-cough is much dreaded by them. It is amenable to treatment. Spring and summer are the best seasons of the year for the disease to occur. This complaint usually lasts from six to twelve weeks—sometimes for a much longer period, more especially if proper means are not employed to relieve it.

"Whooping-cough commences as a common cold and cough. The cough, for ten days or a fortnight, increases in intensity; at about which time it puts on the characteristic " whoop." The attack of cough comes on in paroxysms.

" In a paroxysm the child coughs so long and so violently, and expires so much air from the lungs without inspiring any, that at times he appears suffocated and exhausted; the veins of the neck swell; his face is nearly purple; his eyes, with the tremendous exertion, seem almost to start from their sockets; at length there is a sudden inspiration of air through the contracted chink of the upper part of the wind-pipe—the glottis—causing the peculiar "whoop; " and, after a little more coughing, he brings up some glairy mucous from the chest; and sometimes, by vomiting, food from the stomach; he is at once relieved, until the next paroxysm occurs, when the same process is repeated, the child during the intervals, in a favorable case, appearing quite well, and after the cough is over, instantly returning either to his play or to his food. Generally, after a paroxysm he is hungry, unless, indeed, there be severe inflammation either of the chest or of the lungs. Sickness, as I before remarked, frequently accompanies whooping-cough; when it does, it might be looked upon as a good symptom. The child usually knows when an attack is coming on; he dreads it, and therefore tries to prevent it; he sometimes partially succeeds; but if he does, it only makes the attack, when it does come, more severe. All causes of irritation and excitement ought, as much as possible, to be avoided, as passion is apt to bring on a severe paroxysm.

"A new-born babe, an infant of one or two months old, commonly escapes the infection ; but if at that tender age he unfortunately catch whooping-cough, it is likely to fare harder with him than if he were older—the younger the child the greater the risk. But still, in such a case, do not despair, as I have known numerous cases of new-born infants, with judicious care, recover perfectly from the attack, and thrive after it as though nothing of the kind had ever happened.

"A new-born babe laboring under whooping-cough is liable to convulsions, which is, in this disease, one, indeed the greatest source, of danger. A child, too, who is teething and laboring under the disease is also liable to convulsions. When the patient is convalescing, care ought to be taken that he does not catch cold, or the "whoop" might return. Whooping-cough may either precede, attend, or follow an attack of measles.

" *What to do.*—In the first stage, the commencement of whooping-cough: For the first ten days give the ipecacuanha wine mixture. A teaspoonful three times a day. If the child be not weaned, use a milk and farinaceous diet. Confine him for the first ten days to the house, more especially if the whooping-cough be attended, as it usually is, with more or less of bronchitis. But take care that the rooms be well ventilated, for good air is essential to the cure. If the bronchitis attending the whooping-cough be severe, confine him to his bed, and treat him as though it were simply a case of bronchitis.

Take of—Diluted nitric acid, two drachms ;
Compound tincture of cardamon, half a drachm ;
Simple Syrup, three ounces ;
Water, two ounces and a half.

Make a mixture.—One or two teaspoonfuls, or a tablespoonful, according to the age of the child—one teaspoonful for an infant of six months, and two teaspoonfuls for a child of twelve months, and one tablespoonful for a child of two years, every four hours, first shaking the bottle.

" Let the chest and the spine be well rubbed every night and morning either with Roche's Embrocation, or with the following stimulating liniment (first shaking the bottle):

Take of—Oil of cloves, one drachm;
Oil of amber, two drachms;
Camphorated oil, nine drachms:

Make a liniment.

" Let him wear a broad band of new flannel, which should extend round from his chest to his back, and which ought to be changed every

night and morning, in order that it may be dried before putting on
again. To keep it in its place, it should be fastened by means of tapes
and with shoulder straps.

"The diet ought now to be improved—he should gradually return to
his usual food; and, weather permitting, should almost live in the open
air—fresh air being, in such a case, one of the finest medicines.

"In the third stage, that is to say, when the complaint has lasted a
month, if by that time the child is not well, there is nothing like a change
of air to a high, dry, healthy country place. Continue the nitric acid
mixture, and either the embrocation or the liniment to the back and
chest, let him continue to almost live in the open air, and be sure he does
not discontinue wearing the flannel until he be quite cured, and then it be
left off by degrees.

"If the whooping-cough has caused debility, give him cod-liver oil,
a teaspoonful twice or three times a day, giving it to him on a full
stomach after meals.

"But, remember, after the first three or four weeks, change of air and
plenty of it, is for whooping cough the grand remedy.

"Do not apply leeches to the chest—it is not wise to take blood out
of a child laboring under whooping-cough; the disease is quite weakening
enough to the system of itself without robbing him of his life's blood;
do not, on any account whatever, administer either emetic tartar or antimonial wine; do not give either paregoric or syrup of white poppies; do
not drug him either with calomel or with gray powder; do not dose him
with quack medicine; do not give him stimulants, but rather give him plenty
of nourishment, such as milk and farinaceous food, but no stimulants;
do not be afraid after the first week or two, of his having fresh air, and
plenty of it—for fresh pure air is the grand remedy, after all that can be said
and done, in whooping-cough. Although occasionally we find that if the
child be laboring under whooping-cough and is breathing a pure country
air, and is not getting well so rapidly as we could wish, change of air to
a smoky, gas-laden town will sometimes quickly effect a cure; indeed,
some persons go so far as to say that the best remedy for an obstinate
case of whooping-cough is for the child to live the greater part of every
day in gas-works.

"*During a paroxysm of Whooping Cough.*—If the child be old enough,
let him stand up; but if he be either too young or too feeble, raise his
head, and bend his body a little forward; then support his back with
one hand, and the forehead with the other. Let the mucus, the moment
it is within reach, be wiped away with a soft handkerchief out of his mouth.

"In an obstinate ease of whooping-cough, the best remedy, provided there be no active inflammation, is change of air to any healthy spot. A farm-house in a high, dry, and salubrious neighborhood, is as good a place as can be chosen. If, in a short time, he be not quite well, take him to the sea-side; the sea breezes will often, as if by magic, drive away the disease."

BRONCHITIS.

To enable the inexperienced to distinguish between an attack of bronchitis and one of inflammation of the lungs, the following description of the differing symptoms of the two diseases is given:

"In bronchitis the skin is warm but moist; in inflammation of the lungs it is hot and dry; in bronchitis the mouth is warmer than usual, but moist; in inflammation of the lungs it is burning hot; in bronchitis the breathing is rather hurried, and attended with wheezing; in inflammation of the lungs it is very short and panting, and is unaccompanied with wheezing, although occasionally a very slight crackling sound may be heard; in bronchitis the cough is long and noisy; in inflammation of the lungs it is short and feeble; in bronchitis the child is cross and fretful; in inflammation of the lungs he is dull and heavy, and his countenance denotes distress.

We have sometimes a combination of bronchitis and of inflammation of the lungs, an attack of the latter following the former. Then the symptoms will be modified, and will partake of the character of the two diseases.

"*Treatment to Pursue.*—Confine the child to his bed-room and, if very ill, to his bed. If it be winter time, have a little fire in the grate, but be sure that the temperature of the chamber is not above 60 degrees Fahrenheit, and let the room be properly ventilated, which may be effected by occasionally leaving the door a little ajar.

"Let him lie outside the bed or on a sofa; if he be very ill, inside the bed, with a sheet and a blanket only to cover him, but no thick coverlid. If he be allowed to lie on the lap, it only heats him and makes him restless. If he will not lie on the bed, let him rest on a pillow placed on the lap; the pillow will cause him to lie cooler, and will more comfortably rest his wearied body. If he be at the breast, keep him to it; let him have no artificial food, unless, if he be thirsty, a little water and toast. If he be weaned, let him have either milk and water, arrow-root made with equal parts of milk and water, toast and water, barley-water, or weak, black tea, with plenty of new milk in it, etc. But, until the inflammation has subsided, neither broth nor beef-tea."

"Now, with regard to medicine, the best medicine is ipecacuanha wine, given in large doses, so as to produce constant nausea. The ipecacuanha abates fever, acts on the skin, loosens the cough, and, in point of fact, in the majority of cases will rapidly effect a cure. Let a teaspoonful of the mixture be taken every four hours.

" It in a day or two he be no better, but worse, by all means continue the mixture, whether it produces sickness or otherwise, and put on the chest a tela vesicatoria, prepared and applied as I recommended when treating of the inflammation of the lungs.

" The ipecacuanha wine and the tela vesicatoria are my sheet-anchors in bronchitis, both of infants and of children. They rarely, even in very severe cases, fail to effect a cure, provided the tela vesicatoria be properly applied, and the ipecacuanha wine be genuine and of good quality.

" If there be any difficulty in procuring good ipecacuanha wine, the ipecacuanha may be given in powder instead of the wine. The following is a pleasant form:

Take of—Powder of ipecacuanha, twelve grains;
White sugar, thirty-six grains.

Mix well together, and divide into twelve powders. One of the powders to be put dry on the tongue every four hours.

" The ipecacuanha powder will keep better than the wine, an important consideration to those living in country places; nevertheless, if the wine can be procured fresh and good, I far prefer the wine to the powder.

"When the bronchitis has disappeared, the diet ought gradually to be improved—rice, sago, tapioca and light batter-pudding, etc., and in a few days either a little chicken or a mutton chop, mixed with a well-mashed potato and crumb of bread, should be given. But let the improvement in the diet be gradual, or the inflammation might return.

" *What not to do.*—Do not apply leeches. Do not give either emetic tartar or antimonial wine, which is emetic tartar dissolved in wine. Do not administer either paregoric or syrup of poppies, either of which would stop the cough, and would thus prevent the expulsion of the phlegm. Any fool can stop a cough, but it requires a wise man to rectify the mischief. A cough is an effort of nature to bring up the phlegm, which would otherwise accumulate, and in the end cause death. Again, therefore, let me urge upon you the immense importance of not stopping the cough of a child. The ipecacuanha wine will, by loosening the phlegm, loosen the cough, which is the only right way to get rid of a cough. Let what I have now said be impressed deeply upon your memory, as thousands of children are annually destroyed by having their coughs stopped. Avoid, until the bronchitis be relieved, giving him broths and meat, and stimulants of all kinds. For further observations on what not to do in bronchitis, turn to what not to do in inflammation of the lungs. That which is injurious in the one case is equally so in the other."

SIMPLE REMEDIES FOR CONSTIPATION.

The practice of giving " opening medicines," cannot be too much deprecated; but where it is *absolutely necessary*, one or two teaspoonfuls of syrup of senna, repeated if needful in four hours, will generally answer the purpose; or, for a change, one or two teaspoonfuls of castor oil may be substituted; honey, too, is excellent, a teaspoonful given either by it self, or on a slice of bread.

But it is infinitely better, when possible, to open the bowels by a judicious regulation of the diet. Bran-bread with molasses is excellent for the purpose, and as molasses is wholesome, it may be substituted for butter when the bowels are inclined to be costive. A roasted apple, eaten with raw sugar, is another excellent mild aperient for a child. Milk-gruel--that is to say milk thickened with oat-meal—forms an excellent food for him, and often keeps his bowels regular, and thus (which is a very important consideration) supersedes the necessity of giving him an aperient. An orange (taking care he does not eat the peel or the pulp), or a fig after dinner, or a few Muscatel raisins, will frequently regulate the bowels.

Stewed prunes is another admirable remedy for the costiveness of a child. The manner of stewing them is as follows: Put a pound of prunes into a brown jar, add two tablespoonfuls of raw sugar, then cover the prunes and the sugar with cold water; place them in the oven, and let them stew for a few hours. A child should, every morning, eat a half dozen or a dozen of them, until the bowels are relieved, taking care that he does not swallow the stones.

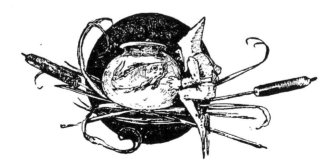

Inexpensive Devices for House Decorations.

THE increasing desire to possess pretty rooms has led to various ingenious devices on the part of those, who, not having a well-filled purse with which to purchase the latest inventions of upholsterers and cabinet-makers, are forced to make deft fingers and busy brains supply their needs. Even articles relegated to lumber-rooms have been brought out and converted into "things of beauty," for the adornment of parlor or chamber, and the woolen rags that accumulate in every house can be turned, by the expenditure of a little time and patience, into rugs that will be very pretty additions to sitting-room or chamber.

COFFEE-BAG RUG.

Cut the coffee-bag—if not procurable, any coarse sacking may be substituted—into the size and shape desired; then cut pieces of wool into strips half an inch wide, and, with a coarse needle, darn them in and out lengthwise through the material, not drawing them flat to the foundation, but leaving loops nearly an inch in height between each stitch. Taste in arranging the colors is of course needed. After the darning is finished, the whole surface is evenly clipped. A very pretty style is to make a black border, and fill in the centre with grey, dotted at intervals with circles of blue or scarlet. Or the centre may be darned hap-hazard with a variety of bright colors. Other combinations will suggest themselves to the worker, who must necessarily be guided somewhat by the hues of the rags from which she is to manufacture the rug.

SET OF FURNITURE.

The most ordinary wooden furniture can be transformed, by the aid of a little paint and some cretonne, into as dainty a set for the "best bed-room," as the heart of woman could desire.

Begin with the bedstead, which we will suppose to be of the ordinary pattern, with head and foot board of nearly the same height. Paint first with white and outline with bands of red, or the color almost every one admires—pale blue—if the paper will permit.

Next take a wooden hoop painted to match the bedstead and suspend from the ceiling by a brass chain above the bed. Buy ten yards of some pretty thin material—dotted swiss, scrim, or cheese-cloth will answer—cut into two lengths, sew them together, then pass through the hoop and sew two of the edges together. This will fall behind the bed and keep the curtains from separating. A ruffle of the same material or a border of lace sewed to the edge will add to the effectiveness of the drapery. Next loop the curtains back just above each corner of the head-board with ribbon bows of a harmonizing color.

DRESSING-TABLE.

Choose a small table with a drawer, and hang above it a mirror in a frame painted to match the colors of the furniture. Cover the top of the table with the same material as the hangings of the bed, lined with a contrasting color, gather around the edge a flounce—also lined if practi-cable—deep enough to reach the floor, and hang above on the wall a mir-ror in a wooden frame painted to match the furniture, with drapery like that of the bed, caught above it with knots of ribbon.

WASH-STAND.

This piece of furniture should be painted to correspond with the other articles, and finished by a dainty white cover, fringed at the ends, with embroidery above. Choose, if possible, a toilet set to match the colors of the room.

CHAIRS.

Common wooden chairs of the kind styled "kitchen" may be made extremely pretty by painting to match the colors of the furniture and put-ting on the seats cushions stuffed with excelsior and covered with cretonne.

To make a delightful little sewing-chair, have the legs of one sawed off about one-third their length, the back ones a trifle shorter than the front.

For the rocker, add a cushion tied across with bows at the top of the back, as well as on the seat. If fortunate enough to possess in addition one of the old-fashioned settees often found in country farm-houses, paint it to match the other pieces of furniture, and tie cretonne covered cushions on the seat and back.

BOOK-CASE.

An old bureau, minus the looking-glass, belonging to any cottage-set, can be converted into a pretty book-case by paint, brass handles, and on the top a set of shelves made by fastening two upright boards on the side of the bureau, and three across. Screw brass rings into each end of the top shelf, slip a bamboo rod through the ends, and hang on the rod curtains of any heavy material that harmonizes in color.

WARDROBE.

A very pretty wardrobe can be improvised from two boards, five feet in height, and one in width, with two other boards crossing at the top and bottom. Fasten casters into the four corners at the bottom, and screw brass rings into each end of the top board.

Make a pair of curtains full and long enough to fall from the top to the bottom, hem the tops, slip a brass wire through the hem, and pass the ends of the wire through the brass hooks. Then screw into the upper board the double hooks that can be obtained in any hardware store for the purpose.

MANTEL-PIECE.

Many houses contain the high old-fashioned wooden mantel-pieces, painted to imitate yellow grained black marble, which are an "eye-sore" to the luckless owner. An artistic friend of the writer, having endured the affliction of one of them till, as she declared, "patience ceased to be a virtue," hit upon a plan which converted the monstrosity into an ornament, all by the aid of a little paint. After ebonizing the entire surface, a spray of flowers was painted in each panel, care being taken to select blossoms whose tints harmonized with the decorations of the room. In a chamber furnished with white and blue, a mantel-piece of this kind would be pretty painted white, with the panels outlined in blue. This demands no skill. If desired, some geometrical design or figure in outline can be painted in each panel. Above the mantel-piece fasten two shelves, the upper one shorter than the lower—supporting them on brackets.

HALL-SEAT.

Still another clever plan for transforming a very ordinary article into a decorative one was devised by a lady with a scanty purse. A plain wooden school bench was stained to imitate cherry, and supplied with a long cushion covered with cretonne, finished at each corner with cords and tassels.

MIRRORS.

A broken looking-glass, usually considered one of the most useless things possible, can be restored to more than its pristine beauty by cutting the fragment into a square, round, or diamond shape, as the fracture best permits, and mounting it in a wooden frame, which may be gilded or painted with any design the worker's skill can compass. Plush frames, too are extremely pretty.

WINDOW DRAPERIES.

A novel window curtain designed by a German lady merits description. It is made of squares of the yellow silk ribbon used for tying bundles of cigars. These squares are joined together by bands of antique lace insertion until the desired length is obtained. The top and bottom are neatly hemmed, and the lower edge is finished by a border of white lace, a row of fringe, or small gilt ornaments.

MORE COSTLY ARTICLES FOR ROOM DECORATION.

The descriptions given for converting inexpensive, old-fashioned, shabby, and dilapidated articles into useful and pretty pieces of furniture will afford suggestions for many other similar plans; but we must not forget to mention more costly bits of decoration, whose manufacture, aided by the description and illustrations, will present no difficulties.

Fig. 1 shows a painted tambourine made to serve the purpose of a photograph frame.

FIG. 1.
PHOTOGRAPH FRAME.

The design of Cupid climbing a bulrush is so clearly given in the illustration that no one who has any skill in painting will have the slightest difficulty in copying it. The drapery is light blue silk, and the ribbons may be either two shades of the same color or in contrasting tints.

TENNIS RACKET WALL-POCKET.

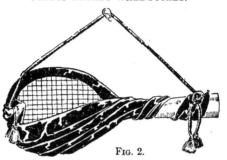

FIG. 2.

Fig. 2 displays a tennis racket decorated with folds of plush so arranged as to form a wall-pocket. A pretty novelty to adorn the room of some college student who is an adept in the game.

BRIC-A-BRAC TABLE.

Fig. 3 shows a novel design for a bric-a-brac table, which will help many a housekeeper to solve the problem of how to conceal a fire-place in summer, or at any time when not in use. The pattern can be easily followed by any cabinet-maker, and the table should then be painted either white and gold, or any tint that harmonizes with the room in which it is to be placed. By means of a removable brass rod, screwed on at the back of the table, curtains of silk or plush are arranged to fall before the fire-place.

FIG. 3.

SCRAP BASKET.

Fig. 4 shows a beautiful scrap basket. The model illustrated was fourteen and a half inches high, lined with soft rose-colored silk, and draped with pale green and rose. The style is not only graceful and pretty in itself,

FIG. 4.

but will afford suggestions for numerous variations, and a tasteful scrap basket is always welcome.

NEWSPAPER HOLDER.

Fig. 5 illustrates one of the new designs for the convenient newspaper wall pockets which are now made in numerous materials and styles. The foundation is usually cloth, embroidered in various ways. The model in the cut is more elaborate. Upon a back-ground of terra-cotta cloth the word newspapers was cut in clear letters from the cloth and appliquéd upon a band of plush. Below it a spray of large marguerites and leaves was traced, under which was inserted a circle of terra-cotta plush. The banner is lined with silk or satin, and a second piece of satin, fastened only at the top and bottom, serves to form the pocket. The top is fastened to a brass or gilt rod, suspended by a cord matching the foundation of the holder.

FIG. 5.

FIG. 6.

DUSTER BAG.

Fig. 6 represents a beautiful duster bag; the material is a rich shade of garnet plush, handsomely embroidered in chenille; but, of course, both fabric and colors can be varied indefinitely to suit the taste of the maker.

FIG. 7.

PALM LEAF WALL POCKET.

Fig. 7 is a new variety of palm leaf wall pocket. The outer fan is cut in the shape seen in the illustration; both are gilded or painted with any of the new metal paints, and then edged with plush and a border of pale green plaited rushes. Other combinations of trimming will suggest themselves. A large bow of ribbon finishes the handle.

CHINESE LANTERN WORK-BASKET.

Fig. 8 is a beautiful work-basket shaped like a Chinese lantern. The height of the model is nine inches and a half. The covering is cream canvas, daintily embroidered in Oriental colorings, and a large full bow of scarlet ribbon decorates it on one side.

FIG. 8.

WHITE AND GOLD SEAT.

Fig. 9 represents a beautiful and novel piece of drawing-room furniture, a seat of unique shape—which any cabinet-maker, however, can copy from the cut—upholstered in bright crimson plush, richly embroidered. After the cabinet-maker has finished the seat in ordinary wood, paint white and varnish,—or use white enamel paint if obtainable—then cover the seat with embroidered or plain plush, brocade, or any material that suits the fancy.

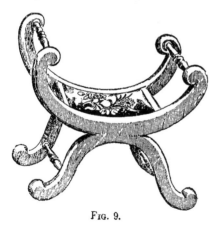

FIG. 9.

WORK-STAND.

Fig. 10 is one of the ever useful work-stands idealized to fill a corner in the drawing-room and hide

FIG. 10.

from sight the half finished embroidery cr more prosaic bit of sewing with which chance moments may be filled. An ordinary " folding stand," which can be shut up if space is narrow, is painted in white enamel, gilded, or stained with cherry, lined with a satin bag of some contrasting color, and tied with long ribbons.

PRETTY LITTLE CONVENIENCES.

PIN SCREEN.

No. 1 is a useful and charming novelty—a pin screen for the dressing-table or bureau—the pattern is cut from stiff paper, according to the following measurements. The first panel is six inches long on one side and five inches on the other, curved at the top, as seen in the illustration; the second is five inches long on one side and four inches on the other, the smallest panel being only four inches on the longest side and three inches on the shortest; each has the same curved top as the first, and all are straight at the bottom. Take cardboard, not too heavy, cut two panels of each size, and cover them with surah of some delicate shade, joining them neatly together with fine sewing silk; then with double thread join the three panels loosely together, that they may be made to stand up like a screen. Each one is then painted with some delicate blossom in water colors. The pins at the top are small English pins; those at the bottom, forming the rollers, are large silver headed or brass headed ones. Those used for pinning the bows of bonnet strings are suitable.

Take twelve inches of three pretty shades of ribbon three or four inches wide ; three shades of green may be chosen, or two white and one yellow, a real buttercup yellow, or the golden browns and yellow are lovely. Join the edges to within an inch of the end, making them only six inches long, and hem the tops neatly—a hem about three-quarters of an inch is a nice size. Now work eyelets, two on each side of each of the three bags, and run a cord of some pretty contrasting color, or one to match, if desired, through them, to draw them up. A little brass ornament of any kind can be put on the outside bag, and may also be sewed on the bottoms. The outside bags should be painted ; on one a flower, on the other a motto for buttons. One seen in New York by the writer had:

> " Three little bags are we,
> All for buttons, one, two, three ;
> Pull the string and then you'll see
> Three little bags are we."

This is a present which will be appreciated by any young girl who likes to see pretty things on her bureau. Cut from satin a circular piece three inches in diameter, then gather a bias piece to fit it and sew firmly to the round. Shirr the upper part of the piece till the opening at the top is the same size as the satin round underneath, thus forming a puff which is stuffed with soft wool wadding.

Next make a second cushion the exact size of the circular opening, cover it with silk, or cotton cloth, and fasten it to the under one. Next cut from black or white cloth or flannel a circle two or three inches larger than the small cushion, and shape the extra size into points. Embroider on each one a small design, and edge with a row of feather-stitching. The round center should also be outlined with a row of feather-stitching, and the middle must then be filled up with an embroidery of bright colored silks in any fancy stitches or patterns to give an Oriental effect.

Finish the end of each point with a tassel, and sew one also between

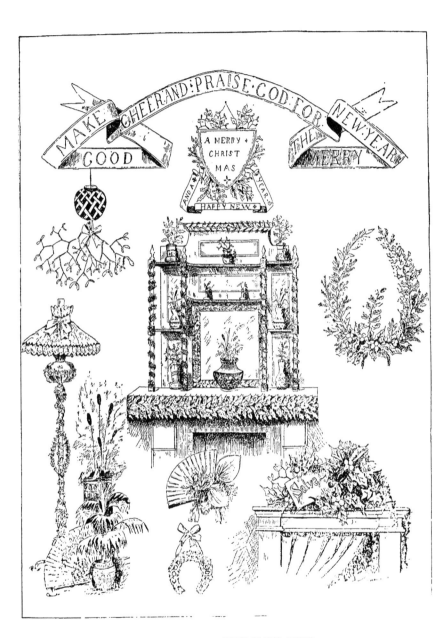

CHRISTMAS DECORATIONS IN THE HOUSE.

every two points. These tassels are prettiest when made of silk, but split zephyr wool combining the colors of the embroidery may be substituted.

When the cloth cover is finished, the circle inside the points should exactly fit the small cushion, over which it must be firmly fastened, the points and tassels lying on the satin puff below, which is larger or smaller according to the width of the bias strip. Since individual taste will vary in regard to this point, it is an excellent plan to cut the round bottom and bias strip from cotton cloth, stuffing the puff loosely and placing above it the upper cushion with its cover, when the effect can be instantly seen. Alterations can then be made when the satin is cut or, if none are desired, the cotton may be kept for a pattern till the next cushion is wanted, for few persons are content with one.

The colors can be varied to suit the room and the taste of the maker. One designed for a bride had a white satin puff, white cloth cover embroidered with white silk and pearl beads, and white silk tassels.

These directions are so explicit that no illustration is necessary.

LETTER HOLDER.

A very ornamental holder for letters answered or unanswered is made of tinted card-board or heavy rough water-color paper, which can be had in delicate pink, blue, and gray. The first piece is ten and one-half inches

long by nine inches wide; the second piece is seven and three-quarters inches long and the same in width; the third is but five inches long, and five wide. Around the top of each sketch a conventional or set row of wild roses; then paint them, adding a few grasses drooping from beneath each. At both ends of every row a few rose leaves are painted. On the largest or longest piece, which we will call No. 1, is painted in gilt letters the word "*lettres ;*" on No. 2 (the second in size) is painted in gold "*repondu*" (answered); on No. 3 (the smallest) is painted, also in gold, "*a repondre*" (to be answered). These three pieces are laid one above another, the largest at the bottom; holes are punched all across the bottom and half way up on the sides of the smallest card. They are then laced together with the narrowest ribbon manufactured, and full bows made at the ends.　A bunch of ribbon also ties the first and second card just above the top of No. 3.　At the top of No. 1 two holes are punched to run the ribbon through, and tie in a full bow some distance (four or five inches) above the top of the pocket to hang the case by.

JEWEL CASE.

A very pretty jewel-case was made by covering an old-fashioned rubber tobacco-pouch with chamois-skin.　This can be done by opening it out and cutting two pieces of chamois just the size of the pouch.　One is then cut in two straight across from one side to the other (this is for the side which is opened).　Join by overcasting the two circles of chamois and slip over the rubber pouch, with the seam inside, hem down the chamois upon the rubber at the opening, and your jewel-case is finished; but a bit of painting adds to its attractiveness.　Pansies are pretty, but any other design can be used.

SHOE-BUTTON CASE.

This pretty and useful little affair is made of ribbons of two colors or shades.

Two pieces of two-inch ribbon, each fourteen inches long, are required. Fringe out the ends for about half an inch, then lay them together so that one will form the lining for the other.　About two inches from the two ends feather stitch them together, forming pockets of this shape for the buttons.　At the top of these pockets, cut very

small holes, through which to run very narrow ribbons tied at the outside edges into small bows, which are extended into ends about four or five inches long and again tied into a full bow.　This loop is used to hang the convenient little article on a gas-jet or keyboard.　In the centre a spool of black linen thread, whose ends, after having the paper soaked off, have been gilded, is tied by running a bit of very narrow ribbon through the two wide ribbons, and then through the hole in the spool, and tying at each end in a little bow.　Near the spool is tacked a piece of white flannel or felt, with pinked or clipped edges, into which coarse needles are thrust. There are now needles made specially for sewing on shoe-buttons.

NECKTIE CASE.

This represents a very pretty necktie case, always an acceptable gift to a gentleman. It is not at all difficult to make by anyone who has the slightest experience in fancy work. Select plush or silk of any favorite color, and ornament with hand painting, embroidery, or any decoration preferred; then line with quilted satin, folding so that it forms the pockets for the ties. When finished and closed like a book, it should measure about half a yard long by five and a half inches wide. A little sachet powder sprinkled on a sheet of wadding should be placed between the cover and the lining. The case illustrated is bronze plush embroidered with a monogram in gold thread, lined with pale blue satin, and finished with a blue and gold cord. One corner is turned down to show the lining.

Another variety is made of the same size and shape; but instead of being soft, firm pieces of card-board are used covered with satin, the inner portion crossed by bands of silk elastic, under which the neckties are to be placed. The cards are then neatly sewed together. If the stitches show, put a small cord along the edges. This kind of case is far better for use in travelling than the soft ones, as it keeps the ties from being crushed, if the trunk or bag is carelessly packed.

WHAT TO DO WITH ODDS AND ENDS.

WHEREVER fancy work is done—and there are few households without some one who is fond of making pretty trifles—scraps accumulate, bits of velvet, plush, and satin, ends of silk and chenille, etc. But ingenious persons find even these bits useful, and the following description of what has been done with them will undoubtedly suggest other plans for utilizing the pile of remnants.

Sofa cushions, of which every fashionable drawing-room now displays an infinite number and variety, can be easily made from odd bits of plush mounted on silk, satin, or serge of any of the new art colors.

Cut the pieces that may be on hand into scrolls, conventional leaves, or any pattern best suited to their shape, and sew them on the foundation, adding veinings and fancy stitches in colored silks and outlining the whole with Japanese gold thread, rope silk, or chenille. Another mode of decoration, if the size of a "left over" bit of plush will permit, is to ornament the upper left hand corner with a spray of painted or embroidered flowers, and then arrange a drapery of plush from the upper right hand corner across the right side of the cushion to the lower corner on the opposite side.

A popular variation of the square shape is the "meal-bag" cushion, stuffed to look like a sack about three-quarters full, and tied around the neck with a bow and ends of ribbon. The portion above the ribbon is lined with a contrasting color, glimpses of which appear here and there among the folds. These "meal-bags" can be made in any material, and may be ornamented either with the conventional pattern described above, or with a large monogram, for which smaller pieces of plush would suffice—outline with rope silk or gold thread.

Two three-cornered pieces of plush, silk, velvet, or brocade can be used by putting them on opposite corners of a square piece of linen or stout calico, and filling the space between with a strip of embroidery placed diagonally across. It is not even necessary that the triangular pieces should be the same size, for if the strip of embroidery does not divide the cushion into two halves of precisely the same size, the effect is equally good. Smaller scraps can be used in the same way for blotters and newspaper holders.

Straight pieces of material can be converted into wall-pockets. A strip thirteen inches long and seven or eight wide will make one of very convenient size, capable of holding a tumbler with a few flowers or small pot of growing ferns, which will be a pretty ornament to hang in any room. To make it, line the two long edges of the material with ribbon or silk for the width of about an inch and a half, then join the ends neatly together, the side which is to form the bottom of the pocket very closely —about an inch and a half from the bottom—and sew it up. The other end is drawn up about the same distance from the top, just tight enough to allow a tumbler of ordinary size to be slipped in and out easily. Add a loop of ribbon, finished with a bow and ends, to hang it by. Quarter of a yard of plush, 27 inches wide, and three yards of ribbon an inch and a half wide, will make two of these little pockets.

The articles mentioned require tolerably large remnants of material, but very small pieces of plush and velvet can be cut into various shapes and used to decorate chairbacks, handkerchief or glove cases. Some persons are very ingenious in inventing designs or copying the quaint figures on Oriental china or rugs, and the queer animals seen on eastern embroideries copied in plush or velvet and mounted on Tussore silk would be very effective. The edges should always be finished with a couching of gold thread or silk. To cut velvet or plush without fraying, it must first be pasted on thin muslin or tissue paper. It should then be pasted on the material to be decorated, and the edges couched or ornamented in any way desired.

The following recipe for embroidery paste will prove very satisfactory. Mix three tablespoonfuls of flour and as much resin as will lie on a shilling with half a pint of water until smooth, pour into an iron saucepan, and stir till it boils. When it has boiled five minutes turn it into a basin. As soon as it is quite cold, it is ready for use. Odd designs of birds and animals cut out of Turkey red cotton and applied to cream-colored material are effective for decorating splashers, night-dress cases, brush-and-comb cases, or shoe-bags.

Patchwork is a convenient way of using small pieces of a variety of materials. The old box, star, and octagon patterns are all popular; and a still more favored design is the crazy-work, which by the exercise of taste can be made very attractive. Any firm material, such as linen, calico, or cretonne can be used for the foundation. This is completely covered with the scraps of material of all shapes and sizes, lightly tacked on, and this is the point where taste is necessary in the selection of harmonizing colors. When all are in place, the edges of each must be secured by working over every joint with fancy stitches, such as herringbone, feather, or coral stitch. The larger pieces are often still further decorated by embroidering or painting flowers, monograms, birds, feathers, etc. Braiding is also used; but though gold braid is extremely effective when first put on, its use is not advisable, as it speedily tarnishes, thus rendering the whole piece of work shabby. It is far better to choose the gold-colored rope silk, whose effect is very similar.

Even scraps of faded or hopelessly ugly silks and velvets, worn ribbons, etc., unfit for patchwork, can be cut in strips from four to ten inches long and about an inch in width—if the silk is very flimsy, it should be cut half an inch wider—sewed together, wound into balls, and then sent to be woven like "rag carpets." A ball weighing one pound and two ounces will make one square yard of the silk fabric, which has a decidedly Oriental effect. It will look better if there is a great deal of red and yellow blended with the dark shades; indeed it is well to put in a bit of some bright hue as often as once in a yard. Soiled silks can be dyed for this purpose.

Portières bordered with plush are very handsome, and the material is also suitable for table-covers, scarfs, book-cases, curtains, etc. A handsome piano scarf was bordered for a quarter of a yard in depth with plain black silk woven in the same manner and finished with a silk fringe combining all the " happy go lucky " colors of the center.

Some persons like to follow their own taste in crazy work, using silks of any color fancy may select; but others can do nothing without explicit directions. For the latter class an effective pattern of patchwork is made by joining pieces about six inches square, arranged in rows of dark and light squares, fastened so that the corners of each light square touch the corners of other light squares, leaving a space between to be filled by the dark piece. It is better, if the scraps will permit, to cut the dark squares from velvet or plush and the light from silk or satin. The joints are covered by working them over in colored silks in herring-bone, or some other fancy stitch, and a design may be worked in the centre of each square. The stitches need not be varied, and can be done in silk of one shade—preferably gold color. But when different shades are employed, it is an excellent way to use up odds and ends of filoselle or embroidery silk.

Another method of utilizing them is by embroidering the corners of the gay silk handkerchiefs, introducing any bits of tinsel, gold and silver thread or spangles left from other work. With the centers covered with plush or velvet, they make very handsome covers for little tables.

Bits of Java canvas, Holbein linen, or any material on which cross-stitch is worked, will make charming little scent-bags, either in the form of " meal-bags " like the sofa-cushions•previously described, or in the shape of a miniature bolster. For this a roll of cotton wool thickly sprinkled with sachet powder is covered with calico, the ends being drawn in. A small design should be worked on the linen in cross-stitch. Then cover the little bolster with the bit of embroidery—first fringing or button-holing the ends—and tie the bows and ends of very narrow ribbon. A full frill of lace can be added at each end, or a remnant of fringe is a graceful addition.

HOME COMFORT.

Hints for the Household.

"Nothing lovelier can be found in woman, than to study household good."—MILTON.

HOME is pre-eminently woman's kingdom, and every "house-mother," using the tender German name, should reign an uncrowned queen. If Heaven has entrusted to her the responsibility of riches, and like Solomon's lilies of the field she need neither toil nor spin, she should still be able to direct, for sooner or later, she must render an account of her stewardship. When she must be at once mistress and maid, subject as well as sovereign, these hints may be of service. The gourmand lives to eat, but the wise man eats to live. Though rules for cooking will not be included in this article, there are a few suggestions that will render that occupation easier; therefore let our first visit be to

THE KITCHEN.

If you burn coal, see that the stove is thoroughly cleaned out in the morning before a fresh fire is started, for in no other way can you secure a clear, bright fire during the day. Be sure that the ashes are sifted, and slightly dampen the cinders before using them, for this promotes combustion.

Since American enterprise has succeeded in supplying reliable time-keepers at so low a figure, every kitchen should reckon a clock among its outfit. Having learned from cookery-books, verified by personal experiment, the average length of time required for cooking the usual meats, poultry, vegetables, etc., make a list of these and hang it up in some convenient place in your kitchen. A small scrubbing-brush for cleaning such vegetables as are cooked in their skins, as potatoes and beets; a pair of sharp-pointed scissors for opening fish, small birds, etc.; a wall pin-cushion containing, besides pins and needles, a large darning-needle for sewing up poultry; a bag with a thimble, coarse thread, soft cotton for the darning-needle, twine, and narrow strips of muslin for tying up bunches of asparagus ready for cooking; a coarsely crocheted or netted bag for boiling cauliflower in; a box containing nails of different sizes, tacks, a gimlet, and a hammer; several small boards to set hot pots and pans on, while dishing their contents, and a linked chain dish-cloth for scouring the inside of pots and pans when they have been used to cook any article that sticks, may all with advantage, be added to the usual kitchen furnishing. All cooking utensils should be kept free from soot, as less fire is required to boil the contents of a bright, clean saucepan or kettle. Should they have been neglected and have become very black, rub them with a flannel rag dipped first in oil, then in powdered brick, and polish with a dry flannel, and a little more brick-dust. All pots and pans are easier to wash if a little hot water is poured into them, when their contents are emptied out, then place them on the rack at the back of the stove or on the hearth until it is convenient to wash them. When onions have been boiled or fried, after washing the vessel, put several spoonfuls of ashes in it, pour on boiling water and let it stand for awhile on the stove.

Silver should always be washed in clean, hot water, as soap dulls the polish. In washing up after meals take the glasses first, next the silver, then such dishes as are not greasy, and lastly, those which are; these are best washed through two waters. Never let knives lie in water, as this discolors and loosens the handles; the practice of placing knives in an old jug and pouring hot water on them, is also to be deprecated, as the intense heat of the blade is communicated to the shank, which melts the cement, and in time loosens the handle. Always have two cloths for cleaning knives; wet the first with water, dip it into fine ashes or brick-dust, and rub the knife free from spots; then polish with the second cloth, dry, add a little more of the ashes or dust; lastly, wipe on a clean, dry towel. Corn-cobs dried in the oven, nut-shells, and bones should all be used for kindling.

Though the tea-towels should be washed and aired every day, it is a good plan to have two sets of them; Monday morning the set that has been used during the previous week, goes into the regular wash, is ironed and darned, should any breaks appear. A small lump of sugar, added to the starch, will keep clothes from sticking to the irons, but there should always be a piece of beeswax sewed in the top of an old stocking, on which to rub the latter. Two or three times a year, the clothes-line, if it is a cotton rope, and the pins, should be placed in the wash-boiler, and clean, hot water poured upon them; after remaining a short time, thoroughly dry them in the sunlight. Though rinsed out as many times a day as necessary, when all the work is done, the sink should be thoroughly flushed with clean, hot water, so as to wash out any impurities that may be lurking in the sewer-trap.

SWEEPING AND CLEANING.

Begin by dusting all the bric-a-brac and carrying it to a place of safety; the smaller articles can be placed in a wide, shallow basket kept for that purpose, or on a tray. Next, with a soft duster, cheese-cloth is the best, and a whisk, thoroughly clean all upholstered furniture, carrying the little articles to the hall or an adjoining room, and covering the larger pieces with dusting sheets; glass globes to the gas fixtures must be washed with warm, soapy water, and rinsed in cold water, in which a little whiting has been dissolved. Shake the window curtains and fold them up as high as you can reach, and pin them there, being careful to avoid all risk of tearing them; dust the shades with a feather brush, and roll them up as high as they will go. Should the stove or grate need attention, spread a piece of coarse canvas or old bed ticking before the fireplace, so as to protect your carpet, remove the ashes, and attend to any polishing necessary. Brush down the walls, carefully dust the picture frames, and then begin your sweeping. Use a whisk to rid the corners and the edges of the carpet of dust, then gently, but with a steady stroke, sweep all the dirt into the middle of the room, and take it up in a dust pan. Repeat this operation to secure any dust that may have blown back. Should the carpet be very dusty, moist tea leaves scattered over the floor before beginning to sweep, will gather up most of the fine dust and prevent its rising and settling on the walls, etc. It freshens and cleans a carpet wonderfully to wipe it thoroughly with a woolen cloth wrung out of water mixed with household ammonia. Ink stains may be removed with salt. If they have dried, slightly moisten the salt with water, scatter it over the stains, and keep gently brushing it back and forth until it is quite black, substitute more salt, and so continue until all the ink is drawn out of the carpet and absorbed by the salt. If the ink is freshly spilled, you need not dampen your salt. Should your window panes need washing in freezingly cold weather, best do it with a soft cloth dipped in alcohol; at other times a little whiting dissolved in the water adds to the brilliant transparency of the glass. In all cases polish with old newspapers. Having attended to your windows, once more carefully dust the walls, pictures, gas-fixtures, and all cornices and mouldings; draw down your shades; unpin and drape your curtains; fold up the dust sheets so as to gather up all the dust that has settled on them, and carry them from the room, which is ready now to be put in order.

If you burn lamps, keep them scrupulously clean. Wicks soaked in strong vinegar and dried before being used, will not smoke. Two or three times a year the part of the lamp containing the wick should be boiled in water in which washing soda has been dissolved; this will improve the quality of the light and obviate the danger of an explosion. Never raise a lighted lamp quickly in a perpendicular direction, as this is apt to send a strong current of air down the chimney, driving the flame into the oil, and causing an explosion. Lift the lamp gently in a slightly slanting direction. Nickel plated lamps must never be washed with soap, as this spoils the polish and makes them look like pewter. Wipe them, instead, with a soft cloth dipped in vinegar. Lamp chimneys, even of flint glass, are less liable to crack if immersed in cold water, which is gradually heated to the boiling point and then allowed to cool. Do not remove the chimney until the water is quite cold. Lamps are more satisfactory when attended to every day.

A dainty addition to any room is one of the now popular rose-jars. A delightful potpourri can be made by the following tested receipt:

½ peck of rose leaves,
½ pound of common salt,
½ pound of bay salt,
½ pound of common brown sugar,
1 oz. of storax,
1 oz. of benzoin,
1 oz. of ground orris root,
1 oz. of ground cinnamon,
1 oz. of ground mace,
1 oz. of ground cloves.

All the above are to be pounded and mixed by a druggist.

Add all sorts of sweet flowers and the leaves of orange and lemon verbena, but no leaves that are not in themselves aromatic. Put the ingredients in a rose-jar and stir frequently with a *wooden* spoon.

After thoroughly cleaning and airing your room, close it, open your rose-jar for a while, and the delicate perfume adds that touch of refinement that proclaims the personal supervision of the mistress.

SUGGESTIONS ABOUT SERVANTS.

SERVANTS' ACCOUNT.

NAME. DATE OF ENGAGEMENT RATE.	CASH PAYMENTS.		CASH PAYMENTS		TOTAL PAID.	TOTAL TIME.	TOTAL DUE.
	DATE	AMOUNT	DATE	AMOUNT			

There is no problem of daily life more difficult to solve than the one frequently termed the "servant question." Rules are hard to give, since establishments vary from a retinue of domestics to a single maid of all work. Widely, however, as the circumstances in which mistresses are placed may differ, the following brief directions are applicable to all cases:

Never reprove servants in the presence of others. Avoid irresolution, undue fault-finding, familiarity, or display of ill-temper, and endeavor to show all possible consideration for their comfort.

Whether the number of domestics is large or small, system is absolutely necessary to ensure comfort, and since the proportion of American families who employ one servant is larger than of those who maintain more extensive establishments, the plan of a well-known writer on household affairs, though it will undoubtedly need alterations to suit the requirements of different families, may afford valuable hints to many a perplexed housekeeper. Her directions, beginning with Monday morning, extend through the week. The one maid must rise early enough to accomplish part of the washing before breakfast. By rising at five,

there will be two hours before it is time to lay the table and prepare the first meal.

A clean cap and long white apron should always be kept hanging in the kitchen closet, ready for the servant to put on to serve the meals or to open the door. It is better for the mistress to own these articles, since if given to the servants they depart with them, and, in our American households, alas, a change of domestics is too apt to be a frequent occurrence.

After having cooked the breakfast and waited at the table, the girl sets before her mistress a neat dish-pan, a mop, and two clean towels; then takes the heavy dishes, knives and forks into the kitchen, while the lady washes the glass, silver, and china.

Having accomplished this task and put the glass and china away, the lady shakes and folds the table-cloth, sweeps the dining-room with a light broom, and dusts it carefully, opening the windows to air the apartment, and then proceeds to set the parlor in order. Meanwhile the servant should go to the chambers, turn the mattresses, make the beds, and then go back to the kitchen, clean the pots and kettles used in preparing the breakfast, and then devote her undivided attention to the heavy work of washing. Care should be taken to choose a plain dinner—steaks or chops, potatoes, and some ready-made dessert. The afternoon is occupied by finishing the washing, hanging out the clothes, and getting the tea, which must be a meal easily cooked; for the "tidying up" of the kitchen is yet to be done before the girl can rest. It will be a great assistance, in places where the visiting is sufficiently informal to permit it, if some member of the family opens the door on busy days.

Tuesday, by general consent, is assigned to the work of ironing; and here it will usually be necessary for the mistress to "lend a hand," and aid in clear-starching and ironing the fine clothing.

Wednesday is devoted to baking part of the cake, bread, and pies that will be needed during the week. In this work the mistress helps by washing the currants, stoning the raisins, beating the eggs, and making the light pastry. Often a lady who has a taste for cooking makes all the desserts, cakes, and pies. She should never consider it extravagant to supply herself with the best cooking utensils—egg-beaters, sugar-sifters, double-boilers, etc., and, if a good house-keeper, she will find both pride and pleasure in her jars of home-made pickles and preserves.

Thursday the maid must sweep the house thoroughly, for this work, if the carpets are heavy, requires strength. The mistress then dusts room after room, and, last of all, the servant follows with a step-ladder to wipe off mirrors and windows.

Friday is commonly occupied in general house-cleaning: scrubbing the floors, cleaning the brasses and silver, scouring the knives, and putting linen-closets and drawers in order.

Saturday is filled with baking bread and cake, preparing the Sunday dinner that the servant may have her Sunday afternoon out, and the toil of the week closes with a thoroughly swept and orderly house, a clean kitchen, and all the cooking done except the meat and vegetables for the Sunday dinner.

Of course the routine given above will not suit all families; many persons may prefer to make a different apportionment their work; but whatever the system fixed upon may be, it should be rigidly carried out, and the maid should receive all the help in her manifold duties that punctuality and order bestow.

Under the most favorable circumstances it is a credit to any mistress to carry on the work of a house through the week, with three meals daily, and to accomplish it she must be capable of doing much of the light work herself and be careful to secure a strong and willing maid servant.

CARE OF THE SPARE ROOM.

One of the joys of house-keeping is the pleasure of exercising hospitality, but it is useless to deny that the enjoyment we derive from our friends' visits is at least somewhat curtailed, if we are compelled to make a general revolution in all the household arrangements in order to secure a chamber in which to place the welcome guest.

Therefore, if possible, every home should have one "spare chamber," only—do not let it be the best and brightest room in the house. A visitor's stay is but short, and to adopt that plan would mean closing one of the cheeriest and sunniest apartments for half the year and relegating some member of the family to an inferior room, which by the exercise of a little taste and skill, might be rendered very charming quarters for friends, who, since they come to spend most of their time with their hostess, are not expected to remain many hours in their rooms.

After the convenience of the regular inmates of the household has been considered, choose the pleasantest room remaining for the guest, or, if but one is left, use every device to render it as pretty and as comfortable as possible.

An excellent plan for the fitting up of a spare room is to put a dado of matting around the walls to protect them from the wear and tear of visitors' trunks, which too often deface the paper, and even by too frequent opening and shutting, make holes in the plaster.

For a summer guest-room an English writer suggests, as exquisitely cool and pretty, white paint, paper of pale green, and green cretonne curtains with a pattern of lillies of the valley, white enamel furniture, and an eider down quilt covered with pale green silk for the bed. Dainty as this would be, however, it is open to two drawbacks—many persons object to green as being liable to contain arsenic, and charming as such decorations might be in summer, they would produce a chilling effect in the dull days of autumn and winter, and the majority of house-keepers need a spare room that will be attractive all the year around.

Nevertheless the description affords valuable hints for fitting up a room. Rose-color could be substituted for the pale-green, or in a chamber facing north, Indian-red would not be too brilliant.

Four pillows and four or five good blankets should always be supplied to the spare room bed, three pairs of sheets, and twelve pillow-cases, four of which should be embroidered with a monogram in the centre or otherwise decorated, as should also one pair of the sheets. The pillow-cases should be removed at bed-time and folded up. A white counter pane is always pretty, and a Madras coverlet flung over the bed in summer has a very dainty effect.

If the household accommodations are limited to *one* spare room, it should always contain a double bed, otherwise only one person could be entertained; married couples thus being excluded from hospitality. Even if the chamber is small, it does not matter, provided that the bed is comfortable.

Spend thought, care, and as much money as the purse can afford in making the spare room cheery and pleasant, and above all let it be always in such order that it can be ready to receive a guest at a half hour's notice.

If there is nothing to be done except to put clean sheets on the bed there will be no domestic turmoil caused by rushing to and fro to procure this, that, and the other necessary article, while our guests are made uncomfortable by the consciousness of the trouble they have occasioned.

Another point to be remembered is not to lumber the drawers and shelves of the spare room with garments or household furnishings put away for storage. Nothing gives a guest a sense of greater discomfort than to see a collection of household goods hurriedly tumbled out of their receptacles to make way for her belongings.

No article intended for the spare room should be allowed to be used elsewhere, otherwise something will be forgotten when the guest arrives to take possession. See that a clothes hamper, a pin-cushion, a match-box, *supplied with matches*, are furnished. Another convenient article is a pretty wall-cupboard for holding medicine and toilet bottles, which if no place is provided for them, are apt to be set on the dainty toilet-cover, where they leave sticky rings.

Of course any careful hostess will see that the soap-dish has a fresh cake of soap, that the water in the pitcher is pure, and that clean towels in abundance, neatly folded, hang on the rack.

SOME WAYS TO MAKE HOME BEAUTIFUL.

Small rooms should always have light paper, as this adds to the apparent size. In choosing a carpet for such a room, avoid large figures; where economy is an object, that carpet wears best which is evenly woven, soft and pliable to the touch, and has but little float work. In hanging pictures, see that the light really comes from the direction that it appears to do in your picture. In the bed-room a dry-goods box, furnished with wooden castors, at the cost of twenty-five cents for the four, and neatly covered with chintz or cretonne, the top stuffed with ten cents' worth of Eureka packing, will be found not only a comfortable seat, but a most welcome addition to the room, should it be without closets, or the furniture not include a wardrobe. A much smaller box, similarly covered, makes a convenient receptacle for shoes. A window with a southern exposure is a real treasure, for with small expense a wide board can be fitted on the sill and two others at equal distances across the window, thus giving you three shelves capable of containing fifteen or twenty pots. All the different varieties of the geranium, coleus, begonia, and ivy, sweet scented violets, Chinese primroses, cyclamen, mignonette, etc., do well in a window garden, and will keep you supplied with a cluster of flowers and bright leaves, or a flowering plant for the center of your dinner table. When the latter is used, if you have not one of the expensive china flower pots in which to set the clay one, a pretty substitute may be made by crocheting a cover of macramé thread. Stiffen this with starch made with strong coffee instead of water, draw it over a clean flower-pot, and let it thoroughly dry; then varnish and add a hint of gilding here and there—gild the handles—and if you desire a bit of color, add a bow of ribbon, which may be varied to suit the requirements of the occasion. Waste no space in your sunny window with palms or ferns, as these do better away from strong sunlight. Fern pans are constant sources of wonder and delight. Any kind of a pan will do—a discarded baking-pan that does not leak, when treated to a coat of green paint, will answer every purpose. Fill your pan in early autumn with wood soil, and then collect your treasures. Here is a pretty arrangement—center, jack-in-the-pulpit, a circle of ferns, at each end a cluster of dandelions with an outer circle of wild strawberry and hepaticas.

FOR THE COMFORT OF THE HOUSEHOLD.

If your house is small and your family large, a folding screen in each bed-room becomes a necessity. Very pretty inexpensive ones may be made by covering the wooden frame—a light clothes-horse will do—with coarse canvas, and on this arranging pictures cut from illustrated papers; when the canvas is entirely covered, var-

nish the whole and be happy in the knowledge that you have added a most important adjunct to your bed-room furniture, as well as provided many an hour's amusement for a sick child in hunting out the various pictures. Should there be a sick person in your household, what greater luxury than cool water, especially if the illness be accompanied with fever. To secure this without ice, melt a handful of coarse salt and a tablespoonful of saltpetre in a quart of water poured into a shallow pan; fill a stone jar with fresh clear water; cover its mouth with a plate; set it in the pan; thoroughly saturate a heavy cloth in water, and with it cover the jar, tucking the ends of the cloth into the shallow pan; set the whole arrangement, if possible, in a draught. Renew the water in the pan each day, but the salt and saltpetre need not be added more than once a month. Firm, sweet butter can be secured in the same way. To return to the sick child, nothing secures a quiet night's rest, after the fatigue of lying in bed all day, better than to rub the body gently all over with a Turkish towel. For delicate persons who cannot bathe freely in cold weather, and who do not take much exercise, this dry rubbing should be part of the daily toilet. Intelligent discrimination in the food selected will add much to the comfort of the household. Solid food may be divided into three classes: those that keep the body warm and give it strength; those that keep the body in repair; and those that keep the brain and nerves in good order and make the bones strong and hard. The first are such as contain *starch*, as potatoes, corn, rice, etc.; *fat*, as in meat, butter, cheese, milk, etc; and *sugar*, which is found in beets, milk, and fruits. The second contain *albumen*, as in the white of an egg; *fibrine*, as in fish and the lean part of meat; *gluten*, as in brown bread, oatmeal, and kindred substances; and *casein*, the solid part of milk in cheese. The third contains *mineral* substances, as water, common salt, and many of the fresh vegetables. A full-grown man requires twenty-one ounces of solid food daily ; sixteen ounces of strength-giving ; four ounces of the flesh-repairing ; and one ounce of mineral food. Then he should take about three pints of liquid every day. Aside from milk and sugar, there is no real nutriment in tea ; but when not allowed to stand too long it is a gentle stimulant to the nerves, and it also hinders the wear and waste of the body. Coffee has the same effect on the body as tea, with a slight difference ; it does not hinder wear and waste so much, but, as it contains a little sugar and a little fat, it adds to our strength. Cocoa and its kindred beverages contain fat, albumen, and gluten in the proportion of one-half its own weight, besides the valuable properties of tea and coffee ; consequently, the wise and truly economical housewife will encourage its use as a preparation. Pure water, besides being refreshing, helps the digestion and supplies much of the requisite one ounce of mineral food. As much of one's comfort depends upon one's health, it would be well to remember what Mrs. Samuel A. Barnett in " The Making of the Home " calls the Seven Golden Rules of Health :

First : Wholesome and regular food, well masticated, is necessary to good health.

Second : Regular heat obtained from food, clothing, fire, and exercise, is necessary.

Third : Cleanliness is necessary ; this includes clean air, clean clothes, clean homes, clean water, and clean skins.

Fourth and Fifth : Light and exercise are necessary to good health.

Sixth : Proper intervals of rest are essential.

Seventh : Self-control is necessary

TO MAKE HOME PLEASANT.

Small courtesies are to home life as the drop of oil to machinery which saves needless wear, and secures smoothness and quiet. Make it a rule to begin the day with a bright good morning and a pleasant smile for each member of your household. If reproof is necessary, let it be given in private and never while you are irritated

yourself. Do not be stingy with your words of praise and always expect that those with whom you associate will do what is right and honorable. It is often a merciful restraint on a child to feel that "mother" believes in him, and a certainty of appreciation and commendation is one of the greatest incentives to exertion. Mark the recurring festivals of Christmas and Easter, the anniversaries of birth and marriage, and even the old-fashioned St. Valentine's Day by some little present for the dear ones. It may be only a knot of flowers from your sunny window ; a delicately browned cake from your orderly kitchen ; a dainty trifle of needlework from your indispensable workbasket, or a loving letter should the dear one be away from home ; but no matter how insignificant the present in itself may be, the love, the kindly thought, the flattering remembrance implied are worth far more than money can ever buy. Good music is a fruitful source of pleasure, and children should be encouraged to sing, as it expands the lungs and strengthens all the respiratory organs. Strive to acquire a voice like Cordelia, "soft and low, an excellent thing in woman," for then, even if your singing is not scientific, it will be a pleasure to listen to your voice. Make a practice of reading aloud yourself, and encourage your children to do so ; good books cultivate and refine while they amuse us. Dancing, when indulged in within the sacred precincts of home, is both a graceful and a healthful recreation ; the home billiard-table, shared with father, the game of cards with mother, the croquet or lawn tennis with sister, would often prove the salvation of the bright, restless boy to whom amusement is a positive necessity which, if not supplied by home, will be sought for elsewhere with what direful results too many heart-broken wives and mothers can testify.

THE CONCLUSION OF THE WHOLE MATTER.

We can give no better summing up of this important matter concerning the making of a home than to quote again from Mrs. Barnett :

"To be a home-maker is not an easy task. It requires much patience, bravery, foresight, and endurance. It calls for some knowledge, thought, and skill. It demands great hopefulness, tenderness, and, above all, unselfishness; but, though it is so difficult, it is none the less a grand privilege— a privilege which none dare think slightingly of; for is not the position of home-maker one which, nobly performed, will bring to every good woman the promise spoken of in the Bible, that 'her children will arise and call her blessed?'"

𝔓leasant 𝔚ork for 𝔑imble 𝔉ingers.

VER since those early days, when Mother Eᵛe made her famous apron of fig leaves, fancy work of some description, the creation of dainty devices out of otherwise useless odds and ends, has been a favorite pastime with women to occupy their spare moments. The work is divided into many branches, and each branch has many subdivisions and modifications, but all are pleasant and each requires nimble fingers.

PATCHWORK.

This is one of the oldest styles of fancy work, but one of the best to use up all the odds and ends that accumulate where a lady is her own dressmaker and milliner. Fig. 1, composed of squares and triangles, is a simple as well as effective design. In the blocks composed of triangles only two colors should be used. For a sofa pillow, the squares might be of plain silk or velvet, embroidered in prettily contrasting silks; while the triangles would look well if made of brocade. A comfort made of scraps of cashmere, wadded with wool and lined with silesia, not only looks bright and pretty thrown across the foot of the bed, but is a light and warming covering during the "forty winks" that "grandma" needs to indulge in at twilight.

Crazy patchwork, to be endurable, must, after all, have "method in its madness." Distinct artistic skill in the grouping and harmonizing of colors is indispensable to the beauty of the final result. The separate bits, if not decidedly handsome in themselves, may be embroidered, painted, or enlivened with a design in appliqué.

KNITTING.

To Cast On:—Measure off a length of thread equal to four times the width required in the completed knitting. For instance, you wish to knit a wash-rag one-quarter of a yard wide then, at a distance of one yard from the end of your thread, make the first stitch. Allowing this take-up, you hold the thread under your second, third, and fourth fingers of your left

288

hand, over your first finger, around your thumb from left to right, over the first finger of your right hand, under the second, over the third, and around the fourth. Hold the needle in your right hand, between the thumb and first finger; let it lie on the thread as it passes from the left to the right hand; insert its point beneath the thread, where it passes over the first finger of the left hand; with the first finger of the right hand pass the thread around the point of the needle; draw the loop so made beneath the thread that lies across the first finger of the left hand, and you will find a small loop on the needle and a large one around your left thumb; slip your thumb from this loop, and with your left hand pull the thread until the large loop has been drawn into a knot close to the base of the small loop on the needle. Repeat until you have the required number of stitches.

To Cast or Bind Off:—Knit the first and second stitches, draw the first over the second, knit the third and draw the second over it; so proceed until all the stitches have been used, pass the thread through the last stitch and draw it up. Always bind off loosely unless directed to do otherwise.

To Knit Plain:—Insert the right-hand needle into the first stitch on the left-hand needle, pass the thread around the point of the right-hand needle, and draw the loop thus formed through the stitch, at the same time dropping the old stitch from the left-hand needle. Continue in this way to the end.

To Purl, Rib, or Seam:—Bring the thread to the front of your work, that is, the side nearest you; pass your right-hand needle through the stitch from right to left, keeping it in front of the left-hand needle; draw the loop thus formed through the stitch on the left-hand needle; slip off the old stitch and, if the next is to be knit plain, remember to pass your thread to the back of the work again, before commencing to knit the plain stitch.

To Rib:—Any given number of stitches knitted plain and purled alternately.

To Widen, Increase, or Make a Stitch:—Pass the thread around the right-hand needle before inserting it in a stitch on the left-hand needle.

To Pick up or Raise a Stitch:—Pick up the thread that lies between the stitches and knit a stitch in it.

To Knit Two Together, Decrease, or Narrow:—Take up two stitches on your right-hand needle and knit them together as if they were one; or, slip one stitch over another as in binding off.

VEST FOR INFANT IN FANCY-RIBBED STITCH.

Required 1 oz. of white Andalusian wool, and a pair of ivory knitting needles, No. 12. Cast on 60 stitches. Knit 1 row plain. The next row begins the pattern. 1st row—knit 2, purl 2, and repeat to the end of the row. 2d row—the same as the 1st, making a ribbing in the usual way. Repeat till 6 rows are done. 7th row—knit plain the whole way. 8th row—purled the whole way. 10th row—purl 2, knit 2, and repeat to the end of the row. This is to reverse the rib of the 1st pattern. Repeat till 6 rows are done. 16th row—knit plain the whole way. 17th row—purled the whole way. Then repeat from the 1st pattern row till 10 patterns in all are completed. 81st row—knit plain, increasing one stitch at the beginning and at the end of the row. 82d row—knit 3, purl the rest till the last 3, which knit plain. 83d row—knit plain, increasing at the beginning and end as before. 84th row—the same as the 82d row. 85th row—the same as the 81st row. 86th row—the same as the 82d row. 87th row—the same as the 81st row. 88th row—you have now 68 stitches; knit 3, purl the rest, knit 3 last. 89th row—knit plain without further increasing. 90th row—the same as the 82d row. 91st row—the same as the 89th row. 92d row—the same as the 82d row. 93d row—knit 13, purl 2, knit 2, purl 2, knit 2, purl 2, knit 2, purl 2, knit 2, purl 2, knit 2, purl 2, knit 2, purl 2, knit 2, purl 2, knit 2, purl 2, knit 2, purl 2, knit 2, purl 2, knit 13. 94th row—knit 3, purl 10, knit 2, purl 2, knit 2, purl 2, knit 2, purl 2, knit 2, purl 2, knit 2, purl 2, knit 2, purl 2, knit 2, purl 2, knit 2, purl 2, knit 2, purl 2, knit 2, purl 10, knit 3. 95th row—the same as the 93d. 96th row—the

Success in Life.

BY WILLIAM MATHEWS.

UCCESS in life is an object of almost universal desire. It is the prize for which men of all professions are contending,—the object for which heads are aching, hearts are panting, hands are working, in all countries and in all ages. Yet, keenly as it is coveted, there are writers who sneer at it and at those who point out the ways of obtaining it. Men who have written on "Self-Help," and the art of "Getting on in the World," have been characterized as authors who have "bowed the knee to the Moloch of Success," and who have taught, explicitly or implicitly, "the most aosolute selfishness." A recent Scotch writer complains that failure has not its Plutarch as well as defeat, "The life of the barrister who was *not* made Lord Chancellor, the life of the curate who did *not* become Bishop of London, the life of the soldier who died a plain lieutenant, are lives," he says, "that I should like to know a little more about." As if anything could be more depressing,—more fatal to all aspiration, hope, or enthusiasm,—than such biographies! That success may be won too dearly,—that it is a positive loss instead of a gain, when attained at the cost of higher interests,—is, indeed, most true; but to win it by legitimate means is not only justifiable, but a duty and an honor. Individual success is essential to the common weal; it implies an increased subjection of the earth to man, a multiplication of the means of common enjoyment, and an improvement of the arts which exalt and embellish life. To prostrate one's self before what success has won, be it power, riches, or

291

luxury, it has been justly said, is flunkeyism; but to honor the qualities that have won success fairly, is worthy worship, not to be condemned or restrained. "It is veneration for that type of manhood which most nearly approaches the divine, by reason of its creative energy."

Properly to estimate success, we must consider what it implies. Success, to an average man, means a tight house, clothing for all weathers, nutritious food, good medical attendance, newspapers and magazines, a good seat in the concert or lecture-room, or in the railway cars, the ability to rest when overtaxed in body or brain, and, above all, personal independence and self-respect. To an educated man, success means, besides all these, books, pictures, and music; intercourse with intellectual, cultivated, and well-bred people; the ability to travel in his own land or in foreign lands; in short, the indulgence of any of the intellectual tastes and pursuits which an advanced civilization creates and fosters, and which can be gratified only by those who inherit wealth or win it in the pursuit of their callings. The love of money may be " *a* root,"—that is, one of the roots—" of all evil ;" but it is the root of a prodigious amount of good, too; and the value of money was never before so great as now. As civilization advances, science multiplies with ever-increasing rapidity the comforts and luxuries of life, and money is the magician that places them at our command. It is precisely because gold and silver mean so much, because life is now so rich in possibilities, that the want of money was never before felt so keenly as to-day.

But what is the secret of this success to which we all aspire? By what act or acts may it be won? I answer first, that success, being the survival of the fittest, implies certain qualities of mind and heart, the germs of which are generally inborn, or implanted so early as to be practically the same thing, but which may be greatly strengthened by culture. For men of a certain constitution there are no rules. For the man of iron frame and quick-pulsing blood, of fierce, indomitable perseverance, of mingled audacity and coolness, and especially of a grim combative religiosity which deepens and concentrates while it sobers all eager acquisitive longings,—for such a man now, as in all ages past, it has been justly said, the world is a prey. " The industrial age is like the age of war. A Napoleon would be the first man in any peaceful profession which he adopted. But men of this stamp, even if it be the highest, are for that very reason rare. It is said that one family of tigers requires a beat as large as Middlesex." But to the mass of men,—to all but one in a hundred thousand,—success is not thus pre-assured. It is a prize for which they must struggle and strain long and late.

The modes in which men win success are almost infinitely diversified, though there are certain ruling qualities common to them all. Some men, ordinarily indolent or negligent, have fits and starts of activity, when they break out in sallies of fortunate boldness,—working double tides, and concentrating years of labor into months,—and absolve their race for power or fame by a series of irregular but giant bounds. Among eminent writers Byron was such a man. He had a volcanic brain, which, in one of its eruptions, threw off "The Corsair" in ten days, and in another, "The Bride of Abydos" in four. "I am like the tiger, " he said; "if I miss the first spring, I go grumbling back to my jungle again; but if I do it, it is crushing." There are other men, who, ever ardent and impetuous, provoke opposition by their vehemence, or overreach the mark, yet succeed in the end. Another class, coldly cautious and silently persevering, seem to weary out the jealousy of fortune by their untiring vigilance and unconquerable patience. Again, there are those who are characterized by an exquisite delicacy of perception and of contrivance,—by a tremulous sensibility which is alive to the most hidden dangers, and a nicety and dexterity of hand that can unravel the most knotty and perplexing difficulties. Finally, there is a class the very opposite of these, who win wealth, place, or honor, by sheer native sense and plodding energy, which ignores all hair-splitting distinctions and over-nice scruples, and cuts the knots it cannot untie.

In reading the lives of successful lawyers, nothing strikes us more than the variety of their natural gifts, plans of study, degrees of industry, and modes of life, when called to the bar. Thurlow at Nando's coffee-house, the idlest of the idle, and Eldon studying with a wet towel round his head; Murray practicing before a looking-glass, and Wedderburn in the green-room; Saunders with a glass of brandy or "a pot of ale at his nose;" and Ellenborough writing and setting before his aching eyes, "Read or starve!"—Kenyon loving law, and Romilly hating it; Story dabbling in politics, and Choate sternly ignoring them; cases like these seem to baffle all speculation, and to show that the ways to legal distinc‧ tion are widely diversified. But to all classes of successful men there are some qualities which are common,—qualities without which their failure would have been inevitable,—and it is these qualities which, in this paper, I wish to point out. But, before doing this, let me say a few words on the notion, so paralyzing to endeavor, which attributes the success or failure of men to luck.

That there is such a thing as luck (that is, that men fail in accomplishing their purposes through causes beyond their control), is beyond dispute. Some of the greatest men have believed in good or bad fortune, or chance. Frederic the Great attributed his conquest of Silesia in part, to " a certain good fortune, which often waits upon youth, and denies itself to advanced age." Napoleon believed in his star and christened Massena, " the spoiled child of fortune." He declared that military science consists in calculating all the chances accurately in the first place, and then in giving accident exactly, almost mathematically, its place in one's calculation. After you have eliminated from any man's career all that can be regarded as the natural results of his conduct, much still remains which is purely fortuitous. Was it not luck when Justin Martyr was converted through a chance meeting with an aged and kindly christian believer? Did not Faust discover the art of printing by looking at the prints of his horse's shoes in the soil, before mounting him? Was not the suspension bridge suggested to Samuel Brown, by the sight of a spider's web? Did not Sir Charles Eastlake owe his first rise in his profession to a chance, which he seized, of painting a portrait of the first Napoleon? On the other hand, did not L'Écure, when young and poor, obtain the place of dentist to King Stanislaus, on the very day on which the king lost his last tooth? Did not Chatterton poison himself just at the very time when the feet of one, who would have relieved his poverty, were turned toward the miserable street in which he died? There is no doubt that " environment " has much to do with success, and turns the scale for or against a man when other things are balanced. Galton has well observed that a certain moral temperature is necessary to develop certain talents,—without it, they prove abortive.

Let us acknowledge, therefore, that there is an element of chance in human affairs,—that man is, to some extent, the creature of circumstances. But let us remember, too, that he is endowed with the power of acting upon circumstances, and shaping them to his will. In a vast majority of cases he may *make* his circumstances. Instead of bemoaning those which are adverse, he should regard them as the very tools he is to work with, —the stepping-stones he is to mount by. The difficulties that determined men conquer are their palaestra,—their gymnasia,—their exercise and stimulant. Did any seeker after knowledge ever battle with greater difficulties than a glover's apprentice of Glasgow, Scotland, of whom it is related that, living with a relative too poor to afford him a candle, or even much fire, he read books in the street by the light of a shop-window, and, when the shop closed, climbed a lamp-post, and, holding on to it with one hand, held his book in the other, and thus mastered its contents? Yet, he persevered in spite of discouragements, till he became the most eminent scholar of his country. Who, again, will whine about his difficulties, when he thinks of Cockraun, the London cab-driver, who, a few years ago, won a prize for the best essay on the effects of Sunday cab-driving, by a paper of 19,000 words, which he wrote in the open air, on the top of his cab?

Need I say that a wise choice of one's profession is essential to high success? As a plant cannot flourish in a temperature contrary to its nature,—as an Arctic animal droops and dies in a tropical climate,—so is it with mental and moral qualities; they require a suitable atmosphere for a vigorous growth. The man who would thrive in his calling must choose one which will enable him to follow the natural bent of his mind, —in which nature will second effort. What can be more painful than for a man to discover, after he has fixed himself in the groove along which he is to work for the rest of his days, that he has mistaken his calling? Waste, it is said, is the law of the world; but none is more conspicuous, more painful to witness, than the waste of talent. In every calling we see men laboring at tasks for which nature never designed them,—cutting blocks with razors, doing fine work with broad axes, fighting with one hand tied. The men who have made their mark in the world have differed from those who have failed, not more in mental power than in their self-knowledge and perception of their inborn apti- tudes. Pope "lisped in numbers," and at twelve feasted his eyes in the picture-galleries of Spencer; Murillo filled the margin of his school books with drawings; Mendelssohn was but sixteen when he read Wieland's Shakespeare, and, with all the vigor of the eagle sunning his newly-per- fected pinions, threw off the immortal overture to the Midsummer Night's Dream. William Pitt was but seven when he told his tutor how glad he was that he was not the eldest son, for he "wanted to speak in the House of Commons, like papa." The late Lord Westbury, Lord High Chancellor of England, was but five years old when his profession was decided upon and his future eminence foretold. Mrs. Martineau did not choose authorship, but wrote because "things were pressing to be said, and there was more or less evidence that I was the person to say them."

On the other hand, what a wretched life was that of Haydon, the painter! A man of great, almost first-rate ability, he failed in his career, not, as he thought, through the world's injustice or insensibility, about which he was perpetually growling, but because he chose the wrong means of making his ability felt and acknowledged. His bitter disappointments, his life-long succession of half-successes worse than defeats, were due to the initial error of mistaking a passion for a power. " A fine critic, a vivid sketcher of character, and a writer of singular clearness, point, and eloquence, was spoiled to make an artist; sometimes noble in conception, but without sense of color, and utterly inadequate to any but the most confused expression of himself by the pencil."

Hardly less than mental ability, are bodily health and vigor necessary to success. In the learned professions, especially, great constitutional strength and power of endurance are absolutely indispensable. The demand on the vitality of a successful clergyman, lawyer, doctor, architect, or engineer, is continuous and exhausting. Talents alone, however fine, will not ensure success. The axe may be sharp, and may be " driven home " with the utmost force; but the power of dealing reiterated and prolonged blows is equally needful. In other words, the mind may be keen, carefully cultured, and full of knowledge and resources; but, to achieve great results it must be capable of sustained energy—of intense and long-continued labor —so as to be fresh and elastic after many hours, and even days, of effort, whether at the desk, in the court-room, the senate, or the chamber of disease. It is true there have been men who, in spite of ill health, have done great and memorable things. Richelieu, baffling conspirators and signing death-warrants, with one foot in the grave; the gouty Torstensohns in a litter, leading armies and astonishing Europe by the rapidity of his movements; Wolfe, capturing Quebec in spite of rheumatism and gravel; Scott, dictating romances with cramp in the stomach, which makes him roll about in agony; Henry Bulwer, going down to the House of Commons with a hectic, suffocating cough, to make a speech on the Irish Church, which is inaudible to more than ten or a dozen members who close up to him—all these are illustrious examples of the soul triumphing over the body's weakness. It is true, also, that it is a working constitution which the professional man needs, not that of an athlete;—the capacity of prolonged mental effort, not the physique of the gymnast or the stroke-oar, or the brawn of the gladiator. It is true, also, that physical vigor is needed more in some professions than in others. But in all it is indispensable to leadership, and he who lacks it must not think to command. Such a constitution is generally inherited, not made; yet, it may often be acquired by strict attention to the health of body and mind. Nutritious food, regular open-air exercise, abstinence from narcotics and unhealthful stimulants, the daily use of the bath and flesh-brush, an abundance of sleep, and regular habits, are the means by which a good working constitution may be gained and secured.

M. EIFFEL.   M. SAUVESTRE.

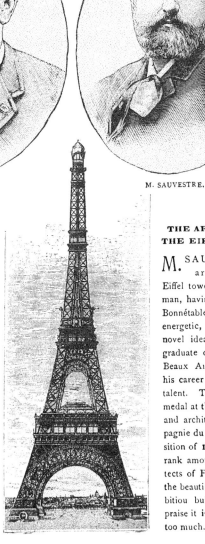

THE BUILDER OF THE EIFFEL TOWER.

THE name of M. Eiffel falls naturally from the pen in connection with that of M. Sauvestre, since the architect and the builder have been co-workers. The man who just at this moment is perhaps the most popular in the world, was born at Dijon in 1832, is a pupil of the Ecole Centrale, and an officer of the Legion of Honor. The number of his successes is limited only by that of his enterprises,—the bridges of Bordeaux, Nive, Bayonne, the metal viaduct of Commentry, that of Douro-Porto, the bridge of Szegedin, and finally the immense viaduct of Garabit.

THE ARCHITECT OF THE EIFFEL TOWER.

M. SAUVESTRE, the architect of the Eiffel tower, is still a young man, having been born at Bonnétable in 1847. Active, energetic, and gifted with novel ideas, though not a graduate of the Ecole des Beaux Arts, he has made his career by sheer force of talent. The recipient of a medal at the Salon of 1869, and architect of the Compagnie du Gaz in the Exposition of 1878, he has taken rank among the first architects of France by erecting the beautiful Colonial Exhibition building, in whose praise it is impossible to say too much.

THE EIFFEL TOWER.

One of the most dangerous gifts is versatility. To be felt in the world, one must be a man of one thing. Having ascertained the thing which he can do best,—which it is his mission to accomplish,—the aspirant must throw into it all the energies of his soul, and sternly confine himself to it alone. " This one thing I do," is not merely an Apostolic resolution,—it is the injunction of universal experience. Singleness ot aim must be added to energy, persistence, and patience, or these qualities will fail of their purpose. Narrow men,—men of single and determined purpose,—are edged men, and cut their way through obstacles more readily than men of broad culture. Many sidedness is desirable, in itself; but a blade which is designed both to shave and carve, will neither shave so well as a razor, nor carve so well as a carving knife. The German scholar who died regretting that he had not confined his labors to the dative case, was one-sided, but he understood the secret of mastery. Compression and concentration are indispensable elements in obtaining the best results of effort. The stream which moves with swiftness and energy, when shouldered between opposite cliffs, becomes an ursightly swamp when left to spread itself over a wide and level plain.

Many men of fine abilities fail through their violation of this rule. Instead of bending all their faculties toward one point, they split themselves in opposite directions, just as a salamander, cut in two, runs forward with its front, and backward with its hind part. In every calling this is disastrous, but emphatically in the learned professions. The lawyer, doctor, and preacher need to steel their hearts against every temptation to scatter their energies. The law is a jealous mistress, impatient of a divided allegiance. It is true that Talfourd was both a successful barrister and a successful author; but " such a phenomenon recalls the black swan, or rather the aloe, that blossoms once in a hundred years." It is true also that concentration does not imply the rejection of collateral aids. It matters not how many are the tributary streams, if they all flow into the great Amazonian river of your action. But hundreds of young lawyers fail because they are impatient of slow results, and turn aside from resolute study to auxiliary pursuits, such as rent-collecting, negotiating loans, etc., that yield an immediate revenue. It almost makes one shiver to think that Daniel Webster came near wrecking his splendid possibilities on this reef. His father, who was poor and had run in debt for the education of Daniel and his brother, obtained for the former an appointment as clerk of the county court, with a salary of fifteen hundred dollars. It seemed a large sum to a family so long pinched by poverty, and Daniel was eager to accept the appointment. " I had felt the *res angustæ domi,"* said he, "till my very bones ached." But Mr. Gore, with whom he was reading law in Boston, advised him to decline acceptance of the appointment, and he did so, though with many pangs, and though his father was nearly heart-broken by his decision. Had he accepted the place, he would, perhaps, have remained a clerk to the end of his days.

Business with Banks.

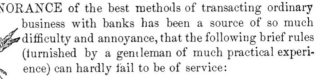

IGNORANCE of the best methods of transacting ordinary business with banks has been a source of so much difficulty and annoyance, that the following brief rules (furnished by a gentleman of much practical experience) can hardly fail to be of service:

1. Before attempting to open a bank account, obtain a proper introduction.

2. Never draw a check unless the money is in the bank, or in your possession to deposit.

3. Never draw a check and send it to any one in another place, expecting to have the funds on deposit before the check can be returned. Inquiry concerning such checks is sometimes made by telegraph.

4. Never exchange checks with any person. It discredits you, and is of no benefit to your friend.

5. Never give your check on condition that it is not to be used for a certain time. There is great danger that it will be presented.

6. Never take a check sent to another person, pass it through your bank without charge, and give him your check for it. Your bank will be certain to discover it.

7. Do not give your check to a stranger. If your bank should lose by it, there would be unkind feeling toward you.

8. When you send your checks out of your own city, to pay bills, write the name and address of the person to whom the payment is made: Pay to Albert Stanley & Co., *of New York*. This will warn your bank, if presented at its counter.

9. Don't be so foolish as to expect that because you deposit your funds in the bank, it ought to pay your overdrafts.

10. Don't imagine that you can treat one bank badly and stand well with others. Remember that there is a Clearing House.

11. Never quarrel with your bank. If you are dissatisfied, go elsewhere, but don't leave your discount line unprotected. Never consider it unreasonable if your bank refuses to discount an accommodation note. Understand that in the estimation of a bank an accommodation note is one for which no value has passed from the endorser to the drawer

12. If you want an accommodation note discounted, tell your bank frankly that it is not, in their opinion, a business note. If you take a note from a debtor with an agreement, verbal or written, that it is to be renewed in part or in whole, and you have the note discounted, and then ask to have a new one discounted to take up the old one, tell your bank about it.

13. Never be so foolish as to say that you will guarantee the payment of a note you have *already endorsed.*

14. Give your bank credit for general intelligence and the understanding of its own business. It is, probably, much better informed than you suppose.

15. Don't try to convince your bank that the paper or security it has declined is better than it supposes. This is sheer folly.

16. Don't quarrel with the teller because he does not pay you in the bills you desire. He probably does the best he can.

17. In your intercourse with bank officers, treat them with the courtesy and frankness you would desire, if you were in their position.

18. Never send stupid or ignorant messengers to transact your business at the bank.

Helpful Suggestions Concerning Ordinary Business Transactions.

FOR THE INEXPERIENCED.

BY WILKING B. COOLEY.

HE purpose of this sketch, the commencement of a woman's business career, is to convey a useful knowledge of the simplest essentials to the successful conduct of everyday business transactions to those who, through lack of experience and training, have no definite conception of the import and purpose of ordinary commercial terms and practices.

There are many who are required by force of circumstances to enter, in a measure, the business world; but, unfortunately for them, the requisite understanding of this subject cannot be readily gained from text-books; and if it could, the aspirant for knowledge often knows not where to seek for it. The widow suddenly bereft, the daughter animated by a praiseworthy desire to add to the scanty family income by embarking in a small business enterprise, are too often confronted at the outset, and retarded in success afterward, by a lack of business experience, and constrained to rely upon the unsympathetic, and perhaps unscrupulous, aid of others.

As of primary importance, I would impress upon all to whom these suggestions may commend themselves, the necessity of keeping an exact record of business transactions of every kind whatsoever. Nothing, even of the most trivial character, should be entrusted to the memory solely. The failure to record a transaction at the time it occurs is apt to lead to disagreement and dispute, and, in financial affairs, may affect the liability of the parties concerned.

In all commercial business, therefore, books should be kept; and here, usually, a mountain of perplexity rises before the timid adventurer.

What account-books shall I buy and keep? is a pertinent query. For your purpose you will probably require a blotter, or day-book, a cash-book, and a ledger, which may be obtained at small cost at any stationer's establishment.

301

You need learn and remember, for the present, but a few essential particulars of the science of book-keeping, and these I shall endeavor to make very plain. For the first lesson, please thoroughly familiarize yourself with the following:

1. When a customer purchases goods, and does not pay for them. you must charge or *debit* him with the value thereof.

2. When a customer who owes you for goods previously bought pays you money on account, or in full of his bill, you must *credit* him with the sum paid.

3. When you receive cash, the cash account must be charged or *debited* with the money.

4. When you pay out cash, the cash account must be *credited* with the amount.

5. When you pay cash to a person whom you owe, you should charge or *debit* the amount to such person.

6. When you buy goods on credit, you must *credit* with the value thereof the person from whom they are purchased.

There is nothing in this that is likely to confuse the beginner.

Debtor is abbreviated Dr., Creditor, Cr.

To elucidate the correct application of the principles mentioned, I shall assume a series of every-day store sales, purchases, and payments, as having occurred, and shall then show, by means of forms, how the several transactions should be entered in the books.

For example:—Mrs. John Brown has rented a convenient little corner store in the town of Empire, and has stocked it with a tempting array of groceries and provisions. She relies for success in the undertaking upon the patronage of neighbors and friends who know her to be deserving and industrious, and to possess excellent judgment as to the quality of the commodities which she is to dispense. With $50.00 in change in the till, she throws open the door of her modest establishment on the first morning of her venture, and customers present themselves. Here is a statement of enough of the business of that memorable first day to answer the present purpose:

Sales on Credit:

To John Smith—10 pounds sugar at 8c.; 25 pounds flour at 4c.; 1 pound ham at 20c.; 2 pounds crackers at 12½c.; 3 loaves bread at 5c. To Richard Jones—2 pounds rice at 8c.; a box cocoa at 25c.; 3 pounds sugar at 8c.; 1 barrel apples at $3.00. To Mary Martin—¼ pound tea at $1.00; ½ bushel of potatoes at 80c.; 1 pound coffee, 28c.

Sales for Cash:

1 pound rice, 8c.; 1 dozen loaves bread at 5c.; 1 pound candles, 20.; 4 pounds sugar at 8c.; 1 dozen eggs, 28c.; 3 pounds butter at 30c.

In addition to these, Richard Jones, who purchased goods to the amount of $3.65, paid $2.00 on account; and Mrs. Brown, encouraged by the extent of her first day's business, paid to Samuel Reed, her landlord, her rent in advance for one week, amounting to $5.00, and purchased from the agent of Barton & Co., of Philadelphia, a choice supply of fancy crackers, costing $8.75, for which she paid cash.

Mrs. Brown, being methodical as well as industrious, had carefully entered each item during the day in her blotter or day-book, and this is the page as it appeared at the close of the day.

1888. Oct.	5							
		John Smith,	Dr.			80		
		To 10 ℔ sugar @ 8			1	00		
		" 25 " flour @ 4				20		
		" 1 " ham				25		
		" 2 " crackers @ 12½				15	2	40
		" 3 loaves bread @ 5						
"	"	Richard Jones,	Dr.			16		
		To 2 ℔ rice @ 8				25		
		" 1 box cocoa				24		
		" 3 ℔ sugar @ 8			3	00	3	65
		" 1 bbl apples						
"	"	Mary Martin,	Dr.			25		
		To ¼ ℔ tea @ $1.00				40		
		" ½ bushel potatoes @ 80				28		93
		" 1 ℔ coffee						
"	"	Richard Jones,	Cr.				2	00
		By cash on account						
"	"	Samuel Reed,	Dr.				5	00
		To cash paid for rent						
"	"	Barton & Co.,	Cr.				8	75
		By goods furnished as follows: (here describe them.)						
"	"	Barton & Co.,	Dr.				8	75
		To cash in full of goods bought						

Mrs. Brown then " posted," as it is called, the day-book entries into her ledger, and the accounts in the latter appeared as follows:

Dr. 1888.		JOHN SMITH.			Cr.
Oct.	5	To sundries...............	2 40		

Dr. 1888		RICHARD JONES. 1888.						Cr.
Oct.	5	To sundries..............	3	65	Oct.	5		2 00

Dr. 1888.		MARY MARTIN.					Cr.
Oct.	5	To sundries..............		93			

Dr. 1888.		SAMUEL REED.					Cr.
Oct.	5	To cash for rent..........	5	00			

Dr. 1888.		BARTON & CO.						Cr.
Oct.	5	To cash.................	8	75	Oct.	5	By goods...............	8 75

She found in the money-drawer in the evening the sum of $40.63, and this amount proved to be correct, as evidenced by the following cash account:

1888.		CASH.	Dr.		Cr.	
Oct.	5	On hand......................................	50	00		
		Cash sales...................................	2	38		
		From Richard Jones...........................	2	00		
		To Samuel Reed...............................			5	00
		To Barton & Co...............................			8	75
		Balance on hand			40	63
			54	38	54	38
Oct.	6	On hand.	40	63		

Mrs. Brown, in her subsequent experience, found it necessary to open a bank account, to draw and receive checks, to give and accept promissory notes, to calculate and charge interest against some of her tardy customers, and to attend to various other details of her thriving business. It will be shown how, with ordinary care and attention, it is easy to become a model merchant.

Mrs. Brown prospered as time went on, as any one may who possesses fair adaptability, and understanding of the branch of business in which he engages, who is industrious, and spends a little less than he earns.

For a time she experienced no little difficulty in making change. Unaccustomed to mental processes, subtraction proved a stumbling-block, until some practical friend, observing her hesitancy, suggested that the calculation of the amount of change due could be very easily made by addition, with less risk of error and considerable diminution of mental labor.

For example, if one purchases goods costing $2.67 and tenders in payment a five dollar bill, the novice would probably attempt to subtract the lesser sum from the greater. The experiment need only be tried to prove how much simpler it is to commence with the amount of the purchase, and add change until the sum total reaches five dollars.

She soon found that it would be very convenient, indeed almost necessary, to mark upon her wares the cost price and the selling price thereof, but did not like to put the former in plain figures, for no merchant desires to advertise his profits. Accordingly she adopted the expedient long resorted to by business men of selecting some word or words of ten letters to represent the ten numerals, and thus avoided the undesirable publicity. It was necessary to find words in which no letter was repeated, and she selected the two words, "Brick House," as her marking guide. A visitor who saw upon a package of goods the characters, $\frac{B \ K \ E.}{3.00}$ would have no conception of their meaning; but Mrs. Brown understood at a glance that the goods in question cost her $2.50, and that she was willing to sell them for $3.00, as may the initiated who know her key, to wit:

BRICK HOUSE

1 2 3 4 5 6 7 8 9 0

Some of Mrs. Brown's patrons were dilatory in discharging their indebtedness to her. She needed the money, and therefore on the first day of the ensuing month transmitted itemized bills to them. This is a specimen bill:

Empire, N. Y., December 1st. 1888.

MR. JACKSON ROE,
            TO MRS. MARY BROWN, DR.

1888.				
Sept. 5	To 6 lbs. ham @ 18c..	$ 1	08	
	" 5 lbs. sugar @ 9c		45	
	" 3 bars soap @ 10c....................................		30	
	" 1 lb. starch		12	
	" 2 loaves of bread @ 5c..............................		10	
	" 1 lb. cheese..		20	
	" 1 lb. of bologna		15	
	" 2 lbs. coffee @ 25c.................................		50	
	" ½ lb. tea @ $1.00...................................		50	
				$ 3 40
Oct. 1	By cash on account,			1 50
	Balance due,			$ 1 90

Mr. Roe, with commendable promptness, called the next day but one
and paid the amount due, whereupon Mrs. Brown receipted the bill in
this form ·

December 3d, 1888.   Received payment in full.
                        (Signed)   MARY BROWN.

Another customer to whom a bill had been sent also presented himself for a like purpose, but had neglected to bring his bill with him, and
requested a separate receipt, which was filled up in this wise

                    Empire, N. Y., December 3d, 1888.
    $5.60.   Received of John Grey five and $\frac{60}{100}$ dollars in full pay-
ment of account to date.   (Signed)   MARY BROWN.

It should be remarked that Mrs. Brown's letters did not often go
astray. The city wholesale houses always received her correspondence
promptly, and commented upon the care with which it was prepared and
the explicitness of detail therein. Unlike many of her sex, she did not
relegate the important part of a letter to the postscript, and she never
forgot to place at the heading the full name of her town and state, with
the number and street of her place of business. As for the envelope, the
address was clearly written, and the postage stamp was *not* placed upon
the back to aid in effectually sealing it, but in the upper right hand
corner of the face. In this way she gained the good-will of the post-
office employés, which sometimes, and especially in a small town, is not
to be undervalued.

At times it was found to be advantageous, as well as convenient, to
buy supplies on credit, and, being known as an honest business woman

whose obligations were invariably met with promptness, no objection was made to the acceptance of her promissory note, payable at a suitable date in the future. This is a good form of note, and the one which was ordinarily employed:

EMPIRE, N. Y., December 1st, 1888.

$65.00.

Ninety days after date I promise to pay to the order of Chubb & Day, the sum of sixty-five dollars, with interest from date, without defalcation, for value received. (Signed) MARY BROWN.

Mrs. Brown soon learned the meaning of *percentage*. One per cent. of any quantity signifies one one-hundredth of that quantity; three per cent., three one-hundredths, etc., abbreviated thus: 1%, 3%, 10%. To calculate percentage, it is only necessary to express the required percentage decimally, that is, to point off the numbers as hundredths, or two places to the right of the decimal point, thus: .01 = 1%, .05 = 5%, and then to multiply the quantity by the rate per cent. As, for example:

What is seven per cent. of $165.

$$\begin{array}{r} \$165 \\ .07 \\ \hline \$11.55 \end{array}$$ — answer.

At first, however, the meaning of a double trade discount was not so clear to her. Goods bought at a discount of 15% will cost a different sum from that which the same goods will cost if purchased at discounts of 10% and 5%, because, in the latter case, the discounts are deducted in succession, first the 10% and then the 5% from the remainder, thus:

$$\begin{array}{lll} \$75 & \$75.00 & \$67.50 \\ .10\% & 7.50 & 3.37 \\ \hline 7.50 & 67.50 & \$64.13 = \text{cost} \\ & .05\% & \\ \hline & 3.37,50 & \end{array}$$

A bank account proves of great convenience to almost all business people, since by its means they become measurably independent of all other modes of transferring money. They need seldom have recourse to the post-office for that purpose, nor are they then required to ask favors of other merchants, or to purchase from banks drafts for which a charge is ordinarily exacted.

What is of quite as much importance, it affords the merchant a handy method, free from expense, of collecting drafts, checks, notes, etc., received in course of business, and, besides, the bank provides a most secure repository for funds which otherwise, in most cases, would be subjected to danger of loss, theft, or destruction.

To the man or woman of business, therefore, it is a good thing to be familiar with banking customs, and if the volume of business be large, dealings of greater or less extent with one or more banks are almost indispensable.

I shall try to state, plainly, some things that Mrs. Brown, whose experiences I have been relating, learned about bank accounts and checks:

She soon ascertained that at least two or three times a week she would have on hand more cash than she needed for the current demands of her business, and more than she cared to keep by her. Having consulted her friend, the cashier of the local bank, she was advised to deposit such moneys therein, and in return for her patronage, was promised every accommodation which the bank could afford. Therefore, from time to time, she placed her surplus, in even dollars, on deposit, first having described the money carefully on a slip furnished by the bank, thus:

DEPOSITED IN FIRST NATIONAL BANK, EMPIRE, N. Y.,
December 10, 1888, by Mrs. Mary Brown.

Bills—Tens, 5...$50
    "   Fives, 3... 15
    "   Twos, 5... 10
Silver coin, Dollars, ... 5
                           —
   Total..$80

She was furnished by the bank with a small pass-book, in which the teller recorded, on the left-hand pages, every sum deposited, and with a book of blank checks, for her use.

Checks may be drawn payable to bearer or to order. Usually the latter is preferred, because, if a check so drawn be lost before presentation, it cannot be collected without the endorsement of the person named as the payee.

A check payable to order is usually in this form·

No. 45.   Empire, N. Y., Dec. 15th, 1888.
                 The First National Bank.
   Pay to Richard Wellston————————or order,
   Fifty-seven——— ————————————Dollars.
$57.00.   MARY BROWN.

If Richard Wellston desire to collect this check in person, he must sign his name across the back, being careful to make his signature agree as to spelling with the designation in the check, and must present it to the paying-teller of the bank. If he desire to transfer it to Mark Jessup, he must make an indorsement in this form:

Pay to Mark Jessup, or order:

RICHARD WELLSTON.

If he desire to transfer it so that any person may collect it he may simply sign his name across the back, and the check is then payable to bearer.

When indorsement is made to a designated individual, the latter may again indorse, specially or generally. The person to whom a check is last indorsed must sign his name across the back to collect the same.

One thing methodical Mrs. Brown did not forget, viz., to keep an exact account upon her check stubs of the amounts deposited in bank, and the amounts drawn out by check. Thus she knew at all times the precise amount remaining to her credit, and was enabled to verify her pass-book at such times as her account was settled by the bank officers. Her check stubs looked like this, the left being the blank backs of the preceding page of stubs:

Balance brought forward.......$110 00 Dec. 1, 1888, Deposited........ 38 00	No. 7. December 3, 1888. To William Johnson, for groceries. $15 00
	No. 8. December 5, 1888. To Robert Paisley, for coffee. $8 00
$148 00 33 00	No. 9. December 6, 1888. To Wistar & Combes, for crackers. $10 00
Balance forward............. $115 00	$33 00

At the close of the first month her account was settled at the bank and stated in the pass-book, in which, on the right-hand side, opposite the entries of the deposits, were given the numbers and amounts of the checks drawn by her, and presented and paid during the course of the month, and a balance was struck. The paid checks, as is customary, were returned to her with the book, and served the purpose of receipts.

It is prudent to be very careful in writing the amounts in checks. Leave no blank spaces in the line for the amount. If there be any spare room, fill it up with heavy dashes. It is, perhaps, the better way to commence at the extreme left, and place the dashes, if there be room, at the right, thus:

Seventy-Five══════════Dollars.

It is also important to exercise great care in writing amounts, particularly such as are susceptible, by means of easy or slight alterations, to change to larger sums. For example, write two very plainly, for nothing is simpler than to change it to five, thus:

Two─────────Five.

Likewise, leave no blank spaces after such small amounts as six, seven, eight, nine, for at most two letters, and, in one case, a single additional letter will multiply the amount ten-fold, thus:

Seven..........
Seventy......
Eight.........
Eighty........

Two may almost as readily be altered to

Twonty.

The business man's, and especially the business woman's path is not, by any means, altogether one of roses, whatever may be the delights of congenial employment and of the anticipation of success in the chosen work. The mercantile field is full of ugly stumps which must needs be pulled up or plowed around or destroyed.

Mrs. Brown's career was no exception in this respect. She had essayed to carry on what is termed a credit business, and some of her customers were none too prompt in meeting obligations. All accounts long unpaid represented to her so much idle capital which might be earning profits if otherwise judiciously employed, and in her own protection she was constrained to charge against and exact from such, "interest" on their unpaid accounts.

Now, without disparagement to the sex, I venture the statement that a knowledge of the mode of computing interest is not often a feminine accomplishment, and that most ladies otherwise shrewd, and perhaps skilled in the ways of the shop-keeper, would be at their wits' end if required to apply such a calculation to a business transaction in which, nevertheless, they might be greatly interested.

Women, in common with men, should be able, when it becomes necessary, to solve such problems for themselves, to the end that they may be proof against the extortions of the usurer and the unscrupulous.

Interest is that which is paid for the use of money. Interest is usually computed at the rate of six per cent. per annum on the basis of twelve months of thirty days each. I shall try to explain what has always seemed to me the easiest rule for ascertaining interest upon this basis.

So long as the period of time for which the interest is to be computed is composed of whole years only, the question is a very simple one. The interest on one dollar for one year at six per cent. is six cents. It is therefore only necessary to multiply the number of years by six cents (.06) and again multiply the result obtained by the number of dollars, thus:

Interest on $55 for 5 years at six per cent.:

$$
\begin{array}{l}
5 \text{ (number of years.)} \\
.06 \text{ (interest on \$1.00 for 1 year.)} \\
\hline
.30 \text{ (interest on \$1.00 for 5 years.)} \\
55 \\
\hline
150 \\
150 \\
\hline
\$16.50 \text{ (interest on \$55 for 5 years.)}
\end{array}
$$

It is really not at all difficult to calculate the interest at the same rate for a part of a year consisting of months without fractions of a month. The interest on $1.00 for one year is six cents; therefore for every two months the interest is one cent, and if we divide the number of months by two and call the result cents we shall be quite correct. Thus the interest on $55 for 5 years and 8 months at six per cent. will be found by the following calculation. I purposely retain the same amount and the same number of years, so that the learner may follow the process step by step.

```
        5 years ——— 2)8  months.
      .06                ——
       ——               .04
      .30               .30
                         ——
                        .34
                        55
                        ——
                       170
                       170
                        ——
                     18.70 answer.
```

Again, the interest for one year is six cents, and for two months is one cent—one cent for every sixty days—ten mills for every sixty days or one mill for every six days. We should then divide the number of days by six and call the result mills. The next calculation will show how to ascertain the interest on $55 at six per cent. for 5 years, 8 months, and 18 days.

```
        5 years — 2)8  months — 6)18  days.
      .06            ——              ——
       ——           .04             .003
      .30                           .04
                                    .30
                                    ——
                                   .343
                                    55
                                    ——
                                  1715
                                  1715
                                    ——
                              $18.86,5 answer.
```

Now that the reader probably understands completely the reasons for the rule, the latter may be concisely stated, thus:

Multiply the year by .06; divide the months by two and call result cents; divide the days by six and call result mills; add the three results thus obtained and multiply the total by the number of dollars.

To find the interest at any other rate, one need only calculate it first at six per cent., divide it by six, thus obtaining the interest at one per cent., and then multiply by the desired rate per cent. For example:

Interest on $55 for 5 years, 8 months, and 18 days at 7 per cent.

5 years — 2)8 months — 6)18 days.

.06   .003

———— .04   .04

.30   .30

        ————

        .343

        55

        ————

        1715

        1715

        ————

6)\$18.86,5 at 6 per cent.

     ————

   3.144 at 1 per cent.

   7

   ————

\$22.00,8 at 7 per cent.

Henry Caller, a business man in a village close by Empire, had long been indebted to our friend for groceries furnished for the use of his family. Mrs. Brown had first politely requested by letter the payment of the money due, but without result. She had even amiably offered to accept payment of the sum in instalments, a good plan often to induce debtors to liquidate their bills; but her efforts proved fruitless. In doubt as to whether to consider the money irrevocably lost or not, she consulted her acquaintance, the cashier of the Empire Bank, who devised a scheme which proved entirely successful, much to her joy.

It transpired in the course of conversation with the cashier that Mrs. Brown had bought of Farmer Conley, living in the neighboring village above mentioned, a considerable quantity of produce, and that the farmer had not yet called for his price. By her friend's advice she drew a draft on the debtor, in favor of Farmer Conley, payable thirty days after date, to be deposited for collection in the bank in the village, "for," said the cashier, " Mr. Caller, your debtor, is in business, and sooner than injure his business reputation in his own village by dishonoring such a draft, he will pay the money, however much against his will such a course may be." The sequel proved the correctness of his conclusions. Mrs. Brown drew the draft in the following form:

\$43.75. Empire, N. Y., January 30th, 1889.

Thirty days from date, pay to Richard Conley, or order, Forty-three and 75/100 dollars, value received.

To Henry Caller, Esq.   Mary Brown.

As a general rule a draft is presented to the person upon whom it is drawn, so that the latter may signify his intention in regard to the payment thereof at maturity. If willing to pay, he signifies that fact by *accepting* the draft; that is writing across its face the word "accepted," the date, and his signature, thus:

Accepted:

February 1, 1889.

HENRY CALLER.

Drafts are customarily deposited for collection in bank.

The time of payment of a draft may be reckoned from the date of the draft or from "sight" thereof, as it is termed. In the latter case the draft would be worded like the following:

> $43.75.   Empire, N. Y., January 30th, 1889.
>   Thirty days after sight pay to the order of Richard Conley, Forty-three and $\frac{75}{100}$ dollars, value received.
>   To Henry Culler, Esq.   Mary Brown.

The time of the draft in such case commences to run from the date of acceptance.

A BANK DRAFT is somewhat different. It is an order by one bank to another to pay a sum of money to a designated person, and is a convenient form of exchange. Banks usually furnish such drafts free of charge for premium as an accommodation, to their patrons or those who keep standing accounts. In form a bank draft is like this:

> No. 58.   Security National Bank of Philadelphia.
>   Philadelphia, Pa., January 31, 1889.
>   At sight, pay to the order of James Johnson, Seven hundred and eighty-six $\frac{51}{100}$ dollars, and charge the same to our account.   Wilson Simpson, Cashier.
>   To Fidelity National Bank, Chicago, Ill.

As stated, such drafts may generally be obtained upon payment of the face value thereof. They are convenient, and, more than that, the employment thereof tends to remove almost wholly the risk of loss of money in transit.

Business.

HE ancients reckoned seven gateways to the soul :—two eyes, two ears, two nostrils, and one mouth — arguing from this, that one should use his gift of speech far less than any of his other senses. Each century that rolls over the world makes the habit of close observation more necessary to success in all the walks of life, and the business man who wishes to reap all the benefits of the passing hour, must keep eyes and ears open, while he weighs his words and prevents his tongue from making rash promises, or giving utterance to any statement other than the truth.

In a recent work on "Business," James Platt enumerates twelve qualities as absolutely necessary for the business man who means to succeed. These are, health, education, observation, industry, perseverance, arrangement, punctuality, calculation, prudence, tact, truthfulness, and integrity.

HEALTH —Our bodies are God's tabernacle, and as such, should be carefully cared for, there is, too, so intimate a relation between the mind and the body that to ensure the best work from the former, we must carefully attend to the demands of the latter. The habit of early rising, the avoidance of late hours, regularity in taking one's meals, simplicity of diet, a recourse to fresh air, bathing, and out-door exercise as tonics rather than to alcoholic stimulants, the faculty of withdrawing the mind from business cares for seasons of rest and relaxation, are all important factors in keeping the body in a healthy condition. Learn, too, to carefully distinguish between strength and health. A uniformly well-developed body, capable of enduring fatigue and climatic changes, is of much greater value than one in which certain sets of muscles have been trained to the performance of some phenomenal feat, at the expense of the rest of the system.

EDUCATION AND OBSERVATION.—Education increases a man's chances of success in a distinct ratio, and the habit of accurate observation is one of nature's best schoolmasters. Every little child proves the truth of the last suggestion. For the first four or five years of its life, how much it learns from observation alone, and how well it generally applies that knowledge, then, when its so-called education begins, how often the habit of observation is lost; the child's head is crammed with isolated dates and facts, but eye and ear are alike closed to what is going on in the world about him. The best education is that which teaches a child to think, and so appropriate what he learns to his own individual needs, that his mind is strengthened and developed by this mental pabulum, as his body is by properly masticated and well-digested food.

INDUSTRY.—"Whatsoever ye do, do it heartily as unto the Lord." Here is the key-note to all true industry. The cheerful, unwearied performance of our daily tasks, dignifies them and lifts them from labor to the higher plane of work. Industry is the "open sesame" to success. The man who spends his time, Micawber-like, waiting for "something to turn up," can rarely profit by the golden opportunity when it does come, but the industrious, like Bacon's wise man "make more opportunities than they find."

PERSEVERANCE.—The ants are "a very little people," yet they teach us the great lesson of perseverance : one grain of sand at a time, they excavate their underground dwelling and pile up the hills around its entrance. But they never try to take more than one grain at a time, however large their excavation is to be. So with human affairs ; do not borrow trouble, do not try to do two days' work in one, do not be discouraged. Nothing is gained by worry, but much by resolution and continuity of purpose. For a lad to try first one occupation and then another is so much lost time, let him rather deliberately and thoughtfully make his choice and then resolutely persevere, remembering that each difficulty conquered, each day's experience gained, are so many rounds in the ladder of life by which he is climbing to ultimate success.

ARRANGEMENT.—"Order is heaven's first law," and the man who systematizes his work has gone a long way toward accomplishing it. If you are in trade, be thoroughly master of your business, appoint each assistant his work; be conversant with every detail, cognizant of your financial position and ready to meet each obligation. As mistress of a household, system in your domestic arrangements will seem to add hours to the day and an extra pair of hands to do the work.

PUNCTUALITY.—If "time is money," then the unpunctual man is a spendthrift that will soon be bankrupt. All engagements or appointments for a fixed time should be as scrupulously fulfilled, as business men valuing their credit, discharge their monetary obligations. Those seeking interviews should enclose a stamp for a reply, which, when received, may, with advantage, be acknowledged, and then the time for the interview having arrived, show your appreciation by presenting yourself punctually. Having promised any merchandise at a certain time, let no cost or trouble deter you from redeeming your promise.

CALCULATION.—This element has been called "the mind of business ; " by it a man can determine what amount of stock to carry, also what expenditure for improvements, what rate of profit, and how many employees the extent of his business will justify. The careful adjustment of outlay in reference to income, will enable one to pay his debts and lay by something for the proverbial "rainy day."

PRUDENCE.—Some one has wittily said, "a prudent man is like a pin, his head keeps him from going too far." Watch carefully the signs of the times, be sure of your own capabilities and resources before you launch out into any larger way of doing business or more expensive manner of living. If you have a good situation, be very sure of your ability to control and direct before attempting to go in business for yourself. Above all, be contented with honest and reliable ways of earning a living and give a wide berth to speculations, though they promise to double your investment each year.

TACT.—If life were represented by a stage coach, tact would be the springs, it lessens the jolting and renders what would otherwise be a wearisome journey, a pleasant trip. True tact is innate, yet it may be acquired to a certain extent by the unflinching and persevering observance of the "golden rule."

TRUTHFULNESS.—Deserve a reputation for truthfulness and, other things being equal, your success is assured. Let your customers, your daily companions, and your friends feel that you are to be relied upon, that in all cases your "word is as good as your bond," and it will be to you in adversity as the rock upon which the wise man builded. Trickery, sharp practice, the tacit falsehood of offering in your business goods which appear well, but will not stand the test of use, the daily lie of marrying for money, influence, or social position, all these may prosper for a time, but they are the shifting sand upon which if a man build, when misfortune comes, as come it surely does to all, his business, his reputation, aye, his character itself, is involved in the mighty ruin because he builded upon the sand.

INTEGRITY.—This is the crowning jewel of human character, the one element of the twelve that includes all the others; for integrity means honesty and he that is strictly honest in all his relations to God, himself, and his fellow man, will conscientiously care for his *health* ; diligently improve every opportunity of enlarging his *education* ; store his mind, and in many instances regulate his conduct by close *observation ;* protect himself from the moral leprosy of idleness by cultivating habits of judicious *industry;* overcome obstacles to success, by *perseverance;* prevent confusion by thoughtful *arrangement;* save precious time by *punctuality ;* adjust his expenditure to his income by *calculation ;* shun snares and pitfalls by *prudence;* avoid cheating any man of his due of courtesy and consideration by *tact ;* and secure respect and confidence by his *truthfulness.* In short the ideal business man is honorable, upright, and just; a man of principle rather than expediency ; a man who could fearlessly say, "if I had to climb even up to Heaven by the mean and crooked ways I have witnessed others adopt, I'd rather stay grovelling in honest dust to the end."

HINTS ON BUSINESS MATTERS.

Letters on Business.—These should be short, clear, and to the point. No unnecessary words, no repetition. The letters should be distinctly formed. Each subject should be in a separate paragraph, the letter written on the full size sheet of note paper, in order that all, or as much as possible, may be contained on the same page. The residence, post-town, and date should be plainly written, and always sign your Christian and Surname *very distinctly.* Many whose writing is clear in other ways, sign their names in such a manner that it is impossible to read them ; and such signatures are far more easily forged than when boldly and simply written. It is advisable to write at the bottom or top of the letter the name of the person to whom it is addressed, as, since envelopes are so much used, it is rarely mentioned otherwise in the letter. If written to a stranger, it is desirable to give your full address at the end of your letter, in order that the person you write to may know how to direct the reply. Suppose the signature is E. Jones; it would be puzzling to know whether to direct to E. Jones, Esq., or Rev. E. Jones, or Captain Jones, or if the letter is from Mrs. or Miss Jones. It makes it much clearer putting a line round the address thus :

Edward Jones, Esq.,
6, Conway Street,
Warwick.

APPLICATION FOR A SITUATION.

132 State St.,
Chicago, Ill., August 30, 189==

Messrs. Holden & Ray,
       Providence, R. I.

Gentlemen:

       Replying to your advertisement in to=day's "Times" for a salesman and office assistant, I beg to offer my services.

       I was in the employ of the well=known firm of Messrs. C. Ingalls & Co., for five years, ending July last, when they sold out. Had the third position in their counting=room, where I had considerable experience in book=keeping, as well as in miscellaneous office work, including corres= pondence. Have had no experience as salesman, but if my application prove successful, shall try to give satisfaction. I enclose a testimonial from my former employers and shall await, with some interest, your reply.

       Yours very respectfully,

                M. E. Baker.

LETTER ORDERING GOODS.

Ivy Seminary, Montrose, N. J.
Shawmut Publishing Co.,
Boston, Mass.

Gentlemen:

Please forward us by Adams'
Express, at earliest possible date, the
following books:

12 Maitland's Language Teaching,
12 Practical Question Books,
16 First Lessons in Arithmetic,
10 Outlines of History.

Enclose bill at your very best
rate, and oblige,

Yours very truly,

William Waters, Prin.

LETTER OF RECOMMENDATION.

Philadelphia, Pa., Dec. 7, 1888.

To whom it may concern

    The bearer, Charles T. Milton, has been in our employ as salesman for eight years. We take pleasure in testifying to his merits, as he has invariably discharged his duties with ability. He was punctual, courteous, and trustworthy.

                C. A. Carter

Put Money in Thy Purse.

HE crucial test of any nation's civilization is the position, domestic and political, of her women. When God crowned His work of creation by making man in His own image, and gave him dominion over the beasts of the field, the fowls of the air, and the fish of the sea, He also gave him woman to be his helpmate. Gradually, however, she sank from this God-given station to be the plaything or worse, the slave, of man. With the dawn of christianity, she began once more to take her rightful place. "Last at the cross, first at the grave," she was no longer the cipher in the world's problem, but a definite quantity possessed of local and individual value.

But greater privileges and higher education imply increased duties and responsibilities. Knowledge is not only power, but it is also the great incentive to human exertion. If she would once more be man's helpmate, she must fit herself for that position, and every year the world is opening more avenues by which she can increase her store of knowledge, either for the sake of education itself or for the increased facilities it will afford her of successfully entering the ranks of bread winners.

To meet the demand for reliable information for those desirous of disposing of their time, books containing either general or specific suggestions are being published from time to time. Some of the ways open to women, alphabetically considered, may be summed up as follows:

AGRICULTURE.—Here is a somewhat neglected field for women, but the raising of medical herbs and such as are used in cooking, with the cultivation of early vegetables, will be found to repay the labor and time expended. Those living in the country have the best chance, but a sunny yard or even a deep window box may be made to yield gratifying crops of lettuce, radishes, curly parsley, cucumbers, or strawberries, which, if not enough to sell, would make pleasant additions to one's bill-of-fare.

ARTIFICIAL FLOWER MAKING.—This trade is soon learned where the person has natural artistic taste and nimble fingers; but the demand for artificial flowers, depending, as it does, upon the fashions, is fluctuating, and the amount to be earned is consequently uncertain.

ATTENDANTS IN ASYLUMS.—These include all grades of service: nurses, cooks, waitresses, laundresses, seamstresses, etc.

BEE-KEEPING.—For those residing in the country, this will be found a pleasant as well as profitable occupation. The prospective bee-keeper should prepare herself by the study of some reliable text-book on the subject and then apply her knowledge patiently and intelligently.

BOARDING-HOUSE KEEPING.—This is a means of livelihood much over crowded and often underpaid, but a good financier and capable housekeeper may reasonably hope for her reward.

BOOKBINDING AND FOLDING.—This trade is now mostly given up to women, and girls can begin as early as thirteen or fourteen. The work is generally paid by the "piece," and can be satisfactorily performed by uneducated persons.

321

BOOKKEEPING.—The chief requisites in this branch are accuracy in figures, correctness in spelling and a good handwriting. The technicalities may be learned at any business college.

BRASS FOUNDING.—Here is a clean and comparatively light employment, but injurious to health. Women now do the polishing, lacquering, burnishing, bronzing, dipping and wrapping up.

CARETAKING.—This is especially suitable for ladies in reduced circumstances who are not young enough to commence training for any especial branch; and a family of means leaving home for any length of time, would gladly entrust the care of the house, and the direction of the servants to such a one.

CHEMISTS druggists)—After a drug clerk has passed a satisfactory examination, she can generally obtain a good situation. The chief requirements are English, Latin, and arithmetic, with three years' experience at a college or with a practising chemist.

CHINA PAINTING.—A girl can begin as soon as she leaves school. Her first work is to cut out the printed paper patterns, next she learns to transfer these to the ware, and gradually rises to the higher grades of the work. There are also merely menial positions that can be filled by the uneducated.

CHRISTMAS CARD MAKING.—This industry gives employment to many ladies, is pleasant and remunerative. Much of it is mechanical, and consists in copying from designs.

CHROMO-LITHOGRAPHING.—At the school of Chromo-lithography in London, the apprenticeship lasts for three years, students receiving a small pay during this time, according to the quality of their work.

CIVIL SERVICE CLERKS.—Applicants for the Classified Department Service must be not less than 18 or over 45 at the time of the examination; must be citizens of the United States; must have previously filed an application upon an official blank, and must not be addicted to the use of intoxicating beverages.

CLERKSHIPS.—In many departments of commercial work, women are superseding men. The requirements differ according to the line of business needing a clerk, but short-hand and book-keeping, with quickness and accuracy in changing money are always desirable.

COURIERS.—A woman with a cheerful disposition, thorough knowledge of the route to be taken, and good business capacity, can often secure a pleasant trip herself, by acting in the capacity of a courier. She must look after the baggage, tickets, hotel accommodations, packing of trunks, and the general comfort and sight-seeing of her employer.

CUTLERY.—Women are employed as scourers and dressers, and their work is the scouring of goods with sand-paper.

DECORATIVE WORK.—Women now are employed extensively in most branches of decorative work; including wood-carving, hand-painting, enameling, gilding, advising as to the furnishing and upholstering of artistic houses, etc.

DENTISTRY.—Women are admitted for training in many of the dental colleges and they are the only dentists permitted to practice in the Eastern harems.

DESIGNING.—Clever designers can always find a ready sale for their work, and it is one of the occupations for a woman that can be carried on in her own home.

DISPENSERS.—This is the latest branch of work taken up by women. A good knowledge of medical Latin, arithmetic, and book-keeping are requisite, with previous hospital training.

DRESSMAKING.—Whether engaged in for profit or to economize, this is an important study for women. When the latter is the object it is sufficient to know how to sew by hand, operate a sewing machine, fit, drape, harmonize colors, copy designs, adapt the prevailing fashion to the individual, and cut the material to the best advantage. When, however, dressmaking is to be one's business, to the above must be added practical knowledge as to the management of work-rooms, giving estimates, buying and selling, corresponding on business matters, making out invoices, estimating rates of profit, calculating prices to be charged, wages to be paid, and the number of dresses that should be turned out weekly by any given number of hands.

ELECTRO-PLATING.—Here is a clean and healthy business, in which about one-sixth of the labor is performed by women.

EMBROIDERY.—Machine work has so far superseded that done by hand that this means of earning one's living is not so remunerative as formerly; it is work, too, that is very trying to the eyes and wearying to the back. A skilful needlewoman may, however, obtain employment with ecclesiastical furnishers, robe-makers, and art needlework establishments.

ENGRAVING. — Here, too, mechanical processes have to a large extent superseded all but the highest class of work. Women make successful engravers, but only those with distinct artistic tastes and strong eyesight should attempt the work. Besides steel and wood engraving, there are gold and silver, which require a course of training lasting from three to six years, but there is one advantage to a woman. As it can be done at home, the accomplished engraver need not lay aside her occupation should she marry.

FACTORY HANDS.—The hours, wages, and requirements differ with the kind of work produced by each establishment, and must be learned by application at the particular factory from which employment is sought.

FEATHER MAKING.—Like artificial flower making, the demand in this branch of trade fluctuates with the fashions, but it is an easy, as well as a pleasant employment for young girls.

FLORICULTURE.—As there is always a demand for sweet-scented flowers, any city lady possessing a window with a southern exposure can add to her income by raising such as do well in pots or boxes. Sweet-scented violets and rose-buds at Christmas command an almost fabulous price.

FRUIT-FARMING. — Many women and girls are employed now to sort, wrap up, pack and label choice fruits prior to their being shipped to market.

GLASS MAKING.—Women are employed in roughing, cleaning, etc., but the wages are small.

GLASS PAINTING AND STAINING.—Comparatively few women are engaged as yet in these industries. Much natural ability, with a knowledge of figure and free-hand drawing are essential, with a thorough training of from three to five years. The extensive use of stained glass in private houses is creating a greater demand for this kind of work.

GLOVE MAKING.—Workers at this trade are employed either in their own homes or at a factory. Work is paid for by the dozen, and is done both by hand and with a machine.

HAIR-DRESSING.—The time required to learn this business, which should include hair-cutting and shaving the head for the sick, varies from nine months to a year. Gentleness and pleasant manners are important characteristics.

HOUSEHOLD SERVANTS.—In no industry is there such a constant demand as for reliable, competent household servants, and many girls seeking employment in the over-crowded, under-paid trades would do well to turn their attention to domestic service, where they would be sure of finding comfortable homes, wholesome food, and high wages.

INDEXING.—Patience, system, exactness, and punctuality are required for success in this occupation. Of a kindred nature is the arranging of literary matter for compilation, much of which is now entrusted to ladies.

INSTRUCTION BY CORRESPONDENCE.—This system was introduced in England in 1871, and was for the benefit of ladies living in the country, who wished to prepare themselves for some of the examinations open to women. The plan is : Questions sent by instructor, answers returned by pupils, corrected and returned by instructor. Short essays and translations written and submitted by pupils. Difficulties solved and general directions as to books by the instructor. Papers are generally returned within a week.

KINDERGARTEN TEACHING.—Those desiring to adopt this style of teaching should receive a thorough training in the true Froebel method; those fitted to give good instruction in this system being always in demand.

LAUNDRY WORK.—Only strong young women, able to labor for ten or twelve hours per day, should engage in this work. In steam laundries, besides the workers, women are also employed as superintendents and clerks.

LIBRARIANS.—Ladies of a literary turn, of good education and address, can fulfil the duties of a librarian or assistant admirably. These duties are entering the names of readers, indexing, booking subscriptions, and attending to the requirements of the readers.

LITERARY WORK.—Women now may be found in every department of literature, and for such as possess real ability there is always employment and fair remuneration.

LITHOGRAPHING.—This is another of the artistic branches in which women could do good work, as it is employed in producing fashion-plates and is not over-crowded.

MASSAGE.—Although women are almost entirely superseding men in this work, none should engage in it but those who are strong and healthy. Practical knowledge of the Swedish gymnastics, anatomy and physiology is absolutely necessary.

MATRONS.—The duties and requirements vary with the institution; but whether it be as matron in an insane asylum, hospital, or home, she should possess a calm, equable disposition, good health, sound judgment, and considerable executive ability.

MEDICAL DRAWINGS.—Though not a pleasant occupation, it has fallen almost exclusively to women, because they are said to be more painstaking and accurate

MILLINERY.—Taste and a good eye for colors are requisite, with practical training, to insure success.

NEEDLE-WOMEN.—Those going out by the day can command higher wages if they can cut and fit children's clothing, undergarments, etc.

NURSING.—There is a growing demand for trained nurses, and every facility for those designing to adopt this profession, to fit themselves for the noble work.

PAPER BAG AND BOX MAKING.—Most of this work is now done by machinery, and the wages for hand-work are low.

PHOTOGRAPHY.—Much of this work is entrusted to ladies, as the retouching of negatives, coloring, mounting on cards, etc., and, as many ladies are learning to take the pictures for amusement, it will not be long before some adopt it as their calling.

PIANO TUNING.—The requirements for this work are a good " ear " and delicate touch; the mechanical part must be learned from a practical tuner.

PLAN TRACING.—Much of this work is now done by ladies. It requires thorough knowledge of mechanical draughting with much practice.

POULTRY RAISING.—No branch of farming pays better than intelligent poultry breeding. Select good stock, give personal supervision each day to your fowls, adopt a regular system whereby you sell your eggs when they command a good price, and use them for hatching when the market is down, and you will find a gratifying balance to your account at the end of the year.

PRINTING.—Women make good compositors and there are some printing establishments in which all the work is done by their sex.

PROOF-READERS.—Female proof-readers are now numerous, but the occupation is fatiguing because of the constant mental exertion. A good general education, familiarity with quotations in foreign languages, accuracy, quickness of eye, and a good knowledge of orthography and punctuation are the essentials.

READERS.—Persons learning short-hand, literary men and women, and invalids often require readers for an hour or two a day. There is no fixed rate of compensation.

REPORTING.—This is a branch of literary work in which a knowledge of short-hand is indispensable.

SHOPPERS.—Ladies engaging in this industry must keep themselves posted in the latest fashions and fabrics, be good judges of quality and probable durability of different materials, and capable of exercising much discretion in their purchasing. Compensation is a certain percentage from employers, and also from the stores patronized.

TEACHING.—Whether in public or private schools or in the family, teaching is always an honorable and fairly remunerative profession. Patience and tact are indispensable to the successful trainer of the young. Besides the English branches necessary for a public school teacher, a governess should be able to give instruction in one or more of the foreign languages, music, calisthenics, painting, dancing, and elegant deportment.

TELEGRAPHING.—Persons wishing to fit themselves for this work must pay particular attention to their spelling and handwriting, and be well up in geography and copying from dictation. The technical part must be learned from a practical telegrapher.

TELEPHONING.—This gives employment to a large number of women. The operator must speak distinctly, and be a person of intelligence, unwearied patience, and good hearing.

TOBACCO STRIPPERS AND SORTERS.—Women earn good wages who engage in this sort of work. Cigarette-making is also profitable, but requires a training of from five to seven years.

TRANSLATING.—Ladies thoroughly conversant with any foreign language can turn it to account by obtaining such work from publishers, though as there is much competition the pay is low.

TYPE-WRITING.—There is no more promising opening for a well educated, pleasant mannered girl than that afforded her by the ability to use the type-writer. With practice a speed of about fifty words per minute may be obtained in six months and gradually increased to eighty or one hundred.

WAITRESSES.—Many women engage in this business. The requirements are neatness and a good appearance generally, with the ability to receive and execute orders with dexterity and despatch. Those who can carve as well as wait command higher wages.

Poor Richard's Almanac.

THE way to wealth, as clearly shown in the preface of an old Pennsylvania almanac, entitled, "Poor Richard Improved."

Courteous reader: I have heard that nothing gives an author so great pleasure as to find his works respectfully quoted by others. Judge, then, how much I must have been gratified by an incident I am going to relate to you. I stopped my horse, lately, where a great number of people were collected at an auction of merchants' goods. The hour of the sale not being come, they were conversing on the badness of the times; and one of the company called to a plain, clean old man, with white locks: "Pray, Father Abraham, what think you of the times? Will not these heavy taxes quite ruin the country? How shall we ever be able to pay them? What would you advise us to do?"

Father Abraham stood up, and replied: "If you would have my advice, I will give it to you in short; 'for a word to the wise is enough,' as poor Richard says."

They joined in desiring him to speak his mind; and, gathering round him, he proceeded as follows:

"Friends," says he, "the taxes are, indeed, very heavy, and, if those laid on by the government were the only ones we had to pay, we might more easily discharge them; but we have many others, and much more grievous to some of us. We are

326

taxed twice as much by our idleness, three times as much by our pride, and four times as much by our folly; and from these taxes the commissioners cannot ease or deliver us, by allowing an abatement. However, let us hearken to good advice, and something may be done for us. 'God helps them that helps themselves,' as poor Richard says.

"1. It would be thought a hard government that should tax its people one-tenth part of their time, to be employed in its service; but idleness taxes many of us much more; sloth, by bringing on diseases, absolutely shortens life. 'Sloth, like rust, consumes faster than labor wears, while the used key is always bright,' as poor Richard says. 'But dost thou love life? then do not squander time, for that is the stuff life is made of,' as poor Richard says. 'How much more than is necessary do we spend in sleep? forgetting that the sleeping fox catches no poultry, and that there will be sleeping enough in the grave,' as poor Richard says.

"'If time be of all things the most precious, wasting time must be,' as poor Richard says, 'the greatest prodigality;' since, as he elsewhere tells us, 'lost time is never found again, and what we call time enough always proves little enough.' Let us then be up and doing, and doing to the purpose; so by diligence shall we do more with less perplexity. 'Sloth makes all things difficult, but industry all easy; and he that riseth late must trot all day, and shall scarce overtake his business at night; while laziness travels so slowly, that poverty soon overtakes him. Drive thy business, let not that drive thee; and early to bed, and early to rise makes a man healthy, wealthy, and wise,' as poor Richard says.

"So what signifies wishing and hoping for better times? We may make these times better, if we bestir ourselves. 'Industry need not wish, and he that lives upon hope will die fasting. There are no gains without pains; then help hands, for I have no lands,' or, if I have, they are smartly taxed. 'He that hath a trade hath an estate; and, he that hath a calling hath an office of profit and honor,' as poor Richard says. But then the trade must be worked at, and the calling well followed, or neither the estate nor the office will enable us to pay our taxes. If we are industrious, we shall never starve; for, 'at the working-man's house hunger looks in, but dares not enter.' Nor will the bailiff or the constable enter; for 'industry pays debts, while despair increaseth them.' What, though you have found no treasure, nor has any rich relation left you a legacy; 'diligence is the mother of good luck, and God gives all things to industry. Then plough deep, while sluggards sleep, and you shall have corn to sell and to keep.' Work while it is called to-day; for you know not how much you may be hindered to-morrow. 'One to day is worth two to-morrows,' as poor Richard says; and, further, 'never leave that till to-morrow which you can do to-day.' If you were a servant, would you not be ashamed that a good master should catch you idle? Are you then your own masters? Be ashamed to catch yourself idle when there is so much to be done for yourself, your family, your country, and your king. Handle your tools without mittens; remember that 'the cat in gloves catches no mice,' as poor Richard says. It is true, there is much to be done, and perhaps you are weak-handed; but stick to it steadily, and you will see great effects, for 'constant dropping wears away stones; and, by diligence and patience the mouse eat in two the cable; and little strokes fell great oaks.'

"Methinks I hear some of you say, 'Must a man afford himself no leisure?' I will tell thee, my friend, what poor Richard says: 'Employ thy time well, if thou meanest to gain leisure; and, since thou art not sure of a minute, throw not away an hour.' Leisure is time for doing something useful; this leisure the diligent man will obtain, but the lazy man never; for 'a life of leisure and a life of laziness are two things. Many, without labor, would live by their wits only, but they break for want of stock;' whereas industry gives comfort, and plenty, and respect. 'Fly pleasures, and they will follow you. The diligent spinner has a large shift; and now I have a sheep and a cow, every one bids me good morrow.'

"2. But, with our industry, we must likewise be steady, settled, and careful, and oversee our own affairs with our own eves, and not trust too much to others; for, as poor Richard says,

'I never saw an oft-removed tree,
Nor yet an oft-removed family,
That throve so well as those that settled be.'

And again, 'three removes is as bad as a fire;' and again; 'keep thy shop, and thy shop will keep thee;' and again, 'if you would have your business done, go,—if not, send;' and again,

'He that by the plough would thrive,
Himself must either hold or drive.'

And again, 'the eye of a master will do more work than both his hands;' and again, 'want of care does us more damage than want of knowledge;' and again, 'not to oversee workmen is to leave them your purse open.'

"Trusting too much to others' care is the ruin of many; for, 'in the affairs of this world, men are saved, not by faith, but by the want of it;' but a man's own care is profitable; for, 'if you would have a faithful servant, and one that you like, serve yourself. A little neglect may breed great mischief; for want of a nail the shoe was lost, and for want of a shoe the horse was lost, and for want of a horse the rider was lost,' being overtaken and slain by the enemy; all for want of a little care about a horse-shoe nail.

"3. So much for industry, my friends, and attention to one's own business. But to these we must add frugality, if we would make our industry more certainly successful. A man may, if he knows not how to save as he gets, 'keep his nose all his life to the grindstone, and die not worth a groat at last. A fat kitchen makes a lean will;' and

'Many estates are spent in the getting,
Since women for tea forsook spinning and knit-
    ting,
And men for punch forsook hewing and split-
    ting.'

"'If you would be wealthy, think of saving, as well as of getting. The Indies have not made Spain rich, becaus: her out-goes are greater than her incomes.'

"Away, then, with your expensive follies, and you will not then have so much cause to complain of hard times, heavy taxes, and chargeable families; for

'Women and wine, game and deceit,
Make the wealth small, and the want great,'

"And further, 'what maintains one vice would bring up two children.' You may think, perhaps, that a little tea, or a little punch now and then, diet a little more costly, clothes a little finer, and a little entertainment now and then, can be no great matter. But remember, ' many a little makes a mickle.' Beware of little expenses : 'A small leak will sink a great ship,' as poor Richard says; and again, 'who dainties love, shall beggars prove ;' and, moreover, 'fools make feasts, and wise men eat them.'

"Here you are all got together to this sale of fineries and knick-knacks. You call them *goods ;* but, if you do not take care, they will prove *evils* to some of you. You expect they will be sold cheap, and perhaps they may, for less than they cost; but, if you have no occasion for them, they must be dear to you. Remember what poor Richard says: 'buy what thou hast no need of, and ere long thou shalt sell thy necessaries.' And again, 'at a great penny-worth pause awhile.' He means that perhaps the cheapness is apparent only, and not real ; or the bargain, by straightening thee in thy business, may do thee more harm than good. For, in another place, he says: 'many have been ruined by buying good pennyworths.' Again, 'it is foolish to lay out money in a purchase of repent-ance ;' and yet this folly is practiced every

day at auctions, for want of minding the almanac. Many a one, for the sake of finery on the back, have gone with a hun-gry belly, and half starved their families; 'silks and satins, scarlet and velvets, put out the kitchen fire,' as poor Richard says. These are not the necessaries of life, they can scarcely be called the conveniences ; and yet, only because they look pretty, how many want to have them ! By these and other extravagances, the genteel are reduced to poverty, and forced to borrow of those whom they formerly despised, but who, through industry and frugality, have maintained their standing; in which case it appears plainly that 'a plowman on his legs is higher than a gentleman on his knees,' as poor Richard says Perhaps they have had a small estate left them, which they knew not the getting of; they think 'it is day, and it will never be night ;' that a little to be spent out of so much is not worth minding; but 'always taking out of the meal-tub, and never putting in, soon comes to the bottom,' as poor Richard says; and then, 'when the well is dry, they know the worth of water.' But this they might have known before, if they had taken his advice : 'if you would know the value of money, go and try to borrow some ; for he that goes a borrowing goes a sorrowing.' As poor Richard says; and, in-deed, so does he who lends to such people, when he goes to get it again. Poor Dick further advises and says :

'Fond pride of dress is sure a curse ;
Ere fancy you consult, consult your purse.'

And again, 'pride is as loud a beggar as want, and a great deal more saucy.' When you have bought one fine thing, you must buy ten more, that your appearance may be all of a piece; but poor Dick says, 'it is easier to suppress the first desire than to satisfy all that follow it ;' and it is as truly folly for the poor to ape the rich, as for the frog to swell in order to equal the ox.

'Vessels large may venture more,
But little boats should keep near shore.'

It is, however, a folly soon punished ; for, as poor Richard says, 'pride, that dines on vanity, sups on contempt; pride breakfasted with plenty, dined with poverty, and supped with infamy.' And, after all, of what use is this pride of appearance, for which so much is risked, so much suffered? It cannot promote health, nor ease pain; it makes no increase of merit in the person; it creates envy, it hastens misfortune.

"But what madness must it be to *run in debt* for these superfluities! We are offered by the terms of this sale six months' credit, and that perhaps has induced some of us to attend it, because we cannot spare the ready money, and hope now to be fine without it. But, ah! think what you do when you run in debt; you give to another power over your liberty. If you cannot pay at the time, you will be ashamed to see your creditor, you will be in fear when you speak to him, when you will make poor, pitiful, sneaking excuses, and by degrees come to lose your veracity, and sink into base, downright lying; for 'the second vice is lying, the *first* is running in debt,' as poor Richard says; and again, to the same purpose, 'lying rides upon debt's back;' whereas a free-born Englishman ought not to be ashamed nor afraid to see or speak to any man living. But poverty often deprives a man of all spirit and virtue. 'It is hard for an empty bag to stand upright.' What would you think of that prince, or of that government, who should issue an edict forbidding you to dress like a gentleman or gentlewoman, on pain of imprisonment or servitude? Would you not say that you were free, have a right to dress as you please, and that such an edict would be a breach of your privileges, and such a government tyrannical? And yet, you are about to put yourself under that tyranny when you run in debt for such dress. Your creditor has authority, at his pleasure, to deprive you of your liberty, by confining you in jail for life, or by selling you for a servant, if you should not be able to pay him. When you have got your bargain, you may, perhaps, think little of payment; but, as poor Richard says, 'creditors have better memories than debtors; creditors are a superstitious sect, great observers of set days and times.' The day comes round before you are aware, and the demand is made before you are prepared to satisfy it; or, if you bear your debt in mind, the term, which at first seemed so long, will, as it lessens, appear extremely short; time will seem to have added wings to his heels, as well as his shoulders. 'Those have a short Lent who have money to be paid at Easter.' At present, perhaps, you may think yourself in thriving circumstances, and that you can bear a little extravagance without injury; but,

'For age and want save while you may,—
No morning sun lasts a whole day.'

Advice to a Young Tradesman.

WRITTEN IN THE YEAR 1748.

To MY FRIEND, A. B. :—As you have desired it of me, I write the following hints, which have been of service to me, and may, if observed, be so to you.

Remember, that *time* is money. He that can earn ten shillings a day by his labor, and goes abroad, or sits idle, one-half of that day, though he spends but sixpence during his diversion or idleness, ought not to reckon *that* the only expense ; he has really spent, or rather thrown away, five shillings besides.

Remember, that *credit* is money. If a man lets his money lie in my hands after it is due, he gives me the interest, or so much as I can make of it during that time. This amounts to a considerable sum where a man has good and large credit, and makes good use of it.

Remember, that money is of the prolific, generating nature. Money can beget money, and its offspring can beget more, and so on. Five shillings turned is six, turned again it is seven and three-pence, and so on till it becomes an hundred pounds. The more there is of it, the more it produces every turning, so that the profits rise quicker and quicker. He that kills a breeding sow, destroys all her offspring to the thousandth generation. He that murders a crown, destroys all that it might have produced, even scores of pounds.

Remember, that six pounds a year is but a groat a day. For this little sum (which may be daily wasted either in time or expense unperceived) a man of credit may, on his own security, have the constant possession of an hundred pounds. So much in stock, briskly turned by an industrious man, produces great advantage.

Remember this saying : *The good paymaster is lord of another man's purse.* He that is known to pay punctually and exactly to the time he promises, may at any time, and on any occasion, raise all the money his friends can spare. This is sometimes of great use. After industry and frugality, nothing contributes more to the raising of a young man in the world than punctuality and justice in all his dealings ; therefore, never keep borrowed money an hour beyond the time you promised, lest a disappointment shut up your friend's purse forever.

The most trifling actions that affect a man's credit are to be regarded. The sound of your hammer at five in the morning, or nine at night, heard by a creditor, makes him easy six months longer ; but, if he sees you at a billiard-table, or hears your voice at a tavern, when you should be at work, he sends for his money the next day ; demands it, before he can receive it, in a lump.

It shows, besides, that you are mindful of what you owe ; it makes you appear a careful as well as an honest man, and that still increases your credit.

Beware of thinking all your own that you possess, and of living accordingly. It is a mistake that many people who have credit fall into. To prevent this, keep an exact account for some time, both of your expenses and your income. If you take the pains at first to mention particulars, it will have this good effect ; you will discover how wonderfully small, trifling expenses mount up to large sums, and will discern what might have been, and may for the future be saved, without occasioning any great inconvenience.

In short, the way to wealth, if you desire it, is as plain as the way to the market. It depends chiefly on two words, *industry* and *frugality;* that is, waste neither *time* nor *money,* but make the best use of both. Without industry and frugality nothing will do and with them everything. He that gets all he can honestly, and saves all he gets (necessary expense excepted), will certainly become *rich,* if that being who governs the world, to whom all should look for a blessing on their honest endeavors, doth not, in his wise providence, otherwise determine. AN OLD TRADESMAN.

330

Civil Service in the United States.

SINCE the organization of the Civil Service Commission, in pursuance of an Act of Congress passed January 16th, 1883, vacancies in the clerical force employed by the Government have been filled by competitive examinations. The act provided for the appointment by the President of three persons as Civil Service Commissioners, not more than two of whom should be adherents of the same political party. It also gave the President the power to remove any commissioner and to fill any vacancy in the commission. It also defined the duties of these three men; the first of which was, "to aid the president, as he may request, in preparing suitable rules for carrying this act into effect; said rules shall provide for open competitive examinations for testing the fitness of applicants for the public service. Such examinations shall be practical in their character, and so far as may be shall relate to those matters which will fairly test the relative capacity and fitness of the persons examined, to discharge the duties of the service into which they seek to be appointed." "Appointments to the public service in the departments at Washington shall be apportioned among the several States and Territories, and the District of Columbia, upon the basis of population as ascertained at the last preceding census." Besides the departmental clerkships in Washington, the Civil Service is applicable to those filling positions in the various custom-houses and post-offices throughout the length and breadth of the land. Examinations to fill such vacancies are held at such times as the public interests require and at such places as best suit the convenience of the greatest number of the applicants; but, "in order to secure uniformity and justice, the questions for all these examinations are prepared at Washington under the supervision of the commission, and the examination papers of all applicants for the departmental service, are marked by the proper Examining Board at Washington." The first thing to be done by an intending applicant is to decide which branch of the service he desires to enter. A consideration which should have weight in settling this question would be where he honestly thinks he can do the best work, which would be determined by his general or special information and the natural bent of his mind. The next step is to obtain proper application blanks. If the department service is the branch selected, then a request for the proper blanks must be addressed to "United States Civil Service Commission, Washington, D. C." If they are wanted for the customs service, then apply to the "Secretary of Customs, Board of Civil Service Examiners, [city, State]." If for the Postal Service, request them of the "Secretary of the Postal Board of Civil Service Examiners [city, State]." In each of the latter cases mention the city in which the custom-house or post-office is located.

The ordinary departmental examinations include the General and the Limited. The first entitles the successful candidate to places having salaries from $1,000 to $1,800 or over; the second commands from $720 to $900 salaries. Those who pass the Limited examination cannot fill a position requiring a General examination; but those who take the General may, with their own consent, be given a low place at first and afterward advanced to the higher without further examination. Tnere are also Special Examinations for places in the departmental service, where technical qualifications are necessary; at present these are given for certain positions in the State Department, the Patent, the Pension, the Signal Office and the Geological Survey. Circulars giving information as to the range of subjects in any of these special examinations will be sent upon application to the Commission. Supplementary examinations in the French, German, Spanish, Italian, and Scandinavian languages, in law, medical science, drafting, stenography, type-writing, telegraphy, and book-keeping are open to those who have passed the general or limited examinations, and a candidate passing in any one of these subjects is placed on a special register, and may be appointed therefrom. In the Customs Service there are three grades of examination: first, for clerks and store-keepers; second, for inspectors; and third, for n'ght inspectors and messengers. In the Postal Service there are also three grades of examination: first, for clerks; second, for carriers; and third, for porters.

"No person who has failed on any examination can, within six months thereafter, be admitted to any other examination without the consent of the Commission, in writing. Consent to a re-examination is given only where sickness or other disabling cause occasioned the failure. No person dismissed from the service for misconduct can be examined within two years thereafter."

" Every false statement knowingly made in the application, or connived at in any certificate which may accompany it, is good cause, not only for exclusion from examination, but for discharge during probation or thereafter."

"The Commission has no wish, on its own account, to conceal the marking of any one, but the injustice and uselessness of making public the failures to pass the examinations, are manifest. The Commission and examining boards will not, therefore, give the standing of applicants to strangers."

"The Commission cannot advise persons as to vacancies in the service, nor furnish information as to the duties, salaries, course of promotion, or other facts as to positions, except such as may be found in its reports."

"The civil service act and the rules make no discrimination in regard to sex. The examinations are open alike to both sexes. The appointing officer in his requests for certifications, declares whether males or females are desired. The Commission must certify from the sex named. If the sex is not specified, the highest in grade, irrespective of sex, must be certified." For deciding what persons may be examined, the Commission has laid down four general rules:

"1st. Only citizens of the United States of the proper age can be admitted to the examinations, and no persons habitually using intoxicating beverages can be appointed.

"2d. Every one seeking to be examined must first file an application upon an official blank.

"3d. No discrimination is made on the ground of political or religious opinions.

"4th. No person shall be entitled to be examined for admission to the Classified Postal Service if under sixteen or over thirty-five years of age, excepting messengers, stampers, and other junior assistants, who must not be under fourteen years of age; or to the Classified Customs Service, or to the Classified Departmental Service, if under eighteen or over forty-five years of age; but no one shall be examined for appointment to any place in the Classified Customs Service except that of clerk or messenger who is under twenty one years of age; but these limitations of age shall not apply to persons honorably discharge l from the military or naval service of the country, who are otherwise duly qualified."

Although each application must be accompanied by a certificate as to good character, general ability, etc., from each of three persons acquainted with the applicant for more than one year previous, more than three certificates will not be received or considered, and for these proper blanks are furnished with the application papers.

Limited examinations embrace the following subjects : dictation exercises ; writing exact copy of printed paragraph ; correcting false spelling in a list of words : arithmetic and letter writing to test the applicants knowledge of English composition and punctuation.

General examinations include, besides the above, additional arithmetical test, and exercise in paraphrasing, grammar, geography, American history, and Constitution of the United States.

Since the Commission has the right to alter its rules and regulations in such manner and at such times as may best secure the public good, candidates would do well, when writing for application blanks, to request also that the last annual report of the Commission should be forwarded to them. Read these rules carefully and follow the directions exactly. During examination, pay attention to neat and legible penmanship, correct grammar and, as far as possible, concise expression.

The Language of Flowers.

E owe to the Oriental nations the invention of a floral language, which was introduced many centuries later into western Europe, and has become to some persons an interesting study. Young girls and lovers, especially, delight in carrying on an exchange of bouquets chosen to express various sentiments, and older persons find a certain pleasure in learning the ideas associated with their favorite blossoms. The following vocabulary, though not intended to be exhaustive, contains most of the flowers best known in this country and England, with their accepted significations.

A novel and pretty entertainment for a summer evening can be given by setting apart an hour for "floral conversation."

Large bunches of the various plants and flowers named must be arranged on tables, from which the guests can select the blossoms needed.

Flowers.	Sentiments.
ACACIA	Concealed love.
ACANTHUS	Arts.
ALMOND	Hope.
ALOE	Superstition.
ALYSSUM, SWEET	Worth beyond beauty.
AMARANTH	Immortality.
AMARYLLIS	Splendid beauty.
AMBROSIA	Love returned.
ANEMONE	Expectation.
ANEMONE, GARDEN	Forsaken.
ANGELICA	Inspiration.
APPLE-BLOSSOM	Preference.
ARBOR VITÆ	Unchanging friendship.
ARBUTUS, TRAILING	Welcome.
ASH, MOUNTAIN, (ROWAN)	Prudence.
ASPEN TREE	Lamentation.
ASPHODEL	Regrets beyond the grave.
AURICULA	Avarice.
AZALEA	Romance.
BACHELOR'S BUTTON	Hope in love.
BALM	Sympathy
BALM OF GILEAD	Healing.
BALSAM	Impatience.
BAY LEAF	No change till death.
BEECH	Prosperity.
BEE-ORCHIS	Industry.
BELL FLOWER	Gratitude.
BILBERRY	Treachery.
BIRCH TREE	Meekness.
BLACK BRYONY	Be my support.
BLUE BOTTLE	Delicacy.
BOX	Constancy.
BROOM	Neatness.
BUGLOSS	Falsehood.
BURDOCK	Importunity.
BUTTERCUP	Riches.

Flowers.	Sentiments.
CALLA LILY	Feminine beauty.
CALYCANTHUS	Benevolence.
CAMELLIA	Pity.
CAMOMILE	Energy in action.
CANDYTUFT	Indifference.
CANTERBURY BELL	Gratitude.
CARDINAL FLOWER	Distinction.
CARNATION, YELLOW	Disdain.
CEDAR	I live for thee.
CELANDINE	Future joy.
CHICKWEED	I cling to thee.
CHINA ASTER	I'll think of it.
CHINA PINK	Aversion.
CHRYSANTHEMUM, ROSE	In love.
CHRYSANTHEMUM, WHITE.	Truth.
CHRYSANTHEMUM. YELLOW.	Slighted love.
CLEMATIS	Artifice.
CLOVER, RED	Industry.
COXCOMB	Foppery.
COLCHICUM	My best days fled
COLUMBINE	Folly.
COLUMBINE, RED	Anxious.
COLUMBINE, PURPLE	Resolved to win
CONVOLVULUS, MAJOR	Dead hope.
COREOPSIS	Love at first sight
COWSLIP	Pensiveness.
COWSLIP, AMERICAN	My divinity.
CROCUS	Cheerfulness
CURRANTS	You please me.
CYPRESS	Mourning.
DAFFODIL	Chivalry.
DAHLIA	Forever thine
DAISY, GARDEN	I share your feelings,
DAISY, MICHAELMAS	Farewell.
DAISY, WHITE	Innocence.
DAISY, WILD	I will think of it.
DANDELION	Coquetry.
DEAD LEAVES	Sadness.

Flowers.	Sentiments.
DOCK	Patience.
DOGWOOD, FLOWERING	Am I indifferent to you?
EGLANTINE	I wound to heal.
ELDER	Compassion.
ELM	Dignity.
ELM, AMERICAN	Patriotism.
EVENING PRIMROSE	Inconstancy.
EVERGREEN	Poverty.
FIR TREE	Elevation.
FLAX	I feel your kindness.
FORGET-ME NOT	True love.
FOXGLOVE	Insincerity.
FUSCHIA	The ambition of my love thus plagues itself.
FUSCHIA, SCARLET	Taste.
GENTIAN, FRINGED	Intrinsic worth.
GERANIUM, APPLE	Present preference.
GERANIUM, IVY	Your hand for next dance.
GERANIUM, NUTMEG	I expect a meeting.
GERANIUM, OAK	Lady, deign to smile.
GERANIUM, ROSE	Preference.
GERANIUM, SILVER LEAF	Recall.
GILLYFLOWER	Lasting beauty.
GLADIOLUS	Ready armed.
GOLDEN ROD	Encouragement.
GORSE	Endearing affection.
GRAPE	Charity.
GUELDER ROSE (SNOWBALL)	Winter.
HAWTHORN	Hope
HEART'S EASE	Think of me.
HEART'S EASE, PURPLE	You occupy my thoughts.
HAZEL	Reconciliation.
HEATH	Solitude.
HELIOTROPE, PERUVIAN	Devotion.
HELLEBORE	Scandal.
HENBANE	Blemish.
HIBISCUS	Delicate beauty
HOLLY	Foresight.
HOLLYHOCK.	Fruitfulness.
HOLLYHOCK, WHITE	Female ambition.
HONEYSUCKLE	Bond of love
HONEYSUCKLE, CORAL	The color of my fate.
HOP	Injustice.
HORSE-CHESTNUT	Luxury.
HOUSE-LEEK	Domestic economy.
HYACINTH	Jealousy.
HYACINTH, BLUE	Constancy.
HYACINTH, PURPLE	Sorrow.
HYDRANGEA	Heartlessness.
ICE PLANT	Your looks freeze me.
IRIS	Message.
IVY	Friendship.
JESSAMINE, WHITE.	Amiability.
JESSAMINE, YELLOW.	Grace ; elegance.
JONQUIL.	Return my affection.
JUDAS-TREE	Betrayed.
JUNIPER.	Protection.
KALMIA (MOUNTAIN LAUREL)	Treachery.
LABURNUM	Pensive beauty.
LADY'S SLIPPER	Capricious beauty.
LAGERSTROEMEA (CRAPE MYRTLE)	Eloquence.
LARCH	Boldness.
LARKSPUR	Fickleness.
LAUREL	Glory.
LAVENDER	Distrust.
LEMON BLOSSOM	Discretion.
LILAC	First emotion of love.
LILAC, WHITE	Youth.
LILY	Purity ; modesty.
LILY OF THE VALLEY	Return of happiness.
LILY, DAY	Coquetry.
LILY, WATER	Eloquence.
LILY, YELLOW	Falsehood.
LIVE OAK	Liberty.
LOCUST	Affection beyond the grave.
LONDON PRIDE	Frivolity.

Flowers.	Sentiments.
LOTUS	Forgetful of the past.
LOVE IN A MIST	You puzzle me.
LUCERNE	Life.
LUPINE	Imagination.
MAIDEN'S HAIR	Discretion.
MAGNOLIA, GRANDIFLORA.	Peerless and proud.
MALLOW	Sweetness.
MANDRAKE.	Honor.
MAPLE	Reserve.
MARIGOLD	Cruelty.
MARIGOLD, FRENCH	Jealousy.
MARSHMALLOW.	Beneficence.
MEADOW SAFFRON	My best days gone.
MIGNONETTE	Your qualities surpass your charms.
MINT	Virtue.
MISTLETOE	I surmount all difficulties.
MOCK ORANGE (SYRINGA)	Counterfeit.
MORNING GLORY	Coquetry.
MOSS	Maternal love.
MOTHERWORT.	Secret love.
MOUSE-EAR CHICKWEED	Simplicity.
MULBERRY, BLACK	I will not survive you.
MULBERRY, WHITE.	Wisdom
MULLEIN	Good nature.
MUSK PLANT	Weakness.
MYRTLE.	Love.
NARCISSUS.	Egotism.
NASTURTIUM	Patriotism.
NETTLE	Cruelty ; slander.
NIGHT-BLOOMING CEREUS.	Transient beauty.
OAK	Hospitality.
OATS	Music.
OLEANDER	Beware.
ORANGE FLOWER	Chastity.
ORCHIS	Beauty.
PANSY	Think of me.
PARSLEY.	Entertainment.
PASSION FLOWER	Religious fervor.
PEA	Appointed meeting.
PEA, SWEET	Departure.
PEACH BLOSSOM	My heart is thine.
PEAR TREE	Affection.
PEONY	Anger.
PENNYROYAL	Flee away.
PETUNIA	Am not proud.
PHLOX	Our souls united.
PINE	Time.
PINEAPPLE	You are perfect.
PINE, SPRUCE	Farewell.
PINK	Pure affection.
PINK, DOUBLE-RED	Pure, ardent love.
PINK, VARIEGATED.	Refusal.
PINK, WHITE	You are fair.
PINK, YELLOW	Disdain
POLYANTHUS	Confidence.
POPLAR, BLACK	Courage.
POPPY	Consolation of sleep.
POMEGRANATE	Foolishness.
POMEGRANATE FLOWER	Elegance.
PRIMROSE	Early youth.
PRIVET	Mildness.
QUINCE	Temptation.
RAGGED ROBIN (LYCHNIS)	Wit.
RANUNCULUS	Radiant with charms.
RHODODENDRON.	Agitation.
ROSE	Beauty.
ROSE, AUSTRIAN	Thou art all that is lovely.
ROSE, BRIDAL.	Happy love.
ROSE, CABBAGE	Love's Ambassador.
ROSE CHINA	Grace.
ROSE DAILY	That smile I would aspire to.
ROSE, DAMASK	Freshness.
ROSE, HUNDRED-LEAVED.	Pride
ROSE, MAIDEN'S BLUSH	If you'll love me, you'll find me out
ROSE, MOSS	Superior merit.
ROSE, MOSS-ROSE BUD	Confessed love.
ROSE, MULTIFLORA.	Grace.

Flowers.	Sentiments.
ROSE, MUSK CLUSTER	Charming.
ROSE, SWEETBRIER	Sympathy.
ROSE, TEA ....., ...	Always lovely.
ROSE, UNIQUE	Call me not beautiful.
ROSE, WHITE	I am worthy of you.
ROSE, WHITE (withered)	Transient impressions.
ROSE, WILD.	Simplicity.
ROSE, YELLOW	Decrease of love.
ROSE, YORK AND LANCASTER.	War.
ROSEBUD	Young girl
ROSEBUD, WHITE.	The heart that knows not love.
ROSEMARY	Your presence revives me.
RUE	Disdain.
SAFFRON	Excess is dangerous.
SAGE	Esteem
SATIN FLOWER (LUNARIA)	Sincerity.
SENSITIVE PLANT	Timidity.
SNAPDRAGON	Presumption.
SNOWBALL ....., ...	Thoughts of heaven.
SOUTHERNWOOD	Jesting
SPEARMINT., ...	Warm feelings.
STAR OF BETHLEHEM.	Reconciliation.
STRAMONIUM, COMMON.	Disguise.
STRAWBERRY.	Perfect excellence.
STRAWBERRY TREE (ARBUTIS)	Esteem and love.

Flowers.	Sentiments.
SUMAC	Splendor
SUNFLOWER, DWARF	Your devoted admirer
SUNFLOWER, TALL	Pride.
SWEET WILLIAM	Finesse.
SYRINGA	Memory
TANSY	I declare against you.
THISTLE	Austerity.
THORNS.	Severity.
THYME .	Activity.
TIGER FLOWER	May pride befriend thee.
TRUMPET FLOWER	Separation.
TUBEROSE	Dangerous pleasures.
TULIP	Declaration of love.
TULIP, VARIEGATED	Beautiful eyes
TULIP, YELLOW	Hopeless love.
VERBENA	Sensibility.
VIOLET, BLUE...	Love
VIOLET, WHITE ., ...	Modesty.
VIOLET, YELLOW...... ..	Modest worth.
WALL FLOWER	Fidelity.
WEEPING WILLOW,	Forsaken.
WHEAT	Prosperity.
WOODBINE	Fraternal love.
WOOD SORREL.	Joy.
WORMWOOD	Absence.
YARROW	Cure for heartache.
YEW	Sorrow.
ZENNÆ	Absent friends.

BOUVARDIAS.

STATE MOTTOES.

UNITED STATES OF AMERICA.—E Pluribus Unum—"Many in one."

ALABAMA.—Here we rest.

ARKANSAS.—Regnant Populi—"The people rule."

CALIFORNIA.—Eureka—"I have found."

COLORADO.—Nil Sine Humine—"Nothing without Divine aid."

CONNECTICUT.—Qui Transtulit Sustinet—"He who planteth still sustains."

DELAWARE.—Liberty and Independence.

GEORGIA.—Constitution, Wisdom, Justice, Moderation.

ILLINOIS. — State Sovereignty, National Union.

IOWA.— Our liberties we prize, and our rights we will maintain.

KANSAS. —Ad Astra per Aspera—"Through rough ways to the stars."

KENTUCKY—United we stand; divided we fall.

LOUISIANA.—Justice, Union, Confidence

MAINE.—Dirigo—"I direct."

MARYLAND.—Crescite et Multiplicamini—"Increase and multiply."

MASSACHUSETTS.—Ense petit placidam sub libertate quietem—"By the sword she seeks peace under liberty."

MICHIGAN.—Tuebor—"I will defend it" Si quoæris peninsulam amœnam circumspice — "If thou seekest a beautiful peninsula, behold it here."

MINNESOTA. — L'Etoile du Nord—"The Star of the North."

MISSOURI.—United we stand; divided we fall. Solus populi suprema lex esto—"The public safety is the supreme law."

NEBRASKA. — Popular Sovereignty, Progress.

NEVADA.—Volens et potens—"Willing and able." All for our country.

NEW YORK.—·Excelsior—"More elevated."

OHIO.—Imperium in imperio.

OREGON. —Alis Volat Propriis—"Union."

PENNSYLVANIA. — Virtue, Liberty, Independence.

RHODE ISLAND.—Hope.

SOUTH CAROLINA.—Animis opibusque parati—"Ready with our lives and property."

TENNESSEE.—Agriculture, commerce·

TEXAS —The lone star.

VERMONT. —Freedom and Unity.

VIRGINIA.—Sic semper tyrannis —"Thus we serve tyrants."

WEST VIRGINIA.—Montani semper liberi—"Mountaineers are always freemen."

WISCONSIN —Civilitas successit barbarum —"Civilization has succeeded barbarism."

ARIZONA.—Sitat Deus.

DAKOTA.—Liberty and union, one and inseparable, now and forever.

DISTRICT OF COLUMBIA.—Justia Omnibus.

NEW MEXICO.—Crescit Eundo— "It increases by going."

WASHINGTON TERRITORY.—Al-Ki — "By and by."

WYOMING.—Cedant arma togae—"Let military yield to the civil power."

Florida, Indiana, Mississippi, New Hampshire, New Jersey, North Carolina, Idaho, Montana, and Utah have no mottoes on their state seals.

FICTITIOUS NAMES OF STATES.

Wisconsin—Badger State.

Massachusetts—Bay State.

Mississippi—Bayou State.

Arkansas—Bear State.

Louisiana—Creole State.

Delaware—Diamond State.

New York—Empire State. Excelsior State.

Connecticut—Freestone State.

New Hampshire—Granite State.

Vermont—Green Mountain State.

Iowa—Hawkeye State.

Indiana—Hoosier State.

Pennsylvania—Keystone State.

Michigan—Lake State.

Texas—Lone-Star State.

Maine—Lumber State. Pine-Tree State.

Virginia—Mother of Presidents. Mother of States.

Connecticut—Nutmeg State.

Massachusetts—Old Colony.

Virginia—Old Dominion.

North Carolina—Old North State.

South Carolina—Palmetto State.

Florida—Peninsular State.

Illinois—Prairie State.

North Carolina—Turpentine State.

FICTITIOUS NAMES OF CITIES.

Hannibal, Missouri—Bluff City
Philadelphia—City of Brotherly love.
Brooklyn, N. Y.—City of Churches.
New Haven, Conn.—City of Elms.
Washington--City of Magnificent Distances.
Boston, Mass.—City of Notions.
Nashville, Tenn.—City of Rocks.
Lowell, Mass.—City of Spindles.
Detroit—City of the Straits.
New Orleans—Crescent City.
New York—Empire City.
Louisville, Ky.—Falls City.
Rochester, N. Y.—Flour City.
Springfield, Ill.—Flower City.
Cleveland, Ohio—Forest City.
Portland, Me.—Forest City.
Chicago, Ill.—Garden City
Keokuk, Iowa—Gate City.
New York—Gotham.
Boston, Mass.—Hub of the Universe.
Pittsburgh, Pa.—Iron City.
Baltimore—Monumental City.
St. Louis, Mo.—Mound City.
Philadelphia, Pa.—Quaker City.
Cincinnati, Ohio—Queen City.
Buffalo, N. Y.—Queen City of the Lakes.
Indianapolis, Ind.—Railroad City.
Pittsburgh—Smoky City.

SIGNS USED BY PHYSICIANS IN WRITING PRESCRIPTIONS.

℔, denotes a pound.
℥, an ounce.
ʒ, a drachm.
℈, a scruple.
gr., a grain.
℞, recipe.
ana. of each alike.
Coch, a spoonful.
P. Æ. equal quantities.
ss. half of anything.
iss. one and a half.
q. s. sufficient quantity.
q. pl. much as you please.
O. a pint.
M. 60th part of a fluid drachm.
i. one of anything.
ij. two of anything.
iij. three of anything.
iv. four of anything.
x. ten of anything.
xij. twelve of anything.
f. prefixed to *dr.* or *oz.* denotes fluid drachm.
gtt. a drop.
℥. *iv.* a cupful.
℥. *iss.* to ℥ *ij.* a wine glass.
f. ℥. *ss.* a tablespoonful.
f. ʒ. *ij.* a dessertspoonful.
f. ʒ. *i.* a teaspoonful.
Pugillas, as much as can be held between the thumb and finger.

HOW TO TELL ANY PERSON'S AGE.

THERE is a good deal of amusement in the following magical table of figures. It will enable you to tell how old the young ladies are. Just hand this table to a young lady, request her to tell you in which column or columns her age is contained, and add together the figures at the top of the columns in which her age is found, and you have the great secret. Thus, suppose her age to be 17, you will find that number in the first and fifth columns; add the first figures of these two columns.

Here is the magic table:

1	2	4	8	16	32
3	3	5	9	17	33
5	6	6	10	18	34
7	7	7	11	19	35
9	10	12	12	20	36
11	11	13	13	21	37
13	14	14	14	22	38
15	15	15	15	23	39
17	18	20	24	24	40
19	19	21	25	25	41
21	22	22	26	26	42
23	23	23	27	27	43
25	26	28	28	28	44
27	27	29	29	29	45
29	30	30	30	30	46
31	31	31	31	31	47
33	34	36	40	48	48
35	35	37	41	49	49
37	38	38	42	50	50
39	39	39	43	51	51
41	42	44	44	52	52
43	43	45	45	53	53
45	46	46	46	54	54
47	47	47	47	55	55
49	50	52	56	56	56
51	51	53	57	57	57
53	54	54	58	58	58
55	55	55	59	59	59
57	58	60	60	60	60
59	59	61	61	61	61
61	62	62	62	62	62
63	63	63	63	63	63

SURELY never was Solomon's saying concerning the making of many books more true than at the present time. From the Atlantic to the Pacific, from Maine to Florida, almost every body, it would appear, is writing poems and prose, fact and fiction;—for the newspapers, the magazines, the publishers, and, as many an editor and reader could testify, a large number of these writers would stand a far better chance of having their wares accepted, did they but heed a few simple rules. It is by no means a rare occurrence to have Mss arrive at newspaper offices and publishing houses with *both* sides of the pages covered with writing.

Therefore the few brief directions which busy editors have not time to write—contained in these pages—may be of service in giving beginners certain information they would otherwise obtain far more slowly, possibly after a long series of Mss had been "returned with thanks."

Never write on both sides of the sheet.

***

Put the lines sufficiently far apart to ensure clearness, and leave a margin at the top and bottom of the page.

***

Write a legible hand, and be very careful to make any foreign or unusual word or proper name especially distinct.

***

Read MS over before offering it for examination—it is hardly fair, because some one is to edit it, to leave the errors to be corrected by him.

***

Make frequent paragraphs, always being careful to put the paragraph mark (¶) before every one.

***

In erasing, show exactly where the erasure is to begin and where it is to end.

***

It will be a valuable aid to the reader of the MS if every period ending a sentence is encircled.

***

Begin every sentence with a capital. If it is not distinct, draw three lines under the letter. When the first words of a sentence are cancelled, or when the sentence is broken in two, draw three lines under the first letter of the first word that is to remain, or the first word of the new sentence.

***

Do not divide a word at the end of a line, it often leads to confusion when the MS. is cut up for the printers. *Never* divide a word at the end of a page.

***

In revising proof, if a word requires erasure, try to put another in the same sentence—if possible in the same line —to fill the space.

***

If an additional bit of paper has been pasted on a leaf, fold the piece forward over the writing so that it may not escape notice.

***

The above directions apply to all MSS., those given below refer to those prepared for newspapers.

Date everything. If intended for use on any day, for instance Sunday, or any department, note it on the envelope.

* *
*

Never address a MS. to any particular person on the staff of a newspaper, unless his personal examination is necessary before it is given to the printers.

* *
*

Put at the top of the first sheet of MS. the name of the writer.

In sending telegrams to a newspaper sign the full name. If a correspondent employs a substitute to forward dispatches, the correspondent's name should be signed.

* *
*

In sending items of news by mail to a newspaper in another city, note the most important ones on the margin or on a separate sheet. If there is anything specially worth inserting, which it is probable no other paper will get, mark "exclusive.'

* *
*

All news of whatever nature should be forwarded as soon as possible.

* *
*

Never permit personal feeling to influence communications, and never write anything whose authorship you would wish to disown. Take the utmost care to be thoroughly accurate.

* *
*

Write the head-lines if time will allow—if not, leave space enough at the top of the first sheet.

SOME PERPLEXING GRAMMATICAL QUESTIONS.

One of the points most puzzling to writers and speakers is the correct use of the pronoun representing a collective noun. Perhaps the clearest rule is the direction to use the singular form if the idea of unity is to be conveyed, and the plural one if the idea is *plurality*. The number of the verb is determined in the same manner.

"The crowd comes on in a compact mass and hurls *itself* at the barrier. Dispersed by a volley of musketry *they* run in every direction and yell fiercely as *they* go." If in doubt as to whether the intention is to convey the idea of unity or plurality it is better to use the singular form.

* *
*

Always repeat a name, rather than permit any uncertainty by using a pronoun.

When comparing only two things, use the comparative form. He is
the younger of the two sons.

**

Put an adverb as near as possible to the word it is intended to
modify.

**

After all forms of the verb to be, use the same case as that which
precedes it. *It is I. I am sure you are she.*

**

When *or, nor, as well as,* and similar disjunctions separate two or
more singular nominatives the verb must be singular ; but if either nominative is plural, the verb should be plural.

**

The active infinitive must never be separated. This is one of the
most frequent errors in speaking and writing; but it is as incorrect to
say *to thoroughly enjoy,* as to say *con rarely cur* for *rarely concur.*

**

The verbs *shall* and *will* are very frequently misused. The following
simple explanation may serve as an aid in doubtful cases. *I will, you shall,
he shall* express resolution on the part of the speaker, while *I shall, you
will, he will* merely predict future events. *Will* used in the first person
expresses either a resolve or a promise, and can never be used in questions
with nominative cases in the first person. *Would* and *should* follow the
same rules as *will* and *shall.*

**

Another frequent error is the use of the present tense in the place of
the future. For instance Mr. Cameron *dines* here two weeks from to-
day, instead of Mr. Cameron *will dine* here two weeks from to-day.

**

The following six verbs often prove stumbling-blocks in the pathway
of the inexperienced. The directions given for their use are taken from
a manual on the art of writing recently published :

Present.	*Past.*	*Participle.*
Transitive, Lay	Laid	Laid (action)
Intransitive, Lie	Lay	Lain (rest)
Transitive, Set	Set	Set (action)
Intransitive, Sit	Sat	Sat (rest)
Transitive, Raise	Raised	Raised
Intransitive, Rise	Rose	Risen.

Correct: He lays the book on the table.

He lay on the bed and laid the book on the table.

After he had lain a while, and had laid the book on the table, he rose, raised the book, and sat down where he had set the chair.

Incorrect: I will lay down a while.

He raised up and then he set still.

I sat him in the chair.

PUNCTUATION MARKS, AND RULES FOR THEIR USE.

A comma (,) is used to mark a slight pause, and to divide a sentence into parts.

A semi-colon (;) denotes a longer pause, and divides compound sentences.

The colon (:) is inserted between the principal divisions of a sentence, when the connection is very slight.

The period (.) marks the end of a sentence.

The dash (—) shows a sudden change of subject.

The interrogation point (?) indicates a question.

The exclamation point (!) shows wonder or astonishment.

The parenthesis ( ) contains something not essential to the sense.

Quotation marks (" ") are used to show that the quotation is verbatim.

The hyphen (-) connects the syllables or parts of a word.

The caret (∧) shows that some word, phrase, or sign has been omitted.

The brackets ([ ]) generally mark a correction.

The ellipsis (* * *) (—) indicates the omission of letters or words.

The index (☞) points to something of special importance.

BRIEF RULES FOR PUNCTUATION.

A *period* is placed:

1. After every declarative and imperative sentence.

2. After all abbreviations.

3. After numbers in the Roman notation.

A *colon* is placed:

1. Between the principal divisions of a sentence, when the connections are slight and the divisions are separated by some other mark.

2. After a sentence that commences a distinct quotation.

3. Between clauses whose connection is so slight that each one might be a distinct sentence.

A *semi-colon* is used:

1. To separate a series of clauses depending upon one principal expression.

2. After an expression that introduces particulars.

3. Before a clause which especially explains the meaning of an expression.

4. To divide a sentence into sections, when the parts are not so independent as to require a colon.

A *comma* is placed:

1. Between the particulars mentioned in a series of words of the same construction.

2. Between each pair of words, when each pair is in the same construction.

3. Before and after every parenthetical expression.

4. Before a quotation closely connected with the preceding words.

5. Between expressions that are repeated.

6. Before a phrase or clause that explains the meaning of a preceding clause.

7. Before all modifying expressions, unless they are closely connected with the rest of the sentence.

8. Whenever a word is understood, unless the connection is close.

An *interrogation point* is placed:

1. After every sentence, phrase, clause, or word which denotes a direct question.

2. Enclosed in parentheses to denote doubt.

An *exclamation point* is placed:

1. After every exclamatory sentence, clause, phrase, or word.

2. Enclosed in parentheses, to denote extreme surprise.

3. After most interjection points.

A *dash* is placed ·

1. After a sudden turn in a sentence.

2. To mark an omission in the regular series.

3. To show the omission of a word, or part of a word.

4. Before the answer to a question, when both are on the same line.

5. Instead of the parenthesis marks.

6. Before an expression repeated for special emphasis.

7. After a sentence introducing a quotation, when the quotation commences a new paragraph.

8. To avoid too many paragraphs.

Quotation marks are placed :

1. At the commencement of every paragraph, when the quotation consists of more than one paragraph, but at the end of the last paragraph alone.

2. To enclose any brief quotation.

3. At the commencement of each line. when a quoted passage requires special attention.

4. When one quotation is included in another, the former has half the first quotation mark before it, and half the second quotation mark after it.

Parenthesis marks are used to enclose matter not connected with the sentence.

Brackets are principally used to enclose corrections.

The *hyphen* is used to separate the syllables of a word.

The *apostrophe* marks a contraction. ·

The *caret* denotes the omission of letters or words.

The *asterisk, dagger,* and similar marks are used to refer to notes at the foot or side of the page.

SIMPLE RULES FOR SPELLING.

Monosyllables ending in *l*, preceded by a single vowel, terminate in *ll*, as *fill, dell.*

Monosyllables ending in *l*, preceded by two vowels, terminate with a single *l*, as *bail, seal.*

The derivatives *instill, distill, foretell, etc.,* follow the rule of their primitives. So, too, do the words *dullness, willful, etc.,* when the accent falls on them.

Words of more than one syllable take the double *l*, if the accent falls on the last syllable, if it does not, they have only the single *l* at the close.

Words which end in *e*, lose the letter before the termination, *able,* as *move, movable,* unless the *e* is preceded by *g*, as in *charge, changeable.*

Monosyllables ending in a consonant preceded by a single vowel double the consonant in derivatives, as *ship, shipping.* But if the consonant is preceded by two vowels, the consonant is not doubled.

Words containing more than one syllable, ending in a consonant, preceded by a single vowel, double the consonant in derivatives, as *commit, committed, etc.* This rule, however, has an exception, *chagrin.*

Participles ending in *ing*, formed from verbs terminating in *e*, drop the final *e*; but verbs ending in double *e* retain both.

There is one exception *dye*, retains its final *e* before *ing*.

Nouns ending in *ment* and adverbs terminating in *ly* retain the final *e* of the words from which they are derived ; as *confine, confinement, brave, bravely*, except words ending in *dge*.

Nouns ending in *y*, preceded by a vowel, take *s* in the plural—but if the *y* is preceded by a consonant, the plural is formed by adding *ies*.

CORRECT USE OF CAPITALS.

A capital letter should be placed ·

1.   At the beginning of every sentence.

2.   At the commencement of all appellations of the Deity, all proper names and adjectives derived from them, and all official and honorary titles.

3.   At the beginning of every line of poetry

4.   Titles of books, headings of chapters and their divisions are printed in capitals.

5.   The exclamation *O*! and the pronoun *I* are always capitals.

6.   The days of the week and the months of the year begin with capitals.

7.   A capital letter should begin every quotation.

8.   Names of religious denominations should begin with capitals.

9.   A capital letter should begin each item of an account.

10.   It is allowable to commence any word of very special importance with a capital.

COME IN OUT OF THE RAIN·

How to Write Clearly.

HE first aim to be kept in view by every writer is to express his or her meaning clearly, and this, fortunately, is an art which can be acquired by all who choose to give the necessary time and attention to its study. Vigor, elegance, variety of style, and forcible expression demand higher powers, and are in a measure the gifts of nature. Yet even those whose talents are of the highest order cannot afford to dispense with instruction concerning the method of clothing their thoughts in the most appropriate form, and the following rules given by a very successful English teacher, though written for beginners, can hardly fail to afford some helpful suggestions, even to experienced writers.

CLEARNESS AND FORCE.

Numbers in brackets refer to the Rules.

WORDS.

1. Use words in their proper sense.

Write, not "His *apparent* guilt justified his friends in disowning him," but "his *evident* guilt." "Conscious" and "aware," "unnatural" and "supernatural," "transpire" and "occur," "circumstance" and "event," "reverse" and "converse," "eliminate" and "elicit," are often confused together.

This rule forbids the use of the same word in different senses. "It is in my *power* to refuse your request, and since I have *power* to do this, I may lawfully do it." Here the second "power" is used for "authority."

This rule also forbids the slovenly use of "nice," "awfully," "delicious," "glorious," &c. See (2).

2. Avoid exaggerations.

"The *boundless* plains in the heart of the empire furnished *inexhaustible* supplies of corn, that would have almost sufficed for twice the population."

547

Here "inexhaustible" is inconsistent with what follows. The words "unprecedented," "incalculable," "very," and "stupendous" are often used in the same loose way.

3. Avoid useless circumlocution and "fine writing."

"Her Majesty here *partook of lunch.*"   Write "*lunched.*"

"Partook of" implies sharing, and is incorrect as well as lengthy.

So do not use "apex" for "top," "species" for "kind," "individual" for "man," "assist" for "help," &c.

4. Be careful how you use the following words: "not and," "any," "only," "not .   or," "that." [1]

AND.—See below, "OR."

ANY.—"I am not bound to receive *any* messenger that you send." Does this mean *every*, or *a single?*   Use "every" or "a single."

NOT.—(1) "I do *not* intend to help you, because you are my enemy, &c.," ought to mean (2), "I intend not to help you, and my reason for not helping you is, because you are my enemy."   But it is often wrongly used to mean (3), "I intend to help you, not because you are my enemy (but because you are poor, blind, &c.)"   In the latter case, *not* ought to be separated from *intend.*   By distinctly marking the limits to which the influence of *not* extends, the ambiguity may be removed.

ONLY is often used ambiguously for *alone.*   "The rest help me to revenge myself; you only *advise* me to wait."   This ought to mean, "you o. ly *advise*, instead of *helping;*" but in similar sentences "you only" is often used for "you alone."   But see 21.

OR.—When "or" is preceded by a negative, as "I do not want butter *or* honey," "or" ought not, strictly speaking, to be used like "and," nor like "nor."   The strict use of "not . . . . or" would be as follows:

You say you don't want both butter *and* honey—you want butter *or* honey; I, on the contrary, *do not want butter or honey*—I want them both."

Practically, however, this meaning is so rare, that "I don't want butter *or* honey" is regularly used for "I want neither butter nor honey." But where there is the slightest danger of ambiguity, it is desirable to use *nor.*

The same ambiguity attends "not . . . . and."   "I do not see Thomas *and* John" is commonly used for "I see neither Thomas nor John;" but it might mean, "I do not see them both—I see only one of them."

---

[1] *For,* at the beginning of a sentence, sometimes causes temporary doubt, while the reader is finding out whether it is used as a conjunction or preposition.

THAT.—The different uses of "that" produce much ambiguity, *e. g.*, "I am so much surprised by this statement *that* I am desirous of resigning, *that* I scarcely know what reply to make." Here it is impossible to tell, till one has read past "resigning," whether the first "that" depends upon "so" or "statement." Write: "The statement that I am desirous of resigning surprises me so much that I scarcely know &c."

4 a. Be careful in the use of ambiguous words, e g "certain."

"Certain" is often used for "some," as in "Independently of his earnings, he has a *certain* property," where the meaning might be "unfailing."

Under this head may be mentioned the double use of words, such as "left" in the same form and sound, but different in meaning. Even when there is no obscurity, the juxtaposition of the same word twice used in two senses is inelegant, *e.g.* (Bain), "He turned to the *left* and *left* the room."

I have known the following slovenly sentence misunderstood: "Our object is that, with the aid of practice, we may sometime arrive at the point where we think eloquence in its most praiseworthy form *to lie*." "To lie" has been supposed to mean "to deceive."

5. Be careful how you use "he," "it," "they," "these," &c.
(For "which" see 8.) The ambiguity arising from the use of *he* applying to different persons is well-known.

"He told his friend that if *he* did not feel better in half an hour he thought *he* had better return." See (6) for remedy.

Much ambiguity is also caused by excessive use of such phrases as *in this way, of this sort*, &c.

"God, foreseeing the disorders of human nature, has given us certain passions and affections which arise from, or whose objects are, these disorders. *Of this sort* are fear, resentment, compassion."

Repeat the noun: "Among these passions and affections are fear, &c."

Two distinct uses of "*it*" may be noted. *It*, when referring to something that precedes, may be called "retrospective;" but when to something that follows, "prospective." In "Avoid indiscriminate charity; *it* is a crime," "it" is retrospective.[1] In "*It* is a crime to give indiscriminately," "it" is prospective.

The prospective "it," if productive of ambiguity, can often be omitted by using the infinitive as a subject: "To give indiscriminately is a crime."

---

[1] *It* should refer (1) either to the noun immediately preceding or (2) to some noun superior to all intervening nouns in emphasis. See (25).

6. Report a speech in the First, not the Third Person, where necessary to avoid ambiguity. Speeches in the third person afford a particular, though very common case, of the general ambiguity mentioned in (5). Instead of " He told his friend that if *he* did not feel better &c.," write "He said to his friend, ' If *I* (or *you*) don't feel better &c.' "

6 a. Sometimes where the writer cannot know the exact words, or where the exact words are unimportant, or lengthy and uninteresting, the Third Person is preferable. Thus, where Essex is asking Sir Robert Cecil that Francis Bacon may be appointed Attorney-General, the dialogue is (as it almost always is in Lord Macaulay's writings) in the First Person, *except where it becomes tedious and uninteresting so as to require condensation*, and then it drops into the Third Person :

" Sir Robert *had nothing to say but* that he thought his own abilities equal to the place which he hoped to obtain, and that his father's long services deserved such a mark of gratitude from the Queen."

6 b. Omission of "that" in a speech reported in the Third Person.—Even when a speech is reported in the third person, " that " need not always be inserted before the dependent verb. Thus, instead of " He said that he took it ill that his promises were not believed," we may write, " ' He took it ill,' he said, ' that &c.' " This gives a little more life, and sometimes more clearness also.

7. When you use a Participle, as "walking," implying "when," "while," "though," "that," make it clear by the context what is implied.

" Republics, in the first instance, are never desired for their own sakes. I do not think they will finally be desired at all, *unaccompanied* by courtly graces and good breeding."

Here there is a little doubt whether the meaning is " *since* they are, or, *if* they are unaccompanied."

THAT or WHEN.—" Men *walking* (*that* walk, or *when* they walk) on ice sometimes fall."

It is better to use " men walking " to mean " men *when* they walk." If the relative is meant, use " men that walk," instead of the participle.

(1) " *While* he was			(1) the road,	
(2) "*Because* he was	} *Walking* on	{	(2) the ice,	} he fell."

When the participle precedes the subject, it generally implies a cause : "*Seeing* this, he retired." Otherwise it generally has its proper participial meaning, *e.g.* " He retired, *keeping* his face towards us." If there is any ambiguity, write " *on* seeing,"— " *at the same time, or while,* keeping."

(1) *"Though* he was ⎫
(2) *"Since* he was ⎬ *Struck* with terror, ⎧ (1) he nevertheless stood his
(3) *"If* he is ⎭   ground."
       (2) he rapidly retreated."
       (3) he will soon retreat."

**8. When using the Relative Pronoun, use " who" and " which"
where the meaning is "and he, it, &c.," "for he, it, &c." In other
cases use " that," if euphony allows.**

I heard this from the inspector, *who* (and he) heard it from the
guard *that* travelled with the train."

" Fetch me (all) the books *that* lie on the table, and also the pam-
phlets, *which* (and these) you will find on the floor."

An adherence to this rule would remove much ambiguity. Thus :
" There was a public-house next door, *which* was a great nuisance," means
and this (i.e. the fact of its being next door) was a great nuisance ; "
whereas *that* would have meant " Next door was a public-house *that (i.e.*
the public-house) was a great nuisance." " Who," " which," &c., introduce a new fact about the antecedent, whereas " that " introduces something without which the antecedent is incomplete or undefined. Thus,
in the first example above, " inspector " is complete in itself, and " who "
introduces a new *fact* about him ; " guard " is incomplete, and requires
" *that* travelled with the train " to complete the meaning.

It is not, and cannot be, maintained that this rule, though observed
in Elizabethan English, is observed by our best modern authors. (Probably
a general impression that " that " cannot be used to refer to persons has
assisted " who " in supplanting " that " as a relative.) But the convenience
of the rule is so great that beginners in composition may with advantage
adhere to the rule. The following are some of the cases where *who* and
which are mostly used, contrary to the rule, instead of *that.*

Exceptions :

(*a*) When the antecedent is defined, *e.g.* by a possessive case, modern English
uses *who* instead of *that.* It is rare, though it would be useful,[1] to say
" His English friends *that* had not seen him," for " the English friends, or
those of his English friends, that had not seen him."

(*b*) *That* sounds ill when separated from its verb and from its antecedents,
and emphasized by isolation : " There are many persons *that,* though
unscrupulous, are commonly good-tempered, and *that,* if not strongly
incited by self-interest, are ready for the most part to think of the interest
of their neighbors." Shakespeare frequently uses *who* after *that* when
the relative is repeated. See " Shakespearian Grammar," par. 260.

---

[1] So useful that, on mature consideration, I am disposed to adopt "that" here and in
several of the following exceptional cases.

(c) If the antecedent is qualified by *that*, the relative must not be *that*. Besides other considerations, the repetition is disagreeable. Addison ridicules such language as " *That* remark *that* I made yesterday is not *that that* I said *that* I regretted *that* I had made."

(d) *That* cannot be preceded by a preposition, and hence throws the preposition to the end. " 'This is the rule *that* I adhere *to*." This is perfectly good English, though sometimes unnecessarily avoided. But, with some prepositions, the construction is harsh and objectionable, *e.g.* " This is the mark *that* I jumped *beyond*." " Such were the prejudices *that* he rose *above*." The reason is that some of these disyllabic prepositions are used as adverbs, and, when separated from their nouns, give one the impression that they are used as abverbs.

(e) After pronominal adjectives used for personal pronouns, modern English prefers *who*. " There are many, others, several, those, *who* can testify, &c.'ı

(f) After *that* used as a conjunction there is sometimes a dislike to use *that* as a relative. See (c).

9. Do not use redundant " and " before " which."[1]

" I gave him a very interesting book for a present, *and which* cost me five shillings."

In short sentences the absurdity is evident, but in long sentences it is less evident, and very common.

" A petition was presented for rescinding that portion of the by-laws which permits application of public money to support sectarian schools over which ratepayers have no control, this being a violation of the principle of civil and religious liberty, *and which* the memorialists believe would provoke a determined and conscientious resistance."

Here *which* ought grammatically to refer to " portion " or " schools." But it seems intended to refer to " violation." Omit " and," or repeat " a violation " before " which," or turn the sentence otherwise.

10. Equivalents for Relative.

(a) PARTICIPLE.—" Men *thirsting* (for ' men *that thirst*') for revenge are not indifferent to plunder." The objection to the participle is that here, as often, it creates a little ambiguity. The above sentence may mean, " men, *when* they thirst," or " *though* they thirst," as well as " men *that* thirst." Often, however, there is no ambiguity : " I have documents *proving* this conclusively."

(b) INFINITIVE.—Instead of " He was the first *that* entered " you can write " *to* enter ; " for " He is not a man *who* will act dishonestly," " *to* act." This equivalent cannot often be used.

---

[1] Of course " and which" may be used where " which" precedes.

(c) WHEREBY, WHEREIN, &c., can sometimes be used for " by *which*," "in *which*," so as to avoid a harsh repetition of "*which*." "The means *whereby* this may be effected." But this use is somewhat antiquated.

(d) IF.—"The man *that* does not care for music is to be pitied " can be written (though not so forcibly), " *If* a man does not care for music, he is to be pitied." It is in long sentences that this equivalent will be found most useful.

(e) AND THIS.—" He did his best, *which* was all that could be expected," can be written, " *and this* was all that, &c."

(f) WHAT.—" Let me repeat *that which* [1] you ought to know, that *that which* is worth doing is worth doing well." " Let me repeat, *what* you ought to know, that *what* is worth doing is worth doing well."

(g) OMISSION OF RELATIVE.—It is sometimes thought ungrammatical to omit the relative, as in " The man (that) you speak of." On the contrary, *that* when an object (not when a subject) may be omitted, wherever the antecedent and the subject of the relative sentence are brought into juxtaposition by the omission.

10 a'. Repeat the Antecedent in some new form, where there is any ambiguity. This is particularly useful after a negative: " He said that he would not even hear me, *which* I confess I had expected."

Here the meaning may be, " I had expected that he would," or " that he would not, hear me." Write " *a refusal*, or *a favor*, that I confess I had expected." See (38).

11. Use particular for general terms. This is a most important rule. Instead of " I have neither the necessaries of life nor the means of procuring them," write (if you can *with truth*), " I have not a crust of bread, nor a penny to buy one."

CAUTION.—There is a danger in this use. The meaning is vividly expressed, but sometimes may be exaggerated or imperfect. *Crust of bread* may be an exaggeration; on the other hand, if the speaker is destitute not only of bread, but also of shelter and clothing, then *crust of bread* is an imperfect expression of the meaning.

In philosophy and science, where the language ought very often to be inclusive and brief, general and not particular terms must be used.

11 a. Avoid Verbal Nouns where Verbs can be used instead. The disadvantage of the use of Verbal Nouns is this, that, unless they

---

[1] "That which," where *that* is an *object, e.g.* " then (set forth) *that which* is worse," *St. John* ii. 10, is rare in modern English.

are immediately preceded by prepositions, they are sometimes liable to be confounded with participles. The following is an instance of an excessive use of Verbal Nouns:

"The pretended confession of the secretary was only collusion to lay the jealousies of the king's *favoring* popery, which still hung upon him, notwithstanding his *writing* on the Revelation, and *affecting* to enter on all occasions into controversy, *asserting* in particular that the Pope was Antichrist."

Write "notwithstanding that he wrote and affected &c."

12. Use a particular Person instead of a class.

"What is the splendor of *the greatest monarch* compared with the beauty of a *flower?*" "What is the splendor of Solomon compared with the beauty of a daisy?"

Under this head may come the forcible use of Noun for Adjective¬ "This fortress is *weakness* itself."

An excess of this use is lengthy and pedantically bombastic, *e.g.*, the following paraphrase for "in every British colony:"—"under Indian palm-groves, amid Australian gum-trees, in the shadow of African mimosas, and beneath Canadian pines."

13. Use Metaphor instead of literal statement.

"The ship *ploughs* the sea" is clearer than "the ship *cleaves* the sea," and shorter than "the ship *cleaves* the sea *as a plough cleaves the land.*"

Of course there are some subjects for which Metaphor should not be used. See (14 *a*) and (14 *b*).

14. Do not confuse Metaphor.

"In a moment the thunderbolt was upon them, *deluging* their country with invaders."

The following is attributed to Sir Boyle Roche: "Mr. Speaker, I smell a rat, I see him brewing in the air; but, mark me, I shall yet nip him in the bud."

Some words, once metaphorical, have ceased to be so regarded. Hence many good writers say "*under* these *circumstances*" instead of "*in* these circumstances."

An excessive regard for disused Metaphor savors of pedantry: disregard is inelegant. Write, not, "*unparalleled* complications," but "*unprecedented* complications;" and "*he threw light on* obscurities," instead of "*he unravelled* obscurities."

14 a. Do not introduce literal statement immediately after Metaphor.

" He was the father of Chemistry, and brother to the Earl of Cork."

" He was a very thunderbolt of war,
And was lieutenant to the Earl of Mar."

14 b. Do not use poetic metaphor to illustrate a prosaic subject.
Thus, we may say " a poet *soars*," or even, though rarely, " a nation *soars* to greatness," but you could not say " Consols *soared* to 94½." Even commonplace subjects may be illustrated by metaphor: for it is a metaphor, and quite unobjectionable, to say " Consols *mounted*, or *jumped* to 94½." But commonplace subjects must be illustrated by metaphor that is commonplace.

ORDER OF WORDS IN A SENTENCE.

15. Emphatic words must stand in emphatic positions; i.e. for the most part, at the beginning or at the end of a sentence.
This rule occasionally supersedes the common rules about position. Thus, the place for an adverb, as a rule, should be between the subject and verb : " He *quickly* left the room;" but if *quickly* is to be emphatic, it must come at the beginning or end, as in " I told him to leave the room slowly, but he left *quickly*."

Adjectives, in clauses beginning with "if" and " though," often come at the beginning for emphasis: " *Insolent* though he was, he was silenced at last."

15 a. Unemphatic words must, as a rule, be kept from the end of the sentence. It is a common fault to break this rule by placing a short and unemphatic predicate at the end of a long sentence.

" To know some Latin, even if it be nothing but a few Latin roots, *is useful*." Write, " It is useful, &c."

So " the evidence proves how kind to his inferiors *he is*."

Often, where an adjective or auxiliary verb comes at the end, the addition of an emphatic adverb justifies the position, *e.g.* above, " is *very* useful," " he has *invariably* been."

A short " chippy " ending, even though emphatic, is to be avoided. It is abrupt and unrhythmical, *e.g.* " The soldier, transfixed with the spear, *writhed*." We want a *longer* ending, " fell writhing to the ground," or " writhed in the agonies of death." A " chippy " ending is common in bad construing from Virgil.

EXCEPTIONS.—Prepositions and pronouns attached to emphatic words need not be moved from the end, *e.g.* "He does no harm that I hear *of.*" "Bear witness how I loved *him.*"

N. B.—In all styles, especially in letter-writing, a final emphasis must not be so frequent as to become obtrusive and monotonous.

15 b. An interrogation sometimes gives emphasis. "No one can doubt that the prisoner, had he been really guilty, would have shown some signs of remorse," is not so emphatic as "Who can doubt, Is it possible to doubt, &c."

Contrast "No one ever names Wentworth without thinking of &c." with "But Wentworth,—who ever names him without thinking of those harsh, dark features, ennobled by their expression into more than the majesty of an antique Jupiter?"

16. The subject, if unusually emphatic, should often be removed from the beginning of the sentence. The beginning of the sentence is an emphatic position, though mostly not so emphatic as the end.   Therefore the principal subject of a sentence, being emphatic, and being wanted early in the sentence to tell us what the sentence is about, comes as a rule, at or near the beginning: "*Thomas* built this house."

Hence, since the beginning is the *usual* place for the subject, if we want to emphasize "Thomas" *unusually*, we must remove "Thomas" from the beginning: "This house was built by *Thomas,*" or "It was *Thomas* that built this house."

Thus, the emphasis on "conqueror" is not quite so strong in "*A mere conqueror* ought not to obtain from us the reverence that is due to the great benefactors of mankind," as in "We ought not to bestow the reverence that is due to the great benefactors of mankind, *upon a mere conqueror.*"   Considerable, but less emphasis and greater smoothness (19) will be obtained by writing the sentence thus: "We ought not to bestow upon a mere conqueror &c."

Where the same subject stands first in several consecutive sentences, it rises in emphasis, and need not be removed from the beginning, even though unusual emphasis be required :

"The captain was the life and soul of the expedition. *He* first pointed out the possibility of advancing; *he* warned them of the approaching scarcity of provisions; *he* showed how they might replenish their exhausted stock, &c."

17. The object is sometimes placed before the verb for emphasis.   This is most common in antithesis.   "*Jesus* I know, and *Paul* I know ; but who are ye?" "*Some* he imprisoned, *others* he put to death."

Even where there is no antithesis, the inversion is not uncommon:

" Military *courage*, the boast of the sottish German, of the frivolous and prating Frenchman, of the romantic and arrogant Spaniard, he neither possesses nor values."

This inversion sometimes creates ambiguity in poetry, *e.g.* " The son the father slew," and must be sparingly used in prose.

Sometimes the position of a word may be considered appropriate by some, and inappropriate by others, according to different interpretations of the sentence. Take as an example, " Early in the morning the nobles and gentlemen who attended on the king assembled in the great hall of the castle; and here they began to talk of what a dreadful storm it had been the night before. But Macbeth could scarcely understand what they said, for he was thinking of something worse.'' The last sentence has been amended by Professor Bain into " *What they said*, Macbeth could scarcely understand." But there appears to be an antithesis between the guiltless nobles who can think about the weather, and the guilty Macbeth who cannot. Hence, " what they said " ought not, and " Macbeth " ought, to be emphasized; and therefore " Macbeth " ought to be retained at the beginning of the sentence.

The same author alters, " The praise of judgment Virgil has justly contested with him, but his invention remains yet unrivalled," into " Virgil has justly contested with him the praise of judgment, but no one has yet rivalled his invention "—an alteration which does not seem to emphasize sufficiently the antithesis between what had been " contested," on the one hand, and what remained as yet " unrivalled " on the other.

More judiciously Professor Bain alters, " He that tells a lie is not sensible how great a task he undertakes; for he must be forced to invent twenty more to maintain one," into " for, to maintain one, he must invent twenty more," putting the emphatic words in their emphatic place, at the end.

18. Where several words are emphatic, make it clear which is the most emphatic. Thus, in " The state was made, under the pretense of serving it, in reality the prize of their contention to each of these opposite parties," it is unpleasantly doubtful whether the writer means (1) *state* or (2) *parties* to be emphatic.

If (1), "As for the *state*, these two parties, under the pretense of serving it, converted it into a prize for their contention." If (2), write, " Though served in profession, the state was in reality converted into a prize for their contention by these two *parties*." In (1) *parties* is subordinated, in (2) *state*.

Sometimes the addition of some intensifying word serves to emphasize. Thus, instead of " To effect this they used all devices," we can write " To effect this they used *every conceivable device*." So, if we want to emphasize fidelity in " The business will task your skill and fidelity," we can write "Not only your skill *but also* your fidelity." This, however, sometimes leads to exaggerations. See (2).

Sometime antithesis gives emphasis, as in " You *do* not know this, but you *shall* know it." Where antithesis cannot be used, the emphasis must be expressed by turning the sentence, as " I *will make you* know it," or by some addition, as " You shall *hereafter* know it."

19. Words should be as near as possible to the words with which they are grammatically connected. See paragraphs 20 to 29. For exceptions see 30.

20. Adverbs should be placed next to the words they are intended to affect. When unemphatic, adverbs come between the subject and the verb, or, if the tense is compound, between the parts of the compound tense : " He *quickly* left the room ; " " He has *quickly* left the room ; " but, when emphatic, after the verb : " He left, or has left, the the room *quickly*." [1]   When such a sentence as the latter is followed by a present participle, there arises ambiguity. " I told him to go slowly, but he left the room *quickly*, dropping the purse on the floor." Does *quickly* here modify *left* or *dropping?* The remedy [2] is, to give the adverb its unemphatic place, " He *quickly* left the room, dropping &c.," or else to avoid the participle, thus: ": He *quickly* dropped the purse and left the room," or " He dropped the purse and *quickly* left the room."

21. " Only " requires careful use. The strict [3] rule is, that " only " should be placed before the word affected by it.
The following is ambiguous
" The heavens are not open to the faithful *only* at intervals."
The best rule is to avoid placing " only " between two emphatic words, and to avoid using " only " where " alone " can be used instead.
In strictness perhaps the three following sentences :
    (1)   He *only* beat three
    (2)   He beat *only* three,
    (3)   He beat three *only*,
ought to be explained, severally, thus :
    (1)   He did no more than beat, did not kill, three.

---

[1] Sometimes the emphatic Adverb comes at the beginning, and causes the transposition of an Auxiliary Verb, " *Gladly* do I consent."
[2] Of course punctuation will remove the ambiguity ; but it is better to express oneself clearly, as far as possible, independently of punctuation.
[3] Professor Bain.

(2) He beat no more than three.

(3) He beat three, and that was all he did. (Here *only* modifies the whole of the sentence and depreciates the action.)

But the best authors sometimes transpose the word. " He *only* lived " ought to mean " he did not die or make any great sacrifice; " but " He *only* l'ved but till he was a man " (*Macbeth*, v. 8. 40) means " He lived *only* till he was a man." Compare also, " Who *only* hath immortality."

Only at the beginning of a statement = *but*. " I don't like to importune you, *only* I know you'll forgive me." Before an imperative it diminishes the favor asked : " *Only* listen to me." This use of *only* is mostly confined to letters.

Very often, *only* at the beginning of a sentence is used for *alone*: " *Only* ten came," " *Only* Cæsar approved." *Alone* is less ambiguous. The ambiguity of *only* is illustrated by such a sentence as, " Don't hesitate to bring a few friends of yours to shoot on my estate at any time. *Only* five (fifteen) came yesterday," which might mean, " I don't mind a *few*; *only* don't bring so many as *fifteen*; " or else " Don't hesitate to bring a few *more*; no more than *five* came yesterday." In conversation, ambiguity is prevented by emphasis; but in a letter, *only* thus used might cause unfortunate mistakes. Write " Yesterday *only* five came," if you mean " no more than five."

22. When "not only " precedes "but also," see that each is followed by the same part of speech.

" He *not only* gave me advice *but also* help " is wrong. Write " He gave me, *not only* advice, *but also* help." On the other hand, " He *not only* gave me a grammar, *but also* lent me a dictionary," is right. Take an instance. " He spoke *not only* forcibly *but also* tastefully (adverbs), and this too, *not only* before a small audience, *but also* in (prepositions) a large public meeting, and his speeches were *not only* successful, *but also* (adjective) worthy of success."

23. "At least," "always," and other adverbial adjuncts, sometimes produce ambiguity.

" I think you will find my Latin exercise, *at all events*, as good as my cousin's." Does this mean (1) " my Latin exercise, though not perhaps my other exercises; " or (2), " Though not very good, yet, at all events, as good as my cousin's ? " Write for (1), " My Latin exercise, at all events, you will find &c." and for (2), " I think you will find my Latin exercise as good as my cousin's, at all events."

The remedy is to avoid placing " at all events " between two emphatic words.

As an example of a misplacing of an adverbial adjunct, take " From abroad he received most favorable reports, but in the City he heard that a panic had broken out on the Enchange, and that the funds were fast falling." This ought to mean that the " hearing," and not (as is intended) that the "breaking out of the panic," took place in the City

In practice, an adverb is often used to qualify a remote word, where the latter is *more emphatic than any nearer word.* This is very common when the Adverbial Adjunct is placed in an emphatic position at the beginning of the sentence : " *On this very spot* our guide declared that Claverhouse had fallen."

24. Nouns should be placed near the nouns that they define. In the very common sentence " The death is announced of Mr. John Smith, an author whose works &c.," the transposition is probably made from a feeling that, if we write "The death of Mr. John Smith is announced," we shall be obliged to begin a new sentence, " He was an author whose works, &c." But the difficulty can be removed by writing " We regret to announce, or, we are informed of, the death of Mr. John Smith, an author, &c."

25. Pronouns should follow the nouns to which they refer without the intervention of another noun. Avoid, " John Smith, the son of Thomas Smith, *who* gave me this book," unless *Thomas Smith* is the antecedent of *who.* Avoid also " John supplied Thomas with money· *he* (John) was very well off."

When, however, one of two preceding nouns is decidedly superior to the other in emphasis, the more emphatic may be presumed to be the noun referred to by the pronoun, even though the noun of inferior emphasis inter venes. Thus : "At this moment the colonel came up, and took the place of the wounded general. *He* gave orders to halt." Here *he* would naturally refer to *colonel,* though *general* intervenes. A *conjunction* will often show that a pronoun refers to the subject of the preceding sentence, and not to another intervening noun. " The sentinel at once took aim at the approaching soldier, and fired. He *then* retreated to give the alarm."

It is better to adhere, in most cases, to Rule 25, which may be called (Bain) the Rule of Proximity. The Rule of Emphasis, of which an instance was given in the last paragraph, is sometimes misleading. A distinction might be drawn by punctuating thus

" David the father of Solomon. who slew Goliath." " David, the father of Solomon who built the Temple." But the propriety of omitting a comma in each case is questionable, and it is better to write so as not to be at the mercy of commas.

26. Clauses that are grammatically connected should be kept as close together as possible. (But see 55.) The introduction of parentheses violating this rule often produces serious ambiguity. Thus, in the following: "The result of these observations appears to be in opposition to the view now generally received in this country, that in muscular effort the substance of the muscle itself undergoes disintegration." Here it is difficult to tell whether the theory of "disintegration" is (1) "the result," or, as the absence of a comma after "be" would indicate, (2) "in opposition to the result of these observations." If (1) is intended, add "and to prove" after "country;" if (2), insert "which is" after "country."

There is an excessive complication in the following:—"It cannot, at all events, if the consideration demanded by a subject of such importance from any one professing to be a philosopher, be given, be denied that &c."

Where a speaker feels that his hearers have forgotten the connection of the beginning of the sentence, he should repeat what he has said; *e.g.* after the long parenthesis in the last sentence he should recommence, " it cannot, I say, be denied." In writing, however, this license must be sparingly used.

A short parenthesis, or modifying clause, will not interfere with clearness, especially if antithesis be used, so as to show the connection between the different parts of the sentence, *e.g.* "A modern newspaper statement, *though probably true,* would be laughed at if quoted in a book as testimony; but the letter of a court gossip is thought good historical evidence if written some centuries ago." Here, to place "though probably true" at the beginning of the sentence would not add clearness, and would impair the emphasis of the contrast between " a modern newspaper statement " and " the letter of a court gossip."

27. In conditional sentences, the antecedent clauses must be kept distinct from the consequent clauses. There is ambiguity in "The lesson intended to be taught by these manœuvres will be lost, if the plan of operations is laid down too definitely beforehand, and the affair degenerates into a mere review." Begin, in any case, with the antecedent, "If the plan," &c. Next write, according to the meaning: (1) "If the plan is laid down, and the affair degenerates &c., then the lesson will be lost;" or (2) " . . . . then the lesson . . . will be lost, and the affair degenerates into a mere review."

28. Dependent clauses preceded by "that" should be kept distinct from those that are independent.

Take as an example:

(1) "He replied that he wished to help them, and intended to make preparations accordingly."

This ought not to be used (though it sometimes is, for shortness) to mean:

(2) "He replied . . . , and he intended."

In (1), "intended," having no subject, must be supposed to oc connected with the nearest preceding verb, in the same mood and tense, that has a subject, *i.e.* "wished." It follows that (1) is a condensation of:

(3) "He replied that he wished . . . , and that he intended."

(2), though theoretically free from ambiguity, is practically ambiguous, owing to a loose habit of repeating the subject unnecessarily. It would be better to insert a conjunctional word or a full stop between the two statements. Thus

(4) "He replied that he wished to help them, and *indeed* he intended," &c., or "He replied, &c. He intended, &c."

Where there is any danger of ambiguity, use (3) or (4) in preference to (1) or (2).

29. When there are several infinitives, those that are dependent on the same word must be kept distinct from those that are not.

"He said that he wished *to* take his friend with him *to* visit the capital and *to* study medicine." Here it is doubtful whether the meaning is—

"He said that he wished to take his friend with him,

(1) *and also* to visit the capital and study medicine," or

(2) "that his friend might visit the capital *and might also* study medicine," or

(3) "on a visit to the capital, *and that he also* wished to study medicine."

From the three different versions it will be perceived that this ambiguity must be met (*a*) by using "that" for "to," which allows us to repeat an auxiliary verb [*e.g.* "might" in (2)], and (*b*) by inserting conjunctions. As to insertions of conjunctions, see (37).

"In order to," and "for the purpose of," can be used to distinguish (wherever there is any ambiguity) between an infinitive that *expresses a purpose*, and an infinitive that does not, *e.g.* "He told his servant to call upon his friend, *to* (in order to) give him information about the trains, and not to leave him till he started."

30. The principle of suspense. Write your sentence in such a way that, until he has come to the full stop, the reader may feel the sentence to be incomplete. In other words, keep your reader in *suspense*. *Suspense* is caused (1) by placing the "if-clause" first, and not last, in a conditional sentence; (2) by placing participles before the words they qualify; (3) by using suspensive conjunctions, *e.g. not only, either, partly, on the one hand, in the first place,* &c.

The following is an example of an *unsuspended* sentence. The sense *draggles*, and it is difficult to keep up one's attention.

"Mr. Pym was looked upon as the man of greatest experience in parliaments, | where he had served very long, | and was always a man of business, | being an officer in the Exchequer, | and of a good reputation generally, | though known to be inclined to the Puritan party; yet not of those furious resolutions (*Mod. Eng.* so furiously resolved) against the Church as the other leading men were,—and wholly devoted to the Earl of Bedford,—who had nothing of that spirit."

The foregoing sentence might have ended at any one of the eight points marked above. When suspended it becomes:—

"Mr. Pym, owing to his long service in Parliament in the Exchequer, was esteemed above all others for his Parliamentary experience and for his knowledge of business. He had also a good reputation generally; for, though openly favoring the Puritan party, he was closely devoted to the Earl of Bedford, and, like the Earl, had none of the fanatical spirit manifested against the Church by the other leading men."

30 a. It is a violation of the principle of Suspense to introduce unexpectedly, at the end of a long sentence, some short and unemphatic clause beginning with (a) " . . . . not " or (b) " . . . . which."

(*a*) "This reform has already been highly beneficial to all classes of our countrymen, and will, I am persuaded, encourage among us industry, self-dependence, and frugality, *and not, as some say, wastefulness.*"

Write "not, as some say, wastefulness, but industry, self-dependence, and frugality."

(*b*) "After a long and tedious journey, the last part of which was a little dangerous owing to the state of the roads, we arrived safely at York, *which is a fine old town.*"

EXCEPTION.—When the short final clause is intended to be unexpectedly unemphatic, it comes in appropriately, with something of the sting of an epigram. See (42). Thus:

"The old miser said that he should have been delighted to give the poor fellow a shilling, but most unfortunately he had left his purse at home—*a habit of his.*"

Suspense naturally throws increased emphasis on the words for which we are waiting, *i.e.* on the end of the sentence. It has been pointed out above that **a monotony of final emphasis is objectionable, especially in letter-writing and conversation.**

31. Suspense must not be excessive.

Excess of suspense is a common fault in boys translating from Latin. " Themistocles, having secured the safety of Greece, the Persian fleet being now destroyed,when he had unsuccessfully attempted to persuade the Greeks to break down the bridge across the Hellespont, hearing that Xerxes was in full flight, and thinking that it might be profitable to secure the friendship of the king, wrote as follows to him :" The more English idiom is : " When Themistocles had secured the safety of Greece by the destruction of the Persian fleet, he made an unsuccessful attempt to persuade the Greeks to break down the bridge across the Hellespont.   Soon afterwards, hearing &c.'

A long suspense that would be intolerable in prose is tolerable in the introduction to a poem.   See the long interval at the beginning of *Paradise Lost* between "Of man's first disobedience " and " Sing, heavenly Muse." Compare also the beginning of *Paradise Lost*, Book **II.** :

> " *High on a throne of royal state, which far*
> *Outshone the wealth of Ormuz and of Ind,*
> *Or where the gorgeous East with richest hand*
> *Showers on her kings barbaric pearl and gold—*
> Satan exalted sat. "

with the opening of Keats' *Hyperion :*

> " *Deep in the shady sadness of a vale,*
> *Far sunken from the healthy breath of morn,*
> *Far from the fiery noon and eve's one star—*
> Sat gray-haired Saturn, quiet as a stone."

32. In a long conditional sentence put the "if-clause," antecedent, or protasis, first.

Every one will see the flatness of "Revenge thy father's most unnatural murder, if thou didst ever love him," as compared with the suspense that forces an expression of agony from Hamlet in—

" *Ghost.*   If thou didst ever thy dear father love ——
Hamlet.   O, God !
Ghost.   Revenge his foul and most unnatural murder."

The effect is sometimes almost ludicrous when the consequent is long and complicated, and when it precedes the antecedent or "if-clause." "I should be delighted to introduce you to my friends, and to show you the objects of interest in our city, and the beautiful scenery in the neighborhood, if you were here." Where the "if-clause" comes last, it ought to be very emphatic: "if you were *only* here."

The introduction of a clause with "if" or "though" in the middle of a sentence may often cause ambiguity, especially when a great part of the sentence depends on "that:" "His enemies answered that, for the sake of preserving the public peace, they would keep quiet for the present, though he declared that cowardice was the motive of the delay, and that for this reason they would put off the trial to a more convenient season." See (27)

33. Suspense[1] is gained by placing a Participle or Adjective that qualifies the Subject, before the Subject.

"*Deserted* by his friends, he was forced to have recourse to those that had been his enemies." Here, if we write, "He, deserted by his friends, was forced &c.," *he* is unduly emphasized; and if we write, "He was forced to have recourse to his enemies, having been deserted by his friends," the effect is very flat.

Of course we might sometimes write "He was deserted and forced &c." But this cannot be done where the "desertion" is to be not stated but implied.

Often, when a participle qualifying the subject is introduced late in the sentence, it causes positive ambiguity: "With this small force the general determined to attack the foe, *flushed* with recent victory and *rendered* negligent by success."

An excessive use of the *suspensive participle* is French and objectionable: *e.g.* "*Careless* by nature, and too much *engaged* with business to think of the morrow, *spoiled* by a long-established liberty and a fabulous prosperity, *having* for many generations forgotten the scourge of war, we allow ourselves to drift on without taking heed of the signs of the times." The remedy is to convert the participle into a verb depending on a conjunction: "Because we are by nature careless, &c.; " or to convert the participle into a verb co-ordinate with the principal verb, *e.g.* "*We are* by nature careless, &c., and therefore we *allow* ourselves, &c."

34. Suspensive Conjunctions, e.g. "either," "not only," "on the one hand," add clearness.—Take the following sentence:—"You

[1] See (30).

must take this extremely perilous course, in which success is úncertain, and failure disgraceful, as well as ruinous, or else the liberty of your country is endangered." Here, the meaning is liable to be misunderstood, till the reader had gone half through the sentence. Write " *Either* you must," &c., and the reader is, from the first, prepared for an alternative. Other suspensive conjunctions or phrases are *partly, for our part ; in the first place ; it is true ; doubtless ; of course ; though ; on the one hand.*

35. Repeat the Subject when the omission would cause ambiguity or obscurity.—The omission is particularly likely to cause obscurity after a Relative standing as Subject:

" He professes to be helping the nation, which in reality is suffering from his flattery, and (he ? or it ?) will not permit anything else to give it advice."

The Relative should be repeated when it is the Subject of several Verbs. "All the pleasing illusions *which* made power gentle and obedience liberal, *which* harmonized the different shades of life, and *which*, by a bland assimilation, incorporated into politics the sentiments that beautify and soften private society, are to be dissolved by this new conquering empire of light and reason."

36. Repeat a Preposition after an intervening Conjunction, especially if a Verb and an Object also intervene.

" He forgets the gratitude that he owes to those that helped all his companions when he was poor and uninfluential, and (*to*) John Smith in particular." Here, omit *to*, and the meaning may be " that helped all his companions, and John Smith in particular." The intervention of the verb and object, " helped " and " companions," causes this ambiguity.

37. When there are several Verbs at some distance from a Conjunction on which they depend, repeat the Conjunction.[1]

" When we look back upon the havoc that two hundred years have made in the ranks of our national authors—and, above all, (*when*) we refer their rapid disappearance to the quick succession of new competitors —we cannot help being dismayed at the prospect that lies before the writers of the present day."

Here omit " when," and we at once substitute a parenthetical statement for what is really a subordinate clause.

In reporting a speech or opinion, " that " must be continually repeated to avoid the danger of confusing what the writer says with what others say.

---

[1] The repetition of Auxiliary Verbs and Pronominal Adjectives is also conductive to clearness.

" We might say that the Cæsars did not persecute the Christians; (*that*) they only punished men who were charged, rightly or wrongly, with burning Rome, and committing the foulest abominations in secret assemblies; and (*that*) the refusal to throw frankincense on the altar of Jupiter was not the crime, but only evidence of the crime." But see (6*b*).

37 a.   Repeat Verbs after the conjunctions "than," "as," &c.

"I think he likes me better *than* you;" *i.e.* either "than you like me," or " he likes you."

" Cardinal Richelieu hated Buckingham as sincerely as *did* the Spaniard Olivares." Omit " did," and you cause ambiguity.

38.   If the sentence is so long that it is difficult to keep the thread of meaning unbroken, repeat the subject, or some other emphatic word, or a summary of what has been said.

" Gold and cotton, banks and railways, crowded ports, and populous cities—*these* are not the elements that constitute a great nation."

The repetition (though useful and, when used in moderation, not unpleasant) is more common with speakers than with writers, and with slovenly speakers than with good speakers.

" The country is in such a condition, that if we delay longer some fair measure of reform, sufficient at least to satisfy the more moderate, and much more, if we refuse all reform whatsoever—I say, if *we adopt so unwise a policy, the country is in such a condition* that we may precipitate a revolution."

Where the relative is either implied (in a participle) or repeated, the antecedent must often be repeated also. In the following sentence we have the Subject repeated not only in the final summary, but also as the antecedent:—

' But if there were, in any part of the world, a national church regarded as heretical by four-fifths of the nation committed to its care ; a *church* established and maintained by the sword; a *church* producing twice as many riots as conversions ; a *church* which, though possessing great wealth and power, and though long backed by persecuting laws, had, in the course of many generations, been found unable to propagate its doctrines, and barely able to maintain its ground ; a *church* so odious that fraud and violence, when used against its clear rights of property, were generally regarded as fair play; a *church* whose ministers were preaching to desolate walls, and with difficulty obtaining their lawful subsistence by the help of bayonets,—*such a church*, on our principles, could not, we must own, be defended."

**39. It is a help to clearness, when the first part of the sen-
tence prepares the way for the middle and the middle for the end,
in a kind of ascent. This ascent is called " climax."**

In the following there are two climaxes, each of which has three
terms:—

" To gossip (a) is a fault (b); to *libel* (a′), a *crime* (b′); to slander (a″),
a *sin* (b″)."

In the following, there are several climaxes, and note how they
contribute to the clearness of a long sentence:—

" Man, working, has *contrived* (a) the Atlantic Cable, but I declare
that it *astonishes* (b) me far more to think that *for his mere amusement* (c),
that to *entertain a mere idle hour* (c′), he has *created* (a′) ' Othello ' and
' Lear,' and I am more than astonished, I am *awe-struck* (b′), at that
inexplicable elasticity of his nature which enables him, instead of *turning
away* (d) from *calamity and grief* (e), or instead of merely *defying* (d′)
them, actually to *make them the material of his amusement* (d″), and to draw
from the *wildest agonies of the human spirit* (e′) a pleasure which is not
only *not cruel* (f′), but is in the highest degree *pure and ennobling* (f′)."

The neglect of climax produces an abruptness that interferes with the
even flow of thought. Thus, if Pope, in his ironical address to mankind, had
written—

> " Go, wondrous creature, mount where science guides;
> Go measure earth, weigh air, and state the tides;
> Go, teach Eternal Wisdom how to rule "—

the ascent would have been too rapid. The transition from earth to heaven,
and from investigating to governing, is prepared by the intervening climax—

> " Instruct the planets in what orbs to run;
> Correct old Time, and regulate the Sun;
> Go, soar with Plato to th' empyreal sphere,
> To the first good, first perfect, and first fair."

**40. When the thought is expected to ascend and yet descends,
feebleness and sometimes confusion is the result. The descent is
called " bathos."**

What pen can describe the tears, the lamentations, the agonies, the
animated remonstrances of the unfortunate prisoners? "

She was a woman of many accomplishments and virtues, graceful
in her movements, winning in her address, a kind friend, a faithful and
loving wife, a most affectionate mother, and she *played beautifully on the
piano forte.*"

INTENTIONAL BATHOS has a humorous incongruity and abruptness that is sometimes forcible. For example, after the climax ending with the line—

"Go' teach Eternal Wisdom how to rule,"

Pope adds

"Then drop into thyself, and be a *fool*."

40 a. A new construction should not be introduced without cause.—

A sudden and apparently unnecessary change of construction causes awkwardness and roughness at least, and sometimes breaks the flow of the sentence so seriously as to cause perplexity. Thus, write "virtuous and accomplished," or "of many virtues and accomplishments," not "of many virtues and accomplished;" "riding or walking" or "on foot or horseback," not "on foot or riding." In the same way, do not put adjectives and participles, active and passive forms of verbs, in too close juxtaposition. Avoid such sentences as the following:—

"He had good reason *to believe* that the delay was not *an accident* (accidental) but *premeditated*, and *for supposing* (to suppose, or else, for believing, above) that the fort, though strong both *by art* and *naturally* (nature), would be forced by the *treachery of the* governor and the *indolent* (indolence of the) general to capitulate within a week."

"They accused him of being *bribed* (receiving bribes from) by the king and *unwilling* (neglecting) to take the city "

41. Antithesis adds force, and often clearness.—

The meaning of *liberal* in the following sentence is ascertained by the antithesis:—

"All the pleasing illusions which made *power* (a) *gentle* (b) and *obedience* (a') *liberal* (b') . . . . are now to be destroyed.'

There is a kind of proportion. As *gentleness* is to *power*, so *liberality* (in the sense here used) is to *obedience*. Now *gentleness* is the check on the excess of power; therefore *liberal* here applies to that which checks the excess of obedience, *i.e.* checks servility. Hence *liberal* here means "free."

The contrast also adds force. "They aimed at the *rule* (a), not at the *destruction* (a), of their country. They were men of great *civil* (b) and great *military* (b') talents, and, if the *terror* (c), the *ornament* (c') of their age."

Excessive antithesis is unnatural and wearisome:—

"Who can persuade where *treason* (a) is above *reason* (a'), and *might* b) ruleth *right* (b'), and it is had for *lawful* (c) whatsoever is *pleasurable* (c'), and *commotioners* (d) are better than *commissioners* (d') and *common woe* (e) is named common *wealth* (e') ? "

42. Epigram.

It has been seen that the neglect of climax results in tameness. Sometimes the suddenness of the descent produces amusement: and when the descent is intentional and very sudden, the effect is striking as well as amusing. Thus:

(1) " You are not only not vicious, you are virtuous," is a *climax.*

(2) " You are not vicious, you are vice," is not *climax,* nor is it *bathos:* it is *epigram.*[1]

Epigram may be defined as a "short sentence expressing truth under an amusing appearance of incongruity." It is often antithetical.

" The Russian grandees came to { and diamonds," *climax.*
    court dropping pearls   { and vermin," *epigram.*

" These two nations were divided { and the bitter remembrance of
    by mutual fear   recent losses," *climax.*
                    { and mountains," *epigram.*

There is a sort of implied antithesis in :—

" He is full of information—(but flat also) like yesterday's *Times.*"

" Verbosity is cured (not by a small, but) by a large vocabulary."

The name of epigram may sometimes be given to a mere antithesis ; *e.g.* "An educated man should know something of everything, and everything of something."

43. Let each sentence have one, and only one, principal subject of thought.

"This great and good man died on the 17th of September, 1683, leaving behind him the memory of many noble actions, and a numerous family, of whom three were sons ; one of them, George, the eldest, heir to his father's virtues, as well as to his principal estates in Cumberland, where most of his father's property was situate, and shortly afterwards elected member for the county, which had for several generations returned this family to serve in Parliament." Here we have (1) the " great and good man," (2) " George," (3) " the country," disputing which is to be considered the principal subject. Two, if not three sentences should have been made, instead of one. Carefully avoid a long sentence like this, treating of many different subjects on one level. It is called *heterogeneous.*

---

[1] Professor Bain says : " In the epigram the mind is roused by a conflict or contradiction between the form of the language and the meaning really conveyed."

44. The connection between different sentences must be kept up by Adverbs used as Conjunctions, or by means of some other connecting words at the beginning of each sentence.—

Leave out the conjunctions and other connecting words, and it will be seen that the following sentences lose much of their meaning:—

"Pitt was in the army for a few months in time of peace. His biographer (*accordingly*) insists on our confessing, that, if the young cornet had remained in the service, he would have been one of the ablest commanders that ever lived. (*But*) this is not all. Pitt (, *it seems,*) was not merely a great poet *in esse* and a great general *in posse*, but a finished example of moral excellence. . . . . (*The truth is, that*) there scarcely ever lived a person who had so little claim to this sort of praise as Pitt. He was (*undoubtedly*) a great man. (*But*) his was not a complete and well-proportioned greatness. The public life of Hampden or of Somers resembles a regular drama which can be criticised as a whole, and every scene of which is to be viewed in connection with the main action. The public life of Pitt (, *on the other hand,*) is," &c.

The following are some of the most common connecting abverbs, or connecting phrases: (1) expressing consequence, similarity, repetition, or resumption of a subject—*accordingly, therefore, then, naturally, so that, thus, in this way, again, once more, to resume, to continue, to sum up, in fact, upon this ;* (2) expressing opposition—*nevertheless, in spite of this, yet, still, however, but, on the contrary, on the other hand ;* (3) expressing suspension— *undoubtedly . . . . but ; indeed   . . yet ; on the one hand . . . . on the other ; partly   . partly ; some . . . . others.*

Avoid a style like that of Bishop Burnet, which strings together a number of sentences with " and " or " so," or with no conjunction at all:

"Blake with the fleet happened to be at Malaga, before he made war upon Spain ; *and* some of his seamen went ashore, *and* met the Host carried about ; *and* not only paid no respect to it, but laughed at those who did." Write "*When* Blake &c."

45. The connection between two long sentences sometimes requires a short intervening sentence, showing the transition of thought.

" Without force or opposition, it (chivalry) subdued the fierceness of pride and power ; it obliged sovereigns to submit to the soft collar [1] of social esteem, compelled stern authority to submit to elegance, and gave a dominating vanquisher of laws to be subdued by manners. But now

---

[1] This metaphor is not recommended for imitation.

(*all is to be changed :*) all the pleasing illusions which made power gentle
and obedience liberal, which harmonized the different shades of life, and
which, by a bland assimilation, incorporated into politics the sentiments
that beautify and soften private society, are to be dissolved by this new
conquering empire of light and reason." If the words italicized were
omitted, the transition would be too abrupt: the conjunction *but* alone
would be insufficient.

Under the Whee

By Will Carleton

SCENE —A cosy cottage in
the outskirts of a city Enter.
a stranger, who is addressed
by the aged lady of the cottage, as follows

You've called to see Jack, **I**
suppose, sir; sit down.

I'm sorry to say't, but the
boy's out of town.

He'll be back in an hour,
if his train is not late,

And, perhaps, you'd be willing to sit here and wait,

While I give you a cup ot
his favorite tea—

Almost ready to pour. Oh !
You called to see me?

You – called – to – see – me?
Strange. I didn't under-
stand !

But you know we old ladies
aren't much in demand—

You—called—to—see—me. And your business is—say!
Let me know, now, at once! Do not keep it away
For an instant!—Oh! pardon!—You wanted to buy
Our poor little house, here. Now thank God on high
That it wasn't something worse that you came for!—
				Shake hands;
I'm so glad!—and forgive an old woman's ado,
While I tell you the facts; till your heart understands
		The reason I spoke up so brusquely to you:

My life lives with Jack;—a plain boy, I confess—
He's a young engineer on the morning express;
But he loves me so true; and though often we part,
He never "pulls out" of one station—my heart.
Poor Jack! how he toils!—he sinks into yon chair
		When he comes home, so tired with the jar and the whirl,
But he fondles my hands, and caresses my hair,
		And he calls me "his love"—till I blush like a girl.
Poor Jack!—but to-morrow is Christmas, you know,
		And this is his present: a gown of fine wool,
Embroidered with silk; my old fingers ran slow,
		But with love from my heart, all the stitches are full!

So when Jack is gone out on his dangerous trip,
		On that hot hissing furnace that flies through the air,
Over bridges that tremble—past sidings that slip—
		Through tunnels that grasp for his life with their snare—
I think of him always; I'm seldom at rest;
		And last night—O God's mercy—the dreams made me see
My boy lying crushed, with a wheel on his breast,
		And a face full of agony, beck'ning to me!
Now to-day, every step that I hear on the street,
		Seems to bring me a tiding of woe and despair;
Each ring at the door bell, my poor heart will beat
		As if Jack, the poor boy, in his grave clothes was there.
		And I thought, when I saw you—I'm nervous and queer—
		You had brought me some news it would kill me to hear.
		Please don't be concerned, sir; I'm bound that in spite
		Of my foolish old fancies, the boy is all right!

No, I don't think we'd sell. For it's this way, you see:
		Jack says that he never will care for the smile
Of a girl till he knows she's in love, too, with me;
		And I tell him—ha! ha!—*that* will be a long while.

So we'll doubtless bide here a good time. And there's some
  Little chance of Jack's leaving the engine, ere long
For a place in the shops ; where they say he'll become
  A master mechanic ;
     Good sir, what is wrong ?

You are death-pale, and trembling ! here, drink some more tea ;
Say ! why are you looking your pity at me ?
What's that word in your face ?—you've a message !—now find
Your tongue !—Then I'll tear the truth out of your mind !

Jack's Hurt! Oh, how hard that you could not at first
    Let me know this black news ! Say ! where is he ? and when
Can he come home with me ?—but my poor heart will burst,
    If you do not speak out !—Speak, I pray you again !
I can stand it ; why, yonder's his own cosy bed ;

I will get it all fixed—Oh ! but I'm a good nurse !
    His hospital's home !—here I'll pillow his head,
I will bring him to life, be he better or worse !
    Oh ! I tell you ! however disfigured he be,
    What is left of the boy; shall be saved, sir, for me !
Thank God for the chance !   Oh, how hard I will work
    For my poor wounded child ! and now let me be led
Where he is.   Do not fear l   I 'll not falter or shrink !

    Turn your face to the light, sir,   *   *   *   *

                 O, God—*Jack is dead* '

BRIDAL SONG.

"DOST thou linger, gentle maiden,
   At the minster door?
Dost thou tremble, tender maiden,
   On the chancel floor?
Dost thou fear and dost thou falter
When thou kneelest at the altar?
With the bridegroom by thee now,
Wilt thou take the marriage vow?

"If thy heart, O loving maiden!
   Thou hast given away,
Without fear, O trustful maiden!
   Give thy hand to-day;
Leaving father, leaving mother,
Give thy life unto another,
Taking back a dearer life
From his love as wedded wife.

"Let him lead thee, wedded maiden,
   From the altar now;
Thou art his forever, maiden,
   By that marriage vow;

His in joy and sorrow ever,
None these holy bonds may sever,
Loving, trusting, stand beside
Him who loves thee, happy bride."

MY OWN SWEET WIFE.

"THERE is a word of common sound
   That's oft pronounced by high and
     low;
Few liquids make it soft or round;
   And yet there comes a sudden glow
As starting from a dreaming mood
Of careless, uneventful life,
I hear a voice best understood,
   Call the charmed name—my own
     sweet—wife.

"What spell weaves joy around that word,
   Brightening the dullest, darkest hour,
That when, or where, or how 'tis heard
   It wields such witching, wondrous
     power?
If Eve, when exiled from lost Eden,
   Wept the soft ease of that charmed
     life,
What need of other gift of heaven
   Than to be Adam's own sweet—wife.

"And so my prayer I make to thee,
   In joy or sadness, grief or pain,
That always you bestow on me
   The name my love would still retain.
No sting can sorrow leave behind,
   No fear of anger nor of strife,
No harsh replies, nor thoughts unkind
   Can mingle with the term—sweet
     wife."

THE JEWEL FOR THE BRIDAL DAY.

THAT is a beautiful custom suggested by legends of the early times to bestow on the bride the well-set stone appropriate to the month of the bride's birth.

For every month there is a stone, and for every stone a motto. Mrs. Julia M. Haderman has set these twelve stones in verse, which cannot fail to charm the readers of the HOME MANUAL:

JANUARY.

By her who in this month is born
No gem save Garnets should be worn;
They will insure her constancy,
True friendship and fidelity.

FEBRUARY.

The February-born will find
Sincerity and peace of mind,
Freedom from passion and from care,
If they the Amethyst will wear.

MARCH.

Who on this world of ours their eyes
In March first open, shall be wise,
In days of peril firm and brave
And wear a Bloodstone to their grave.

APRIL.

She who from April dates her years
Diamonds should wear, lest bitter tears
For vain repentance flow; this stone,
Emblem of innocence is known.

MAY.

Who first beholds the light of day
In Spring's sweet flow'ry month of May,
And wears an Emerald all her life,
Shall be a loved and happy wife.

JUNE.

Who comes with Summer to this earth,
And owes to June her day of birth,
With ring of Agate on her hand,
Can health, wealth, and long life command.

JULY.

The glowing Ruby should adorn
Those who in warm July are born;
Then will they be exempt and free
From love's doubts and anxiety.

AUGUST.

Wear a Sardonyx, or for thee
No conjugal felicity;
The August-born, without this stone,
'Tis said must live unloved and lone.

SEPTEMBER.

A maiden born when Autumn leaves
Are rustling in September's breeze,
A Sapphire on her brow should bind,
'Twill cure diseases of the mind.

OCTOBER.

October's child is born for woe,
And life's vicissitudes must know;
But lay an Opal on her breast,
And hope will lull those woes to rest.

NOVEMBER.

Who first comes to this world below
With drear November's fog and snow,
Should prize the Topaz, amber hue—
Emblem of friends and lovers true.

DECEMBER.

If cold December gave you birth,
The month of snow and ice and mirth,
Place on your hand a Turquoise blue;
Success will bless whate'er you do.

HOME, WHERE THERE'S ONE TO LOVE US.

HOME'S not merely four square walls,
   Though with pictures hung and gilded,
Home is where affection calls—
   Filled with shrines the heart hath builded
Home!—go watch the faithful dove
   Sailing 'neath the heaven above us—
Home is where there's one to love!
   Home is where there's one to love us!

Home's not merely roof and room,
   It needs something to endear it;
Home is where the heart can bloom:
   Where there's some kind lip to cheer it!
What is home with none to meet?
   None to welcome—none to greet us!
Home is sweet—and only sweet—
   When there's one we love to meet us!
                        —CHARLES SWAIN.

THE FAMILY.

"THE Family is like a Book,
    The Children are the leaves,
The Parents are the cover, that
    Protective beauty gives.

"At first the pages of the book
    Are blank and purely fair,
But time soon writeth memories
    And painteth pictures there.

"Love is the little golden clasp
    That bindeth up the trust;
Oh, break it not, lest all the leaves
    Shall scatter and be lost."

DE TOUT MON CŒUR.

THE sweetest songs I ever sing
    Are those I sing to you,
The deepest thoughts that I can bring
    Are thoughts I never knew
Until your soft eyes questioning
    Had made me question, too.
My soul lies open to your sight,
    When all the world's away,
Like that pale flower that at night,
    As ancient legends say,
Unfolds beneath the moon's clear light,
    And dies at dawn of day.

—G. H. DUFFIELD.

BABY.

WHERE did you come from, baby dear?
    Out of the everywhere into here.

Where did you get those eyes so blue?
Out of the sky as I came through.

What makes the light in them sparkle and
    spin?
Some of the starry spikes left in.

Where did you get that little tear?
I found it waiting when I got here.

What makes your forehead so smooth and
    high?
A soft hand stroked it as I went by.

What makes your cheek like a warm white
    rose?
I saw something better than anyone knows.

Whence that three-cornered smile of bliss?
Three angels gave me at once a kiss.

Where did you get this pearly ear?
God spoke, and it came out to hear.

Where did you get those arms and hands?
Love made itself into bonds and bands.

Feet, whence did you come, you darling
    things?
From the same box as the cherub's wings.

How did they all just come to be you?
God thought about me, and so I grew.

But how did you come to us, you dear?
God thought about you, and so I am here

—GEORGE MACDONALD.

TEN YEARS.

'TIS said ten years are tin,
  Whether or not you win
Knowledge, or power, or fame;
'Tis always TIN, the same.
With this philosophy
I hardly can agree,
'Tis surely more than this
Unless great thought you miss.

Ten years, foundations laid
With stone of finest grade,
Chiseled and laid in course,
So solid that no force
Can ever make a breach,
Or its warm color bleach.
Ten years, the walls arise
Up t'wards the blessed skies;
So that e'en now I see
More than mortality.

Behold the wondrous tint
Which Heaven's golden glint
Reveals to our glad eyes;
A tint that never dies—
The glory of God's grace
Waving from either face.

Ten years give more than signs
Of deep, exhaustless mines.
No, no, not mines of tin,
Of rust, and dust, and din!
But mines of virgin gold
That ne'er were bought or sold;
Of Christian thought, deed-born,
That richer glows when worn;
Of doctrine pure and strong;
The girdle and the song;
Opening yon pearly gate,
Where royal servants wait,
Till pilgrims thither come,
Their earthly mission done.

Of LOVE that spreads its breast
Wherever sobs unrest,
And turns a tearful eye
On men condemned to die.
The Rose that never fades;
The Light that lightens glades;
The Arm of mighty power
That shields in terror's hour;
The Lullaby of God,
When smitten by the rod;
The soul's "Thy will be done,"
Crying when shines no sun,
Rough sea, or thorny land,
"O Father, take my hand!"

Well, this I have to say,
On this decadal day,
With Bride and Bridegroom here.
And rosy children dear,
If this be tin, when old,
How bright will be the gold!

ONLY HALF A SCORE.

TEN years have silent swept
  With all their train along;
Time and our hearts have kept
  The echoes of their voiceless song.

Their music—that of dreams—
  Floats in upon my soul.
Its silent sweetness seems
  To soothe, like distant church bells' toll.

Those years! How bright they seemed!
  With hopes and joys so filled.
Their promise half redeemed
  Has left our lives with gladness thrilled.

Ten years have passed, and ten
  Or more, or less, are yet.
The memories of the past remain,
  And joy in all the rest beget.
—REV. FREDERICK B. PULLAN.

THE CRYSTAL WEDDING.

IN olden time, I have been told,
 When husband chose a wife,
One wedding served the twain, to hold
 Through all their mortal life.

In modern times, if for five years
 The bond has holden good,
People are coming, it appears,
 To wed again with Wood.

If for ten years the twain abide,
 Again the friends come in
To clasp the knot so firmly tied,
 In wedding called the Tin.

And yet again the tried and true,
 When five years more shall pass,
Are wont to celebrate anew
 Their wedding termed the Glass.

Thus Hymen's bond, the people learn,
 Grows dear in growing old,
And hence they celebrate in turn
 With China, Silver, Gold.

Thus far we've journeyed on the way,
 Till fifteen years from starting,
And are not yet prepared to say
 That we are bent on parting.

A cordial greeting we extend
 To all whose presence bright,
Combines a social joy to lend
 On this our Crystal night.

Unitedly we pledge you all,
 But not in sparkling wine;
Oh, may our loved ones never fall
 Before its mocking shrine.

Then fill the glass for each to-night
 From Nature's crystal tide,
That which has sparkled, pure and bright,
 Since Eve became a bride.

We know our Lord, 'tis truly said,
 Turned water into wine,
And by the power He thus displayed
 Proved that he was divine ;

And at the Supper gave command
 That we partake the same,
Throughout all time, in every land,
 Remembering His name.

An emblem of our Saviour's blood,
 Let wine forever be,
Reminding of the crimson flood
 That flowed for you and me.

But not fermented, madd'ning wine,
 Which hath such ruin wrought,
Of that vile product of the vine
 The Word saith "Touch it not."

Then fill the glass for each, to-night,
 From Nature's crystal tide,
That which has sparkled, pure and bright,
 Since Eve became a bride.

How rapidly through all these years.
 Life's moments have been fleeting,
Bringing us mingled joys and tears,
 Sad parting and fond greeting.

Four children form our little band,
 And call us Father, Mother,
While two are in the " Happy Land,
 A sister and a brother.

And thus our God, in giving joy,
Hath not forgotten chiding;
All earthly bliss hath some alloy,
And may not prove abiding.

Yet all along the light hath shone
Above the fleeting shadows,
Which sometimes settle darkly down
As fog upon the meadows.

And while the rain may fall to-day,
The sun will shine to-morrow;
And thus our Father hath alway
Dispelled our clouds of sorrow.

Now, grateful for the tender care
Which thus far has been o'er us,
We'll trust our Father to prepare
The way that lies before us.

MRS. L. H. WASHINGTON.

THE SILVER GREETING.

AFTER twenty-five years of wedded life, loved ones come together with their silver greeting, thus:

" DEAR friends, we come to greet you
And chant in humble lay,
Your first bright silver crescent
Now waning fast away.
How each unto the other
In plighted faith ye gave,
And in your little life-boat
Launched out upon the wave.

"The morning sun beams brightly
O'er life's broad, silvery sea,
As down the smiling harbor
Ye drop confidingly.
And with your heavenly Pilot
Your fragile bark to guide,
Securely float, or safely
Defy the rolling tide.

"Tho' silvery skies may vanish,
Yet many a silver shower
Dispels the clouds' foreboding,
And gilds the dark'ning hour.
While gentler dews descending
In blessings from above,
In sparkling brilliants blending,
Reflect the Father's love."

THE SILVER WEDDING.

A QUARTER of a century
Has rolled upon Time's tide,
Since thou, a youthful lover, came
To claim thy chosen bride.

How beautiful Life's pathway seemed
In those fresh early years,
Decked all along with buds of hope,
Undimmed by cares or tears!

For it has wisely ever been,
Since Love's first blushing morn,
We grasp the rose without a thought
Of underlying thorn.

And yet to all Life's changing hours
Some cares and sorrows bring;
Some thorns are placed amid the flowers,
Lest we too fondly cling

To earthly joys, which must decay,
Alas, that they may prove
Reminders of that better life,
Where all is light and love.

LAY THY HAND IN MINE.

OH, lay thy hand in mine, dear!
We're growing old;
But Time hath brought no sign, dear,
That hearts grow cold.
'Tis long, long since, our new love
Made light divine;
But age enricheth true love
Like noble wine.

And lay thy cheek to mine, dear,
And take thy rest;
Mine arms around thee twine, dear,
And make thy nest.
A-many cares are pressing
On this dear head;
But sorrow's hands in blessing
Are surely laid.

Oh, lean thy life on mine, dear!
'Twill shelter thee.
Thou wert a winsome vine, dear,
On my young tree;
And so, till boughs are leafless,
And song-birds flown,
We'll twine, then lay us griefless
Together down.

—GERALD MASSEY.

WHEN THE OLD RING WAS NEW.

The wedding-ring, which has now been worn twenty-five years, has not been laid aside a single day, and has grown thin by use; beautiful, beautiful ring! He who gave it in tenderness says :

"YOUR wedding-ring grows thin, dear
  wife ; ah, summers not a few,
Since I put it on your finger first have
  passed o'er me and you ;
And love, what changes have we seen—
  what cares and pleasures too—
Since you became my own dear wife, when
  this old ring was new.

" O blessings on that happy day, the hap-
  piest of my life,
When, thanks to God, your low, sweet ' yes'
  made you my loving wife !
Your heart will say the same, I know; that
  day's as dear to you,—
That day that made me yours, dear wife,
  when this old ring was new.

"Years bring fresh links to bind us, wife,—
  young voices that are here,
Young faces round our fire that make their
  mother's yet more dear ;
Young loving hearts, your care each day
  makes yet more like to you,
More like the loving heart made mine when
  this old ring was new.

"The past is dear; its sweetness still our
  memories treasure yet—
The griefs we've borne together, we would
  not now forget.
Whatever, wife, the future brings, heart
  unto heart still true,
We'll share as we have shared all else, since
  this old ring was new.

'And if God spare us 'mongst our sons
  and daughters to grow old,
We know His goodness will not let your
  heart or mine grow cold ;
Your aged eyes will see in mine still all
  they've shown to you,
And mine in yours, all they've seen since
  this old ring was new."
     —W. COX BENNETT.

THE PLEDGE.

FROM this hour the pledge is given,
 From this hour my soul is thine ·
Come what will from earth or Heaven,
 Weal or woe thy fate be mine.

     —MOORE.

FIFTIETH ANNIVERSARY.

OUR hearts are young as ever, now,
    Though fifty years are gone
Since vows were made, and words were said
    That of the twain made one.

Our hearts are young as ever, now,—
    That was a happy home
Where first we lit the lamp of love,
    Nor thought a grief could come.

Our hearts are young as ever, now,
    And God has kindly smiled
On each long year, since that in which
    We hailed our first-born child.

Our hearts are young as ever, now,
    Though changes we have seen;
For now the girls are women grown
    And all our boys are men.

Our hearts are young as ever, now,—
    See our grandchildren run!
A little great-granddaughter comes
    And stands with great-grandson.

Our hearts are young as ever, now,
    God hath His blessing given,
We wedded once for earthly bliss,
    We now are wed for Heaven.

Our hearts are young as ever, now,—
    Fifty years more gone by,
Our hearts will then be younger still,
    There's youth for aye on high.—

            —D. W. FAUNCE, D. D.

THE OLD MAN TO HIS WIFE.

JUST fifty years have passed away
    Since you and I were wed,
How swiftly since that bridal day
    The fifty years have sped.
God's providence on us hath shone,
    His gracious hand hath led,
And ne'er in vain before His throne
    We've said, "Our daily bread."

Together struggling up the hill
    Of life's uneven way,
Our hearts are knit more closely till
    We've reached this golden day.
We've known the bliss which joy imparts,
    Life's raptures and its tears,
But God has let us youthful hearts
    Bring into ripened years.

In children God to us hath given,
    We live our youth anew,
Some wait for us to-day in Heaven,
    They all to us are true:
And yet by "silver threads" entwined
    Among the "threads of gold,"
And furrows down our cheeks, we find
    That we are growing old.

Just fifty years ago we wed,
    Just fifty years to-day;
We two are one, the preacher said,
    And so we've held our way.
The ties of love which bound us then
    To-day are golden thread,
And this will never break, till when
    We're numbered with the dead.

            —J. BYINGTON SMITH, D.D.

THE HOME-BOUND HOST.

THE sound of a host advancing,
    Tramp! tramp! tramp!
Under the windy flicker
    And flare of the evening lamp,
Under the steady whiteness
    Of the clear electric light,
The sound of an army marching
    Is in the streets to-night.

Not to the clamor of bugles,
    Nor the stormy beat of drums,
Not to the battle's tocsin,
    The jubilant army comes.
A sweeter music summons
    And thrills along the line,
Though each for himself may hear it,
    And make to the next no sign.

The patter of tiny footfalls
    That run to an open door,
The mother's tender singing,
    Her step on the nursery floor,
The boyish shout of welcome
    The girlish ripple of glee,
At the click in the guarded portal
    Of the home-bound father's key.

This is the army's music:
    Cheerily calls good-night
The merry voice of the comrade
    As he passes out of sight
Into the heart of the household
    When the day's long work is done,
And wife and bairns are waiting
    With a kiss for their dearest one.

Under the windy flicker
    And flare of the evening lamp
I hear a host advancing
    With steady and resolute tramp
A host of the strong and gentle,
    A throng of the brave and true,
Dear little wives and mothers,
    Hastening home to you!

IF WE KNEW.

IF we knew the baby fingers
    Pressed against the window-pane
Would be cold and stiff to-morrow—
    Never trouble us again;
Would the bright eyes of our darling
    Catch the frown upon our brow?
Would the prints of rosy fingers
    Vex us then as they do now?

Ah, these little ice-cold fingers,
    How they point our memories back
To the hasty words and actions
    Strewn along our backward track!
How those little hands remind us,
    As in snowy grace they lie,
Not to scatter thorns—but roses—
    For our reaping by and by!

Strange we never prize the music
    Till the sweet-voiced bird has flown;
Strange that we should slight the violets
    Till the lovely flowers are gone;
Strange that Summer skies and sunshine
    Never seem one-half so fair
As when Winter's snowy pinions
    Shake their white down in the air!

Lips from which the seal of silence
    None but God can roll away,
Never blossomed in such beauty
    As adorns the mouth to-day;
And sweet words that freight our memory
    With their beautiful perfume,
Come to us in sweeter accents
    Through the portals of the tomb.

Let us gather up the sunbeams
    Lying all along our path;
Let us keep the wheat and roses,
    Casting out the thorns and chaff;
Let us find our sweetest comfort
    In the blessings of *to-day;*
With a patient hand removing
    All the briars from our way.

MY MOTHER.

THE sweetest face in all the world to me,
  Set in a frame of shining silver hair,
With eyes whose language is fidelity:
  This is my mother. Is she not most fair?

Ten little heads have found their sweetest
    rest
  Upon the pillow of her loving breast:
The world is wide; yet nowhere does it keep
  So safe a haven, so secure a rest.

'Tis counted something great to be a queen,
  And bend a kingdom to a woman's will.
To be a mother such as mine, I ween,
  Is something better and more noble still.

O mother! in the changeful years now
    flown,
  Since, as a child I leant upon your knee,
Life has not brought to me, nor fortune
    shown,
  Such tender love! such yearning sympa-
    thy!

Let fortune smile or frown, whiche'er she
    will;
  It matters not, I scorn her fickle ways!
I never shall be quite bereft until
  I lose my mother's honest blame and
    praise!

TIRED MOTHERS.

A LITTLE elbow leans upon your knee,
  Your tired knee, that has so much to
    bear;
A child's dear eyes are looking lovingly
  From underneath a thatch of shining hair:
Perhaps you do not heed the velvet touch
  Of warm, moist fingers, folding yours so
    tight,
You do not prize this blessing overmuch—
  You almost are too tired to pray, to-night!

But it *is* blessedness! A year ago
  I did not see it as I do to-day,
We are so dull and thankless; and too slow
  To catch the sunshine e'er it slips away.
And now it seems surpassing strange to me,
  That while I wore the badge of mother-
    hood,
I did not kiss more oft and tenderly
  The little child that brought me only good!

And if some night when you sit down to rest,
  You miss this elbow from your tired knee;
This restless, curling head from off your
    breast,
  This lisping tongue that chatters con-
    stantly;
If from your own the dimpled hand had
    slipped,
  And ne'er would nestle in your palm
    again;
If the white feet into their grave had tripped
  I could not blame you for your heartache
    then!

I wonder so that mothers ever fret
  At little children, clinging to their gown;
Or that the footprints, when the days are
    wet,
  Are ever black enough to make them
    frown!
If I could find a little muddy boot,
  Or cap, or jacket, on my chamber floor;
If I could kiss a rosy, restless foot,
  And hear its music in my home once
    more;

If I could mend a broken cart to-day,
  To-morrow make a kite to reach the sky
There is no woman in God's world could say
  She was more blissfully content than I.
But, ah! the dainty pillow next my own
  Is never rumpled by a shining head;
My singing birdling from its nest is flown—
  The little boy I used to kiss is dead!

DAN'S WIFE.

UP in early morning light,
  Sweeping, dusting, "setting right,"
Oiling all the household springs,
Sewing buttons, tying strings,
Telling Bridget what to do,
Mending rips in Johnny's shoe,
Running up and down the stair,
Tying baby in his chair,
Cutting meat and spreading bread,
Dishing out so much per head,
Eating as she can by chance,
Giving husband kindly glance,
Toiling, working, busy life :
      Smart woman,
      Dan's wife.

Dan comes home at fall of night—
Home so cheerful, neat and bright—
Children meet him at the door,
Pull him in and look him o'er,
Wife asks "how the work has gone?
"Busy times with us at home !"
Supper done—Dan reads at ease,
Happy Dan, but one to please.
Children must be put to bed—
All their little prayers are said;
Little shoes are placed in rows,
Bed-clothes tucked o'er little toes,
Busy, noisy, wearing life :
      Tired woman,
      Dan's wife.

Dan reads on, and falls asleep,
See the woman softly creep ;
Baby rests at last, poor dear,
Not a word her heart to cheer ;
Mending-basket full to top—
Stockings, shirts, and little frock—
Tired eyes and weary brain,
Side with darting ugly pain—
"Never mind, 'twill pass away !"
She must work, but never play ;
Closed piano, unused books,
Done the walks to cosy nooks,
Brightness faded out of life :
      Saddened woman,
      Dan's wife.

Upstairs, tossing to and fro,
Fever holds the woman low ;
Children wander, free to play,
When and where they will to-day,
Bridget loiters—dinner's cold,
Dan looks anxious, cross, and old ,
Household screws are out of place,
Lacking one dear, patient face ;
Steady hands, so weak but true—
Hands that knew just what to do,
Never knowing rest or play,
Folded now, and laid away
Work of six in one short life :
      Shattered woman,
      Dan's wife.

———

I LOVE YOU.

SHE climbed upon my willing knee,
  And softly whispered unto me,
      " I love you."

Her dainty arms were around my neck,
Her sunny curls were in my face ;
And in her tender eyes I saw
The soul of innocence and grace.

And like a sunbeam gliding through
The clouds that hide the skies of blue,
Her smile found access to my heart,
And bade the shadows all depart.

O, moment of apocaly-pse,
In which I saw the stately ships,
That erstwhile sailed away from me,
Come riding back across the sea ;
I would you might return and stay
Within my lonely heart alway.

God bless the darling little child
Who looked up in my face and smiled
And wrought into my heart a spell
More sweet than songs of Israel.

O, angels, listen while I pray
That you will make her life as sweet
As that brief moment was to me,
When'er I heard her lips repeat,
      " I love you."

THE BALLAD OF BABIE BELL.

HAVE you not heard the poets tell
   How came the dainty Babie Bell
    Into this world of ours?
The gates of heaven were left ajar;
With folded hands and dreamy eyes,
Wandering out of Paradise,
She saw this planet, like a star,
   Hung in the glistening depths of even,—
Its bridges running to and fro,
O'er which the white-winged angels go,
   Bearing the holy dead to heaven.
She touched a bridge of flowers,—those
    feet,
So light they did not bend the bells
Of the celestial asphodels!
They fell like dew upon the flowers,
Then all the air grew strangely sweet—
And thus came dainty Babie Bell
   Into this world of ours.
She came and brought delicious May.
   The swallows built beneath the eaves ·
   Like sunlight in and out the leaves,
The robins went the livelong day;
The lily swung its noiseless bell,
   And o'er the porch the trembling vine
   Seemed bursting with its veins of wine.
How sweetly, softly, twilight fell!
O, earth was full of singing-birds,
And opening spring-tide flowers,
When the dainty Babie Bell
   Came to this world of ours!

O Babie, dainty Babie Bell,
How fair she grew from day to day!
What woman-nature filled her eyes,
What poetry within them lay!
Those deep and tender twilight eyes,
   So full of meaning, pure and bright,
   As if she yet stood in the light
Of those oped gates of Paradise.
And so we loved her more and more;
Ah, never in our hearts before
   Was love so lovely born:
We felt we had a link between
This real world and that unseen
   The land beyond the morn.
And for the love of those dear eyes,
For love of her whom God led forth
(The mother's being ceased on earth
When Babie came from Paradise),—
For love of Him who smote our lives,
   And woke the chords of joy and pain,
We said, *Dear Christ!*—our hearts bent
   down
   Like violets after rain.

And now the orchards, which were white
And red with blossoms when she came,
Were rich in autumn's mellow prime.
The clustered apples burnt like flame,
The soft-cheeked peaches blushed and
   fell,
The ivory chestnut burst its shell,
The grapes hung purpling in the grange;
And time wrought just as rich a change
   In little Babie Bell.
Her lissome form more perfect grew,
   And in her features we could trace,
   In softened curves, her mother's face
Her angel-nature ripened too.
We thought her lovely when she came
But she was holy, saintly now:—
Around her pale angelic brow
We saw a slender ring of flame.

God's hand had taken away the seal
   That held the portals of her speech;
And oft she said a few strange words
   Whose meaning lay beyond our reach.

She never was a child to us,
We never held her being's key,
We could not teach her holy things;
    She was Christ's self in purity.

It came upon us by degrees:
We saw its shadow ere it fell,
The knowledge that our God had sent
His messenger for Babie Bell.
We shuddered with unlanguaged pain,
And all our hopes were changed to fears,
And all our thoughts ran into tears
    Like sunshine into rain.
We cried aloud in our belief,
" O, smite us gently, gently, God !
Teach us to bend and kiss the rod,
And perfect grow through grief."
Ah, how we loved her, God can tell;
Her heart was folded deep in ours.
    Our hearts are broken, Babie Bell !

At last he came, the messenger,
    The messenger from unseen lands:
And what did dainty Babie Bell?
She only crossed her little hands,
She only looked more meek and fair !
We parted back her silken hair,
We wove the roses round her brow,
White buds, the summer's drifted snow,
Wrapt her from head to foot in flowers;
And then went dainty Babie Bell
    Out of this world of ours !
             —T. B. ALDRICH.

JOHN ANDERSON MY JO.

JOHN Anderson, my jo, John,
  When we were first acquent,
Your locks were like the raven,
Your bonnie brow was brent;
But now your brow is beld, John,
Your locks are like the snaw;
But blessings on your frosty pow,
John Anderson, my jo.

John Anderson, my jo, John,
We clamb the hill thegither;
And monie a canty day, John,
We've had wi' ane anither:

Now we maun totter down, John,
But hand in hand we'll go,
And sleep thegither at the foot,
John Anderson, my jo.

PHILIP MY KING.

LOOK at me with thy large brown eyes,
    Philip my king,
Round whom the enshadowing purple lies
Of babyhood's royal dignities:
Lay on my neck thy tiny hand
With love's invisible sceptre laden;
I am thine Esther to command
Till thou shalt find a queen-handmaiden,
    Philip my king.

O the day when thou goest a-wooing,
    Philip my king !
When some beautiful lips are suing,
And some gentle heart's bars undoing,
Thou dost enter, love-crowned, and there
Sittest love glorified. Rule kindly,
Tenderly, over thy kingdom fair,
For we that love, ah ! we love so blindly,
    Philip my king.

Up from thy sweet mouth,—up to thy brow,
    Philip my king !
The spirit that lies sleeping, now
May rise like a giant and make men bow
As to one heaven-chosen among his peers
My Saul, than thy brethren taller and
    fairer,
Let me behold thee in future years;
Yet thy head needeth a circlet rarer,
    Philip my king.

—A wreath not of gold, but palm, one day,
    Philip my king
Thou too must tread, as we trod, a way
Thorny and cruel and cold and grey:
Rebels within thee and foes without,
Will snatch at thy crown. But march on,
    glorious
Martyr, yet monarch : till angels shout
As thou sit'st at the feet of God victorious
    " Philip the king !"

To A Pair of Slippers in the Egyptian Exhibition

TINY slippers of gold and green,
   Tied with a mouldering golden cord!
What pretty feet they must have been
   When Cæsar Augustus was Egypt's Lord!
Somebody graceful and fair you were!
   Not many girls could dance in these!
When did the Shoemaker make you, dear,
   Such a nice pair of Egyptian 'threes.'

Where were you measured? In Saïs, or On,
   Memphis, or Thebes, or Pelusium?—
Fitting them neatly your brown toes upon,
   Lacing them deftly with finger and thumb
I seem to see you!—so long ago!
   Twenty centuries—less or more!
And here are the sandals; yet none of us know
What name, or fortune, or face you bore!

Your lips would have laughed, with a
     rosy scorn,
   If the merchant or slave had mock-
     ingly said :
'The feet will pass, but the shoes they
     have worn
   Two thousand years onward Time's
     road shall tread,
And still be foot-gear, as good as new !'
   To think that calf-skin, gilded and
     stitched,
Should Rome and her Cæsars outlive ;
     and you
Be gone like a dream from the world
     you bewitched !

    Not that we mourn you ; 'twere too absurd !
     You have been such a very long while away !
    Your dry spiced dust would not value a word
     Of the soft regrets that a verse could say.
   Sorrow and Joy, and Love and Hate,
     If you ever felt them, are vaporized hence
   To this odor—subtle and delicate—
     Of cassia, and myrrh, and frankincense.

Of course they embalmed you ! But not
    so sweet
  Were aloes and nard as your youthful
    glow
Which Amenti took, when the small
    dark feet
  Wearied of treading our Earth below.
Look ! It was flood-time in valley of
    Nile,
  Or a very wet day in the Delta, dear!
When your gilded shoes tripped their
    latest mile !
    The mud on the soles renders that
    fact clear.

You died believing in Horus and Pasht,
  Isis, Osiris, and priestly lore;
And found, of course, such theories
    smashed
  By actual fact, on the heavenly shore!
What next did you do? did you trans-
    migrate ?
Have we seen you since, all modern and fresh?
Your charming soul—as I calculate—
Mislaid its mummy, and sought new flesh.

You knew Cleopatra no doubt ! You saw
  Anthony's galleys from Actium come!
But there !—if questions could answers draw
  From lips so many a long age dumb—
I would not tease you for history,
  Nor vex your heart with the men which were;
The one point to know that would fascinate me,
  Is, where and what are you, to-day, my dear !

Were you she whom I met at dinner last week,
  With eyes and hair of the Ptolemy black.
Who still of this 'find' in the Fayoum would speak,
  And to scarabs and Pharaohs would carry us back
A scent of lotus around her hung,
  She had such a far-away wistful air
As of somebody born when the Earth was young,
  And wore of gilt slippers a lovely pair !

Perchance you were married? These
  might have been
Part of your *trousseau*—the wedd-
  ing shoes ;
And you laid them aside with the
  lote-leaves green,
And painted clay gods which a
  Bride did use.
And, maybe, to-day by Nile's bright
  waters
Damsels of Egypt in gowns of
  blue—
Great-great-great-very-great grand-
  daughters—
Owe their shapely insteps to you!

But vainly I knock at the bars of the Past,
  Little green slippers with golden strings!
For all you can tell is that leather will last
  When loves and delights and beautiful things
Have vanished, forgotten! Nay, not quite that!
  I catch some light of the grace you wore
When you finished with Life's daily pit-a-pat,
  And left your shoes at Time's bed-room door!

You were born in the Old World which did not
  doubt ;
  You were never sad with our new-fashioned
    sorrow ;
You were sure, when your gladsome days ran out,
  Of day-times to come, as we of to-morrow !
Oh, dead little Maid of the Delta ! I lay
  Your shoes on your mummy-chest back again,
And wish that one game we might merrily play
  At ' Hunt-the-slipper '—to see it all plain !

Schooner yacht " Hadassah," July, 1888.   EDWIN ARNOLD.

ON THE SHORES OF TENNESSEE.

"MOVE my arm-chair, faithful Pompey,
  In the sunshine bright and strong,
For this world is fading, Pompey,—
  Massa won't be with you long;
And I fain would hear the south wind
  Bring once more the sound to me,
Of the wavelets softly breaking
  On the shores of Tennessee.

" Mournful though the ripples murmur,
  As they still the story tell,
How no vessels float the banner
  That I've loved so long and well.
I shall listen to their music,
  Dreaming that again I see
Stars and stripes on sloop and shallop
  Sailing up the Tennessee.

"And, Pompey, while old massa's waiting
  For Death's last despatch to come,
If that exiled starry banner
  Should come proudly sailing home,
You shall greet it, slave no longer ;—
  Voice and hand shall both be free
That shout and point to Union colors
  On the waves of Tennessee."

" Massa's berry kind to Pompey;
  But ole darkey's happy here,
Where he's tended corn and cotton
  For 'ese many a long gone year.
Over yonder Missis' sleeping,—
  No one tends her grave like me ;
Mebbie she would miss the flowers
  She used to love in Tennessee.

"'Pears like she was watching, Massa—
  If Pompey should beside him stay;
Mebbe she'd remember better
  How for him she used to pray ;
Telling him that way up yonder
  White as snow his soul would be,
If he served the Lord of Heaven
  While he lived in Tennessee."

Silently the tears were rolling
  Down the poor, old dusky face,
As he stepped behind his master,
  In his long-accustomed place.

Then a silence fell around them,
  As they gazed on rock and tree
Pictured in the placid waters
  Of the rolling Tennessee.

Master, dreaming of the battle
  Where he fought on Marion's side,
When he bid the haughty Tarleton
  Stoop his lordly crest of pride.
Man, remembering how yon sleeper
  Once he held upon his knee,
Ere she loved the gallant soldier,
  Ralph Vervair, of Tennessee.

Still the south wind fondly lingers
  'Mid the veteran's silver hair ;
Still the bondman close beside him
  Stands behind the old arm-chair.
With his dark-hued hand uplifted,
  Shading eyes, he bends to see
Where the woodland, boldly jutting,
  Turns aside the Tennessee.

Thus he watches cloud-born shadows
  Glide from tree to mountain crest,
Softly creeping, aye and ever,
  To the river's yielding breast.
Ha ! above the foliage yonder
  Something flutters wild and free !
"Massa ! Massa ! Hallelujah !
  The flag's come back to Tennessee!

"Pompey, hold me on your shoulder,
  Help me stand on foot once more,
That I may salute the colors
  As they pass my cabin door ;
Here's the paper signed that frees you,
  Give a freeman's shout with me,—
'God and Union !' be our watchword,
  Evermore in Tennessee."

Then the trembling voice grew fainter
  And the limbs refused to stand ;
One prayer to Jesus—and the soldier
  Glided to that better land.
When the flag went down the river,
  Man and master both were free,
While the ring-dove's note was mingled
  With the rippling Tennessee.

THE PICKET-GUARD.

"ALL quiet along the Potomac," they
say,
"Except now and then a stray picket
Is shot, as he walks on his beat, to and fro,
By a rifleman hid in the thicket.
'Tis nothing—a private or two, now and
then,
Will not count in the news of the bat-
tle ;
Not an officer lost—only one of the men,
Moaning out, all alone, the death-rat-
tle."

All quiet along the Potomac to-night,
Where the soldiers lie peacefully dream-
ing ;
Their tents, in the rays of the clear autumn
moon,
Or the light of the watch-fires are gleam-
ing.
A tremulous sigh, as the gentle night-
wind
Through the forest leaves softly is creep-
ing ;
While stars up above, with their glittering
eyes
Keep guard—for the army is sleeping.

There's only the sound of the lone sentry's
tread,
As he tramps from the rock to the fountain,
And thinks of the two in the low trundle-
bed,
Far away in the cot on the mountain.

His musket falls slack—his face, dark and
grim,
Grows gentle with memories tender,
As he mutters a prayer for the children
asleep,—
For their mother—may Heaven defend
her.

The moon seems to shine just as brightly
as then,
That night, when the love yet unspoken,
Leaped up to his lips,—when low, mur-
mured vows
Were pledged to be ever unbroken.
Then drawing his sleeve roughly over his
eyes,
He dashes off tears that are welling,
And gathers his gun closer up to its place,
As if to keep down the heart-swelling.

He passes the fountain, the blasted pine-
tree—
The footstep is lagging and weary ;
Yet onward he goes, through the broad
belt of light,
Toward the shades of the forest so dreary.
Hark ! was it the night-wind that rustled
the leaves ?
Was it moonlight so wondrously flashing ?
It looked like a rifle—"Ha ! Mary, good-
by !"
And the life-blood is ebbing and plashing.

All quiet along the Potomac to-night—
No sound save the rush of the river ;
While soft falls the dew on the face of the
dead,—
The picket's off duty forever.

SHIPS AT SEA.

I HAVE ships that went to sea
 More than fifty years ago:
None have yet come home to me
 But keep sailing to and fro.
I have seen them, in my sleep,
Plunging through the shoreless deep,
With tattered sails and battered hulls
While around them screamed the gulls.
  Flying low, flying low.

I have wondered why they staid
 From me, sailing round the world·
And I've said, "I'm half afraid
 That their sails will ne'er be furled."
Great the treasures that they hold,—
Silks and plumes, and bars of gold·
While the spices which they bear
Fill with fragrance all the air,
  As they sail, as they sail.

Every sailor in the port
 Knows that I have ships at sea,
Of the waves and winds the sport;
 And the sailors pity me.
Oft they come and with me walk
Cheering me with hopeful talk,
Till I put my fears aside,
And contented watch the tide
  Rise and fall, rise and fall.

I have waited on the piers,
　Gazing for them down the bay,
Days and nights, for many years,
　Till I turned heart-sick away.
But the pilots, when they land,
Stop and take me by the hand,
Saying, "You will live to see
Your proud vessels come from sea,
　One and all, one and all."

So I never quite despair,
　Nor let hope or courage fail;
And some day, when skies are fair,
　Up the bay my ships will sail.
I can buy then all I need,—
Prints to look at, books to read,
Horses, wines, and works of art,
Every thing except a heart:
　That is lost, that is lost.

Once when I was pure and young,
　Poorer, too, than I am now,
Ere a cloud was o'er me flung,
　Or a wrinkle creased my brow,
There was one whose heart was mine;
But she's something now divine,
And though come my ships from sea,
They can bring no heart to me,
　Evermore, evermore.
　　　　—ROBERT BARRY COFFIN.

CARCASSONNE.
From the French of Gustave Nadaud.

I'M growing old, I'm sixty years;
　I've labored all my life in vain;
In all that time of hopes and fears
　I've failed my dearest wish to gain
I've seen full well that here below
　Bliss unalloyed there is for none;
My prayer will ne'er fulfillment know—
　I never have seen Carcassonne,
　I never have seen Carcassonne!

You see the city from the hill,—
　It lies beyond the mountains blue,—
And yet, to reach it, one must still
　Five long and weary leagues pursue,
And to return, as many more!
　Ah, had the vintage plenteous grown!
The grape withheld its yellow store,—
　I shall not look on Carcassonne,
　I shall not look on Carcassonne!

They tell me every day is there
　Not more nor less than Sunday gay,—
In shining robes and garments fair
　The people walk upon their way;
One gazes there on castle walls
　As grand as those of Babylon,
A bishop and two generals.
　I do not know fair Carcassonne,
　I do not know fair Carcassonne!

The Vicar's right, he says that we
　Are ever wayward, weak, and blind;
He tells us in his homily
　Ambition ruins all mankind—
Yet could I there two days have spent
　While still the autumn sweetly shone,
Ah me! I might have died content
　When I had looked on Carcassonne,
　When I had looked on Carcassonne!

Thy pardon, Father; I beseech,
　In this my prayer, if I offend!
One something sees beyond his reach
　From childhood to his journey's end;
My wife, our little boy Aignan,
　Have travelled even to Narbonne,
My grandchild has seen Perpignan,—
　And I have not seen Carcassonne,
　And I have not seen Carcassonne!

So crooned one day, close by Limoux,
　A peasant, double-bent with age,
"Rise up, my friend," said I; "with you
　I'll go upon this pilgrimage."
We left next morning his abode,
　But (heaven forgive him!) half way on,
The old man died upon the road:
　He never gazed on Carcassonne,
　Each mortal has his Carcassonne!

THE RAIN.

WE knew it would rain, for all the morn
　A spirit on slender robes of mist
Was lowering its golden buckets down
　Into the vapory amethyst
Of marshes and swamps and dismal fens,
　Scooping the dew that lay in the flowers,
Dipping the jewels out of the sea,
To sprinkle them over the land in showers.
We knew it would rain, for the poplars
　showed
The white of their leaves, the amber grain
Shrunk in the wind, and the lightning now
Is tangled in tremulous skeins of rain.
　　　　—T. B. ALDRICH.

SANDALPHON.

HAVE you read in the Talmud of old,
   In the Legends the Rabbins have told
     Of the limitless realms of the air,
Have you read it,—the marvelous story
Of Sandalphon, the Angel of Glory,
     Sandalphon, the Angel of Prayer?

How, erect, at the outermost gates
Of the City Celestial he waits,
     With his feet on the ladder of light,
That, crowded with angels unnumbered,
By Jacob was seen, as he slumbered
     Alone in the desert at night?

The Angels of Wind and of Fire
Chant only one hymn, and expire
     With the song's irresistible stress;
Expire in their rapture and wonder,
As harp-strings are broken asunder
     By music they throb to express.

But serene in the rapturous throng,
Unmoved by the rush of the song,
     With eyes unimpassioned and slow,
Among the dead angels, the deathless
Sandalphon stands listening breathless
     To sounds that ascend from below;

From the spirits on earth that adore,
From the souls that entreat and implore
     In the fervor and passion of prayer;

From the hearts that are broken with losses,
And weary with dragging the crosses
     Too heavy for mortals to bear.

And he gathers the prayers as he stands,
And they change into flowers in his hands,
     Into garlands of purple and red;
And beneath the great arch of the portal,
Through the streets of the City Immortal
     Is wafted the fragrance they shed.

It is but a legend, I know,
A fable, a phantom, a show,
     Of the ancient Rabbinical lore;
Yet the old mediæval tradition,
The beautiful, strange superstition,
     But haunts me and holds me the more.

When I look from my window at night,
And the welkin above is all white,
     All throbbing and panting with stars,
Among them majestic is standing
Sandalphon the angel, expanding
     His pinions in nebulous bars.

And the legend, I feel, is a part
Of the hunger and thirst of the heart,
     The frenzy and fire of the brain,
That grasps at the fruitage forbidden,
The golden pomegranates of Eden,
     To quiet its fever and pain.
            —H. W. LONGFELLOW.

OVER THE RIVER.

OVER the river they beckon to me,
　Loved ones who've crossed to the
　　farther side ;　　　•
The gleam of their snowy robes I see,
　But their voices are lost in the dashing
　　tide.
There's one with ringlets of sunny gold,
　And eyes the reflection of heaven's own
　　blue ;
He crossed in the twilight gray and cold,
　And the pale mist hid him from mortal
　　view.
We saw not the angels that met him
　　there—
　The gates of the city we could not see ;
Over the river, over the river,
　My brother stands waiting to welcome
　　me.

Over the river the boatman pale
　Carried another, the household pet ;
Her brown curls waved in the gentle
　　gale—
　Darling Minnie ! I see her yet.
She crossed on her bosom her dimpled
　　hands,
　And fearlessly entered the phantom
　　bark ;
We felt it glide from the silver sands,
　And all our sunshine grew strangely
　　dark.
We know she is safe on the farther side,
　Where all the ransomed and angels be ;
Over the river, the mystic river,
　My childhood's idol is waiting for me.

For none return from those quiet shores,
　Who cross with the boatman cold and
　　pale ;
We hear the dip of the golden oars,
　And catch a gleam of the snowy sail,

And lo ! they have passed from our yearning
　　hearts,
　They cross the stream and are gone for aye.
We may not sunder the veil apart
　That hides from our vision the gates of
　　day ;
We only know that their barks no more
　May sail with us o'er life's stormy sea ;
Yet, somewhere, I know, on the unseen
　shore,
　They watch and beckon, and wait for
　　me.

And I sit and think, when• the sunset's
　　gold
　Is flushing river and hill and shore,
I shall one day stand by the water cold,
　And list to the sound of the boatman's
　　oar ;
I shall watch for the gleam of the flapping
　　sail,
　I shall hear the boat as it gains the
　　strand,
I shall pass from sight with the boatman pale
　To the better shore of the spirit land.
I shall know the loved who have gone be-
　　fore,
　And joyfully sweet will the meeting be,
When over the river, the peaceful river,
　The angel of death shall carry me.
　　　　　　—NANCY A. W. PRIEST.

AFTER THE BALL.

THEY sat and combed their beautiful hair,
  Their long, bright tresses, one by one,
As they laughed and talked in the chamber
      there,
    After the revel was done.

Idly they talked of waltz and quadrille,
  Idly they laughed, like other girls,
Who over the fire, when all is still,
    Comb out their braids and curls.

Robe of satin and Brussels lace,
  Knots of flowers and ribbons, too,
Scattered about in every place,
    For the revel is through.

And Maud and Madge in robes of white,
  The prettiest night-gowns under the sun,
Stockingless, slipperless, sit in the night,
    For the revel is done,—

Sit and comb their beautiful hair,
  Those wonderful waves of brown and
      gold,
Till the fire is out in the chamber there,
    And the little bare feet are cold.

Then out of the gathering winter chill,
  All out of the bitter St. Agnes weather,
While the fire is out and the house is still,
    Maud and Madge together,—

Maud and Madge in robes of white,
  The prettiest night-gowns under the sun,
Curtained away from the chilly night,
    After the revel is done,—

Float along in a splendid dream,
  To a golden gittern's tinkling tune,
While a thousand lustres shimmering
      stream,
    In a palace's grand saloon.

Flashing of jewels, and flutter of laces,
  Tropical odors sweeter than musk,
Men and women with beautiful faces
    And eyes of tropical dusk,—

And one face shining out like a star,
  One face haunting the dreams of each,
And one voice, sweeter than others are,
    Breaking into silvery speech,

Telling, through lips of bearded bloom,
  An old, old story over again,
As down the royal bannered room,
    To the golden gittern's strain,

Two and two, they dreamily walk,
  While an unseen spirit walks beside,
And, all unheard in the lovers' talk,
    He claimeth one for a bride.

Oh, Maud and Madge, dream on together,
  With never a pang of jealous fear !
For, ere the bitter St. Agnes weather
    Shall whiten another year,

Robed for the bridal, and robed for the
      tomb,
  Braided brown hair, and golden tress,
There'll be only one of you left for the
      bloom
    Of the bearded lips to press,—

Only one for the bridal pearls,
  The robe of satin and Brussels lace,—
Only one to blush through her curls
    At the sight of a lover's face.

Oh, beautiful Madge, in your bridal white,
  For you the revel has just begun ;
But for her who sleeps in your arms to-
      night
    The revel of life is done !

But robed and crowned with your saintly
      bliss,
  Queen of heaven and bride of the sun,
Oh, beautiful Maud, you'll never miss
    The kisses another hath won !
                        —NORA PERRY.

WHAT MY LOVER SAID.

BY the merest chance, in the twilight
   gloom,
  In the orchard path he met me ;
In the tall, wet grass, with its faint perfume,
And I tried to pass, but he made no room,
  Oh I tried, but he would not let me.
So I stood and blushed till the grass grew
  red,
  With my face bent down above it,
While he took my hand as he whispering
  said—
(How the clover lifted each pink, sweet
  head,
To listen to all that my lover said ;
  Oh, the clover in bloom, I love it!)

In the high wet grass went the path to hide,
  And the low, wet leaves hung over ;
But I could not pass upon either side,
For I found myself, when I vainly tried,
  In the arms of my steadfast lover.
And he held me there and he raised my
  head,
  While he closed the path before me,
And he looked down into my eyes and said—
(How the leaves bent down from the boughs
  o'er head,
To listen to all that my lover said.
  Oh, the leaves hanging lowly o'er me !)

Had he moved aside but a little way,
  I could surely then have passed him ;
And he knew I never could wish to stay,
And would not have heard what he had to
  say,
  Could I only aside have cast him.
It was almost dark, and the moments sped,
  And the searching night-wind found us,

But he drew me nearer and softly said—
(How the pure, sweet wind grew still,
  instead,
To listen to all that my lover said ;
  Oh, the whispering wind around us !)

I am sure he knew when he held me fast,
  That I must be all unwilling ;
For I tried to go, and I would have passed,
As the night was come with its dew, at last,
  And the sky with its stars was filling.
But he clasped me close when I would have
  fled,
  And he made me hear his story,
And his soul came out from his lips and
  said—
(How the stars crept out where the white
  moon led,
To listen to all that my lover said ;
  Oh, the moon and the stars in glory !)

I know that the grass and the leaves will
  not tell,
  And I'm sure that the wind, precious
   rover,
Will carry my secrets so safely and well
  That no being shall ever discover
One word of the many that rapidly fell
  From the soul-speaking lips of my lover ;
  And the moon and the stars that looked
   over
Shall never reveal what a fairy-like spell
They wove round about us that night in
  the dell,
  In the path through the dew-laden
   clover,
Nor echo the whispers that made my heart
  swell,
  As they fell from the lips of my lover.
          —HOMER GREENE.

WHEN MY SHIP WENT DOWN.

SANK a palace in the sea,
    When my ship went down;
Friends whose hearts were gold to me—
Gifts that ne'er again can be—
    'Neath the waters brown.
There you lie, O Ship, to-day,
In the sand-bar stiff and gray!
You who proudly sailed away
    From the splendid town.

II.

Now the ocean's bitter cup
    Meets your trembling lips;
Now your gilded halls look up
    From Disaster's grip.
Ruin's nets around you weave;
But I have no time to grieve;
I will promptly, I believe,
    Build another ship.

                    —WILL CARLETON.

AT THE MAKING OF THE HAY.

WHEN the whip-poor-wills are calling,
And the apple-blooms are falling,
With a tender tint forestalling
Summer's blush upon the grass ;
Where the little stars are keeping
Watch above the meadow sleeping,
And the jack-o'-lantern's peeping,
I will meet my bonnie lass.
I will seek her. I will find her.
I will slyly steal behind her ;
And with kisses I will blind her
Till she sets the happy day !
And when the barley's heading,
And the summer rose is shedding,
Oh, there 'll be a merry wedding
At the making of the hay !

SAMUEL M. PECK.

"GOOD BYE, GOD BLESS YOU."

I LOVE the words—perhaps because,
When I was leaving mother,
Standing at last in solemn pause,
We looked at one another.
And I—I saw in mother's eyes
The love she could not tell me—
A love eternal as the skies ;
Whatever fate befell me ;
She put her arms about my neck,
And soothed the pain of leaving,
And, though her heart was like to break,
She spoke no word of grieving ;
She let no tear bedim her eye,
For fear that might distress me,
But, kissing me, she said good-bye,
And asked our God to bless me.

—EUGENE FIELD.

WHEN BABY WAS SICK.

WHEN the baby wuz sick, I tell yeh the
days
Fergot 'et they ever could fly,
An' acted right like they wuz clipped i' the
wings,
The way they went crawfishin' by.
An' gran'pappy's clock on the landin', yeh
see
Ez yeh come up the steers f'om the hall,
Felt mean ez the rest o' the fambly an
strek
'Bout like it wuz ready to bawl.

When the baby wuz sick, thar wuz maw an'
paw,
An' sister an' me an' my wife,
Went tip-toein' round with faces ez peak'd
Ez a passel o' ghosts kem to life ;
An' we spoke in the way ye h've heerd
folks speak
In a room whar thar's somethin' dead,
An' the women folks sniffled a heap—an',
well—
My eyes an' pap's wuz red.

When the baby wuz sick, our old maltee cat,
With the white strip crossin' her face
Picked up an' put out, fer she seemed to
sense
Thar was somethin' wrong on the place.
An' the yeller houn' dog let loose an'
yowled
Thoo the hull of a night—the limb !
Tell I jes strek out an' natchelly wiped
The barnyard up with him.

When the baby wuz sick, an' the doctor
would come,
We'd all keep a-scrougin' around,
A-countin' our breaf, while he counted the
pulse,
Watching out ef he smiled or he frowned ;
An' the day when he 'lowed in his gruffy
old voice
Thet the danger wuz over an' done,
We gripped thet old man round the keen
an' we says,
" You're a angel ef ever wuz one !"

—EVA W. McGLASSON.

BATTLE HYMN OF THE REPUBLIC.

MINE eyes have seen the glory of the
    coming of the Lord ;
He is trampling out the vintage where
    the grapes are stored ;
He hath loosed the fateful lightning of his
    terrible swift sword :
      His truth is marching on.

I have seen Him in the watch-fires of a
    hundred circling camps ;
They have builded Him an altar in the
    evening dews and damps ;
I have read His righteous sentence by the
    dim and flaring lamps ;
      His day is marching on.

I have read a fiery gospel writ in burnished
    rows of steel :
  " As he deal with my contemners, so with
    you my grace shall deal ;
Let the Hero, born of woman, crush the
    serpent with his heel,
      Since God is marching on."

He has sounded forth the trumpet that shall
    never call retreat ;
He is sifting out the hearts of men before
    His judgment-seat ;
Oh ! be swift, my soul, to answer Him ! be
    jubilant, my feet !
      Our God is marching on.

In the beauty of the lilies Christ was born
    across the sea,
With a glory in his bosom that transfig-
    ures you and me ;
As he died to make men holy, let us die to
    make men free,
      While God is marching on.
        —Mrs. Julia Ward Howe.

THE BABY AND THE SOLDIERS.

ROUGH and ready the troopers ride,
    Great bearded men with swords by
      side ;
They have ridden long, they have ridden
    hard,
They are travel-stained and battle-scarred ;
The hard ground shakes with their mar-
    tial tramp,
And coarse is the laugh of the men in
    camp.

They reach the spot where the mother
    stands
With a baby clapping its little hands,
Laughing aloud at the gallant sight
Of the mounted soldiers fresh from the
    fight.
The captain laughs out : "I'll give you
    this,
A handful of gold, your baby to kiss."

Smiles the mother : "A kiss can't be sold,
But gladly he'll kiss a soldier bold."
He lifts the baby with manly grace
And covers with kisses its smiling face,
Its rosy cheeks and its dimpled charms,
And it crows with delight in the soldier's
    arms.

"Not all for the captain," the soldiers call ;
"The baby, we know, has one for all."
To the soldiers' breasts the baby is pressed
By the strong, rough men, and by turns
    caressed ;
And louder it laughs, and the mother fair
Smiles with mute joy as the kisses they
    share.

"Just such a kiss," cries one trooper grim,
"When I left my boy I gave to him ;"
"And just such a kiss on the parting day
I gave to my girl as asleep she lay."
Such were the words of the soldiers brave,
And their eyes were moist as the kiss they
    gave.

WHEN THE FROST IS ON THE PUNKIN.

WHEN the frost is on the punkin and
   the fodder's in the shock,
And you hear the kyouck and gobble of
   the struttin' turkey-cock,
And the clackin' of the guineys, and the
   cluckin' of the hens,
And the rooster's hallylooyer as he tiptoes
   on the fence ;
O its then's the times a feller is a-feelin' at
   his best,
With the risin' sun to greet him from a
   night of peaceful rest,
As he leaves the house, bare-headed, and
   goes out to feed the stock,
When the frost is on the punkin and the
   fodder's in the shock.

They's something kindo' harty-like about
   the atmosphere
When the heat of summer's over and the
   coolin' fall is here—
Of course we miss the flowers, and the
   blossoms on the trees,
And the mumble of the hummin'-birds and
   buzzin' of the bees ;
But the air's so appetizin'; and the land-
   scape through the haze
Of a crisp and sunny morning of the airly
   autumn days
Is a pictur' that no painter has the colorin'
   to mock—
When the frost is on the punkin and the
   fodder's in the shock.

The husky, rusty rustle of the tossels of
   the corn,
And the raspin' of the tangled leaves, as
   golden as the morn ;
The stubble in the furries—kindo' lone-
   some-like, but still
A-preachin' sermons to us of the barns
   they growed to fill;
The strawstack in the medder, and the
   reaper in the shed ;
The hosses in theyr stalls below—the clover
   overhead !—
O, it sets my heart a-clickin' like the tickin'
   of a clock,
When the frost is on the punkin and the
   fodder's in the shock !
     —JAMES WHITCOMB RILEY.

CUDDLE DOON.

The bairnies cuddle doon at nicht
   Wi' muckle faucht an' din.
"Oh, try and sleep, ye waukrife rogues :
   Your father's comin' in."
They never heed a word I speak.
   I try to gie a froon ;
But aye I hap them up, an' cry,
   "Oh, bairnies, cuddle doon !"

Wee Jamie wi' the curly heid—
   He aye sleeps next the wa'—
Bangs up an' cries, "I want a piece"—
   The rascal starts them a'.
I rin an' fetch them pieces, drinks—
   They stop awee the soun'—
Then draw the blankets up, and cry,
   "Noo, weanies, cuddle doon !"

But ere five minutes gang, wee Rab
   Cries oot, frae 'neath the claes,
"Mither, mak' Tam gie ower at ance :
   He's kittlin' wi' his taes."
The mischief's in that Tam for tricks :
   He'd bother half the toon.
But aye I hap them up, and cry,
   "Oh, bairnies, cuddle doon !"

At length they hear their father's fit ;
   An', as he steeks the door,
They turn their faces to the wa',
   While Tam pretends to snore.
"Hae a' the weans been gude?" he asks,
   As he pits aff his shoon.
"The bairnies, John, are in their beds,
   An' lang since cuddled doon."

An' just afore we bed oorsels,
   We look at oor wee lambs.
Tam has his airm roun' wee Rab's neck,
   An' Rab his airm roun' Tam's.
I lift wee Jamie up the bed,
   An' as I straik each croon,
I whisper, till my heart fills up,
   "Oh, bairnies, cuddle doon !"

The bairnies cuddle doon at nicht
   Wi' mirth that's dear to me ;
But soon the big warl's cark an' care
   Will quaten doon their glee.
Yet, come what will to ilka ane,
   May He who sits aboon
Aye whisper, though their pows be bauld,
   "Oh, bairnies, cuddle doon !"
     —ALEXANDER ANDERSON.

SO SHE REFUSED HIM.

LAST night, within the little curtained
     room
   Where the gay music sounded faintly
     clear,
And silver lights came stealing through the
     gloom,
   You told the tale that women love to
     hear;
You told it well, with firm hands clasping
     mine,
   And deep eyes glowing with a tender
     light.
Mere acting? But your prayer was half
     divine
       Last night, last night.

Ah, you had much to offer; wealth enough
   To gild the future, and a path of ease
For one whose way is somewhat dark and
     rough;
   New friends—life calm as summer seas,
And something (was it love?) to keep us
     true
   And make us precious in each other's
     sight—
Ah, then indeed my heart's resolve I
     knew!
       Last night, last night.

Let the world go, with all its dross and
     pelf!
   Only for one, like Portia, could I say,
"I would be trebled twenty times myself;"
   Only for one, and he is far away;
     His voice came back to me, distinct
       and dear,
     And thrilled me with the pain of lost
       delight,
   The present faded, but the past was
     clear,
       Last night, last night.

If others answered, as I answered then,
   We would hear less, perchance, of
     blighted lives;
There would be truer women, nobler men,
   And fewer dreary homes and faithless
     wives.
Because I could not give you all my best,
   I gave you nothing. Judge me—was I
     right?
You may thank heaven, that I stood the
     test
       Last night, last night.

———

LAUGHING IN HER SLEEP.

I CAUGHT my love reclining
     Beside the ingle warm,
Her silken tresses twining
   About her snowy arm,
A silver rippling murmur,
   A dimple half a-peep,
Proclaimed my little sweetheart
   Laughing in her sleep.

As she lay there a-dreaming,
   Had Cupid crept a-near,
Beside the embers gleaming,
   To whisper in her ear?
Some plan for man's confusion,
   Some plot for heartaches deep,
It filled her soul with rapture,
   Laughing in her sleep.

Ah, woe betide the morrow
   When she shall come to wake;
My soul is wrung with sorrow
   To think how hearts will ach
For gallant beaux may tremble,
   And pitying seraphs weep,
When Cupid talks with Beauty
   Laughing in her sleep!
             —S. M. PECK.

"THE NORWAY SHEEP."

THE fierce wind breaking from his bond
  comes roaring from the west ;
On every long, deep rolling wave the white
  horse shows his crest,
As if a million mighty steeds had burst
  their master's hold ;
For the wild white sheep of Norway are
  coming to the fold.

The storm-drum shows its warning sign ;
  the sea-gulls swoop and cry ;
The fleecy clouds are driven fast across the
  stormy sky ;
Along the sands the fresh foam-gouts in
  ghastly sport are rolled ;
For the wild white sheep of Norway are
  coming to the fold.

Wistful the fisher seaward looks, out from
  the great stone pier,
Wistful he stands, the breakers' call along
  the cliffs to hear,
To hear across the flowing tide, the cease-
  less rock-bells tolled,
While fast and fierce the Norway sheep are
  coming to the fold.

'The wife and bairns will get no bread
  from yonder sea," he thinks,
As his idle coble by the staithes strains at
  its cable's links ;
Small use to bait the lines, or see the broad,
  brown sails unrolled,
When the wild white sheep of Norway are
  coming to the fold.

"God guard the ships at sea to-night !" the
  stern old sailors say,
Straining keen eyes across the waste of
  heaving, tossing spray,
Recalling many a bitter night of storm and
  dread of old,
When the wild white sheep of Norway
  were coming to the fold.

Oh ! there is many an aching heart, here in
  the red-roofed town,
As wives and mothers hear the blast come
  wailing from the down ;
Who knows what tale of death or wreck
  to-morrow may be told?
For the wild white sheep of Norway are
  coming to the fold.

TIDES.

IN my innermost soul is a deep, deep sea,
  Never furrowed by stately ships ;
Where many a pleasure, many a pain,
In their shotted shrouds for ages have lain
  Where the sea-gull never dips.

There are tides to this sea which ebb and
  shift
  At the wave of Memory's hand ;
And I would I could close my eyes to the
  drift,
The waves with their cruel fingers lift,
  And leave, in their flow, on the sand !

There are memories, buried fathoms deep,
  Lying, all bare, on the beach ;
There are withered flowers I thought I had
  hurled
To the uttermost depths of that sunless
  world,
  Where the plummet could never reach.

There are bundles of letters, tied with blue,
  Throbbing a faint perfume
Of love which the water could never drown,
Though it plunged their sunny sweetness
  down
  To a drear and flowerless tomb.

And the surges which break on that Lethean
  reach
  Leave the sea weed writhing there ;
But the sea-weed that strands on that lonely
  shore—
Sad flotsam from the nevermore—
  Is wavy and brown—like hair.
    *   *   *   *   *   *   *

Would God that the croon of this sea might
  cease ;
  That its billows might sing instead ;
That its tides might sleep forever ;—or yet,
From its sobbing caverns of dull regret,
  The sea might give up its dead !

        —JULIUS DEXTER.

WHITTIER'S CENTENNIAL POEM.

THE sword was sheathed ; in April's sun
  Lay green the fields by Freedom won.
And severed sections, weary of debates,
Joined hands at last and were United States.

O City sitting by the Sea !
  How proud the day that dawned on thee,
When the new era, long desired, began,
And, in its need, the hour had found the
    man !

One thought the cannon salvos spoke ;
  The resonant bell-tower's vibrant stroke,
The voiceful street, the plaudit-echoing
    halls,
And prayer and hymn borne heavenward
    from St. Paul's.

How felt the land in every part
  The strong throb of a nation's heart,
As its great leader gave, with reverent awe,
His pledge to Union, Liberty, and Law !

That pledge the heavens above him heard,
  That vow the sleep of centuries stirred ;
In world-wide wonder listening peoples bent
Their gaze on Freedom's great experiment.

Could it succeed ! Of honor sold
  And hopes deceived all history told,
Above the wrecks that strewed the mourn-
    ful past,
Was the long dream of ages true at last ?

Thank God ! the people's choice was just,
  The one man equal to his trust,
Wise beyond lore, and without weakness
    good,
Calm in the strength of flawless rectitude !

His rule of justice, order, peace,
  Made possible the world's release ;
Taught prince and serf that power is but a
    trust,
And rule, alone, which serves the ruled, is
    just ;

That Freedom generous is, but strong
  In hate of fraud and selfish wrong.
Pretence that turns her holy truths to lies,
And lawless license masking in her guise.

Land of his love ! with one glad voice
  Let thy great sisterhood rejoice ;
A century's suns o'er thee have risen and set,
And, God be praised, we are one nation yet.

And still, we trust, the years to be
  Shall prove his hope was destiny,
Leaving our flag with all its added stars
Unrent by faction and unstained by wars!

Lo ! where with patient toil he nursed
  And trained the new-set plant at first,
The widening branches of a stately tree
Stretch from the sunrise to the sunset sea.

And in its broad and sheltering shade,
  Sitting with none to make afraid,
Were we now silent, through each mighty
    limb
The winds of heaven would sing the praise
    of him

Our first and best !—his ashes lie
  Beneath his own Virginian sky.
Forgive, forget, O true and just and brave,
The storm that swept above thy sacred
    grave !

For, ever in the awful strife,
  And dark hours of the Nation's life,
Through the fierce tumult pierced his warn-
    ing word,
Their father's voice his erring children
    heard !

The change for which he prayed and
    sought
  In that sharp agony was wrought ;
No partial interest draws its alien line
'Twixt North and South, the cypress and
    the pine.

One people now, all doubt beyond,
  His name shall be our Union-bond ;
We lift our hands to Heaven, and here and
    now,
Take on our lips the old Centennial vow.

For rule and trust must needs be ours ;
  Chooser and chosen both are powers
Equal in service as in rights ; the claim
Of Duty rests on each and all the same.

Then let the sovereign millions, where
  Our banner floats in sun and air,
From the warm palm-lands to Alaska's cold,
Repeat with us the pledge a century old !

           —J. G. WHITTIER.

Child's Guide to Knowledge.

WHAT is alabaster?

It is a species of limestone found in masses, hanging like immense icicles from the roofs of caverns. The finest comes from the cave of Antiparos, in the Grecian Archipelago. The ancients used it for windows and for incense and funeral urns.

What are aloes?

The juice of the Socotrine aloe, prepared from the leaves when fresh cut, which juice, when dried in the sun, becomes a hard substance. A valuable violet dye is also obtained from these leaves, and the tree is held sacred by Mohammedans and Egyptians, the former hanging it over their doors when they return from the holy journey to Mecca.

What is amber?

A substance usually of a golden yellow color, found on the south coast of the Baltic, and also on the shores of Sicily, and the Adriatic.

What is aqua-marine or beryl?

It is a stone of a light sea-green color; the most beautiful are brought from the borders of China, and from Siberia and Brazil.

By whom were the Arabic figures introduced in Europe?

By the Saracens; and arithmetic was considered so complex in the time of the Saxons in England, that it was said to be a study *too difficult for the mind of man.*

What is arrow-root?

The root of a plant growing in the East and West Indies. There are three species of it; that used for food is called the starch plant, and requires a long preparation. The name originated in the use of another species of it, called *galanga*, by the Indian, as an antidote to the venom communicated by their poisoned arrows.

What is asbestos?

It is a silvery white mineral, of silky, long, slender filaments, which is found in mountainous countries abroad. The ancients made it into a kind of cloth in which they burned their dead, and were thus enabled to collect the ashes without admixture, as the cloth could not be burnt.

What does the name Bab-el-Mandeb mean?

The Gate of Tears; the straits are so called from the number of vessels that are wrecked while attempting to pass through them.

Who invented the game called backgammon?

The Welsh: as derived from their language, it means *a little* battle; but as derived from the Saxon, it means *back-game*, because the players bring back their men from their opponent's tables into their own.

409

What are bananas or plantains?

The fruit of a tropical tree which forms the chief means of subsistence to the negroes of the West Indies and the wild tribes of South America. The fruit is produced in clusters weighing forty pounds and upwards.

What is the origin of the name banker?

The Italian Jews kept benches in the market-places for the exchange of bills, etc.; *banco*, being the Italian for *bench*, was in time corrupted to *banker* in English.

What is the barometer?

An instrument for telling the changes in the weather, by means of the variations in the state of the air. It was invented by Torricelli, the pupil of Galileo, in 1644.

Which is the largest bell ever founded?

The great bell at Moscow, in the Kremlin. It is 67 feet 4 inches in circumference, and was kept in a deep pit, where it was originally cast, and weighs 443,772 pounds.

Was it ever moved?

Not until 1837, when the Emperor Nicholas had it placed on a low circular wall. It is visited as one of the wonders of Moscow, which is celebrated for its bells.

What well-known perfume is made from the rind of the orange?

Bergamot; it is made near the town of Bergamo, in Italy; the rind is cut into small pieces, and the oil pressed out into glass vessels.

What Emperor learnt the trade of a blacksmith, in order to set an example to his subjects?

Peter the Great, the Czar or Emperor of Russia.

When he worked at the forge, what did he make his noblemen do?

He obliged them to blow the bellows, stir the fire, carry coals, and perform all the other offices of blacksmiths.

Where were blankets first made?

At Bristol; they are so named from Thomas Blanket, who, in 1340, first set up the looms there for weaving these comfortable articles.

From what language do we derive the word *book*?

From the Danish word *bock*, which was the beech-tree, because that, being the most plentiful in Denmark, was used to engrave on.

What is borax?

It is a salt of a brownish-grey color and a sweetish taste, and is found in Thibet, East Indies, South America and Italy. It is used in making the finest glass, as a medicine, and by jewellers in soldering gold and silver.

What sort of wood is box?

It is remarkable for its hardness, weight, and readiness to take a polish; mathematical instruments, screws, chessmen, etc., are made of it, and all fine wood prints are done on box.

What is the light called bude light?

A very brilliant flame, obtained by introducing a current of fresh air into a common gaslight.

What are cantharides, or Spanish flies?

Insects about an inch long, valuable for blistering purposes. Being torpid during the day, they are shaken from the trees upon a cloth, collected in bags, killed by being suspended in the steam of boiling vinegar, dried in the sun, and pounded to a paste.

When were carriages introduced into France?

In 1550; but for a long time there were but three carriages in Paris, and it was considered very effeminate to be seen in one.

From what are fine Cashmere shawls made?

From the delicate wool of a species of goat found in Thibet and Cashmere. They are very costly, because, if elaborately worked, not one-quarter of an inch is completed in a day by three persons, and it is no unusual thing for a shop to be employed an entire year in the manufacture of a single shawl.

What is charcoal?

Wood half-burnt or charred by being heaped up into piles or stacks, covered with turf, and made to burn; but, as the air cannot get to it, it smoulders. It is used when a strong fire is wanted without smoke.

Who is said to have invented chess?

Ulysses. William the Conqueror, King John and Charles I were dotingly fond of this scientific game.

Why is the dragon china from China so much valued?

Because it is so difficult to procure, the grotesque figure on it being the Imperial arms, and only permitted for the Emperor's use.

How is chocolate obtained?

Each pod of the chocolate or cocoa plant contains from twenty to thirty seeds resembling almonds. These are gently roasted, pounded in a mortar, ground, mixed with water, sugar, and spices, and, while hot, poured into tin molds.

What is cinnabar?

A red ore from which mercury is chiefly obtained; there are large mines of it at Almaden, in Spain; also in Hungary and in Transylvania.

What is cochineal?

A very beautiful scarlet dye, produced from insects about the size of a small pea, which adhering in a torpid state to the leaves of the prickly pear are carefully picked or brushed off with an instrument like a pen.

What is coffee?

The berry of an evergreen shrub. When ripe, it is red, not unlike a cherry, and is dried on mats in the sun; this causes the pulp to shrivel so that it can easily be removed, the kernel is then dried again.

Do not different countries adopt different colors for mourning?

Yes, in Europe the ordinary color for mourning is *black :* in China it is *white,* a color which was the mourning of the ancient Spartan and Roman ladies. In Turkey it is *blue* or *violet;* in Egypt, *yellow;* in Ethiopia, *brown,* and kings and cardinals mourn in *purple.*

Does not every nation give a particular reason for the color they assume in mourning?

Yes, *black,* which is the privation of light, indicates the privation of life; *white* is an emblem of the purity of the spirit, separated from the body; *yellow* is to represent that death is the end of all our earthly hopes, because this is the color of leaves when they fall, and flowers when they fade.

What does *brown* denote?

The earth to which the dead return; *blue* is an emblem of happiness, which it is hoped the dead enjoy; and *purple* and *violet* express a mixture of sorrow and hope.

Are not colors in China emblematical of rank?

Yes; *yellow* is the imperial color for the Emperor and his sons; *purple* for the grandsons; *red* is the symbol of virtue, truth, and sincerity; the Emperor writes his edicts in *vermilion ; black* denotes guilt and vice; *white,* moral purity.

What is coral?

A beautiful branched substance, formed at the bottom of the sea by small animals called polypi, and it is their habitation. It is of three colors; red, white, and black ; the last is the rarest and most esteemed.

What is cork?

The bark of a beautiful tree, which is a kind of large green oak; it grows in Italy, Spain, Portugal, and most of the southern countries of Europe. Removing the bark does not hurt the tree, for cork is really dead bark, and when the tree is fifteen years' old it is fit to be barked; but it cannot be done oftener than every eight or ten years.

What is a cypress-tree?

A dark evergreen tree, which takes its name from the island of Cyprus in the Mediterranean Sea. It was sacred to Pluto and was used at the funerals of people of eminence. It takes a high polish and is very durable. The doors of the temple of Diana at Ephesus were of cypress, as also the gates of St. Peters at Rome; the latter were a thousand years' old when they were replaced by brazen ones.

What is the peculiar property of the diamond?

It is the hardest and most brilliant of all natural productions, and can only be cut and polished by its own powder.

What do you mean by distilling?

It is to draw off, drop by drop, the spirit of any body by means of fire placed above or under the vessels that contain the liquor to be distilled; the spirit or alcohol rises in vapor and passes into a tube surrounded by cold water, which condenses it into a liquid.

What is dragon's blood?

A red kind of resin, forced out of the fruit of the rotang plant, when exposed by the Japanese over the steam of boiling water. It is chiefly used in coloring, but sometimes as a medicine.

Which is the most ancient game still in common practice?

Draughts. Rameses, the king of Egypt, is represented on the walls of his palace at Thebes, engaged in the game of draughts.

When were drinking-glasses first made in England?

In Queen Mary's time; but horn drinking-cups were in use from the time of the Saxons.

What nations have adopted the eagle as an emblem?

The Romans, and in later times, France, Austria, Prussia, Russia and the United States.

What was the Edict of Nantes?

A law made by the good king, Henry IV, of France, granting the Huguenots, or Protestants, the free use of their religion, and protecting their persons and property.

Why were the ancient Egyptians so anxious about preserving their dead?

They believed in the immortality of the soul, and thought that by preserving the body from corruption, they were retaining the soul within it till the day of resurrection.

What was the size of the largest emerald ever known?

It was as large as an ostrich's egg, and was worshipped by the Peruvians under the name of the Goddess, or Mother of Emeralds.

What is emery?

A hard, heavy iron ore, found in large masses, mixed with other minerals; the best comes from the Levant, and the Isle of Naxos, in the Archipelago.

Is the use of the fan very ancient?

Yes; the custom was borrowed from the East, where they were made principally of feathers. The ladies in Queen Mary's time carried fans with handles a yard long, and often used them to correct their children and servants.

How are figs prepared for exportation?

They are dried in a furnace, or in the sun, after being dipped in a scalding preparation, made from the ashes of the fig-tree. The fruit always precedes the leaves.

What is flax?

The product of a beautiful grass-like annual plant, with slender stalks, small leaves, and blue blossoms.

To what country are we indebted for the flax plant?

To those parts of Egypt annually inundated by the Nile. The yarn was all spun by hand, in which they had attained such perfection, that some of the linen made from it was so exquisitely fine as to be called "woven air."

When does history record the first use of forks?

At the table of John the Good, Duke of Burgundy, and he had only two.

What is frankincense?

A gum, which, upon the application of heat, emits a most fragrant smell.

What is gas?

A sort of inflammable air, found in many substances, but most plentifully in coal. It was not generally used to light the streets of London until 1814.

Who was the celebrated carver in wood in James the Second's time?

Gibbons; some of the finest specimens of his festoons and flowers are to be seen at Windsor, and at Petworth, in Sussex.

What is ginger?

The dried root and underground stem of a reed-like plant. It derives its name from and abounds in the mountainous district of Gingi, to the east of Pondicherry, and is cultivated all over the tropics of Asia and America.

What sum of money did the Emperor Nero give for two small cups of transparent glass?

It is recorded in history that he paid a sum of money for them nearly equal to £50,000 sterling.

When was the Gobelin tapestry introduced into France?

In the reign of Francis I, by Giles Gobelin, a celebrated dyer, particularly in worsteds, who brought to the greatest perfection the fine scarlet dye which bears his name.

What is the guava?

A West Indian fruit, both delicious and wholesome; it is eaten raw, but it is prepared as a sweetmeat in many ways, particularly in that form called guava jelly.

What is hartshorn?

It is now distilled from bones, but formerly it was only prepared from the horns of the deer or hart, and hence its name.

In what country is heron's crest a mark of sovereignty?

In Persia.

Was the holly esteemed by the ancient Romans?

Yes; it was customary with them to send branches of holly to their friends with new year's gifts, as emblematical of *good wishes*. The use of holly at Christmas is partly owing to this old custom.

What is the origin of the term honeymoon?

It originated from a custom prevailing among the ancient Gothic people of Germany of drinking mead or metheglin, as it was called, for thirty days after a wedding.

What English king prohibited the putting of hops and sulphur into ale?

Henry VIII.

What is the ichneumon?

A quadruped found in Egypt and Asia. It is the natural enemy of serpents and will destroy them by seizing them by the throat. It digs the eggs of the crocodile from the sand and devours great numbers of them.

What is isinglass?

A glue made of the sounds and air-bladders of fish.

What is japaning?

The art of painting and varnishing ornaments on wood, metals, leather and paper prepared for the purpose.

What is jasper?

A variegated, very hard stone, with stripes and shades of yellow, red, green, and white, with black dots.

How is the kaleidoscope useful?

The beautiful objects it produces in endless variety often suggest patterns which are adopted in our arts and manufactures.

Through how many hands does a table knife pass before it is finished?

Through sixteen hands in one hundred and forty-four stages of workmanship.

What is the lamprey?

A small eel-shaped fish, much esteemed by epicures, particularly when potted or stewed.

Is there not a splendid festival held in China, called the feast of lanterns?

Yes; on the 15th day after the commencement of their new year, when such a profusion of rich transparent lanterns are hung out of the houses, that to a stranger the whole empire looks like Fairy-land.

What is laudanum?

A liquid made from opium and spirits of wine.

What are leeches?

A worm-shaped animal found in muddy waters; used for drawing congested or bruised blood.

What nation wears the leek as a badge of honor?

The Welsh; on the 1st of March, the day of their patron saint, St. David. This curious custom had its origin in the circumstance that during the Welsh wars, a party of Welshmen wanted a mark of distinction, and, passing through a field of leeks, they seized and stuck the plants in their caps, and under this signal they were victorious.

Which were the two most valuable libraries among the ancients?

That of Alexandria, collected by the Ptolemies, kings of Egypt, and the other at Pergamus, collected by Eumenes. Mark Antony gave the latter to Cleopatra, and these valuable collections were then united, and most unfortunately lost by being burnt by the Saracens in the year 642.

What people eat locusts?

The Hottentots and African tribes delight in them; they make the eggs into soup and boil the insects in milk.

What are lucifer matches?

Small splinters of wood, tipped with a preparation of phosphorus; they came into use about the year 1834.

What is macaroni?

Fine wheat flour, mixed with the white of eggs; it comes from Italy, Sicily, and Germany.

What is malachite?

A beautiful green copper ore, very like green jasper, capable of being cut and polished as a gem.

What prince is said to have been drowned in a butt of Malmsey wine?

The Duke of Clarence, brother to Edward IV.

What is the mariner's compass?

The valuable needle or magnet, which always turns to the north.

What is mother-of-pearl?

The internal layer of the shell of the pearl-oyster, and of other mussels of the oyster kind.

Who invented musical notes?

Guido Aretine, an Italian monk, in the reign of Henry I; he formed the musical scale we now use, an invention which he thought "atoned for all his sins."

What is myrrh?

A gum obtained by incision from a tree resembling the acacia; it grows on the eastern coast of Arabia Felix, and that part of Abyssinia near the Red Sea; also in the Levant, and the East Indies.

What nation makes the best needles?

English needles are considered the best in the world.

What are nutmegs?

The kernels of a fruit which grows in the East India Islands.

Who invented painting in oils?

John Van Eyck, in Henry the Fifth's time.

Who is said to have been cast into a cauldron of boiling oil at Rome?

St. John the Evangelist, by the order of the Emperor Domitian; but instead of killing him, he was not even hurt. He was afterwards banished to the island of Patmos, where he wrote the Revelation, and died at Ephesus, in Asia Minor.

What is neat's-foot oil?

It is procured from the feet of oxen, and is of great use in preparing and softening leather.

What is train oil?

An oil extracted from the fat of whales. This fat is called blubber and lies beneath the skin to the thickness of ten or twelve inches.

Whence have we olives?

From Italy, Spain, and the southern parts of France.

What are opals?

Half-transparent kinds of stone which have a milky cast, and when held betwixt the eye and light, appear blue, green, red, and yellow.

What is otto of roses?

The oil of the flower whose name it bears.

By whom were oysters considered a great luxury?

By the Romans, who were supplied with them by the Britons.

What is papier-mâché?

A preparation of moistened paper of considerable thickness, which is made into tea-trays, dressing-cases, port-folios, and other articles of great beauty.

What is Parmesan cheese?

The most celebrated foreign cheese, made wholly from the milk of cows feeding in the rich pasturage of Lombardy, about Parma and Pavia. It is prepared in a peculiar way, with much care and trouble, and flavored with saffron.

During the days of chivalry, what fowl was considered a distinguished dish?

The pea-fowl, it was called "the food of lovers and the meat of lords." At the banquet it was served up on a golden dish, and carried to the table by a lady of rank, attended by a train of high-born dames and damsels, accompanied by music.

Who was appointed to carve it?

On the occasion of a tournament, the successful knight. He was obliged to regulate his portions so that each individual, be the company ever so numerous, might taste; and if he had any oath or vow to make, rising from his seat, and extending his hand over the bird, he exclaimed, I vow to God, to the blessed Virgin, to the dames, and to the *peacock.*

How was the bird served up in Shakespeare's time?

In a pie, the head, richly gilt, being placed at one end of the dish, and the tail spread out in its full circumference at the other.

By what people are their feathers much valued?

By the Chinese, for decorating the caps of the mandarins; *three peacocks' feathers* marking the highest honor to which a Chinese mandarin can aspire.

What is peat?

It is formed by the partial decay of vegetable matter, especially of various mosses. The largest peat beds are in Ireland, where they cover 3,000,000 acres to the depth of 19 feet.

When were pins first used and made?

They were invented in France, in 1543, in the reign of Frances I; before this art was discovered, the ladies used small skewers made of wood, bone, and ivory.

What queen first made use of pins in England?

Catherine Howard, the fifth wife of Henry VIII.

Were they not considered a great luxury, and not fit for common use?

Yes; the maker was not allowed to sell them in an open shop, except on two days of the year, at the beginning of January.

What old custom did this give rise to?

To husbands giving their wives money at the beginning of the year, to buy a few pins; therefore money allowed to a wife for her own private spending, is even now called *pin-money.*

By whom was the first post-office set up in England?

By Charles I; he appointed a post to carry letters once a week between London and Edinburgh.

What is potash?

It is a salt or alkali, found in vegetable substances, obtained by burning them. It is so called because formerly it was prepared in large pots.

What great man is said to have introduced white potatoes into Ireland?

Sir Walter Raleigh, at Youghal, in the county of Cork, in the reign of James I.

What is putty?

It is made of pulverized chalk and linseed oil, well mixed together.

What is quassia?

A very bitter drug; the root of a tree, so called from a slave of the name of Quassi, who used it with great success in the malignant fevers which prevail in Surinam.

What is quicksilver?

An imperfect metal, resembling melted silver, of great use in manufactures and medicine; it is the heaviest of all fluids.

What are raisins?

Very ripe grapes, prepared by drying them in the sun. Damascus, the capital of Syria, produces the finest, called jar-raisins.

Are not razors made of the finest steel?

Yes: each razor passes through a dozen hands; it is ground and polished upon wheels, so as to make the blade hollow and give it a very fine edge.

What is rhubarb?

The root of a plant which grows wild in Turkey in Asia and Arabia Felix. It is valuable as a medicine, and is a different species from that used for pies.

What is rosewood?

A beautiful wood of a dark color, fine grain, and susceptible to a high polish. It comes from the island of Jamaica and from Brazil, where it is called the Jacaranda tree.

What is the sable?

A small animal resembling the marten and weasel. It is found in Siberia, Kamschatka, Russia, and America. It is trapped to avoid injuring the fur, and is hunted in winter, because of its greater beauty at that season.

By whom was the safety lamp invented? Describe it.

By Sir Humphry Davy, in 1816. The flame is covered with such fine wire that whilst it gives light. it will not allow the gas to explode.

What is saffron?

The orange-colored stigma, or centre part of a purple crocus, which is gathered every morning as soon as the flower opens. These stigmas are dried in a kiln and made into cakes. Saffron is dissolvable in water, is used in making yellow dye, and sometimes as a medicine.

What is sago?

The inner pith of a species of palm-tree growing in the Moluccas and Ceram.

Where is salt considered very valuable?

In Abyssinia, where every person who can carries a small piece of it suspended in a bag from his girdle; when friends meet, each offers his bit of salt to the other to lick as a great mark of civility and friendship.

What is bay-salt?

That which is obtained by the evaporation of sea water wholly by the heat of the sun.

What is sealing-wax?

It is made of shell-lac, cinnabar, and Venetian turpentine, which are melted, prepared, and colored with vermilion, according to fancy.

Is there not a beautiful ware made in France?

Yes; it is called Sèvres china; the manufactory near Paris is carried on at the public expense, and no cost is spared to carry it to perfection.

What distinguishing ornaments did the Patricians, among the Romans, wear in their shoes?

An ivory crescent, and Isaiah speaks of the moons which the Jewish women wore in their shoes.

What peculiar fashion in shoes and sleeves prevailed during the reign of Edward IV of England?

The shoes had long peaks turning upward from the toes and fastened by silver chains to the knees. Men wore their sleeves hanging from the elbow to such a length that Edward IV used to tie his behind his back to avoid tumbling over them.

What is spermaceti?

It is a white, fatty substance found in an immense cavity in the skull of the sperm whale, but distinct from the brain. The spermaceti is fluid during life but hardens into lumps after death. The sperm whale is distinguished from all others by having a hump on its back.

Who invented the art of weaving stockings in a frame?

William Lee, a native of Woodborough, England, in 1589. The stocking-knitters, fearing it would spoil their trade, drove him away. He died of grief, but his invention did not die with him.

What is storax?

A fragrant balsam, like benzoin, used in medicine and burnt as a perfume.

Is there not a tree called the tallow-tree?

Yes; it is a native of China. The fruit of this tree is enclosed in a husk like that of the chestnut and consists of three white kernels. The Chinese melt these kernels, add a little wax, color them with vermilion, and use little slips of wood entwined with the pith of rushes for wicks. They are better than tallow, but not so good as wax candles.

Whence have we tamarinds?

From both the Indies; they make a delicious preserve and a cooling, agreeable drink.

At whose tomb were tapers kept burning, day and night, for nearly one hundred years?

At the tomb of Henry V, but all of these customs were abolished at the Reformation.

What great painter has immortalized his name by his designs for tapestry?

Raphael, who executed twenty-five Scriptural subjects as copies for tapestry hangings, at the request of Pope Leo X; one set was intended to adorn the palace at Rome, the other as a present to Henry VIII of England.

What is teasel?

A plant used in woolen manufacture; the crooked scales connected with the flowers are so hard and rough that the heads are employed for raising the nap on woolen cloths. No mechanical contrivance has yet been invented to take its place.

Who invented thimbles?

The Dutch

What great king was nursed in the shell of a tortoise?

Henry IV of France.

What is turmeric?

The root of an East Indian plant, like ginger, used in India and Europe in medicine, in making curry powder, in seasoning dishes, for giving a rich-yellow dye to silk and linen, and in improving the red dye of cochineal.

Are not umbrellas of great antiquity?

Yes; the Greeks, Romans, and all Eastern nations used them to keep off the sun; "*ombrello*," in Italian, signifies "*a little shade*."

What is vellum?

The skin of young calves; it is finer, whiter, and smoother than common parchment.

What is verde-antique?

A beautiful green marble found only in Egypt; if it ever came from Italy, the quarries are not now known.

What is verdigris?

It is that green substance so often seen on dirty copper, and may be called its rust. It is a rank poison, but is useful for dyeing a fine black when mixed with logwood, a beautiful green to porcelain, in making green paint, etc.

What are wafers?

They are made of flour, isinglass, and a small quantity of yeast. After being colored, the mixture is spread out in thin cakes on tin plates, dried in an oven, and cut into wafers.

What great Emperor amused himself by making watches?

Charles V of Germany; one day he exclaimed: " What an egregious fool must I have been, to have squandered so much blood and treasure in an absurd attempt to make all men think alike, when I cannot even make a few watches keep time together! "

What are Westphalia hams?

The thighs of wild hogs and boars; their singular flavor is the result of smoking them several months in chimneys where nothing but wood is burnt.

What is whalebone?

A fibrous horny substance attached to the upper jaw of one kind of whale in thin, long, flat pieces, three or four yards long; it supplies the place of teeth.

What does the wolf afford us?

Nothing valuable but its skin, which makes a warm and durable fur.

How many churches did Sir Christopher Wren build in London?

Fifty-eight; of these St. Paul's is his greatest work.

Why was the yew-tree formerly much cultivated in England?

Because before the introduction of fire-arms, they made their bows of its hard, smooth, tough wood.

What is zinc?

A metal of a brilliant white color, with a shade of blue, extremely useful and valuable, as it mixes well with most other metals.

100
Questions and Answers on General History.

1. What is General History?

A history of all Nations and Peoples. It is treated under three great divisions : *Ancient*, from remote antiquity to the Fall of the Roman Empire, 476 A. D., *Mediæval*, from 476 A. D. to the close of the 15th century ; and *Modern*, from the beginning of the year 1500 to the present time.

2. What country has the oldest authentic history?

Egypt ; dating to about 2700 B. C.

3. What is the date of the building of the Pyramids?

About 2400 to 2200 B. C.

4. What is the title of the ruler of Egypt?

Khedive. He receives a salary of one million three hundred and fifty thousand dollars, the highest of any ruler in the world.

5. Name some great curiosities in Egypt.

Pyramids, Sphinxes, Obelisks, Petrified Forests, etc.

6. Where are the Pyramids?

In the western valley of the Nile, from near Cairo to about 100 miles up the river. They are built of brick or stone, are four-sided and are but sixty-five in number, though originally there were one hundred of them. They were built as monuments over the remains of noted rulers.

7. What is a Sphinx?

A fabulous monster of Greek Mythology. The Egyptian Sphinxes were large statues having the head of a woman and the body of a lion. The Great Sphinx is made of solid rock ; the paws are 50 feet long, the body 143 feet long, and the height from the paws to the top of the head is 62 feet long.

8. What is an Obelisk?

A large shaft of stone, usually square, and covered with hieroglyphics.

9. Where is the Petrified Forest?

In Egypt, West of the Nile. Logs, trees blown up by the roots and small shrubs have been turned to stone and are now completely covered by the sandy soil.

10. Where is the Lake of Salt?*

Near Cairo, east of the Nile. During high water it is a lake, and then evaporation causes it to dry up, and leaves the white Lake of Salt?

11. Where does the History of the Chinese begin?

About the year 2697 B. C. They count time by cycles of 60 years each, instead of by centuries and would express 1889 as the 26th year of the 77th cycle.

12. Who was the greatest writer in Chinese literature?

Confucius; born June 19th, 551 B. C.; died 479 B. C.

13. Give the dates of the Three Periods in Chinese History.

The Legendary, from 2697 to 1122 B. C.; the Semi-Historical, from 1122 to 770 B. C.; and the Historical, from 770 B. C. to the present time.

14. Why was the Great Wall built?

To keep out the hordes of Tartars who were constantly making invasions on the north. It is 1,500 miles long, averages 25 feet high by 20 feet thick with brick towers at regular intervals; is doubled at important passes and is still in well-preserved condition.

15. Who was the first European to visit China?

Marco Polo, in 1290 A. D.; followed by the first missionaries four years later.

16. Give two events in Chinese history that caused great loss of life.

The Great Famine in China in 1342 A. D., by which 13,000,000 lost their lives; and the earthquake at Pekin in 1700 A. D., by which 400,000 persons perished.

17. When did Great Britain get a hold in Southern Asia?

About the end of the 17th century.

18. What great evil has resulted from commercial intercourse with China?

The introduction of opium from India by the British.

19. When was a Treaty made between the United States and China?

July 3d, 1844.

20. Are the Chinese a wandering race?

They are not, but are home-loving, and when they emigrate it is with the expectation of returning to their " Flowery Land."

21. From the best authority what is thought to be the origin of the Japanese?

The weight of history is in favor of the idea that they migrated from northeastern Asia, through Corea, to Japan. Their legendary chronicles date back to 650 B. C.

22. What governmental changes occurred in 604 A. D?

A Monarchical Government was established; the officials were divided into civil and military grades.

23. When was the war of the Red and White Flags?

In 1159 A. D. It was a war between the ruling families, and took its name from the color of their banners.

24. When was Japan opened to commerce?

In 1872.

25. What is Japan's present condition?

She holds intercourse with all nations, and her Sovereign rules a " Land of Great Peace."

26. By what name is the Babylonian Empire known at present?
The Province of Bagdad.

27. Who founded the Empire?
Nimrod, who passed on to the East and founded Nineveh.

28. Describe the chief city of the Empire.
Babylon; it was 209 years in building; it was 15 miles square, was surrounded by a wall 350 feet high, with a thickness at the base of 87 feet, and a chariot road on top. Its most imposing structure was the Palace of Nebuchadnezzar, built 600 B.C. Its greatest curiosity was its Hanging Gardens.

29. Who was the last King of Babylon?
Belshazzar, whose reign was brought to a close by the invasion of Cyrus and the destruction of the city, 538 B.C.

30. Who was the greatest monarch of Persia?
Darius I.

31. Who commanded the largest army in the world?
Xerxes, the son of Darius, whose army numbered over 2 000,000 fighting men.

32. Who were the first Rulers of Palestine?
The descendants of Ham; the country was then called the land of Canaan.

33. Who first conquered the Canaanites?
Moses, in the Fifteenth Century, B.C. The Romans came into possession of Palestine about 100 B C. Jerusalem was first taken in 70 A.D., by Titus, and the Jews were scattered as slaves or exiles.

34. When was Jerusalem again taken?
In 610 A.D., by the Persians, who were assisted by the rebellious Jews. It was retaken by the Romans in 622, but fell into the hands of the Arabs, in 637 A. D. The Egyptians got control of it in 696 A.D., but it has been in rebellion between Egypt and Turkey ever since.

35. What were the principal cities of Greece?
Athens, Sparta, Corinth, and Thebes, founded about 1500 B.C.

36. Describe the Olympic Games?
They were held every four years at Olympia; races of all kinds were engaged in, the ballads of Homer were cited, and the victor was crowned with olive or laurel. Greeks from all over the world contended in these games, but they were open to no other nation.

37. Who gave a code of laws to Athens?
Draco. He defended their severity by saying: " The smallest crime deserves death, and I can find no heavier penalty for the greatest."

38. What military event took place in 431 B.C.?
The long continued jealousy between Sparta and Athens broke out in the Peloponnesian War which lasted thirty-seven years and resulted in the triumph of Sparta.

39. When was the Theban period?

From 371 to 361 B.C. It was so called because of the war between the Spartans and Thebans. Epaminondas was the leading Theban general. He defeated the Spartans at the battle of Leuctra.

40. Who built Corinth?

The Romans after their conquest of Greece in 146 B.C.

41. When does trustworthy history of Rome begin?

About 281 B. C., all earlier records having been destroyed by the Gauls who sacked and burnt the city about this time.

42. Who was the first king of Rome?

Romulus, who built the city, and to furnish it with inhabitants, made it an asylum for murderers, slaves, and thieves; for wives they kidnapped the Latin and Sabine virgins.

43. Who were the two great Classes of Rome?

The Patricians, the wealthy, ruling class; and the Plebeians, the working class.

44. Who was Cicero?

He was the greatest of Roman orators; having made an oration against Antony; he was killed by that general's friends, and his head nailed to the Rostra where he had spoken.

45. Who was the wickedest ruler of Rome?

Nero II; he murdered his mother; persecuted the Christians, burned the city, and finally committed suicide 68 A. D.

46. What was the religion of the Romans?

Idol worship of the heathen gods.

47. When was the Roman Empire divided?

In 395 A. D., into an Eastern and Western Empire.

48. Into how many periods is English History divided?

Into five: The Prehistoric, from antiquity to the Invasion by the Romans under Cæsar, 55 B. C.; the Roman, from 55 B. C. to 449 A. D.; the Saxon, from 449 to 827 A. D.; the Norman, from 827 to 1399 A. D.; and the Royal, from 1399 to the present time.

49. How many different Houses have reigned during the Royal Period?

Five: the Houses of Lancaster, York, Tudor, Stuart, and Hanover.

50. What was the Magna Charta, and by whom signed?

It was the basis of the English Constitution and was signed by King John 1215 A. D.

51. What promise did Edward I make to the Welsh?

To give them a ruler born in their own land, who could not speak a word of English or French.

52. How did he keep his promise?

By giving them his own son born in their palace the day previous.

53. To what custom did this give rise?

Calling the eldest son of the Sovereign of England, the Prince of Wales.

54. In what battle did the English use gunpowder for the first time?

At the battle of Crecy, against the French, in 1346 A. D.

55. What war began in 1455?

The "Wars of the Roses," between the Yorkists, who adopted a white rose, and the Lancasters, who wore a red rose as their symbol.

56. When was printing introduced into England?

In 1476, by Caxton, of London.

57. What war broke out during the reign of Charles I?

The Civil Wars, ending in the defeat of the Royal party, the execution of the king, and the establishment of the Commonwealth, with Oliver Cromwell as its head.

58. When was the kingdom restored?

In 1660; Charles II, nicknamed the Merry Monarch, was proclaimed king.

59. When was the union of England and Scotland?

In 1707, under the name of Great Britain.

60. Who first translated the Bible into English?

Venerable Bede, born 673 A.D., died 755 A.D.

61. Who was Frederic Barbarosa?

The most powerful Emporor that Germany ever had. He died in 1190 A.D., while on the third Crusade.

62. Who were the Seven Wise Men of Greece?

Bias, Cleobus, Chilo, Pittacus, Periander, Solon, and Thales.

63. Name fourteen Decisive Battles of the Old World.

Marathon (490 B. C.); Syracuse (413 B. C.); Arbela (331 B. C.); Metansus (207 B. C.); Hercynian Forest, or Victory of Arminius (9 A. D.); Chalons (451 A. D.); Tours (732 A. D.); Hastings (1066 A. D.); Orleans (1429 A. D.); Defeat of the Spanish Armada (1588 A.D.); Blenheim (1704 A. D.); Pultowa (1709 A. D.); Volmy (1792); and Waterloo (1815 A. D.)—*Cresy.*

64. Give a short description of the Batle of Marathon.

Fought in September, 490 B. C., on the plains of Marathon, in Greece, between the Persian invaders under Datis, a Median General, and Artaphemes, a nephew of Darius. They had under their commands over 100,000 men. They were met by the Greeks, numbering 11,000, under the command of several Generals, the chief of whom was Miltiades. The Persians were defeated by a loss of 6,000 men, while the Greeks lost but 200; and thus a stunning blow was given to the Persian invasion.

65. Give a short description of the Battle of Syracuse.

In 413 B. C. the Athenians, with a great number of vessels under the commands of Nicias and Demosthenes, invaded Sicily and laid siege to Syracuse. The siege lasted for some time, but was finally repelled with great loss to the Athenians, whose progress was thus stopped in the West. Gylippus had command of the besieged city.

66. Give a short description of the Battle of Arbela.

On the left bank of the Tigris River, on October 1, 331 B. C., between the Persian Army, under Darius, and the Macedonian invaders, under Alexander the Great. The result was a complete victory of Alexander over Darius, and thus the Great Commander became the ruler of the Eastern World.

67. Give a short description of the Battle of Metansus.

On the River Metanso, in northern Italy, Hasdrubal, with the Carthaginians and Africans, were met by the Romans under Nero, in the spring of 207 B. C. Hasdrubal was utterly defeated by the Romans, and his invasion of Italy from the north was ended. Hasdrubal, who fell in this battle, was a brother of Hannibal.

68. Describe Arminius' victory.

In Germany, near the town of Driburg, the Roman Army, under Varus, was met by the Germans, under Arminius, in the year 9 A. D. Varus was killed, and the Roman Army totally defeated. The Romans never again attempted to invade Germany.

69. Describe the Battle of Chalons.

Near the city of Chalons, in the northeast of France, the Huns, under Attila, met the Romans, under Aetius, in the year 451 A. D. The Romans were victorious, and from thence the name of Huns ceased to be a terror in Europe.

70. Describe the Battle of Tours.

Near the city of Tours, on the River Loire, in the year 732 A. D., Charles Martel, with the Frank warriors, defeated the Saracens, or Arabs, under Abderrahman, and thus the Moslems were driven out of Western Europe.

71. Describe the Battle of Hastings.

Near Hastings, in England, the Norman Army, under Harold, met the English, under William. It was a Norman victory (1066 A. D.)

72. Describe the Battle of Orleans.

The city of Orleans is on the River Loire, and was besieged by the English, under the Earl of Salisbury, on the 12th of October, 1428 A. D. Finally Salisbury was killed, and Lord Suffolk took his place and renewed the siege with vigor in the spring of 1429. The city was about to surrender when Jenette, or Joan of Arc, a poor peasant girl, came to their assistance with a few followers, and after being severely wounded she succeeded in raising the siege and defeating the English.

73. Describe the defeat of the Armada.

The great Spanish fleet under Philip II met the English in the English Channel. Lord Effingham commanded the English vessels. The Spanish Armada was nearly all destroyed, and the result was an English victory (1588 A. D.)

74. Describe the Battle of Blenheim.

This decisive battle, near the village of Blenheim, between the English, under the Duke of Marlborough and Prince Eugene, and the French, under

Tallard and Marsin.   Thus Germany was delivered from France, as the English were the conquerors.   This battle was fought in August, 1704 A. D.

75.   Describe the Battle of Pultowa.

In the spring of the year 1709 A. D., on the River Vorksla, the town of
Pultowa was fortified by Charles, King of Sweden, who was making an invasion of Russia.   But here he was met by the Czar, Peter, with the Russian
army, and defeated, and thus ended the invasion of his country.

76.   Describe the Battle of Volmy.

Near the village of Volmy, in the northeast of France, in the year 1792
A. D., the German invaders, consisting of Prussians, Russians, Hessians and
Germans, under the Duke of Brunswick, were met by the French under
the command of Kellerman, who defeated them and ended their intended destruction of Paris.

77.   Describe the Battle of Waterloo.

On the 18th of June, 1816 A. D., the French Army, under Napoleon, was
met near Brussels by the Allied English Army of 68,000 men, under the Duke
of Wellington.   Napoleon's Army consisted of about 70,000 men.   Napoleon
was completely defeated in this battle, and was taken prisoner by the British.

78.   Name four Decisive Battles of the New World.

Quebec (1759 A. D.) ; Saratoga (1777 A. D.) ; Perry's Victory (1813 A.D.) ;
and Gettysburg (1863 A. D.)

79.   Describe the Battle of Quebec.

In September, 1759, the English, under General Wolf, on the Plains of
Abraham, just above the city of Quebec, stood ready to meet the French,
under Montcalm.   Both Generals were killed, the French defeated, and Quebec
surrendered.   This battle decided that the English people should rule America.

80   Describe the Battle of Saratoga.

The American Army, under General Gates, defeated and captured the
British, under General Burgoyne, and thus freed America from all fear of invasion from Canada, and greatly inspired the American Army.   The battle was
fought in the fall of 1777.

81.   Describe Perry's Victory.

In September of 1813, Commodore Perry, with his fleet of nine American
vessels, went out to meet Commodore Barclay, who had command of the
British fleet.   The engagement was a complete victory for the Americans,
thus giving them undisputed control of the Lakes.   The dispatch Perry sent
to General Harrison at the close of this battle was :—" We have met the
enemy and they are ours—two ships, two brigs, one schooner, and a sloop."

82.   Describe the Battle of Gettysburg ?

On July 1, 2, and 3, the great Battle of Gettysburg, in Pennsylvania, was
fought, between the Confederate Army, under General Lee, and the Union
Army, under General Meade.   The result was a Union victory, and thus the
Southern invasion of the North was checked.

83. What is the form of government of the United States of America

Pure republic. President elected for four years, Senate for six years, and House of Representatives for two years.

84. Name ten ruined cities of the world.

Abydos, Agrigentum, Arsinoe, Corinth, Carthage, Delphi, Ephesus, Pompeii, Tyre and Veii.

85. When was Abydos destroyed?

This city of Asia Minor was destroyed by the Turks in the year 1330 A. D.

86. When and by whom was Agrigentum destroyed?

This ancient city of Sicily was destroyed by the Carthaginians in the year 205 B. C.

87. What happened to the city of Arsinoe, in Egypt?

It was allowed to go to ruin by neglect.

88. When and by whom was Corinth destroyed?

By Alaric, in the year 396 A. D.

89. When and by whom was Carthage destroyed?

This city of Africa was captured at different times by the Romans, and was finally destroyed by Hassan in the year 698 A. D.

90. What caused the destruction of Delphi?

This city, in Greece, was destroyed by war and decay, and was abandoned in the year 395 A. D.

91. What happened the city of Ephesus?

Inundation and war plundered the city, which was finally destroyed by an earthquake in the year 17 A. D.

92. What destroyed the city of Pompeii?

This city of Italy was destroyed by an eruption of Mt. Vesuvius in the year 79 A. D.

93. What happened the City of Tyre?

The city of Tyre was sacked several times, and finally destroyed by the Turks in the year 1516 A. D.

94. What destroyed the city of Veii?

After a ten years' siege, it was taken by the Romans in the year 396 B. C.

95. Name ten of the most important inventions of history.

Steam engine, by James Watt, 1769 A. D. Sewing machine, 1790. Cotton-gin by Eli Whitney, 1793. Steam locomotive, 1802. Gas light, 1815. Telegraph, 1844. Submarine Cable, 1850. Photo-engraving, 1852. Telephones, 1874. Phonograph, 1877.

96. Name five Great Public Works of history.

Suez Canal, opened November, 1869. Pacific Railway, completed 1869. Mont Cenis Tunnel, completed September, 1871. Hoosac Tunnel, completed November, 1873. The Submarine Cable from Ireland to Newfoundland, 1858 to 1866.

97.   What is the most northern point ever reached by man?

83° 24', by the members of the Greely Expedition.

98.   From the observations of the explorers what is the belief in regard to the North Pole?

They express the belief that around the pole there is an open sea, where the temperature is not so severe as it is some distance from the pole.

99.   What has been the result of explorations into the Antartic Regions?

Navigators have never succeeded in getting as far south as they have north, on account of the climate being more severe.

100.   Why is it colder at the South Pole than it is at the North Pole?

On account of the great extent of water in the region of the South Pole and the absence of land areas.

MY NAME IS_____AND I THINK

1. That Poetry _____

_____

2. That my Favorite Poets are _____

3. That History_____

_____

4. That the Greatest Historians are_____

5. That Fiction_____

_____

6. That the Novelists I prefer are_____

7. That a Country Life_____

_____

8. That a Town Life_____

_____

9. That the Greatest Living Statesmen are_____

10. That my Favorite Heroes and Heroines are_____

11. That Music_____

_____

12. That the most Delightful Composers are_____

13. That the Fine Arts_____

_____

14. That the Finest Painters and Sculptors are_____

15. That Reading _____

_____

16. That my favorite Books are _____

17. That Love _____

_____

18. That Marriage _____

_____

19. That Dress _____

_____

20. That my Favorite Pursuits are _____

21 That my Favorite Amusements are _____

22. That my Favorite Flower is _____

23. That my Favorite Fruit is _____

24. That I would like my Friends to be _____

25 That the Wittiest Saying I know is _____

_____

_____

26. That the Finest Passage of Poetry I remember is _____

_____

_____

_____

_____

MY NAME IS＿＿＿＿＿＿＿＿＿＿＿＿＿＿AND I THINK

1. That Poetry ＿＿＿＿＿＿＿＿＿＿＿＿＿＿＿＿＿＿＿＿.

＿＿＿＿＿＿＿＿＿＿＿＿＿＿＿＿＿＿＿＿＿＿＿

2. That my Favorite Poets are＿＿＿＿＿＿＿＿＿＿＿

3. That History＿＿＿＿＿＿＿＿＿＿＿＿＿＿＿＿＿＿

＿＿＿＿＿＿＿＿＿＿＿＿＿＿＿＿＿＿＿＿＿＿＿

4. That the Greatest Historians are＿＿＿＿＿＿＿＿

5. That Fiction＿＿＿＿＿＿＿＿＿＿＿＿＿＿＿＿＿＿

＿＿＿＿＿＿＿＿＿＿＿＿＿＿＿＿＿＿＿＿＿＿＿

6. That the Novelists I prefer are＿＿＿＿＿＿＿＿＿

7. That a Country Life＿＿＿＿＿＿＿＿＿＿＿＿＿＿

＿＿＿＿＿＿＿＿＿＿＿＿＿＿＿＿＿＿＿＿＿＿＿

8. That a Town Life＿＿＿＿＿＿＿＿＿＿＿＿＿＿＿

＿＿＿＿＿＿＿＿＿＿＿＿＿＿＿＿＿＿＿＿＿＿＿

9. That the Greatest Living Statesmen are＿＿＿＿＿

10. That my Favorite Heroes and Heroines are＿＿＿

11. That Music＿＿＿＿＿＿＿＿＿＿＿＿＿＿＿＿＿＿

＿＿＿＿＿＿＿＿＿＿＿＿＿＿＿＿＿＿＿＿＿＿＿

12. That the most Delightful Composers are＿＿＿＿＿

13. That the Fine Arts＿＿＿＿＿＿＿＿＿＿＿＿＿＿＿

＿＿＿＿＿＿＿＿＿＿＿＿＿＿＿＿＿＿＿＿＿＿＿

14. That the Finest Painters and Sculptors are＿＿＿＿

15. That Reading _____

_____

16. That my favorite Books are _____

17. That Love _____

_____

18. That Marriage_____

_____

19. That Dress _____

_____

20. That my Favorite Pursuits are_____ _____

21 That my Favorite Amusements are_____

22. That my Favorite Flower is_____

23. That my Favorite Fruit is_____

24. That I would like my Friends to be _____

25. That the Wittiest Saying I know is_____

____ _____

____ _____

26. That the Finest Passage of Poetry I remember is_____

_____

_____

_____

_____

MY NAME IS_____AND I THINK

1. That Poetry _____

_____

That my Favorite Poets are_____

3. That History_____

_____

4. That the Greatest Historians are_____

5. That Fiction_____

_____

6. That the Novelists I prefer are_____

7. That a Country Life_____

_____

8. That a Town Life_____

_____

9. That the Greatest Living Statesmen are_____

10. That my Favorite Heroes and Heroines are_____

11. That Music_____

_____

12. That the most Delightful Composers are_____

13. That the Fine Arts_____

_____

14. That the Finest Painters and Sculptors are_____

15. That Reading _____

_____

16. That my favorite Books are _____

17. That Love _____

_____

18. That Marriage _____

_____

19 That Dress _____

_____

20. That my Favorite Pursuits are _____

21 That my Favorite Amusements are _____

22. That my Favorite Flower is _____

23. That my Favorite Fruit is _____

24. That I would like my Friends to be _____

25. That the Wittiest Saying I know is _____

_____

_____

26. That the Finest Passage of Poetry I remember is _____

_____

_____

_____

_____

MY NAME IS————————————————————AND I THINK

1. That Poetry _____

_____

2. That my Favorite Poets are _____

3. That History_____

_____

4. That the Greatest Historians are _____

5 That Fiction_____

_____

6. That the Novelists I prefer are_____

7. That a Country Life_____

_____

8. That a Town Life_____

_____

9. That the Greatest Living Statesmen are _____

10. That my Favorite Heroes and Heroines are_____

11. That Music_____

_____

12. That the most Delightful Composers are_____

13. That the Fine Arts_____

_____

14. That the Finest Painters and Sculptors are_____

15. That Reading _____

_____

16. That my favorite Books are _____

17. That Love _____

_____

18. That Marriage _____

_____

19. That Dress _____

_____

20. That my Favorite Pursuits are _____

21 That my Favorite Amusements are _____

22. That my Favorite Flower is _____

23. That my Favorite Fruit is _____

24. That I would like my Friends to be _____

25. That the Wittiest Saying I know is _____

_____

_____

26. That the Finest Passage of Poetry I remember is _____

_____

_____

_____

_____

MY NAME IS_____AND I THINK

1. That Poetry _____

    That my Favorite Poets are _____

3. That History_____

4. Tnat the Greatest Historians are_____

5. That Fiction_____

6. That the Novelists I prefer are_____

7. That a Country Life_____

8. That a Town Life_____

9. That the Greatest Living Statesmen are_____

10. That my Favorite Heroes and Heroines are_____

11. That Music_____

12. That the most Delightful Composers are_____

13. That the Fine Arts_____

14. That the Finest Painters and Sculptors are_____

15. That Reading _____

_____

16. That my favorite Books are _____

17. That Love _____

_____

18. That Marriage_____

_____

19. That Dress _____

_____

20. That my Favorite Pursuits are_____

21 That my Favorite Amusements are _____

22. That my Favorite Flower is_____

23. That my Favorite Fruit is_____

24. That I would like my Friends to be _____

25. That the Wittiest Saying I know is_____

_____

_____

26. That the Finest Passage of Poetry I remember is _____

_____

_____

_____

_____

Come, my best friends, my books! and lead me on.—COWLEY.

MY NAME IS..AND I THINK

1. That Poetry _____

2. That my Favorite Poets are_____

3. That History_____

4. That the Greatest Historians are_____

5. That Fiction_____

6. That the Novelists I prefer are_____

7. That a Country Life_____

8. That a Town Life_____

9. That the Greatest Living Statesmen are_____

10. That my Favorite Heroes and Heroines are_____

11. That Music_____

12. That the most Delightful Composers are_____

13. That the Fine Arts_____

14. That the Finest Painters and Sculptors are_____

15. That Reading _____

_____

16. That my favorite Books are _____

17. That Love _____

_____

18. That Marriage _____

_____

19. That Dress _____

_____

20. That my Favorite Pursuits are _____

21 That my Favorite Amusements are _____

22. That my Favorite Flower is _____

23. That my Favorite Fruit is _____

24. That I would like my Friends to be _____

25. That the Wittiest Saying I know is _____

_____

_____

26. That the Finest Passage of Poetry I remember is _____

_____

_____

_____

_____

MY NAME IS .... AND I THINK

1. That Poetry ....

2. That my Favorite Poets are ....

3. That History ....

4. That the Greatest Historians are ....

5. That Fiction ....

6. That the Novelists I prefer are ....

7. That a Country Life ....

8. That a Town Life ....

9. That the Greatest Living Statesmen are ....

10. That my Favorite Heroes and Heroines are ....

11. That Music ....

12. That the most Delightful Composers are ....

13. That the Fine Arts ....

14. That the Finest Painters and Sculptors are ....

15. That Reading _____

_____

16. That my favorite Books are _____

17. That Love _____

_____

18. That Marriage _____

_____

19. That Dress _____

_____

20. That my Favorite Pursuits are _____

21 That my Favorite Amusements are _____

22. That my Favorite Flower is _____

23. That my Favorite Fruit is _____

24. That I would like my Friends to be _____

25. That the Wittiest Saying I know is _____

_____

_____

26. That the Finest Passage of Poetry I remember is _____

_____

_____

_____

_____

MY NAME IS_____ AND I THINK

1. That Poetry _____

_____

That my Favorite Poets are_____

That History_____

_____

4. That the Greatest Historians are_____

5. That Fiction_____

_____

6. That the Novelists I prefer are_____

7. That a Country Life_____

_____

8. That a Town Life_____

_____

9. That the Greatest Living Statesmen are _____

10. That my Favorite Heroes and Heroines are_____

11. That Music_____

_____

12. That the most Delightful Composers are_____

13. That the Fine Arts_____

_____

14. That the Finest Painters and Sculptors are_____

15. That Reading _____

_____

16. That my favorite Books are _____

17. That Love _____

_____

18. That Marriage_____

_____

19. That Dress _____

_____

20. That my Favorite Pursuits are_____

21 That my Favorite Amusements are_____

22. That my Favorite Flower is_____

23. That my Favorite Fruit is_____

24. That I would like my Friends to be _____

25 That the Wittiest Saying I know is_____

_____

_____

26. That the Finest Passage of Poetry I remember is _____

_____

_____

_____

_____

ANUARY.

WHEN icicles hang by the wall,
    And Dick the shepherd blows his nail,
And Tom bears logs into the hall,
    And milk comes frozen home in pail,

  *   *   *   *   *

When all aloud the wind doth blow,
And birds sit brooding in the snow.

Love's Labour's Lost, Act V. Sc. 2.

January

In the great hand of God I stand.
    Macbeth, Act II. Sc. 3

January

    God shall be my hope,
My stay, my guide, and lantern to my feet.
    Second Part of Henry VI, Act II. Sc. 8.

January 3.

Pleasure and action make the hours seem short.
    Othello, Act II. Sc. 8.

January 4.

Sure, He that made us with such large discourse,
Looking before and after, gave us not
That capability and God-like reason
To rust in us unsued.
    Hamlet, Act IV. Sc. 4.

January 5.

    Let our old acquaintance be renewed.
    Second Part of Henry IV, Act III. Sc. 2.

January 6.

He hath known you but three days, and already
you are no stranger.
Twelfth Night, Act I. Sc. 4.

January 7.

Lay aside life-harming heaviness,
And entertain a cheerful disposition.
Richard II, Act II. Sc. 2.

January 8.

The Lord bless you .
God prosper your affairs ! God send us peace !
Second Part of Henry IV, Act III. Sc. 2.

January 9.

The life is dear ; for all that life can rate
Worth name of life in thee hath estimate,
Youth, beauty, wisdom, courage, all
That happiness and prime can happy call.
All's Well that Ends Well, Act II. Sc. 1.

January 10.

Your gentleness shall force
More than your force move us to gentleness.
As You Like It, Act II. Sc. 7.

January 11.

Here comes a man of comfort, whose advice
Hath often stilled my brawling discontent.
Measure for Measure, Act IV. Sc. 1.

January 12.

Love, give me strength ! and strength shall help
afford.
Romeo and Juliet, Act IV. Sc. 1.

———————————————————— *January 13.* ————————————————————

A man of good repute, carriage, bearing, and estimation.
                  Love's Labour's Lost, Act I. Sc. 1.

———————————————————— *January 14.* ————————————————————

I cannot hide what I am.
                  Much Ado about Nothing, Act I. Sc. 3.

———————————————————— *January 15.* ————————————————————

Kindness in women, not their beauteous looks,
shall win my love.
                  Taming of the Shrew, Act V. Sc. 2.

———————————————————— *January 16.* ————————————————————

           Happy thou art not;
For what thou hast not, still thou strivest to get,
And what thou hast, forget'st.
                  Measure for Measure, Act III. Sc. 1.

———————————————————— *January 17.* ————————————————————

Why should a man be proud? How doth pride
   grow?
I know not what pride is.
                  Troilus and Cressida, Act II. Sc. 3.

———————————————————— *January 18.* ————————————————————

What stature is she of?
Just as high as my heart.
                  As You Like It, Act III. Sc. 2.

———————————————————— *January 19.* ————————————————————

Well, I am not fair; and therefore I pray the
Gods make me honest.
                  As You Like It, Act III. Sc. 3.

January 20.

Heaven bless thee!
Thou hast the sweetest face I ever looked on.
Henry VIII, Act IV. Sc. 1.

January 21.

You do so grow in my requital
As nothing can unroot you.
All's Well that Ends Well, Act V. Sc. 1.

January 22.

The dearest friend to me, the kindest man,
The best condition'd and unwearied spirit
In doing courtesies.
Merchant of Venice, Act III. Sc. 2.

January 23.

He will keep that good name still.
Henry V, Act III. Sc. 7.

January 24.

I swear he is truehearted, and a soul
None better in my kingdom.
Henry VIII, Act V. Sc. 1.

January 25.

Men at some time are masters of their fates:
The fault, dear Brutus, is not in our stars,
But in ourselves.
Julius Cæsar, Act I. Sc. 2.

January 26.

But I'll endeavour deeds to match these words.
Troilus and Cressida, Act IV. Sc. 5.

———————————————— *January 27.* ————————————————

Be to yourself
As you would to your friend.

Henry VIII, Act I. Sc. 1.

———————————————— *January 28.* ————————————————

I have heard of the lady, and good words went
with her name.

Measure for Measure, Act III. Sc. 1.

———————————————— *January 29.* ————————————————

As much good stay with thee as go with me.

Richard II, Act I. Sc. 2.

———————————————— *January 30.* ————————————————

You have deserved
High commendation, true applause, and love.

As You Like It, Act I. Sc. 2.

———————————————— *January 31.* ————————————————

His years but young, but his experience old ;
His head unmellowed, but his judgment ripe.

Two Gentlemen of Verona, Act II. Sc. 4.

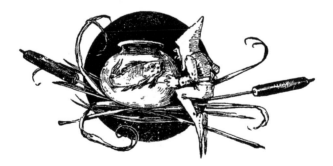

EBRUARY.

THE seasons alter: hoary-headed frosts
Fall in the fresh lap of the crimson rose,
And on old Hiems' thin and icy crown
An odorous chaplet of sweet summer buds
Is, as in mockery, set: the spring, the summer,
The childing autumn, angry winter, change
Their wonted liveries, and the mazed world,
By their increase, now knows not which is which.

Midsummer Night's Dream, Act II. Sc. 12.

———————————— *February 1.* ————————————

For there is nothing either good or bad, but
thinking makes it so.

Hamlet, Act II. Sc. 2.

———————————— *February 2.* ————————————

If reasons were as plentiful as blackberries, I
would give no man a reason upon compulsion, I.

First Part of Henry IV, Act II. Sc. 4.

———————————— *February 3.* ————————————

Constant you are,
But yet a woman, and for secrecy
No lady closer, for I well believe
Thou wilt not utter what thou dost not know.

First Part of Henry IV, Act II. Sc. 3.

———————————— *February 4.* ————————————

O ye gods, render me worthy of this noble wife.

Julius Cæsar, Act II. Sc. 1.

———————————— *February 5.* ————————————

She taketh most delight in music instruments,
and poetry.

Taming of the Shrew, Act I. Sc. 2.

---------- *February 6.* ----------

A double blessing is a double grace.

Hamlet, Act I. Sc. 3.

---------- *February 7.* ----------

Our contentment is our best having.

Henry VIII, Act II. Sc. 3

---------- *February 8.* ----------

Yet I do fear thy nature,
It is too full of the milk of human kindness.

Macbeth, Act I. Sc. 5.

---------- *February 9.* ----------

One touch of nature makes the whole world kin.

Troilus and Cressida, Act. III Sc. 3.

---------- *February 10.* ----------

Let myself and fortune
Tug for the time to come.

Winter's Tale, Act. IV. Sc. 4.

---------- *February 11.* ----------

Those friends thou hast, and their adoption tried,
Grapple them to thy soul with hoops of steel.

Hamlet, Act I. Sc. 3.

---------- *February 12.* ----------

I will chide no breather in the world but myself,
Against whom I know most faults.

As You Like It, Act III. Sc. 2.

February 13.

She's a good creature.
Merry Wives of Windsor, Act II. Sc. 2.

February 14.

(St. Valentine.)
. . . Sleep in peace and wake in joy;
Good angels guard thee.
Richard III, Act v. Sc. 3.

February 15.

Be sure of this,
What I can help thee to thou shalt not miss.
All's Well that Ends Well, Act I. Sc. 3.

February 16.

She is a woman, therefore may be woo'd;
She is a woman, therefore may be won.
Titus Andronicus, Act II. Sc. 1.

February 17.

I remember him well, and I remember him
worthy of thy praise.
Merchant of Venice, Act I. Sc. 2.

February 18.

O, this boy
Lends mettle to us all !
First Part of Henry IV, Act v. Sc. 4.

February 19.

Look, what is best, that best I wish in thee.
Sonnet, XXXVII.

— *February 20.* —

Her whose worth makes other worthies nothing.
She is alone.
Two Gentlemen of Verona, Act II. Sc. 4.

— *February 21.* —

God in heaven bless thee!
Romeo and Juliet, Act II. Sc. 4.

— *February 22.* —

Frank Nature, rather curious than in haste
Hath well composed thee.
All's Well that Ends Well, Act I. Sc. 2.

— *February 23.* —

Do as the heavens have done, forget your evil
With them forgive yourself.
Winter's Tale, Act v. Sc. 1.

— *February 24.* —

All places that the eye of Heaven visits
Are to a wise man ports and happy havens.
Richard II, Act I. Sc. 3.

— *February 25.* —

It never yet did hurt
To lay down likelihoods and forms of hope.
Second Part of Henry IV, Act I. Sc. 3.

— *February 26.* —

Nothing do I see in you
That I can find should merit any hate.
King John, Act II. Sc. 1.

——————— *February 27.* ———————

Day serves not light more faithful than I'll be.

Pericles, Act I. Sc. 2.

——————— *February 28.* ———————

And those about her
From her shall read the perfect ways of honour.

Henry VIII, Act v. Sc. 5.

——————— *February 29.* ———————

Let men take heed of their company.

Second Part of Henry IV, Act v. Sc. 1.

ARCH.

WHEN daffodils begin to peer,
With heigh ! the doxy over the dale,
Why, then comes in the sweet of the year;
For the red blood reigns in the Winter's pale.
Winter's Tale, Act IV. Sc. 3.

—— *March 1.* ——

Joy, gentle friends ! joy and fresh days of love
Accompany your hearts !
Midsummer Night's Dream, Act V. Sc. 1.

—— *March 2.* ——

Exceeding wise, fair-spoken, and persuading.
Henry VIII, Act IV. Sc. 2.

—— *March 3.* ——

The gentleman is full of virtue, bounty, worth
and qualities.
Two Gentlemen of Verona, Act III. Sc. 1.

—— *March 4.* ——

Valiant as a lion,
And wondrous affable, and as bountiful
As mines of India.
First Part of Henry IV, Act III. Sc. 1.

—— *March 5.* ——

In thy face I see
The map of honour, truth, and loyalty.
Second Part of Henry VI, Act III. Sc. 1.

---------------------------- *March 6.* ----------------------------

I pray thee sort thy heart to patience.
>>> *Second Part of Henry VI*, Act II. Sc. 4.

---------------------------- *March 7.* ----------------------------

Since this fortune falls to you,
Be content and seek no new.
>>> *Merchant of Venice*, Act III. Sc. 2.

---------------------------- *March 8.* ----------------------------

Ill blows the wind that profits nobody.
>>> *Third Part of Henry VI*, Act II. Sc. 5.

---------------------------- *March 9.* ----------------------------

I have a man's mind, but a woman's might.
>>> *Julius Cæsar*, Act II. Sc. 4.

---------------------------- *March 10.* ----------------------------

Honour, riches, marriage-blessing,
Long continuance, and increasing,
Hourly joys be still upon you!
Juno sings her blessings on you.
>>> *Tempest*, Act IV. Sc. 1.
God be wi' you, with all my heart.
>>> *Troilus and Cressida*, Act III. Sc. 3.

---------------------------- *March 11.* ----------------------------

Sir, I praise the Lord for you and so may my
parishioners.
>>> *Love's Labour's Lost*, Act IV. Sc. 2.

---------------------------- *March 12.* ----------------------------

But there's more in me than thou understand'st.
>>> *Troilus and Cressida*, Act IV. Sc. 5.

March 13.

Sir, I am a true labourer, I earn that I get, get that I wear, owe no man hate, envy no man's happiness.

As You Like It, Act III. Sc. 2.

March 14.

I do beseech you—
Chiefly that I might set it in my prayers—
What is your name?

Tempest, Act III. Sc. 1.

March 15.

How poor are they that have no patience !
What wound did ever heal but by degrees?

Othello, Act II. Sc. 3.

March 16.

What touches us ourself should be last served.

Julius Cæsar, Act III. Sc. 1.

March 17.

(ST. PATRICK'S DAY.)
'Tis not enough to help the feeble up,
But to support him after. Fare you well,
All happiness to your honour !

Timon of Athens, Act I. Sc. 1.

March 18.

Women will love her, that she is a woman
More worth than any man ; men, that she is
The rarest of all women.

Winter's Tale, Act v. Sc. 1.

March 19.

When love begins to sicken and decay,
It useth an enforced ceremony.
There are no tricks in plain and simple faith.

Julius Cæsar, Act IV. Sc. 2.

March 20.

For I profess not talking; only this—
Let each man do his best.
> *First Part of Henry IV*, Act v. Sc. 3.

March 21.

Firm of word,
Speaking in deeds and deed'ess in his tongue;
Not soon provoked, nor being provoked soon
  calm'd ;
His heart and hand both open and both free.
> *Troilus and Cressida*, Act iv. Sc. 5.

March 22.

My bosom is full of kindness.
> *Twelfth Night*, Act ii. Sc. I.

March 23.

He reads much ;
He is a great observer, and he looks
Quite through the deeds of men.
> *Julius Cæsar*, Act i. Sc. 2.

March 24.

If he serve God,
We'll serve Him too, and be his fellow so.
> *Richard II*, Act iii. Sc. 2.

March 25.

The gentleness of all the gods go with thee.
> *Twelfth Night*, Act ii. Sc. 1.

March 26.

Truth shall nurse her,
Holy and heavenly thoughts still counsel her :
She shall be loved and feared : her own shall bless
  her.
> *Henry VIII*, Act v. Sc. 5.

—————————————— *March 27.* ——————————————

The world is full of rubs.
                    Richard II, Act III. Sc. 4.

—————————————— *March 28.* ——————————————

Many days shall see her,
And yet no day without a deed to crown it.
                    Henry VIII, Act V. Sc. 5.

—————————————— *March 29.* ——————————————

There's little of the melancholy element in her!
                    Much Ado about Nothing, Act II. Sc. 1.

—————————————— *March 30.* ——————————————

And now am I, if a man should speak truly,
little better than one of the wicked.
                    First Part of Henry IV, Act I. Sc. 2.

—————————————— *March 31.* ——————————————

Not fearing death, nor shrinking for distress,
But always resolute in most extremes.
                    First Part of Henry VI, Act IV. Sc. 1.

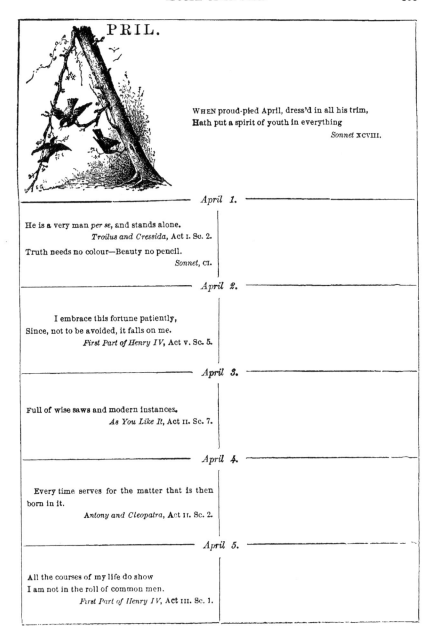

PRIL.

WHEN proud-pied April, dress'd in all his trim,
Hath put a spirit of youth in everything
Sonnet XCVIII.

———————— *April 1.* ————————

He is a very man *per se*, and stands alone.
Troilus and Cressida, Act I. Sc. 2.

Truth needs no colour—Beauty no pencil.
Sonnet, CI.

———————— *April 2.* ————————

I embrace this fortune patiently,
Since, not to be avoided, it falls on me.
First Part of Henry IV, Act v. Sc. 5.

———————— *April 3.* ————————

Full of wise saws and modern instances.
As You Like It, Act II. Sc. 7.

———————— *April 4.* ————————

Every time serves for the matter that is then
born in it.
Antony and Cleopatra, Act II. Sc. 2.

———————— *April 5.* ————————

All the courses of my life do show
I am not in the roll of common men.
First Part of Henry IV, Act III. Sc. 1.

April 6.

All happiness bechance to thee !
> *Two Gentlemen of Verona*, Act I. Sc. 1.

April 7.

Who is it that says most? which can say more
Than this rich praise, that you alone are you?
> *Sonnet*, LXXXIV.

April 8.

A learned spirit, of human dealings.
> *Othello*, Act III. Sc. 3.

April 9.

God's benison go with you; and with those
That would make good of bad, and friends of foes !
> *Macbeth*, Act II. Sc. 4.

April 10.

I am not lean enough to be thought a good student !
> *Twelfth Night*, Act IV. Sc. 2.

April 11.

A merrier man,
Within the limit of becoming mirth,
I never spent an hour's talk withal.
> *Love's Labour's Lost*, Act II. Sc. 1.

April 12.

More is thy due than more than all can pay.
> *Macbeth*, Act I. Sc. 4.

April 13.

I ear not flatter; I do defy
The tongues of soothers ; but a braver place
In my heart's love hath no man than yourself.
First Part of Henry IV, Act IV. Sc. 1.

April 14.

Fair thoughts and happy hours attend on you !
Merchant of Venice, Act III. Sc. 4.

April 15.

What cannot be avoided,
'Twere childish weakness to lament or fear.
Third Part of Henry VI, Act V. Sc. 4.

April 16.

This above all, to thine own self be true,
And it must follow as the night the day,
Thou canst not then be false to any man.
Hamlet, Act I. Sc. 3.

April 17.

Most prudent, of an excellent
And unmatched wit and judgment.
Henry VIII, Act II. Sc. 4.

April 18.

He was a man, take him for all in all,
I shall not look upon his like again.
Hamlet, Act I. Sc. 2.

April 19.

Our kindred, though they be long ere they are
wooed, they are constant being won.
Troilus and Cressida, Act III. Sc. 2.

——————————— *April 20.* ———————————

He was a scholar, and a ripe good one.

> *Henry VIII*, Act IV. Sc. 2.

——————————— *April 21.* ———————————

.   . I know the gentleman
To be of worth and worthy estimation,
And not without desert so well reputed.

> *Two Gentlemen of Verona*, Act II. Sc. 3.

——————————— *April 22.* ———————————

What's in a name? That which we call a rose,
By any other name would smell as sweet.

> *Romeo and Juliet*, Act II. Sc. 2.

——————————— *April 23.* ———————————

(ST. GEORGE'S DAY.)

But here's the joy, my friend and I are one.

> *Sonnet*, XLII.

——————————— *April 24.* ———————————

And I feel within me
A peace above all earthly dignities,
A still and quiet conscience   . .
My hopes in heaven do dwell

> *Henry VIII*, Act III. Sc. 2.

——————————— *April 25.* ———————————

Certainly a woman's thought runs before her
actions

> *As You Like It*, Act IV. Sc. 1.

——————————— *April 26.* ———————————

Remember this,
God and our good cause fight upon our side.

> *Richard III*, Act V. Sc. 3.

―――― *April 27.* ――――

She was the sweet marjoram of the salad, or
rather, the herb of grace
   All's Well that Ends Well, Act IV. Sc. 5.

―――― *April 28.* ――――

Sleep that knits up the ravell'd sleeve of care,
The death of each day's life, sore labour's bath,
Balm of hurt minds, great nature's second course,
Chief nourisher in life's feast.
   Macbeth, Act II. Sc. 2.

―――― *April 29.* ――――

Our life, exempt from public haunt,
Finds tongues in trees, books in the running brocks,
Sermons in stones, and good in everything.
   As You Like It, Act II. Sc. 1.

―――― *April 30.* ――――

The April's in her eyes   it is love's spring,
And these the showers to bring it on.
   Antony and Cleopatra, Act III. Sc. 2

APRIL SHOWERS.

AY.

As it fell upon a day
In the merry month of May,
Sitting in a pleasant shade
Which a grove of myrtles made,
Beasts did leap, and birds did sing,
Trees did grow, and plants did spring
Everything did banish moan,
Save the nightingale alone.

Sonnets set to Music, XXI.

--- May 1. ---

. . . Take arms against a sea of troubles,
And by opposing end them.

Hamlet, Act III. Sc. 1.

--- May 2. ---

. . . . I am a man
That from my first have been inclined to thrift.

Timon of Athens, Act I. Sc. 1.

--- May 3. ---

Thou art thy mother's glass, and she in thee
Calls back the lovely April of her prime ;
So thou through windows of thine age shalt see
Despite of wrinkles this thy golden time.

Sonnet III.

--- May 4. ---

Some are born great, some achieve greatness, and
some have greatness thrown upon them.

Twelfth Night, Act V. Sc. 1.

--- May 5. ---

Ay, me ! for aught that I could ever read,
Could ever hear by tale or history,
The course of true love never did run smooth.

Midsummer Night's Dream, Act I. Sc. 1.

——————————————————————— *May 6.* ———————————————————

The elements be kind to thee, and make
Thy spirits all of comfort !
    Antony and Cleopatra, Act III. Sc. 2.

——————————————————————— *May 7.* ———————————————————

    The God of heaven
Both now and ever bless her !
    Henry VIII, Act v. Sc. 1.

——————————————————————— *May 8.* ———————————————————

Old fashions please me best ; I am not so nice,
To change true rules for old inventions.
    Taming of the Shrew, Act III. Sc. 1.

——————————————————————— *May 9.* ———————————————————

    Shall we serve Heaven
With less respect than we do minister
To our gross selves?
    Measure for Measure, Act II. Sc. 2.

——————————————————————— *May 10.* ———————————————————

Holy, fair, and wise is she.
    Two Gentlemen of Verona, Act IV. Sc. 2.

——————————————————————— *May 11.* ———————————————————

The good I stand on is my truth and honesty :
 . . . . I fear nothing
What can be said against me.
    Henry VIII. Act v. Sc. 1.

——————————————————————— *May 12.* ———————————————————

Comfort's in heaven ; and we are on the earth,
Where nothing lives but crosses, cares and grief.
    Richard II. Act II. Sc. 2.

May 13.

What poor an instrument may do a noble deed!
Antony and Cleopatra, Act v. Sc. 2.

May 14.

How green you are, and fresh, in this old world!
King John, Act III. Sc. 4.

May 15.

Welcome ever smiles,
And farewell goes out sighing.
Troilus and Cressida, Act III. Sc. 3.

May 16.

He hath a daily beauty in his life.
Othello, Act v. Sc. 1.

May 17.

Thou art as wise as thou art beautiful.
Midsummer Night's Dream, Act III. Sc. 1.

May 18.

You are very welcome to our house.
Merchant of Venice, Act v. Sc. 1.

May 19.

One of the noblest note, to whose kindnesses I
am most infinitely tied.
Cymbeline, Act I. Sc. 6.

May 20.

His worth is warrant for his welcome hither.
Two Gentlemen of Verona, Act II. Sc. 4.

May 21.

Were man but constant he were perfect.
Two Gentlemen of Verona, Act V. Sc. 4.

May 22.

But Heaven in thy creation did decree
That in thy face sweet love should ever dwell.
Sonnet XCIII.

May 23.

The hand that made you fair hath made you good.
Measure for Measure, Act III. Sc. 1.

May 24.

His better does not breathe upon the earth.
Richard III, Act I. Sc. 2.

May 25.

The Lord in heaven bless thee !
Henry V, Act IV. Sc. 1.

May 26

Fair thoughts be your fair pillow !
Troilus and Cressida, Act III. Sc. 1.

May 27.

There is no darkness but ignorance.
Twelfth Night, Act IV. Sc. 1.

May 28.

He has my heart yet, and shall have my prayers
While I shall have my life.
Henry VIII, Act III. Sc. 1.

May 29.

My salad days,
When I was green in judgment.
Antony and Cleopatra, Act I. Sc. 5.

May 30.

O, what may man within him hide,
Though angel on the outward side !
Measure for Measure, Act III. Sc. 2.

May 31.

Love thyself last.
Henry VIII, Act III. Sc. 2.

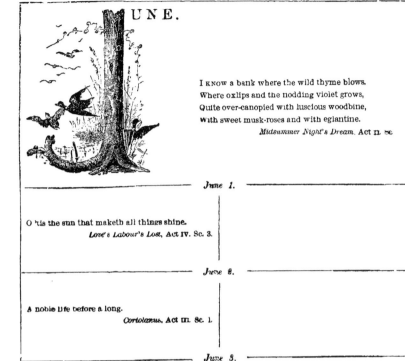

UNE.

I KNOW a bank where the wild thyme blows,
Where oxlips and the nodding violet grows,
Quite over-canopied with luscious woodbine,
With sweet musk-roses and with eglantine.

Midsummer Night's Dream. Act II. Sc

June 1.

O 'tis the sun that maketh all things shine.
Love's Labour's Lost, Act IV. Sc. 3.

June 2.

A noble life before a long.
Coriolanus, Act III. Sc. 1.

June 3.

I will be the pattern of all patience · I will say
nothing.
King Lear. Act III. Sc. 2

June 4.

Pray that the right may thrive.
King Lear. Act V. Sc. 2

June 5.

And having sworn troth. ever will be true.
Twelfth Night, Act IV. Sc. 3.

————————————— *June 6.* —————————————

She is young, and of a noble modest nature
Henry VIII, Act IV. Sc. 2.

————————————— *June 7.* —————————————

He is simply the rarest man i' the world.
Coriolanus, Act IV. Sc. 5.

————————————— *June 8.* —————————————

Bliss and goodness on you.
Measure for Measure, Act III. Sc. 2.

————————————— *June 9.* —————————————

Polonius. What do you think of me?
King. As of a man faithful and honourable
Hamlet, Act II. Sc. 2.

————————————— *June 10.* —————————————

All the world's a stage,
And all the men and women merely players.
As You Like It, Act II. Sc. 6.

————————————— *June 11.* —————————————

Striving to better, oft we mar what's well.
King Lear, Act I. Sc. 4.

————————————— *June 12.* —————————————

God, the best maker of all marriages,
Combine your hearts in one.
Henry V, Act v. Sc. 2

───────────────── June 13. ─────────────────

Wise men ne'er sit and wail their loss,
But cheerly seek how to redress their harms.
Third Part of Henry VI. Act v Sc. 4.

───────────────── June 14. ─────────────────

I would not wish any companion in the world
but you.
Tempest, Act III. Sc. 1.

───────────────── June 15. ─────────────────

Quick is mine ear to hear of good towards him.
Richard II. Act II. Sc. 1.

───────────────── June 16. ─────────────────

. . . Spirits are not finely touch'd
But to fine issues.
Measure for Measure, Act I. Sc. 1.

───────────────── June 17. ─────────────────

Be cheerful · wipe thine eyes:
Some falls are means the happier to arise.
Cymbeline, Act IV. Sc. 2.

───────────────── June 18. ─────────────────

Thy truth then be thy dower.
King Lear, Act I. Sc. 1.

───────────────── June 19. ─────────────────

Happy in that we are not over-happy.
Hamlet, Act II. Sc. 2.

———————————————— *June 20.* ————————————————

The purest treasure mortal times afford
Is spotless reputation.

            Richard II, Act I. Sc. 1.

———————————————— *June 21.* ————————————————

Happy are they that hear their own detraction,
and can put them to mending.

           Much Ado About Nothing, Act II. Sc. 3.

———————————————— *June 22.* ————————————————

Men of few words are the best men.

            Henry V, Act III. Sc. 2.

———————————————— *June 23.* ————————————————

        There be many Cæsars
Ere such another Julius.

            Cymbeline, Act III. Sc. 1.

        Things done well,
And with a care, exempt themselves from fear.

            Henry VIII, Act I. Sc. 2.

———————————————— *June 24.* ————————————————

And He that doth the ravens feed,
Yea, providently caters for the sparrow,
Be comfort to my age!

          As You Like It, Act II. Sc. 3.

———————————————— *June 25.* ————————————————

We know what we are, but know not what we
may be.

           Hamlet, Act IV. Sc. 5,

———————————————— *June 26.* ————————————————

Be great in act, as you have been in thought.

          King John, Act V. Sc. 1.

June 27.

Give sorrow words: the grief that does not speak
Whispers the o'erfraught heart and bids it break.
Macbeth, Act IV. Sc. 3.

June 28.

For 'tis the mind that makes the body rich;
And as the sun breaks through the darkest clouds,
So honour peereth in the meanest habit.
Taming of the Shrew, Act IV. Sc. 3.

June 29.

And creep time ne'er so slow,
Yet it shall come for me to do thee good.
King John, Act III. Sc. 3.

June 30.

Be not too tame neither; but let your own discretion be your tutor: suit the action to the word,
the word to the action.
Hamlet, Act III. Sc. 2.

ULY

HERE's flowers for you;
Hot lavender, mints, savory, marjoram;
The marigold, that goes to bed wi' the sun
And with him rises weeping: these are flowers
Of middle summer, and I think they are given
To men of middle age.

Winter's Tale, Act. IV. Sc. 4.

July

O, how full of briers is this working-day world!
As You Like It, Act I. Sc. 3.

July 2.

With thoughts so qualified as your charities
shall best instruct you, measure me.
Winter's Tale, Act II. Sc. 1.

July 3.

Thou art not farther than my thoughts canst move,
And I am still with them, and they with thee.
Sonnet, XLVII.

July 4.

I have no other but a woman's reason:
I think him so because I think him so.
Two Gentlemen of Verona. Act I. Sc. 2

July 5.

He's truly valiant that can wisely suffer.
Timon of Athens, Act III. Sc. 5.

---------------- *July 6.* ----------------

Heaven give you many many merry days.
Merry Wives of Windsor, Act v. Sc. 5.

---------------- *July* ----------------

Let me be that I am, and seek not to alter me.
Much Ado about Nothing, Act i. Sc. 2.

---------------- *July 8.* ----------------

This day
Shall change all griefs and quarrels into love.
Henry V, Act v. Sc 2

---------------- *July 9* ----------------

For truth can never be confirmed enough,
Though doubts did ever sleep.
Pericles, Act v Sc. 1.

---------------- *July 10.* ----------------

Thou bringst me happiness and peace.
Second Part of Henry IV, Act iv Sc. 5

---------------- *July 11.* ----------------

Truth hath a quiet breast . . .
For gnarling sorrow hath less power to bite
The man that mocks at it and sets it light.
Richard II, Act i. Sc. 3.

---------------- *July 12.* ----------------

The best wishes that can be forged in your
thoughts be servants to you!
All's Well that Ends Well, Act i. Sc. 1.

July 13.

For to be wise and love
Exceeds man's might: that dwells with gods above
Troilus and Cressida, Act III. Sc. 3.

July 14.

Nature hath formed strange fellows in her time.
Merchant of Venice, Act I. Sc. I.

July 15.

We must take the current when it serves,
Or lose our ventures.
Julius Cæsar, Act IV. Sc. 3

July 16.

True hope is swift, and flies with swallow's wings·
Kings it makes gods, and meaner creatures kings
Richard III, Act v. Sc. ?

July 17.

Thou art a summer bird,
Which ever in the haunch of winter sings
The lifting up of day.
Second Part of Henry IV, Act IV Sc 4.

July 18.

I do love nothing in the world so well as you is
not that strange?
Much Ado about Nothing, Act IV. Sc. 1.

July 19.

The blessed gods
Purge all infection from our air whilst you
Do climate here!
Winter's Tale. Act I. Sc. 1.

July 20.

It was not born under a rhyming planet, nor I
cannot woo in festival terms.

Much Ado about Nothing, Act V. Sc. 2.

July 21.

A woman's gentle heart, but not acquainted
With shifting change, as is false women's fashion.

Sonnet, XX.

July 22.

There's no art
To find the mind's construction in the face:
He was a gentleman on whom I built
An absolute trust.

Macbeth, Act I. Sc. 4.

July 23.

The setting sun, and music at the close,
As the last taste of sweets, is sweetest last,
Writ in remembrance more than things long past.

Richard II, Act II. Sc. 1.

July 24.

My crown is in my heart, not on my head;
Not decked with diamonds and Indian stones,
Nor to be seen; my crown is called, Content.

Third Part of Henry VI, Act III. Sc. 1.

July 25.

I know you have a gentle noble temper,
A soul as even as a calm.

Henry VIII, Act III. Sc. 1.

July 26.

The sweetest lady that ever I looked on.

Much Ado about Nothing, Act I. Sc. 1.

—————————— *July 27.* ——————————

She is of so free, so kind, so apt, so blessed a
disposition.

Othello, Act II. Sc. 3.

—————————— *July 28.* ——————————

Her voice was ever soft,
Gentle, and low; an excellent thing in woman.

King Lear, Act v. Sc. 3.

—————————— *July 29.* ——————————

A heart unspotted is not easily daunted.

Second Part of Henry VI, Act III. Sc. 1.

—————————— *July 30.* ——————————

He is no hypocrite, but prays from his heart.

Much Ado about Nothing, Act I. Sc. 1.

—————————— *July 31.* ——————————

The noblest mind he carries
That ever govern'd man.
Long may he live in fortunes!

Timon of Athens, Act I. Sc. 1.

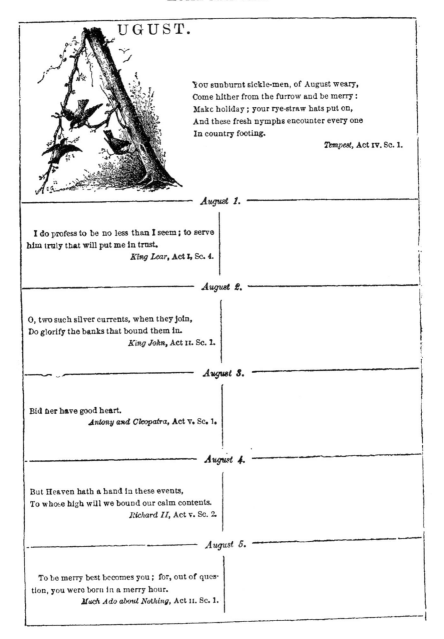

AUGUST.

You sunburnt sickle-men, of August weary,
Come hither from the furrow and be merry :
Make holiday ; your rye-straw hats put on,
And these fresh nymphs encounter every one
In country footing.

Tempest, Act IV. Sc. 1.

——— *August 1.* ———

I do profess to be no less than I seem ; to serve
him truly that will put me in trust.
King Lear, Act I, Sc. 4.

——— *August 2.* ———

O, two such silver currents, when they join,
Do glorify the banks that bound them in.
King John, Act II. Sc. 1.

——— *August 3.* ———

Bid her have good heart.
Antony and Cleopatra, Act V. Sc. 1.

——— *August 4.* ———

But Heaven hath a hand in these events,
To whose high will we bound our calm contents.
Richard II, Act v. Sc. 2.

——— *August 5.* ———

To be merry best becomes you ; for, out of question, you were born in a merry hour.
Much Ado about Nothing, Act II. Sc. 1.

—————————————— *August 6.* ——————————————

Hope is a lover's staff; walk hence with that
And manage it against despairing thoughts.
Two Gentlemen of Verona, Act III. Sc. 1.

—————————————— *August 7.* ——————————————

Who is't can say ' I am at the worst?'
King Lear, Act IV. Sc. 1.

—————————————— *August 8.* ——————————————

You have too much respect upon the world,
They lose it that do buy it with much care.
Merchant of Venice, Act I. Sc. 1.

—————————————— *August 9.* ——————————————

Thrice is he armed that hath his quarrel just.
Second Part of Henry VI, Act III. Sc. 2.

—————————————— *August 10.* ——————————————

Ignorance is the curse of God,
Knowledge the wing wherewith we fly to heaven.
Second Part of Henry VI, Act IV. Sc. 7.

—————————————— *August 11.* ——————————————

Your fair discourse hath been as sugar,
Making the hard way sweet and delectable.
Richard II, Act II. Sc. 3.

—————————————— *August 12.* ——————————————

We will not from the helm to sit and weep,
But keep our course, though the rough wind say no.
Third Part of Henry VI, Act V. Sc. 4.

— *August 13.* —

But He, that hath the steerage of my course,
Direct my sail !
  Romeo and Juliet, Act I. Sc. 4.

— *August 14.* —

When fortune means to men most good,
She looks upon them with a threatening eye.
  King John, Act III. Sc. 4.

— *August 15.* —

God bless thee; and put meekness in thy mind,
Love, charity, obedience, and true duty !
  Richard III, Act II. Sc. 2.

— *August 16.* —

She looks as clear
As morning roses newly washed with dew.
  Taming of the Shrew, Act II. Sc. 1.

— *August 17.* —

The better part of valour is discretion.
  First Part of Henry IV, Act V. Sc. 4.

— *August 18.* —

In the reproof of chance
Lies the true proof of men. . . . Even so
Doth valour's show and valour's worth divide
In storms of fortune.
  Troilus and Cressida, Act I. Sc. 3.

— *August 19.* —

Thou hast a perfect thought :
I will upon all hazards well believe
Thou art my friend, that know'st my tongue so well.
  King John, Act V. Sc. 6.

—————————————— *August 20.* ——————————————

For man is a giddy thing, and this is my conclusion.
Much Ado about Nothing, Act v. Sc. 4.

—————————————— *August 21.* ——————————————

A good heart's worth gold.
Second Part of Henry IV, Act ii. Sc. 4.

—————————————— *August 22.* ——————————————

Take my blessing: God protect thee!
Into whose hand *I* give thy life. . .
When I am in heaven I shall desire
To see what this child does, and praise my Maker.
Henry VIII, Act v. Sc. 5.

—————————————— *August 23.* ——————————————

Look, he's winding up the watch of his wit; by
and by it will strike.
Tempest, Act ii. Sc. 1.

—————————————— *August 24.* ——————————————

Is not birth, beauty, good shape, discourse, manhood, learning, gentleness, virtue, youth, liberality,
and such-like, the spice and salt that season a man?
Troilus and Cressida, Act i. Sc. 2.

—————————————— *August 25.* ——————————————

Win straying souls . . . .
Cast none away.
Henry VIII, Act v. Sc. 3.

—————————————— *August 26.* ——————————————

Is she not passing fair?
Two Gentlemen of Verona, Act iv. Sc. 4.

August 27.

Then speak the truth by her ; if not divine,
Yet let her be a principality,
Sovereign to all the creatures on the earth.
Two Gentlemen of Verona, Act II. Sc. 4.

August 28.

The strawberry grows underneath the nettle.
Henry V, Act I. Sc. 1.

August 29.

Every one can master a grief but he that has it.
Much Ado about Nothing, Act III. Sc. 2.

August 30.

The quality of mercy is not strain'd.
It droppeth as the gentle rain from heaven
Upon the place beneath: it is twice blest ;
It blesseth him that gives and him that takes.
Merchant of Venice, Act IV. Sc. 1.

August 31.

There's nothing ill can dwell in such a temple.
If the ill spirit have so fair a house,
Good things will strive to dwell with 't.
Tempest, Act I. Sc. 2.

EPTEMBER.

ROUGH winds do shake the darling buds of May,
And summer's lease hath all too short a date :
Sometimes too hot the eye of heaven shines,
And often is his gold complexion dimm'd ;
And every fair from fair sometime declines,
By chance or nature's changing course untrimm'd.

Sonnet, XVIII.

September 1.

Is it possible he should know what he is and be that he is?

All's Well that Ends Well, Act IV. Sc. 1.

September 2.

The time is worth the use on't.

Winter's Tale, Act III. Sc. 1.

September 3.

To thee and thy company I bid
A hearty welcome.

Tempest, Act v. Sc. 1.

September 4.

But, in the verity of extolment,
I take him to be a soul of great article.

Hamlet, Act v. Sc. 2.

September 5.

You were born under a charitable star.

All's Well that Ends Well, Act I. Sc. 1.

———————————— *September 6.* ————————————

My words fly up, my thoughts remain below.
Words without thoughts never to Heaven go.
    Hamlet, Act III. Sc. 3.

———————————— *September 7.* ————————————

What stronger breastplate than a heart untainted?
    Second Part of Henry VI, Act III. Sc. 2.

———————————— *September 8.* ————————————

In maiden meditation fancy free.
    Midsummer Night's Dream, Act II. Sc. 1.

———————————— *September 9.* ————————————

Happy is your Grace,
That can translate the stubbornness of fortune
Into so quiet and so sweet a style.
    As You Like It, Act II. Sc. 1.

———————————— *September 10.* ————————————

I am sure care's an enemy to life.
    Twelfth Night, Act I. Sc. 3.

———————————— *September 11.* ————————————

Small cheer and great welcome make a merry
feast.
    Comedy of Errors, Act III, Sc. 1.

———————————— *September 12.* ————————————

He is as full of valour as of kindness
    Henry V, Act IV. Sc. 3.

September 13.

A good man's fortune may grow out at heels.
King Lear, Act II. Sc. 2.

September 14.

Hast any philosophy in thee, shepherd?
As You Like It, Act III. Sc. 2.

September 15.

When remedies are past, the griefs are e ded
By seeing the worst, which late on hopes depended.
Othello, Act I. Sc. 3.

September 16.

I am ashamed that women are so simple
To offer war where they should kneel for peace;
Or seek for rule, supremacy, and sway,
When they are bound to serve, love, and obey.
Taming of the Shrew, Act V. Sc 2.

September 17.

I'll note you in my book of memory.
First Part of Henry VI, Act II. Sc. 4.

September 18.

I am not merry; but I do beguile
The thing I am, by seeming otherwise.
Othello, Act II, Sc. 1.

September 19.

I have bought
Golden opinions from all sorts of people, . . .
I dare do all that may become a man;
Who dares do more is none.
Macbeth, Act I. Sc. 7.

September 20.

He that is thy friend indeed,
He will help thee in thy need.
Sundry Sonnets, XXI.

September 2 .

I am the very pink of courtesy.
Romeo and Juliet, Act II. Sc. 4.

September 22.

He tells you flatly what his mind is.
Taming of the Shrew, Act I. Sc. 2.

September 23.

His life was gentle, and the elements
So mix'd in him that Nature might stand up
And say to all the world, 'This was a man !'
Julius Cæsar, Act V. Sc. 5.

September 24.

I to the world am like a drop of water,
That in the ocean seeks another drop.
Comedy of Errors, Act I. Sc. 2.

September 25.

Sir, as I have a soul, she is an angel.
Henry VIII, Act IV. Sc. 1.

September 26.

Frame your mind to mirth and merriment,
Which bars a thousand harms and lengthens life.
Taming of the Shrew, Act I. Sc. 1.

September 27.

The time of life is short!
To spend that shortness basely were too long,
If life did ride upon a dial's point,
Still ending at the arrival of an hour.
First Part of Henry IV, Act v. Sc. 2.

September 28.

My gentle lady,
I wish you all the joy that you can wish.
Merchant of Venice, Act iii. Sc. 2.

September 29.

When I said I would die a bachelor, I did not
think I should live till I were married.
Much Ado about Nothing, Act ii. Sc. 3.

September 30.

Friendship is constant in all other things
Save in the office and affairs of love:
Therefore all hearts in love use their own tongues;
Let every eye negotiate for itself,
And trust no agent.
Much Ado about Nothing. Act ii Sc. 1.

CTOBER.

I BEHELD the violet past prime,
And sable curls all silver'd o'er with white;
When lofty trees I see barren of leaves,
Which erst from heat did canopy the herd
And Summer's green all girded up in sheaves,
Borne on the bier with white and bristly beard.

Sonnet XII.

October *1.*

The air of Paradise did fan the house,
And angels officed all.

All's Well that Ends Well, Act III. Sc. 2.

October *2*

Here is a dear, a true industrious friend.

First Part of Henry IV, Act I. Sc. 1.

October *3.*

Do you not know I am a woman? When I think,
I must speak.

As You Like It, Act III. Sc. 2.

October *4.*

He is a marvellous good neighbour.

Love's Labour's Lost, Act V. Sc. 2.

October *5.*

Give every man thine ear, but few thy voice;
Take each man's censure, but reserve thy judgment.

Hamlet, Act I. Sc. 3.

——————————————— *October 6.* ———————————————

A kinder gentleman treads not the earth.
         Merchant of Venice, Act II. Sc. 8.

——————————————— *October 7.* ———————————————

God in thy good cause make thee prosperous !
         Richard II, Act I. Sc. 3.

——————————————— *October 8.* ———————————————

Life every man holds dear; but the brave man
Holds honour far more precious dear than life.
         Troilus and Cressida, Act V. Sc. 3.

——————————————— *October 9.* ———————————————

A son who is the theme of honour's tongue,
Amongst a grove the very straightest plant.
         First Part of Henry IV, Act I. Sc. 1.

——————————————— *October 10.* ———————————————

All this day an unaccustomed spirit
Lifts me above the ground with cheerful thoughts.
         Romeo and Juliet, Act V. Sc. 1.

——————————————— *October 11.* ———————————————

Fortune brings in some boats that are not steer'd.
         Cymbeline, Act IV. Sc. 3.

——————————————— *October 12.* ———————————————

Heaven give your spirits comfort.
         Measure for Measure, Act IV. Sc. 2.

—————————————————— *October 13.* ——————————————————

I had rather seal my lips, than, to my peril,
Speak that which is not.
  Antony and Cleopatra, Act v. Sc. 2.

—————————————————— *October 14.* ——————————————————

May the gods direct you to the best!
  Cymbeline, Act III. Sc. 4.

—————————————————— *October 15.* ——————————————————

Age cannot wither her, nor custom stale
Her infinite variety.
  Antony and Cleopatra, Act II. Sc. 2.

—————————————————— *October 16.* ——————————————————

  Our doubts are traitors,
And make us lose the good we oft might win
By fearing to attempt.
  Measure for Measure, Act I. Sc. 4.

—————————————————— *October 17* ——————————————————

Here's one, a friend, and one that knows you well.
  Romeo and Juliet, Act V. Sc. 3.

—————————————————— *October 18.* ——————————————————

There is a kind of character in thy life,
That to the observer doth thy history
Fully unfold.
  Measure for Measure, Act I. Sc. 1.

—————————————————— *October 19.* ——————————————————

We are in God's hand. brother.
  Henry V, Act III. Sc. 6.

October 20.

The benediction of these covering heavens
Fall on their heads like dew!
                        Cymbeline, Act v. Sc. 5.

October 21.

There is a tide in the affairs of men,
Which, taken at the flood, leads on to fortune ;
Omitted, all the voyage of their life
Is bound in shallows and in miseries.
                        Julius Cæsar, Act IV. Sc. 3.

October 22.

Keep your fellows' counsels and your own.
                        Much Ado about Nothing, Act III. Sc. 3.

October 23.

                    I will hope
Of better deeds to-morrow. Rest you happy!
                        Antony and Cleopatra, Act I. Sc. 1.

October 24.

The force of his own merit makes his way.
                        Henry VIII, Act I. Sc. 1.

October 25.

Of a cheerful look, a pleasing eye, and a most
noble carriage.
                        First Part of Henry IV, Act II. Sc. 4.

October 26.

I do not think a braver gentleman,
More active-valiant, or more valiant-young,
More daring or more bold, is now alive
To grace this latter age with noble deeds.
                        First Part of Henry IV, Act v. Sc. 1.

October 27.

Many years of happy days befall.
> *Romeo and Juliet*, Act I. Sc. 1

October 28.

Then Heaven, set ope thy everlasting gates,
To entertain my vows of thanks and praise!
> *Second Part of Henry VI*, Act IV. Sc. 9.

October 29.

I count myself in nothing else so happy
As in a soul remembering my good friends.
> *Richard II*, Act II. Sc. 3.

October 30.

I cannot but remember such things were,
That were most precious to me.
> *Macbeth*, Act IV. Sc. 3.

October 31.

(HALLOW E'EN.)
Though fortune's malice overthrow my state,
My mind exceeds the compass of her wheel.
> *Third Part of Henry VI*, Act IV. Sc. 3.

OVEMBER.

WITH hey, ho, the wind and the rain,—
Must make content with his fortunes fit,
For the rain it raineth every day.

King Lear, Act III. Sc 2.

─────────────── *November 1.* ───────────────

All the world is cheered by the sun.

Richard III, Act I. Sc. 2.

─────────────── *November 2.* ───────────────

Thou hast mettle enough in thee to kill care.

Much Ado about Nothing, Act v. Sc. 1.

─────────────── *November 3.* ───────────────

'Tis beauty that doth oft make woman proud,
'Tis virtue that doth make them most admired,
'Tis government that makes them seem divine.

Third Part of Henry VI, Act I. Sc. 4.

─────────────── *November 4.* ───────────────

For I know thou 'rt full of love and honesty,
And weigh'st thy words before thou givest them
breath.

Othello, Act III. Sc. 3.

─────────────── *November 5.* ───────────────

My endeavours
Have ever come too short of my desires.

Henry VIII, Act III. Sc. 2.

November 6.

This must my comfort be,
That sun that warms you here shall shine on me.
                Richard II, Act I, Sc. 3.

November 7.

Her that loves him with that excellence
That angels love good men with.
                Henry VIII, Act II. Sc. 2.

November 8.

He is complete in feature and in mind,
With all good grace to grace a gentleman.
                Two Gentlemen of Verona, Act II. Sc. 1.

November 9.

All the gods go with you! upon your sword
Sit laurel victory! and smooth success
Be strew'd before your feet!
                Antony and Cleopatra, Act I. Sc. 3.

November 10.

But men may construe things after their fashion,
Clean from the purpose of the things themselves.
                Julius Cæsar, Act I. Sc. 3.

November 11.

Direct not him whose way himself will choose:
'Tis breath thou lack'st, and that breath wilt thou
lose.
                Richard II, Act II. Sc. 1.

November 12.

Model to thy inward greatness,
Like little body with a mighty heart.
                Henry V, Act II. Chorus.

———————————————— *November 13.* ————————————————

Men should be what they seem.

Othello, Act III. Sc. 3.

———————————————— *November 14.* ————————————————

Things at the worst will cease.

Macbeth, Act IV. Sc. 2.

———————————————— *November 15.* ————————————————

The dews of heaven fall thick in blessings on her i

Henry VIII, Act IV. Sc. 2.

———————————————— *November 16.* ————————————————

You bear a gentle mind, and heavenly blessings
Follow such creatures.

Henry VIII, Act II. Sc. 3.

———————————————— *November 17.* ————————————————

God send every one their heart's desire.

Much Ado about Nothing, Act III. Sc. 4.

———————————————— *November 18.* ————————————————

Be checked for silence, but never taxed for speech.

All's Well that Ends Well, Act I. Sc. 1.

———————————————— *November 19.* ————————————————

I forgive and quite forget old faults.

Third Part of Henry VI, Act III. Sc. 3.

November 20.

Our indiscretion sometimes serves us well,
When our deep plots do pall: and that should
    teach us
There's a divinity that shapes our ends,
Rough hew them how we will.
                    Hamlet, Act V. Sc. 2

November 21.

        Now the fair goddess Fortune,
Fall deep in love with thee ; and her great charms
Misguide thy opposers' swords!
                    Coriolanus, Act I. Sc. 5.

November 22.

It is religion that doth make vows kept.
                    King John, Act III. Sc. 1.

November 23.

Good name in man and woman, dear my lord,
Is the immediate jewel of their souls: . . .
Poor and content is rich and rich enough,
But riches fineless is as poor as winter
To him that ever fears he shall be poor.
                    Othello, Act III. Sc. 3.

November 24.

        Sudden sorrow
Serves to say thus, some good thing comes to-
    morrow.
                    Second Part of Henry IV, Act IV. Sc. 2.

November 25.

Bosom up my counsel, you'll find it wholesome.
                    Henry VIII, Act I. Sc. 1.

November 26.

There is no time so miserable but a man may be
    true.
                    Timon of Athens, Act IV. Sc. 3.

———————————— *November 27.* ————————————

Full of noble device, of all sorts enchantingly
    beloved.
                            As You Like It, Act I. Sc. 1.

———————————— *November 28.* ————————————

Our separation so abides, and flies,
That thou, residing here, go'st yet with me,
And I, hence fleeting, here remain with thee.
                            An'ony and Cleopatra, Act I. Sc. 3.

———————————— *November 29.* ————————————

I'll take thy word for faith, not ask thine oath:
Who shuns not to break one will sure crack both.
                            Pericles, Act I. Sc. 2.

———————————— *November 30.* ————————————

(St. Andrew's Day.)
Remember thee! Ay, while memory holds
A seat in this distracted globe.
                            Hamlet, Act I. Sc. 4.

 ECEMBER.

THAT time of year thou may'st in me behold
When yellow leaves, or none, or few, do hang
Upon those boughs which shake against the cold
Bare ruin'd choirs, where late the sweet birds sang.

Sonnet LXXIII.

December 1.

Her peerless feature, joined with her birth,
Approves her fit for none but for a king.

First Part of Henry VI, Act v. Sc. 5.

December 2.

But we all are men,
In our own natures frail, and capable
Of our flesh; few are angels.

Henry VIII, Act v. Sc. 3.

December 3.

Be just, and fear not:
Let all the ends thou aim'st at be thy country's,
Thy God's, and truth's; then if thou fall'st, . . .
Thou fall'st a blessed martyr.

Henry VIII. Act III. Sc. 2.

December 4.

Let's teach ourselves that honourable stop,
Not to outsport discretion.

Othello, Act II. Sc. 3.

December 5.

Silence is the perfectest herald of joy: I were but
little happy, if I could say how much.

Much Ado about Nothing, Act II. Sc. 1.

December 6.

I am not of many words, but I thank you.
Much Ado about Nothing, Act I. Sc. 1.

December 7.

In winter's tedious nights, sit by the fire with good old folks.
Richard II. Act V. Sc. 1.

December 8.

Me, poor man, my library was dukedom large enough.
Tempest, Act 1. Sc. 2.

December 9.

Full of wise care is this your counsel.
Richard III, Act III. Sc. 1.

December 10.

I hear, yet say not much, but think the more.
Third Part of Henry VI, Act IV. Sc. 1.

December 11.

Let gentleness my strong enforcement be.
As You Like It, Act II. Sc. 7.

December 12.

He hath indeed a good outward happiness!
Much Ado about Nothing, Act II. Sc. 3.

December 13.

There is some soul of goodness in things evil,
Would men observingly distil it out.
Henry V, Act iv. Sc. 1.

December 14.

He gave his honours to the world again,
His blessed part to Heaven, and slept in peace.
Henry VIII, Act iv. Sc. 2.

December 15

All may be well; but, if God sort it so,
'Tis more than we deserve, or I expect.
Richard III, Act ii. Sc. 3.

December 16.

He's honest, on mine honour.
Henry VIII, Act v. Sc. 1.

December 17.

For mine own part, I could be well content
To entertain the lag-end of my life
With quiet hours.
First Part of Henry IV, Act v. Sc. 1.

December 18.

You shall hear from me still; the time shall not
Out-go my thinking on you.
Antony and Cleopatra, Act iii. Sc. 2.

December 19.

Time comes stealing on by night and day.
Comedy of Errors, Act iv. Sc. 2.

--- *December 20.* ---

A virtuous and a Christian-like conclusion,
To pray for them that have done scathe to us.
Richard III, Act I. Sc. 3.

--- *December 21.* ---

The web of our life is of a mingled yarn, good
and ill together.
All's Well that Ends Well, Act IV. Sc. 3.

Jog on, jog on, the foot-path way,
And merrily hent the stile-a :
A merry heart goes all the day,
Your sad tires in a mile-a.
Winter's Tale, Act IV. Sc. 3.

--- *December 22.* ---

Cease to lament for that thou canst not help,
And study help for that which thou lament'st.
Two Gentlemen of Verona, Act III. Sc. 1.

--- *December 23.* ---

O Lord, that lends me life,
Lend me a heart replete with thankfulness!
Second Part of Henry VI, Act I. Sc 1.

--- *December 24.* ---

Look, what thy soul holds dear, imagine it
To lie that way thou go'st, not whence thou comest.
Richard II, Act I. Sc. 3.

--- *December 25.* ---

(CHRISTMAS DAY.)
Alas, alas!
Why, all the souls that were were forfeit once;
And He that might the vantage best have took
Found out the remedy.
Measure for Measure, Act II. Sc. 2.

--- *December 26.* ---

Therefore my age is as a lusty winter,
Frosty, but kindly.
As You Like It, Act II. Sc. 3.

—————————— *December 27.* ——————————

Pray you, bid
These unknown friends to 's welcome; for it is
The way to make us better friends, more known.
Winter's Tale, Act IV. Sc. 4.

—————————— *December 28.* ——————————

. . . . So we'll live
And pray, and sing, and tell old tales.
King Lear, Act V. Sc. 2.

—————————— *December 29.* ——————————

We see which way the stream of time doth run,
And are enforced from our most quiet there
By the rough torrent of occasion.
Second Part of Henry IV, Act IV. Sc. 1.

—————————— *December 30.* ——————————

He sits high in all the people's hearts.
Julius Cæsar, Act I. Sc. 3.

—————————— *December 31.* ——————————

Watch to-night, pray to-morrow.
First Part of Henry IV, Act II. Sc. 4.

Parting is such sweet sorrow
That I shall say good-night till it be morrow.
Romeo and Juliet, Act II. Sc. 3.

Then let us take a ceremonious leave
And loving farewell of our several friends.
Richard II, Act I. Sc. 3.

God be with you all !
Henry V, Act IV. Sc. 3.

CPSIA information can be obtained
at www.ICGtesting.com
Printed in the USA
BVHW04s0220140618
519036BV00018B/155/P

9 781331 787655